THE
COMPLETE WORKS
OF
SWAMI VIVEKANANDA

Mayavati Memorial Edition

VOLUME III

Advaita Ashrama
(Publication Department)
5 Dehi Entally Road
Calcutta 700 014

Published by
Swami Mumukshananda
President, Advaita Ashrama
Mayavati, Champawat, Himalayas
from its Publication Department, Calcutta
Email: advaita@vsnl.com • Website: www.advaitaonline.com

Eighteenth Reprint, February 2001
3M3C

ISBN 81-85301-47-6 (P.B. Set)   ISBN 81-85301-75-1 (H.B. Set)
ISBN 81-85301-78-6 (Vol. 3)

Printed in India at
Gipidi Box Co.
3B Chatu Babu Lane
Calcutta 700 014

PREFACE TO THE NINTH EDITION

In this edition, Buddhistic India, a lecture hitherto unpublished in this series, is included.

The *Index* has been revised to include new references.

September, 1964   PUBLISHER

PREFACE TO THE EIGHTH EDITION

In this edition are added some reports about Swami Vivekananda and his speeches appearing in the American press of those days. These were published in 1958 in our book, *Swami Vivekananda in America : New Discoveries*, copyrighted by the Vedanta Society of Northern California, San Francisco, U.S.A. The reports are reproduced without any change of spelling or correction of factual mistakes, which are obvious, though footnotes are often added for helping the readers. The headings are mostly ours, and some explanatory words are inserted in the texts within square brackets. The *Index* which was added in the last printing has been revised accordingly.

May, 1960   PUBLISHER

CONTENTS

LECTURES AND DISCOURSES

After the Parliament of Religions

UNITY, THE GOAL OF RELIGION

(Delivered in New York, 1896)

This universe of ours, the universe of the senses, the rational, the intellectual, is bounded on both sides by the illimitable, the unknowable, the ever unknown. Herein is the search, herein are the inquiries, here are the facts ; from this comes the light which is known to the world as religion. Essentially, however, religion belongs to the supersensuous and not to the sense plane. It is beyond all reasoning and is not on the plane of intellect. It is a vision, an inspiration, a plunge into the unknown and unknowable, making the unknowable more than known, for it can never be "known". This search has been in the human mind, as I believe, from the very beginning of humanity. There cannot have been human reasoning and intellect in any period of the world's history without this struggle, this search beyond. In our little universe, this human mind, we see a thought arise. Whence it arises we do not know ; and when it disappears, where it goes, we know not either. The macrocosm and the microcosm are, as it were, in the same groove, passing through the same stages, vibrating in the same key.

I shall try to bring before you the Hindu theory that religions do not come from without, but from within. It is my belief that religious thought is in man's very constitution, so much so that it is impossible for him to give up religion until he can give up his mind and body, until he can give up thought and life. As long as a man thinks, this struggle must go on, and so long man must have some form of religion. Thus we see various forms of religion in the world. It is a bewildering study; but it is not, as many of us think, a vain speculation. Amidst this chaos there is harmony, throughout these discordant sounds there is a note of concord; and he who is prepared to listen to it will catch the tone.

The great question of all questions at the present time is this: Taking for granted that the known and the knowable are bounded on both sides by the unknowable and the infinitely unknown, why struggle for that infinite unknown? Why shall we not be content with the known? Why shall we not rest satisfied with eating, drinking, and doing a little good to society? This idea is in the air. From the most learned professor to the prattling baby, we are told that to do good to the world is all of religion, and that it is useless to trouble ourselves about questions of the beyond. So much is this the case that it has become a truism.

But fortunately we *must* inquire into the beyond. This present, this expressed, is only one part of that un-expressed. The sense universe is, as it were, only one portion, one bit of that infinite spiritual universe projected into the plane of sense consciousness. How can this little bit of projection be explained, be understood, without knowing that which is beyond? It is said of Socrates that one day while lecturing at Athens, he met a Brâhmin who had travelled into Greece, and Socrates told the Brahmin that the greatest study for mankind is man. The Brahmin sharply retorted: "How can you know man until you know God?" This God, this eternally Un-knowable, or Absolute, or Infinite, or without name—you may call Him by what name you like—is the rationale, the only explanation, the *raison d'être* of that which is known and knowable, this present life. Take anything before you, the most material thing—take one of the most material sciences, as chemistry or physics, astronomy or biology—study it, push the study forward and forward, and the gross forms will begin to melt and become finer and finer, until they come to a point where you are bound to make a tremendous leap from these material things into the immaterial. The gross melts into the fine, physics into metaphysics, in every department of knowledge.

Thus man finds himself driven to a study of the beyond. Life will be a desert, human life will be vain, if we cannot know the beyond. It is very well to say: Be contented with the things of the present. The cows and the dogs are, and so are all animals ; and that is what makes them animals. So if man rests content with the present and gives up all search into the beyond, mankind will have to go back to the animal plane again. It is religion, the inquiry into the beyond, that makes the difference between man and an animal. Well has it been said that man is the only animal that naturally looks upwards ; every other animal naturally looks down. That looking upward and going upward and seeking perfection are what is called salvation; and the sooner a man begins to go higher, the sooner he raises himself towards this idea of truth as salvation. It does not consist in the amount of money in your pocket, or the dress you wear, or the house you live in, but in the wealth of spiritual thought in your brain. That is what makes for human progress, that is the source of all material and intellectual progress, the motive power behind, the enthusiasm that pushes mankind forward.

Religion does not live on bread, does not dwell in a house. Again and again you hear this objection advanced: "What good can religion do? Can it take away the poverty of the poor?" Supposing it cannot, would that prove the untruth of religion? Suppose a baby stands up among you when you are trying to demonstrate an astronomical theorem, and says, "Does it bring gingerbread?" "No, it does not", you answer. "Then," says the baby, "it is useless." Babies judge the whole universe from their own standpoint, that of producing gingerbread, and so do the babies of the world. We must not judge of higher things from a low standpoint. Everything must be judged by its own standard and the infinite must be judged by the standard of infinity. Religion permeates the whole of man's life, not only the present, but the past, present, and future. It is, therefore, the eternal relation between the eternal soul and the eternal God. Is it logical to measure its value by its action upon five minutes of human life? Certainly not. These are all negative arguments.

Now comes the question: Can religion really accomplish anything? It can. It brings to man eternal life. It has made man what he is, and will make of this human animal a god. That is what religion can do. Take religion from human society and what will remain? Nothing but a forest of brutes. Sense-happiness is not the goal of humanity. Wisdom (Jnâna) is the goal of all life. We find that man enjoys his intellect more than an animal enjoys its senses; and we see that man enjoys his spiritual nature even more than his rational nature. So the highest wisdom must be this spiritual knowledge. With this knowledge will come bliss. All these things of this world are but the shadows, the manifestations in the third or fourth degree of the real Knowledge and Bliss.

One question more: What is the goal? Nowadays it is asserted that man is infinitely progressing, forward and forward, and there is no goal of perfection to attain to. Ever approaching, never attaining, whatever that may mean and however wonderful it may be, it is absurd on the face of it. Is there any motion in a straight line? A straight line infinitely projected becomes a circle, it returns to the starting point. You must end where you begin; and as you began in God, you must go back to God. What remains? Detail work. Through eternity you have to do the detail work.

Yet another question: Are we to discover new truths of religion as we go on? Yea and nay. In the first place, we cannot know anything more of religion, it has all been known. In all religions of the world you will find it claimed that there is a unity within us. Being one with divinity, there cannot be any further progress in that sense. Knowledge means finding this unity. I see you as men and women, and this is variety. It becomes scientific knowledge when I group you together and call you human beings. Take the science of chemistry, for instance. Chemists are seeking to resolve all known substances into their original elements, and if possible, to find the one element from which all these are derived. The time may come when they will find one element that is the source of all other elements. Reaching that, they can go no further; the science of chemistry will have become perfect. So it is with the science of religion. If we can discover this perfect unity, there cannot be any further progress.

The next question is: Can such a unity be found? In India the attempt has been made from the earliest times to reach a science of religion and philosophy, for the Hindus do not separate these as is customary in Western countries. We regard religion and philosophy as but two aspects of one thing which must equally be grounded in reason and scientific truth.

The system of the Sânkhya philosophy is one of the most ancient in India, or in fact in the world. Its great exponent Kapila is the father of all Hindu psychology; and the ancient system that he taught is still the foundation of all accepted systems of philosophy in India today which are known as the Darshanas. They all adopt his psychology, however widely they differ in other respects.

The Vedanta, as the logical outcome of the Sankhya, pushes its conclusions yet further. While its cosmology agrees with that taught by Kapila, the Vedanta is not satisfied to end in dualism, but continues its search for the final unity which is alike the goal of science and religion.

THE FREE SOUL

(Delivered in New York, 1896)

The analysis of the Sânkhyas stops with the duality of existence—Nature and souls. There are an infinite number of souls, which, being simple, cannot die, and must therefore be separate from Nature. Nature in itself changes and manifests all these phenomena; and the soul, according to the Sankhyas, is inactive. It is a simple by itself, and Nature works out all these phenomena for the liberation of the soul; and liberation consists in the soul discriminating that it is not Nature. At the same time we have seen that the Sankhyas were bound to admit that every soul was omnipresent. Being a simple, the soul cannot be limited, because all limitation comes either through time, space, or causation. The soul being entirely beyond these cannot have any limitation. To have limitation one must be in space, which means the body; and that which is body must be in Nature. If the soul had form, it would be identified with Nature; therefore the soul is formless, and that which is formless cannot be said to exist here, there, or anywhere. It must be omnipresent. Beyond this the Sankhya philosophy does not go.

The first argument of the Vedantists against this is that this analysis is not a perfect one. If their Nature be absolute and the soul be also absolute, there will be two absolutes, and all the arguments that apply in the case of the soul to show that it is omnipresent will apply in the case of Nature, and Nature too will be beyond all time, space, and causation, and as the result there will be no change or manifestation. Then will come the difficulty of having two absolutes, which is impossible. What is the solution of the Vedantist? His solution is that, just as the

Sankhyas say, it requires some sentient Being as the motive power behind, which makes the mind think and Nature work, because Nature in all its modifications, from gross matter up to Mahat (Intelligence), is simply insentient. Now, says the Vedantist, this sentient Being which is behind the whole universe is what we call *God*, and consequently this universe is not different from Him. It is He Himself who has become this universe. He not only is the instrumental cause of this universe, but also the material cause. Cause is never different from effect, the effect is but the cause reproduced in another form. We see that every day. So this Being is the cause of Nature. All the forms and phases of Vedanta, either dualistic, or qualified-monistic, or monistic, first take this position that God is not only the instrumental, but also the material cause of this universe, that everything which exists is He. The second step in Vedanta is that these souls are also a part of God, one spark of that Infinite Fire. "As from a mass of fire millions of small particles fly, even so from this Ancient One have come all these souls." So far so good, but it does not yet satisfy. What is meant by a part of the Infinite? The Infinite is indivisible ; there cannot be parts of the Infinite. The Absolute cannot be divided. What is meant, therefore, by saying that all these sparks are from Him? The Advaitist, the non-dualistic Vedantist, solves the problem by maintaining that there is really no part; that each soul is really not a part of the Infinite, but actually *is* the Infinite Brahman. Then how can there be so many? The sun reflected from millions of globules of water appears to be millions of suns, and in each globule is a miniature picture of the sun-form; so all these souls are but reflections and not real. They are not the real "I" which is the God of this universe, the one undivided Being of the universe. And all these little different beings, men and animals etc. are but reflections, and not real. They are simply illusory reflections upon

Nature. There is but one Infinite Being in the universe, and that Being appears as you and as I; but this appearance of divisions is after all a delusion. He has not been divided, but only appears to be divided. This apparent division is caused by looking at Him through the network of time, space, and causation. When I look at God through the network of time, space, and causation, I see Him as the material world. When I look at Him from a little higher plane, yet through the same network, I see Him as an animal, a little higher as a man, a little higher as a god, but yet He is the One Infinite Being of the universe, and that Being we are. I am That, and you are That. Not parts of It, but the whole of It. "It is the Eternal Knower standing behind the whole phenomena; He Himself is the phenomena." He is both the subject and the object, He is the "I" and the "You". How is this? "How to know the Knower? The Knower cannot know Himself; I see everything but cannot see myself. The Self, the Knower, the Lord of all, the Real Being, is the cause of all the vision that is in the universe, but it is impossible for Him to see Himself or know Himself, excepting through reflection. You cannot see your own face except in a mirror, and so the Self cannot see Its own nature until It is reflected, and this whole universe therefore is the Self trying to realise Itself. This reflection is thrown back first from the protoplasm, then from plants and animals, and so on and on from better and better reflectors, until the best reflector, the perfect man, is reached—just as a man who, wanting to see his face, looks first in a little pool of muddy water, and sees just an outline; then he comes to clear water, and sees a better image; then to a piece of shining metal, and sees a still better image; and at last to a looking-glass, and sees himself reflected as he is. Therefore the perfect man is the highest reflection of that Being who is both subject and object. You now find why man instinctively worships everything, and how perfect

men are instinctively worshipped as God in every country.
You may talk as you like, but it is they who are bound to
be worshipped. That is why men worship Incarnations,
such as Christ or Buddha. They are the most perfect
manifestations of the eternal Self. They are much higher
than all the conceptions of God that you or I can make.
A perfect man is much higher than such conceptions. In
him the circle becomes complete ; the subject and the
object become one. In him all delusions go away and in
their place comes the realisation that he has always been
that perfect Being. How came this bondage then? How
was it possible for this perfect Being to degenerate into the
imperfect? How was it possible that the free became
bound? The Advaitist says, he was never bound, but
was always free. Various clouds of various colours come
before the sky. They remain there a minute and then pass
away. It is the same eternal blue sky stretching there
for ever. The sky never changes : it is the cloud that is
changing. So you are always perfect, eternally perfect.
Nothing ever changes your nature, or ever will. All these
ideas that I am imperfect, I am a man, or a woman, or a
sinner, or I am the mind, I have thought, I will think—all
are hallucinations; you never think, you never had a
body; you never were imperfect. You are the blessed Lord
of this universe, the one Almighty ruler of everything that
is and ever will be, the one mighty ruler of these suns
and stars and moons and earths and planets and all the
little bits of our universe. It is through you that the sun
shines and the stars shed their lustre, and the earth
becomes beautiful. It is through your blessedness that they
all love and are attracted to each other. You are in all,
and you are all. Whom to avoid, and whom to take?
You are the all in all. When this knowledge comes,
delusion immediately vanishes.

I was once travelling in the desert in India. I travelled
for over a month and always found the most beautiful

landscapes before me, beautiful lakes and all that. One day I was very thirsty and I wanted to have a drink at one of these lakes; but when I approached that lake it vanished. Immediately with a blow came into my brain the idea that this was a mirage about which I had read all my life; and then I remembered and smiled at my folly, that for the last month all the beautiful landscapes and lakes I had been seeing were this mirage, but I could not distinguish them then. The next morning I again began my march ; there was the lake and the landscape, but with it immediately came the idea, "This is a mirage." Once known it had lost its power of illusion. So this illusion of the universe will break one day. The whole of this will vanish, melt away. This is realisation. Philosophy is no joke or talk. It has to be realised; this body will vanish, this earth and everything will vanish, this idea that I am the body or the mind will for some time vanish, or if the Karma is ended it will disappear, never to come back; but if one part of the Karma remains, then as a potter's wheel, after the potter has finished the pot, will sometimes go on from the past momentum, so this body, when the delusion has vanished altogether, will go on for some time. Again this world will come, men and women and animals will come, just as the mirage came the next day, but not with the same force; along with it will come the idea that I know its nature now, and it will cause no bondage, no more pain, nor grief, nor misery. Whenever anything miserable will come, the mind will be able to say, "I know you as hallucination." When a man has reached that state, he is called Jivanmukta, living-free", free even while living. The aim and end in this life for the Jnâna-Yogi is to become this Jivanmukta, "living-free". He is Jivanmukta who can live in this world without being attached. He is like the lotus leaves in water, which are never wetted by the water. He is the highest of human beings, nay, the highest of all beings, for he has realised his identity with

the Absolute, he has realised that he is one with God. So
long as you think you have the least difference from God,
fear will seize you, but when you have known that you are
He, that there is no difference, entirely no difference, that
you are He, all of Him, and the whole of Him, all fear
ceases. "There, who sees whom? Who worships whom?
Who talks to whom? Who hears 'whom? Where one
sees another, where one talks to another, where one
hears another, that is little. Where none sees none,
where none speaks to none, that is the highest, that is the
great, that is the Brahman." Being That, you are always
That. What will become of the world then? What good
shall we do to the world? Such questions do not arise
"What becomes of my gingerbread if I become old?"
says the baby! "What becomes of my marbles if I grow?
So I will not grow," says the boy! "What will become
of my dolls if I grow old?" says the little child! It is the
same question in connection with this world; it has no
existence in the past, present, or future. If we have
known the Âtman as It is, if we have known that there is
nothing else but this Atman, that everything else is but a
dream, with no existence in reality, then this world with
its poverties, its miseries, its wickedness, and its goodness
will cease to disturb us. If they do not exist, for whom and
for what shall we take trouble? This is what the Jnana-
Yogis teach. Therefore, dare to be free, dare to go as far
as your thought leads, and dare to carry that out in your
life. It is very hard to come to Jnâna. It is for the
bravest and most daring, who dare to smash all idols, not
only intellectual, but in the senses. This body is not I; it
must go. All sorts of curious things may come out of this.
A man stands up and says, "I am not the body, therefore
my headache must be cured"; but where is the headache
if not in his body? Let a thousand headaches and a
thousand bodies come and go. What is that to me? I
have neither birth nor death; father or mother I never

had; friends and foes I have none, because they are all I.
I am my own friend, and I am my own enemy. I am
Existence-Knowledge-Bliss Absolute. I am He, I am He.
If in a thousand bodies I am suffering from fever and
other ills, in millions of bodies I am healthy. If in a
thousand bodies I am starving, in other thousand bodies
I am feasting. If in thousands of bodies I am suffering
misery, in thousands of bodies I am happy. Who shall
blame whom, who praise whom? Whom to seek, whom
to avoid? I seek none, nor avoid any, for I am all the
universe. I praise myself, I blame myself, I suffer for
myself, I am happy at my own will, I am free. This is the
Jnâni, the brave and daring. Let the whole universe
tumble down; he smiles and says it never existed, it was
all a hallucination. He sees the universe tumble down.
Where was it! Where has it gone!

Before going into the practical part, we will take up
one more intellectual question. So far the logic is
tremendously rigorous. If man reasons, there is no place
for him to stand until he comes to this, that there is but
One Existence, that everything else is nothing. There is
no other way left for rational mankind but to take this
view. But how is it that what is infinite, ever perfect, ever
blessed, Existence-Knowledge-Bliss Absolute, has come
under these delusions? It is the same question that has
been asked all the world over. In the vulgar form the
question becomes, "How did sin come into this world?"
This is the most vulgar and sensuous form of the question,
and the other is the most philosophic form, but the answer
is the same. The same question has been asked in various
grades and fashions, but in its lower forms it finds no
solution, because the stories of apples and serpents and
women do not give the explanation. In that state, the
question is childish, and so is the answer. But the question
has assumed very high proportions now: "How did this
illusion come?" And the answer is as fine. The answer

is that we cannot expect any answer to an impossible question. The very question is impossible in terms. You have no right to ask that question. Why? What is perfection? That which is beyond time, space, and causation —that is perfect. Then you ask how the perfect became imperfect. In logical language the question may be put in this form: "How did that which is beyond causation become caused?" You contradict yourself. You first admit it is beyond causation, and then ask what causes it. This question can only be asked within the limits of causation. As far as time and space and causation extend, so far can this question be asked. But beyond that it will be nonsense to ask it, because the question is illogical. Within time, space, and causation it can never be answered, and what answer may lie beyond these limits can only be known when we have transcended them; therefore the wise will let this question rest. When a man is ill, he devotes himself to curing his disease without insisting that he must first learn how he came to have it.

There is another form of this question, a little lower, but more practical and illustrative: What produced this delusion? Can any reality produce delusion? Certainly not. We see that one delusion produces another, and so on. It is delusion always that produces delusion. It is disease that produces disease, and not health that produces disease. The wave is the same thing as the water, the effect is the cause in another form. The effect is delusion, and therefore the cause must be delusion. What produced this delusion? Another delusion. And so on without beginning. The only question that remains for you to ask is: Does not this break your monism, because you get two existences in the universe, one yourself and the other the delusion? The answer is: Delusion cannot be called an existence. Thousands of dreams come into your life, but do not form any part of your life. Dreams come and go; they have no existence. To call delusion existence will be sophistry. Therefore there is only one individual existence in the universe, ever free, and ever blessed; and that is what you are. This is the last conclusion reached by the Advaitists.

It may then be asked: What becomes of all these various forms of worship? They will remain ; they are simply groping in the dark for light, and through this groping light will come. We have just seen that the Self cannot see Itself. Our knowledge is within the network of Mâyâ (unreality), and beyond that is freedom. Within the network there is slavery, it is all under law; beyond that there is no law. So far as the universe is concerned, existence is ruled by law, and beyond that is freedom. As long as you are in the network of time, space, and causation, to say you are free is nonsense, because in that network all is under rigorous law, sequence, and consequence. Every thought that you think is caused, every feeling has been caused; to say that the will is free is sheer nonsense. It is only when the infinite existence comes, as it were, into this network of Maya that it takes the form of will. Will is a portion of that being, caught in the network of Maya, and therefore "free will" is a misnomer. It means nothing—sheer nonsense. So is all this talk about freedom. There is no freedom in Maya.

Every one is as much bound in thought, word, deed, and mind, as a piece of stone or this table. That I talk to you now is as rigorous in causation as that you listen to me. There is no freedom until you go beyond Maya. That is the real freedom of the soul. Men, however sharp and intellectual, however clearly they see the force of the logic that nothing here can be free, are all compelled to think they are free; they cannot help it. No work can go on until we begin to say we are free. It means that the freedom we talk about is the glimpse of the blue sky through the clouds and that the real freedom—the blue sky itself—is behind. True freedom cannot exist in the

midst of this delusion, this hallucination, this nonsense of
the world, this universe of the senses, body, and mind. All
these dreams, without beginning or end, uncontrolled and
uncontrollable, ill-adjusted, broken, inharmonious, form
our idea of this universe. In a dream, when you see a giant
with twenty heads chasing you, and you are flying from
him, you do not think it is inharmonious; you think it is
proper and right. So is this law. All that you call law is
simply chance without meaning. In this dream state you
call it law. Within Maya, so far as this law of time, space,
and causation exists, there is no freedom; and all these
various forms of worship are within this Maya. The idea
of God and the ideas of brute and of man are within this
Maya, and as such are equally hallucinations; all of them
are dreams. But you must take care not to argue like some
extraordinary men of whom we hear at the present time.
They say the idea of God is a delusion, but the idea of
this world is true. Both ideas stand or fall by the same
logic. He alone has the right to be an atheist who denies
this world, as well as the other. The same argument is for
both. The same mass of delusion extends from God to the
lowest animal, from a blade of grass to the Creator. They
stand or fall by the same logic. The same person who
sees falsity in the idea of God ought also to see it in the
idea of his own body or his own mind. When God
vanishes, then also vanish the body and mind; and when
both vanish, that which is the Real Existence remains
for ever. "There the eyes cannot go, nor the speech, nor
the mind. We cannot see it, neither know it." And we
now understand that so far as speech and thought and
knowledge and intellect go, it is all within this Maya,
within bondage. Beyond that is Reality. There neither
thought, nor mind, nor speech, can reach.

So far it is intellectually all right, but then comes the
practice. The real work is in the practice. Are any
practices necessary to realise this Oneness? Most

decidedly. It is not that you become this Brahman. You
are already that. It is not that you are going to become
God or perfect; you are already perfect; and whenever
you think you are not, it is a delusion. This delusion which
says that you are Mr. So-and-so or Mrs. So-and-so can
be got rid of by another delusion, and that is practice.
Fire will eat fire, and you can use one delusion to conquer
another delusion. One cloud will come and brush away
another cloud, and then both will go away. What are
these practices then? We must always bear in mind that
we are not going to be free, but are free already. Every
idea that we are bound is a delusion. Every idea that we
are happy or unhappy is a tremendous delusion; and
another delusion will come—that we have got to work
and worship and struggle to be free—and this will chase
out the first delusion, and then both will stop.

The fox is considered very unholy by the Mohammedans and by the Hindus. Also, if a dog touches any bit
of food, it has to be thrown out, it cannot be eaten by any
man. In a certain Mohammedan house a fox entered and
took a little bit of food from the table, ate it up, and fled.
The man was a poor man, and had prepared a very nice
feast for himself, and that feast was made unholy, and he
could not eat it. So he went to a Mulla, a priest, and
said, "This has happened to me; a fox came and took a
mouthful out of my meal. What can be done? I had prepared a feast and wanted so much to eat it, and now comes
this fox and destroys the whole affair." The Mulla thought
for a minute and then found only one solution and said,
"The only way for you is to get a dog and make him eat
a bit out of the same plate, because dogs and foxes are
eternally quarrelling. The food that was left by the fox
will go into your stomach, and that left by the dog will
go there too, and both will be purified." We are very
much in the same predicament. This is a hallucination
that we are imperfect; and we take up another, that we

have to practise to become perfect. Then one will chase
the other, as we can use one thorn to extract another and
then throw both away. There are people for whom it
is sufficient knowledge to hear, "Thou art That". With
a flash this universe goes away and the real nature shines,
but others have to struggle hard to get rid of this idea of
bondage.

The first question is: Who are fit to become Jnana-
Yogis? Those who are equipped with these requisites:
First, renunciation of all fruits of work and of all enjoyments in this life or another life. If you are the creator of
this universe, whatever you desire you will have, because
you will create it for yourself. It is only a question of time.
Some get it immediately; with others the past Samskâras
(impressions) stand in the way of getting their desires. We
give the first place to desires for enjoyment, either in this
or another life. Deny that there is any life at all, because
life is only another name for death. Deny that you are a
living being. Who cares for life? Life is one of these
hallucinations, and death is its counterpart. Joy is one
part of these hallucinations, and misery the other part,
and so on. What have you to do with life or death?
These are all creations of the mind. This is called giving
up desires of enjoyment either in this life or another.

Then comes controlling the mind, calming it so that it
will not break into waves and have all sorts of desires,
holding the mind steady, not allowing it to get into waves
from external or internal causes, controlling the mind
perfectly, just by the power of will. The Jnana-Yogi does
not take any one of these physical helps or mental helps:
simply philosophic reasoning, knowledge, and his own will,
these are the instrumentalities he believes in. Next comes
Titikshâ, forbearance, bearing all miseries without mur-
muring, without complaining. When an injury comes, do
not mind it. If a tiger comes, stand there. Who flies? There
are men who practise Titiksha, and succeed in it. There

are men who sleep on the banks of the Ganga in the mid-summer sun of India, and in winter float in the waters of the Ganga for a whole day; they do not care. Men sit in the snow of the Himalayas, and do not care to wear any garment. What is heat? What is cold? Let things come and go, what is that to me, I am not the body. It is hard to believe this in these Western countries, but it is better to know that it is done. Just as your people are brave to jump at the mouth of a cannon, or into the midst of the battlefield, so our people are brave to think and act out their philosophy. They give up their lives for it. "I am Existence-Knowledge-Bliss Absolute; I am He, I am He." Just as the Western ideal is to keep up luxury in practical life, so ours is to keep up the highest form of spirituality, to demonstrate that religion is not merely frothy words, but can be carried out, every bit of it, in this life. This is Titiksha, to bear everything, not to complain of anything. I myself have seen men who say, "I am the soul; what is the universe to me? Neither pleasure nor pain, nor virtue nor vice, nor heat nor cold is anything to me." That is Titiksha; not running after the enjoyments of the body. What is religion? To pray, "Give me this and that"? Foolish ideas of religion! Those who believe them have no true idea of God and soul. My Master used to say, "The vulture rise higher and higher until he becomes a speck, but his eye is always on the piece of rotten carrion on the earth." After all, what is the result of your ideas of religion? To cleanse the streets and have more bread and clothes? Who cares for bread and clothes? Millions come and go every minute. Who cares? Why care for the joys and vicissitudes of this little world? Go beyond that if you dare; go beyond law, let the whole universe vanish, and stand alone. "I am Existence-Absolute, Knowledge-Absolute, Bliss-Absolute; I am He, I am He."

ONE EXISTENCE APPEARING AS MANY

(Delivered in New York, 1896)

Vairâgya or renunciation is the turning point in all the various Yogas. The Karmi (worker) renounces the fruits of his work. The Bhakta (devotee) renounces all little loves for the almighty and omnipresent love. The Yogi renounces his experiences, because his philosophy is that the whole Nature, although it is for the experience of the soul, at last brings him to know that he is not in Nature, but eternally separate from Nature. The Jnâni (philosopher) renounces everything, because his philosophy is that Nature never existed, neither in the past, nor present, nor will It in the future. The question of utility cannot be asked in these higher themes. It is very absurd to ask it; and even if it be asked, after a proper analysis, what do we find in this question of utility? The ideal of happiness, that which brings man more happiness, is of greater utility to him than these higher things which do not improve his material conditions or bring him such great happiness. All the sciences are for this one end, to bring happiness to humanity; and that which brings the larger amount of happiness, man takes and gives up that which brings a lesser amount of happiness. We have seen how happiness is either in the body, or in the mind, or in the Âtman. With animals, and in the lowest human beings who are very much like animals, happiness is all in the body. No man can eat with the same pleasure as a famished dog or a wolf; so in the dog and the wolf the happiness is entirely in the body. In men we find a higher plane of happiness, that of thought; and in the Jnani there is the highest plane of happiness in the Self, the Atman. So to the philosopher this knowledge of the Self is of the highest utility, because it gives him the highest happiness possible. Sense-gratifications or physical things cannot be of the highest utility to him, because he does not find in them the same pleasure that he finds in knowledge itself; and after all, knowledge is the one goal and is really the highest happiness that we know. All who work in ignorance are, as it were, the draught animals of the Devas. The word Deva is here used in the sense of a wise man. All the people that work and toil and labour like machines do not really enjoy life, but it is the wise man who enjoys. A rich man buys a picture at a cost of a hundred thousand dollars perhaps, but it is the man who understands art that enjoys it; and if the rich man is without knowledge of art, it is useless to him, he is only the owner. All over the world, it is the wise man who enjoys the happiness of the world. The ignorant man never enjoys; he has to work for others unconsciously.

Thus far we have seen the theories of these Advaitist philosophers, how there is but one Atman; there cannot be two. We have seen how in the whole of this universe there is but One Existence; and that One Existence when seen through the senses is called the world, the world of matter. When It is seen through the mind, It is called the world of thoughts and ideas; and when It is seen as it is, then It is the One Infinite Being. You must bear this in mind; it is not that there is a soul in man, although I had to take that for granted in order to explain it at first, but that there is only One Existence, and that one the Atman, the Self; and when this is perceived through the senses, through sense-imageries, It is called the body. When It is perceived through thought, It is called the mind. When It is perceived in Its own nature, It is the Atman, the One Only Existence. So it is not that there are three things in one, the body and the mind and the Self, although that was a convenient way of putting it in the course of explanation; but all is that Atman, and that one Being is sometimes called the body, sometimes the mind, and sometimes the Self, according to different vision. There is but one Being which the ignorant call the world. When a man goes higher in knowledge, he calls the very same Being the world of thought. Again, when knowledge itself comes, all illusions vanish, and man finds it is all nothing but Atman. I am that One Existence. This is the last conclusion. There are neither three nor two in the universe; it is all One. That One, under the illusion of Mâyâ, is seen as many, just as a rope is seen as a snake. It is the very rope that is seen as a snake. There are not two things there, a rope separate and a snake separate. No man sees these two things there at the same time. Dualism and non-dualism are very good philosophic terms, but in perfect perception we never perceive the real and the false at the same time. We are all born monists, we cannot help it. We always perceive the one. When we perceive the rope, we do not perceive the snake at all; and when we see the snake, we do not see the rope at all—it has vanished. When you see illusion, you do not see reality. Suppose you see one of your friends coming at a distance in the street; you know him very well, but through the haze and mist that is before you, you think it is another man. When you see your friend as another man, you do not see your friend at all, he has vanished. You are perceiving only one. Suppose your friend is Mr. A; but when you perceive Mr. A as Mr. B, you do not see Mr. A at all. In each case you perceive only one. When you see yourself as a body, you are body and nothing else; and that is the perception of the vast majority of mankind. They may talk of soul and mind, and all these things, but what they perceive is the physical form, the touch, taste, vision, and so on. Again, with certain men in certain states of consciousness, they perceive themselves as thought. You know, of course, the story told of Sir Humphrey Davy, who was making experiments before his class with laughing-gas, and suddenly one of the tubes broke, and the gas escaping, he breathed it in. For some moments he remained like a statue. Afterwards he told his class that when he was in that state, he actually perceived that the whole world is made up of ideas. The gas, for a time, made him forget the consciousness of the body, and that very thing which he was seeing as the body, he began to perceive as ideas. When the consciousness rises still higher, when this little puny consciousness is gone for ever, that which is the Reality behind shines, and we see it as the One Existence-Knowledge-Bliss, the one Atman, the Universal. "One that is only Knowledge itself, One that is Bliss itself, beyond all compare, beyond all limit, ever free, never bound, infinite as the sky, unchangeable as the sky. Such a One will manifest Himself in your heart in meditation."

How does the Advaitist theory explain these various phases of heaven and hells and these various ideas we find in all religions? When a man dies, it is said that he goes to heaven or hell, goes here or there, or that when a man dies he is born again in another body either in heaven or in another world or somewhere. These are all hallucinations. Really speaking nobody is ever born or dies. There is neither heaven nor hell nor this world; all three never really existed. Tell a child a lot of ghost stories, and let him go out into the street in the evening. There is a little stump of a tree. What does the child see? A ghost, with hands stretched out, ready to grab him. Suppose a man comes from the corner of the street, wanting to meet his sweetheart; he sees that stump of the tree as the girl. A policeman coming from the street corner sees the stump as a thief. The thief sees it as a policeman. It is the same stump of a tree that was seen in various ways. The stump is the reality, and the visions of the stump are the projections of the various minds. There is one Being, this Self; It neither comes nor goes. When a man is ignorant, he wants to go to heaven or some place, and all his life he has been thinking and thinking of this; and when this earth-dream vanishes, he sees this world as a heaven with Devas and angels flying about, and all such things. If a man all his life desires to meet his forefathers, he gets them all from Adam downwards, because he creates them. If a man is still more ignorant and has always been frightened by fanatics with ideas of hell, with all sorts of punishments, when he dies, he will see this very world as hell. All that is meant by dying or being born is simply changes in the plane of vision. Neither do you move, nor does that move upon which you project your vision. You are the permanent, the unchangeable. How can you come and go? It is impossible ; you are omnipresent. The sky never moves, but the clouds move over the surface of the sky, and we may think that the sky itself moves, just as when you are in a railway train, you think the land is moving. It is not so, but it is the train which is moving. You are where you are ; these dreams, these various clouds move. One dream follows another without connection. There is no such thing as law or connection in this world, but we are thinking that there is a great deal of connection. All of you have probably read *Alice in Wonderland*. It is the most wonderful book for children that has been written in this century. When I read it, I was delighted; it was always in my head to write that sort of a book for children. What pleased me most in it was what you think most incongruous, that there is no connection there. One idea comes and jumps into another, without any connection. When you were children, you thought that the most wonderful connection. So this man brought back his thoughts of childhood, which were perfectly connected to him as a child, and composed this book for children. And all these books which men write, trying to make children swallow their own ideas as men, are nonsense. We too are grown-up children, that is all. The world is the same unconnected thing—*Alice in Wonderland*—with no connection whatever. When we

III—3

see things happen a number of times in a certain sequence, we call it cause and effect, and say that the thing will happen again. When this dream changes, another dream will seem quite as connected as this. When we dream, the things we see all seem to be connected; during the dream we never think they are incongruous; it is only when we wake that we see the want of connection. When we wake from this dream of the world and compare it with the Reality, it will be found all incongruous nonsense, a mass of incongruity passing before us, we do not know whence or whither, but we know it will end; and this is called Maya, and is like masses of fleeting fleecy clouds. They represent all this changing existence, and the sun itself, the unchanging, is you. When you look at that unchanging Existence from the outside, you call it God; and when you look at it from the inside, you call it yourself. It is but one. There is no God separate from you, no God higher than you, the real "you". All the gods are little beings to you, all the ideas of God and Father in heaven are but your own reflection. God Himself is your image. "God created man after His own image." That is wrong. Man creates God after his own image. That is right. Throughout the universe we are creating gods after our own image. We create the god and fall down at his feet and worship him; and when this dream comes, we love it!

This is a good point to understand—that the sum and substance of this lecture is that there is but One Existence, and that One-Existence seen through different constitutions appears either as the earth, or heaven, or hell, or gods, or ghosts, or men, or demons, or world, or all these things. But among these many, "He who sees that One in this ocean of death, he who sees that One Life in this floating universe, who realises that One who never changes, unto him belongs eternal peace; unto none else, unto none else." This One existence has to be realised. How, is the next question. How is it to be realised? How is this dream

to be broken, how shall we wake up from this dream that
we are little men and women, and all such things? ·We
are the Infinite Being of the universe and have become
materialised into these little beings, men and women,
depending upon the sweet word of one man, or the angry
word of another, and so forth. What a terrible depen-
dence, what a terrible slavery! I who am beyond all
pleasure and pain, whose reflection is the whole universe,
little bits of whose life are the suns and moons and stars—
I am held down as a terrible slave! If you pinch my body,
I feel pain. If one says a kind word, I begin to rejoice.
See my condition—slave of the body, slave of the mind,
slave of the world, slave of a good word, slave of a bad
word, slave of passion, slave of happiness, slave of life,
slave of death, slave of everything! This slavery has to be
broken. How? "This Atman has first to be heard, then
reasoned upon, and then meditated upon." This is the
method of the Advaita Jnâni. The truth has to be heard,
then reflected upon, and then to be constantly asserted.
Think always, "I am Brahman". Every other thought
must be cast aside as weakening. Cast aside every thought
that says that you are men or women. Let body go, and
mind go, and gods go, and ghosts go. Let everything go
but that One Existence. "Where one hears another, where
one sees another, that is small; where one does not hear
another, where one does not see another, that is Infinite."
That is the highest when the subject and the object
become one. When I am the listener and I am the speaker,
when I am the teacher and I am the taught, when I am
the creator and I am the created—then alone fear ceases ;
there is not another to make us afraid. There is nothing
but myself, what can frighten me? This is to be
heard day after day. Get rid of all other thoughts.
Everything else must be thrown aside, and this is to be
repeated continually, poured through the ears until it
reaches the heart, until every nerve and muscle, every

drop of blood tingles with the idea that I am He, I am He.
Even at the gate of death say, "I am He". There was a
man in India, a Sannyâsin, who used to repeat **"Shivoham"**
—"I am Bliss Eternal" ; and a tiger jumped on him one
day and dragged him away and killed him; but so long as
he was living, the sound came, "Shivoham, Shivoham".
Even at the gate of death, in the greatest danger, in the
thick of the battlefield, at the bottom of the ocean, on the
tops of the highest mountains, in the thickest of the forest,
tell yourself, "I am He, I am He". Day and night say,
"I am He". It is the greatest strength; it is religion. "The
weak will never reach the Atman." Never say, "O Lord,
I am a miserable sinner." Who will help you? You are
the help of the universe. What in this universe can help
you? Where is the man, or the god, or the demon to help
you? What can prevail over you? You are the God of
the universe; where can you seek for help? Never help
came from anywhere but from yourself. In your ignorance,
every prayer that you made and that was answered, you
thought was answered by some Being, but you answered
the prayer yourself unknowingly. The help came from
yourself, and you fondly imagined that some one was
sending help to you. There is no help for you outside of
yourself ; you are the creator of the universe. Like the
silkworm you have built a cocoon around yourself. Who
will save you? Burst your own cocoon and come out as
the beautiful butterfly, as the free soul. Then alone you
will see Truth. Ever tell yourself, "I am He." These are
words that will burn up the dross that is in the mind,
words that will bring out the tremendous energy which is
within you already, the infinite power which is sleeping
in your heart. This is to be brought out by constantly
hearing the truth and nothing else. Wherever there is
thought of weakness, approach not the place. Avoid all
weakness if you want to be a Jnani.

Before you begin to practise, clear your mind of all

doubts. Fight and reason and argue; and when you have established it in your mind that this and this alone can be the truth and nothing else, do not argue any more ; close your mouth. Hear not argumentation, neither argue yourself. What is the use of any more arguments? You have satisfied yourself, you have decided the question. What remains? The truth has now to be realised, therefore why waste valuable time in vain arguments? The truth has now to be meditated upon, and every idea that strengthens you must be taken up and every thought that weakens you must be rejected. The Bhakta meditates upon forms and images and all such things and upon God. This is the natural process, but a slower one. The Yogi meditates upon various centres in his body and manipulates powers in his mind. The Jnani says, the mind does not exist, neither the body. This idea of the body and of the mind must go, must be driven off ; therefore it is foolish to think of them. It would be like trying to cure one ailment by bringing in another. His meditation therefore is the most difficult one, the negative; he denies everything, and what is left is the Self. This is the most analytical way. The Jnani wants to tear away the universe from the Self by the sheer force of analysis. It is very easy to say, "I am a Jnani", but very hard to be really one. "The way is long", it is, as it were, walking on the sharp edge of a razor; yet despair not. "Awake, arise, and stop not until the goal is reached", say the Vedas.

So what is the meditation of the Jnani? He wants to rise above every idea of body or mind, to drive away the idea that he is the body. For instance, when I say, "I Swami", immediately the idea of the body comes. What must I do then? I must give the mind a hard blow and say, "No, I am not the body, I am the Self." Who cares if disease comes or death in the most horrible form? I am not the body. Why make the body nice? To enjoy the illusion once more? To continue the slavery? Let it go,

I am not the body. That is the way of the Jnani. The Bhakta says, "The Lord has given me this body that I may safely cross the ocean of life, and I must cherish it until the journey is accomplished." The Yogi says, "I must be careful of the body, so that I may go on steadily and finally attain liberation." The Jnani feels that he cannot wait, he must reach the goal this very moment. He says, "I am free through eternity, I am never bound; I am the God of the universe through all eternity. Who shall make me perfect? I am perfect already." When a man is perfect, he sees perfection in others. When he sees imperfection, it is his own mind projecting itself. How can he see imperfection if he has not got it in himself? So the Jnani does not care for perfection or imperfection. None exists for him. As soon as he is free, he does not see good and evil. Who sees evil and good? He who has it in himself. Who sees the body? He who thinks he is the body. The moment you get rid of the idea that you are the body, you do not see the world at all; it vanishes for ever. The Jnani seeks to tear himself away from this bondage of matter by the force of intellectual conviction. This is the negative way—the "Neti, Neti"—"Not this, not this."

BHAKTI-YOGA

OR

THE YOGA OF LOVE AND DEVOTION

BHAKTI-YOGA

PRAYER

स तन्मयो ह्यमृत ईशसंस्थो ज्ञः सर्वगो भुवनस्यास्य गोप्ता ।
य ईशेऽस्य जगतो नित्यमेव नान्यो हेतुर्विद्यत ईशनाय ॥
यो ब्रह्माणं विदधाति पूर्वं यो वै वेदांश्च प्रहिणोति तस्मै ।
तं ह देवं आत्मबुद्धिप्रकाशं मुमुक्षुर्वै शरणमहं प्रपद्ये ॥

"He is the Soul of the Universe; He is Immortal; His is the Rulership; He is the All-knowing, the All-pervading, the Protector of the Universe, the Eternal Ruler. None else is there efficient to govern the world eternally. He who at the beginning of creation projected Brahmâ (i.e. the universal consciousness), and who delivered the Vedas unto him— seeking liberation I go for refuge unto that Effulgent One, whose light turns the understanding towards the Âtman."

Shvetâshvatara-Upanishad, VI. 17-18.

DEFINITION OF BHAKTI

Bhakti-Yoga is a real, genuine search after the Lord, a search beginning, continuing, and ending in love. One single moment of the madness of extreme love to God brings us eternal freedom. "Bhakti", says Nârada in his explanation of the Bhakti-aphorisms, "is intense love to God"; "When a man gets it, he loves all, hates none; he becomes satisfied for ever"; "This love cannot be reduced to any earthly benefit", because so long as worldly desires last, that kind of love does not come; "Bhakti is greater than Karma, greater than Yoga, because these are intended for an object in view, while Bhakti is its own fruition, its own means and its own end."

Bhakti has been the one constant theme of our sages. Apart from the special writers on Bhakti, such as Shândilya or Narada, the great commentators on the *Vyâsa-Sutras,* evidently advocates of knowledge (Jnâna), have also something very suggestive to say about love. Even when the commentator is anxious to explain many, if not all, of the texts so as to make them import a sort of dry knowledge, the *Sutras,* in the chapter on worship especially, do not lend themselves to be easily manipulated in that fashion.

There is not really so much difference between knowledge (Jnana) and love (Bhakti) as people sometimes imagine. We shall see, as we go on, that in the end they converge and meet at the same point. So also is it with Râja-Yoga, which when pursued as a means to attain liberation, and not (as unfortunately it frequently becomes in the hands of charlatans and mystery-mongers) as an instrument to hoodwink the unwary, leads us also to the same goal.

The one great advantage of Bhakti is that it is the easiest and the most natural way to reach the great divine end in view; its great disadvantage is that in its lower forms it oftentimes degenerates into hideous fanaticism. The fanatical crew in Hinduism, or Mohammedanism, or Christianity, have always been almost exclusively recruited from these worshippers on the lower planes of Bhakti. That singleness of attachment (Nishthâ) to a loved object, without which no genuine love can grow, is very often also the cause of the denunciation of everything else. All the weak and undeveloped minds in every religion or country have only one way of loving their own ideal, i.e. by hating every other ideal. Herein is the explanation of why the same man who is so lovingly attached to his own ideal of God, so devoted to his own ideal of religion, becomes a howling fanatic as soon as he sees or hears anything of any other ideal. This kind of love is somewhat like the canine instinct of guarding the master's property from intrusion; only, the instinct of the dog is better than the reason of man, for the dog never mistakes its master for an enemy in whatever dress he may come before it. Again, the fanatic loses all power of judgment. Personal considerations are in his case of such absorbing interest that to him it is no question at all what a man says—whether it is right or wrong; but the one thing he is always particularly careful to know is who says it. The same man who is kind, good, honest, and loving to people of his own opinion, will not hesitate to do the vilest deeds when they are directed against persons beyond the pale of his own religious brotherhood.

But this danger exists only in that stage of Bhakti which is called the *preparatory* (Gauni). When Bhakti has become ripe and has passed into that form which is called the *supreme* (Parâ), no more is there any fear of these hideous manifestations of fanaticism; that soul which is overpowered by this higher form of Bhakti is too near the God of Love to become an instrument for the diffusion of hatred.

It is not given to all of us to be harmonious in the building up of our characters in this life: yet we know that that character is of the noblest type in which all these three—knowledge and love and Yoga—are harmoniously fused. Three things are necessary for a bird to fly—the two wings and the tail as a rudder for steering. Jnana (Knowledge) is the one wing, Bhakti (Love) is the other, and Yoga is the tail that keeps up the balance. For those who cannot pursue all these three forms of worship together in harmony and take up, therefore, Bhakti alone as their way, it is necessary always to remember that forms and ceremonials, though absolutely necessary for the progressive soul, have no other value than taking us on to that state in which we feel the most intense love to God.

There is a little difference in opinion between the teachers of knowledge and those of love, though both admit the power of Bhakti. The Jnânis hold Bhakti to be an instrument of liberation, the Bhaktas look upon it both as the instrument and the thing to be attained. To my mind this is a distinction without much difference. In fact, Bhakti, when used as an instrument, really means a lower form of worship, and the higher form becomes inseparable from the lower form of realisation at a later stage. Each seems to lay a great stress upon his own peculiar method of worship, forgetting that with perfect love true knowledge is bound to come even unsought, and that from perfect knowledge true love is inseparable.

Bearing this in mind let us try to understand what the great Vedantic commentators have to say on the subject. In explaining the Sutra Âvrittirasakridupadeshât[1], Bhagavân Shankara says, "Thus people say, 'He is devoted to the king, he is devoted to the Guru'; they say this of him who follows his Guru, and does so, having that following as the one end in view. Similarly they say, 'The loving wife meditates on her loving husband'; here also a kind of eager and continuous remembrance is meant." This is devotion according to Shankara.

"Meditation again is a constant remembrance (of the thing meditated upon) flowing like an unbroken stream of oil poured out from one vessel to another. When this kind of remembering has been attained (in relation to God) all bondages break. Thus it is spoken of in the scriptures regarding constant remembering as a means to liberation. This remembering again is of the same form as seeing, because it is of the same meaning as in the passage, 'When He who is far and near is seen, the bonds of the heart are broken, all doubts vanish, and all effects of work disappear.' He who is near can be seen, but he who is far

---

[1] Meditation is necessary, that having been often enjoined.

can only be remembered. Nevertheless the scripture says
that we have to see Him who is near as well as Him who
is far, thereby indicating to us that the above kind of
remembering is as good as *seeing*. This remembrance
when exalted assumes the same form as seeing. . . .
Worship is constant remembering as may be seen from the
essential texts of scriptures. Knowing, which is the same
as repeated worship, has been described as constant
remembering. . . . Thus the memory, which has attained
to the height of what is as good as direct perception, is
spoken of in the Shruti as a means of liberation. 'This
Atman is not to be reached through various sciences, nor
by intellect, nor by much study of the Vedas. Whomsoever this Atman desires, by him is the Atman attained,
unto him this Atman discovers Himself.' Here, after
saying that mere hearing, thinking and meditating are not
the means of attaining this Atman, it is said, 'Whom this
Atman desires, by him the Atman is attained.' The extremely beloved is desired ; by whomsoever this Atman is
extremely beloved, he becomes the most beloved of the
Atman. So that this beloved may attain the Atman, the
Lord Himself helps. For it has been said by the Lord:
'Those who are constantly attached to Me and worship
Me with love—I give that direction to their will by which
they come to Me.' Therefore it is said that, to whomso-
ever this remembering, which is of the same form as
direct perception, is very dear, because it is dear to the
Object of such memory perception, he is desired by the
Supreme Atman, by him the Supreme Atman is attained.
This constant remembrance is denoted by the word
Bhakti." So says Bhagavân Râmânuja in his commentary
on the Sutra Athâto Brahma-jijnâsâ.[1]

In commenting on the Sutra of Patanjali, Ishvara
pranidhânâdvâ, i.e. "Or by the worship of the Supreme

[1] Hence follows a dissertation on Brahman.

Lord"—Bhoja says, "Pranidhâna is that sort of Bhakti in which, without seeking results, such as sense-enjoyments etc., all works are dedicated to that Teacher of teachers." Bhagavan Vyâsa also, when commenting on the same, defines Pranidhana as "the form of Bhakti by which the mercy of the Supreme Lord comes to the Yogi, and blesses him by granting him his desires". According to Shândilya, "Bhakti is intense love to God." The best definition is, however, that given by the king of Bhaktas, Prahlâda: या प्रीतिरविवेकानां विषयेष्वनपायिनी । त्वामनुस्मरतः सा मे हृदयान्मापसर्पतु ॥ "That deathless love which the ignorant have for the fleeting objects of the senses—as I keep meditating on Thee—may not that love slip away from my heart!" *Love!* For whom? For the Supreme Lord Ishvara. Love for any other being, however great cannot be Bhakti; for, as Ramanuja says in his *Shri Bhâshya*, quoting an ancient Âchârya, i.e. a great teacher: आब्रह्मस्तम्बपर्यन्ताः जगदन्तर्व्य- वस्थिताः । प्राणिनः कर्मजनितसंसारवशवर्तिनः ॥ यतस्ततो न ते ध्याने ध्यानिनामुपकारकाः । अविद्यान्तर्गतास्सर्वं ते हि संसारगोचराः ॥ "From Brahmâ to a clump of grass, all things that live in the world are slaves of birth and death caused by Karma; therefore they cannot be helpful as objects of meditation, because they are all in ignorance and subject to change." In commenting on the word Anurakti used by Shandilya, the commentator Svapneshvara says that it means Anu, after, and Rakti, attachment; i.e. the attachment which comes after the knowledge of the nature and glory of God; else a blind attachment to any one, e.g. to wife or children, would be Bhakti. We plainly see, therefore, that Bhakti is a series or succession of mental efforts at religious realisation beginning with ordinary worship and ending in a supreme intensity of love for Ishvara.

THE PHILOSOPHY OF ISHVARA

Who is Ishvara? Janmâdyasya yatah—"From whom is the birth, continuation, and dissolution of the universe," —He is Ishvara—"the Eternal, the Pure, the Ever-Free, the Almighty, the All-Knowing, the All-Merciful, the Teacher of all teachers"; and above all, Sa Ishvarah anirvachaniya-premasvarupah—"He the Lord is, of His own nature, inexpressible Love." These certainly are the definitions of a Personal God. Are there then two Gods— the "Not this, not this," the Sat-chit-ânanda, the Existence-Knowledge-Bliss of the philosopher, and this God of Love of the Bhakta? No, it is the same Sat-chit-ananda who is also the God of Love, the impersonal and personal in one. It has always to be understood that the Personal God worshipped by the Bhakta is not separate or different from the Brahman. All is Brahman, the One without a second ; only the Brahman, as unity or absolute, is too much of an abstraction to be loved and worshipped; so the Bhakta chooses the relative aspect of Brahman, that is, Ishvara, the Supreme Ruler. To use a simile: Brahman is as the clay or substance out of which an infinite variety of articles are fashioned. As clay, they are all one; but form or manifestation differentiates them. Before every one of them was made, they all existed potentially in the clay, and, of course, they are identical substantially; but when formed, and so long as the form remains, they are separate and different; the clay-mouse can never become a clay-elephant, because, as manifestations, form alone makes them what they are, though as unformed clay they are all one. Ishvara is the highest manifestation of the Absolute Reality, or in other words, the highest possible reading of the Absolute by the human mind. Creation is eternal, and so also is Ishvara.

In the fourth Pâda of the fourth chapter of his *Sutras*, after stating the almost infinite power and knowledge which will come to the liberated soul after the attainment of Moksha, Vyâsa makes the remark, in an aphorism, that none, however, will get the power of creating, ruling, and dissolving the universe, because that belongs to God alone. In explaining the Sutra it is easy for the dualistic commentators to show how it is ever impossible for a subordinate soul, Jiva, to have the infinite power and total independence of God. The thorough dualistic commentator Madhvâchârya deals with this passage in his usual summary method by quoting a verse from the *Varâha Purâna*.

In explaining this aphorism the commentator Râmânuja says, "This doubt being raised, whether among the powers of the liberated souls is included that unique power of the Supreme One, that is, of creation etc. of the universe and even the Lordship of all, or whether, without that, the glory of the liberated consists only in the direct perception of the Supreme One, we get as an argument the following: It is reasonable that the liberated get the Lordship of the universe, because the scriptures say, 'He attains to extreme sameness with the Supreme One and all his desires are realised.' Now extreme sameness and realisation of all desires cannot be attained without the unique power of the Supreme Lord, namely, that of governing the universe. Therefore, to attain the realisation of all desires and the extreme sameness with the Supreme, we must all admit that the liberated get the power of ruling the whole universe. To this we reply, that the liberated get all the powers except that of ruling the universe. Ruling the universe is guiding the form and the life and the desires of all the sentient and the non-sentient beings. The liberated ones from whom all that veils His true nature has been removed, only enjoy the unobstructed perception of the Brahman, but do not possess the power of ruling the universe. This is proved from the scriptural text, "From whom all these things are born, by which all that are born live, unto whom they, departing, return—

ask about it. That is Brahman.' If this quality of ruling the universe be a quality common even to the liberated, then this text would not apply as a definition of Brahman, defining Him through His rulership of the universe. The uncommon attributes alone define a thing; therefore in texts like—'My beloved boy, alone, in the beginning there existed the One without a second. That saw and felt, "I will give birth to the many." That projected heat.' —'Brahman indeed alone existed in the beginning. That One evolved. That projected a blessed form, the Kshatra. All these gods are Kshatras: Varuna, Soma, Rudra, Parjanya, Yama, Mrityu, Ishâna.'—'Atman indeed existed alone in the beginning; nothing else vibrated; He thought of projecting the world; He projected the world after.'—'Alone Nârâyana existed; neither Brahmâ, nor Ishâna, nor the Dyâvâ-Prithivi, nor the stars, nor water, nor fire, nor Soma, nor the sun. He did not take pleasure alone. He after His meditation had one daughter, the ten organs, etc.'—and in others as, 'Who living in the earth is separate from the earth, who living in the Atman, etc.'—the Shrutis speak of the Supreme One as the subject of the work of ruling the universe. . . . Nor in these descriptions of the ruling of the universe is there any position for the liberated soul, by which such a soul may have the ruling of the universe ascribed to it."

In explaining the next Sutra, Ramanuja says, "If you say it is not so, because there are direct texts in the Vedas in evidence to the contrary, these texts refer to the glory of the liberated in the spheres of the subordinate deities." This also is an easy solution of the difficulty. Although the system of Ramanuja admits the unity of the total, within that totality of existence there are, according to him, eternal differences. Therefore, for all practical purposes, this system also being dualistic, it was easy for Ramanuja to keep the distinction between the personal soul and the Personal God very clear.

We shall now try to understand what the great representative of the Advaita School has to say on the point. We shall see how the Advaita system maintains all the hopes and aspirations of the dualist intact, and at the same time propounds its own solution of the problem in consonance with the high destiny of divine humanity. Those who aspire to retain their individual mind even after liberation and to remain distinct will have ample opportunity of realising their aspirations and enjoying the blessing of the qualified Brahman. These are they who have been spoken of in the *Bhâgavata Purâna* thus: "O king, such are the glorious qualities of the Lord that the sages whose only pleasure is in the Self, and from whom all fetters have fallen off, even they love the Omnipresent with the love that is for love's sake." These are they who are spoken of by the Sânkhyas as getting merged in nature in this cycle, so that, after attaining perfection, they may come out in the next as lords of world-systems. But none of these ever becomes equal to God (Ishvara). Those who attain to that state where there is neither creation, nor created, nor creator, where there is neither knower, nor knowable, nor knowledge, where there is neither *I*, nor *thou*, nor *he*, where there is neither subject, nor object, nor relation, "there, who is seen by whom?"—such persons have gone beyond everything to "where words cannot go nor mind", gone to that which the Shrutis declare as "Not this, not this"; but for those who cannot, or will not reach this state, there will inevitably remain the triune vision of the one undifferentiated Brahman as nature, soul, and the interpenetrating sustainer of both— Ishvara. So, when Prahlâda forgot himself, he found neither the universe nor its cause; all was to him one Infinite, undifferentiated by name and form; but as soon as he remembered that he was Prahlada, there was the universe before him and with it the Lord of the universe— "the Repository of an infinite number of blessed qualities".

So it was with the blessed Gopis. So long as they had lost
sense of their own personal identity and individuality, they
were all Krishnas, and when they began again to think of
Him as the One to be worshipped, then they were Gopis
again, and immediately तासामाविरभूच्छौरिः स्मयमानमुखाम्बुजः ।
पीताम्बरधरः स्रग्वी साक्षान्मन्मथमन्मथः ॥ (*Bhagavata*)—"Unto them
appeared Krishna with a smile on His lotus face, clad in
yellow robes and having garlands on, the embodied
conqueror (in beauty) of the god of love."

Now to go back to our Acharya Shankara: "Those",
he says, "who by worshipping the qualified Brahman
attain conjunction with the Supreme Ruler, preserving
their own mind—is their glory limited or unlimited? This
doubt arising, we get as an argument: Their glory should
be unlimited because of the scriptural texts, 'They attain
their own kingdom', 'To him all the gods offer worship',
'Their desires are fulfilled in all the worlds'. As an answer
to this, Vyasa writes, 'Without the power of ruling the
universe.' Barring the power of creation etc. of the universe, the other powers such as Animâ etc. are acquired
by the liberated. As to ruling the universe, that belongs
to the eternally perfect Ishvara. Why? Because He is the
subject of all the scriptural texts as regards creation etc.,
and the liberated souls are not mentioned therein in any
connection whatsoever. The Supreme Lord indeed is
alone engaged in ruling the universe. The texts as to creation etc. all point to Him. Besides, there is given the
adjective 'ever-perfect'. Also the scriptures say that the
powers Anima etc. of the others are from the search after
and the worship of God. Therefore they have no place
in the ruling of the universe. Again, on account of their
possessing their own minds, it is possible that their
wills may differ, and that, whilst one desires creation,
another may desire destruction. The only way of avoiding
this conflict is to make all wills subordinate to some one
will. Therefore the conclusion is that the wills of the lib-

erated are dependent on the will of the Supreme Ruler."

Bhakti, then, can be directed towards Brahman, only
in His personal aspect. क्लेशोऽधिकतरस्तेषामव्यक्तासक्तचेतसाम्—
"The way is more difficult for those whose mind is attached
to the Absolute!" Bhakti has to float on smoothly with
the current of our nature. True it is that we cannot have
any idea of the Brahman which is not anthropomorphic,
but is it not equally true of everything we know? The
greatest psychologist the world has ever known, Bhagavān
Kapila, demonstrated ages ago that human consciousness
is one of the elements in the make-up of all the objects of
our perception and conception, internal as well as external.
Beginning with our bodies and going up to Ishvara, we may
see that every object of our perception is this consciousness plus something else, whatever that may be; and this
unavoidable mixture is what we ordinarily think of as
reality. Indeed it is, and ever will be, all of the reality that
is possible for the human mind to know. Therefore to
say that Ishvara is unreal, because He is anthropomorphic,
is sheer nonsense. It sounds very much like the occidental
squabble on idealism and realism, which fearful-looking
quarrel has for its foundation a mere play on the word
"real". The idea of Ishvara covers all the ground ever denoted and connoted by the word real, and Ishvara is as
real as anything else in the universe ; and after all, the word
real means nothing more than what has now been pointed
out. Such is our philosophical conception of Ishvara.

SPIRITUAL REALISATION, THE AIM OF
BHAKTI-YOGA

To the Bhakta these dry details are necessary only to
strengthen his will; beyond that they are of no use to him.
For he is treading on a path which is fitted very soon
to lead him beyond the hazy and turbulent regions of
reason, to lead him to the realm of realisation. He, soon,
through the mercy of the Lord, reaches a plane where

pedantic and powerless reason is left far behind, and the mere intellectual groping through the dark gives place to the daylight of direct perception. He no more reasons and believes, he almost perceives. He no more argues, he senses. And is not this seeing God, and feeling God, and enjoying God higher than everything else? Nay, Bhaktas have not been wanting who have maintained that it is higher than even Moksha—liberation. And is it not also the highest utility? There are people—and a good many of them too—in the world who are convinced that only that is of use and utility which brings to man crea-ture-comforts. Even religion, God, eternity, soul, none of these is of any use to them, as they do not bring them money or physical comfort. To such, all those things which do not go to gratify the senses and appease the appetites are of no utility. In every mind, utility, how-ever, is conditioned by its own peculiar wants. To men, therefore, who never rise higher than eating, drinking, begetting progeny, and dying, the only gain is in sense-enjoyments; and they must wait and go through many more births and reincarnations to learn to feel even the faintest necessity for anything higher. But those to whom the eternal interests of the soul are of much higher value than the fleeting interests of this mundane life, to whom the gratification of the senses is but like the thoughtless play of the baby, to them God and the love of God form the highest and the only utility of human existence. Thank God there are some such still living in this world of too much worldliness.

Bhakti-Yoga, as we have said, is divided into the Gauni or the preparatory, and the Parâ or the supreme forms. We shall find, as we go on, how in the prepara-tory stage we unavoidably stand in need of many concrete helps to enable us to get on ; and indeed the mythological and symbological parts of all religions are natural growths which early environ the aspiring soul and help it Godward. It is also a significant fact that spiritual giants have been produced only in those systems of religion where there is an exuberant growth of rich mythology and ritualism. The dry fanatical forms of religion which attempt to eradicate all that is poetical, all that is beautiful and sublime, all that gives a firm grasp to the infant mind tottering in its Godward way—the forms which attempt to break down the very ridge-poles of the spiritual roof, and in their ignorant and superstitious conceptions of truth try to drive away all that is life-giving, all that furnishes the formative material to the spiritual plant growing in the human soul—such forms of religion too soon find that all that is left to them is but an empty shell, a contentless frame of words and sophistry with perhaps a little flavour of a kind of social scavengering or the so-called spirit of reform.

The vast mass of those whose religion is like this, are conscious or unconscious materialists—the end and aim of their lives here and hereafter being enjoyment, which indeed is to them the alpha and the omega of human life, and which is their Ishtâpurta ; work like street-cleaning and scavengering, intended for the material comfort of man is, according to them, the be-all and end-all of human existence ; and the sooner the followers of this curious mixture of ignorance and fanaticism come out in their true colours and join, as they well deserve to do, the ranks of atheists and materialists, the better will it be for the world. One ounce of the practice of righteousness and of spiritual Self-realisation outweighs tons and tons of frothy talk and nonsensical sentiments. Show us one, but one gigantic spiritual genius growing out of all this dry dust of ignorance and fanaticism ; and if you cannot, close your mouths, open the windows of your hearts to the clear light of truth, and sit like children at the feet of those who know what they are talking about—the sages of India. Let us then listen attentively to what they say.

THE NEED OF GURU

Every soul is destined to be perfect, and every being, in the end, will attain the state of perfection. Whatever we are now is the result of our acts and thoughts in the past ; and whatever we shall be in the future will be the result of what we think and do now. But this, the shaping of our own destinies, does not preclude our receiving help from outside ; nay, in the vast majority of cases such help is absolutely necessary. When it comes, the higher powers and possibilities of the soul are quickened, spiritual life is awakened, growth is animated, and man becomes holy and perfect in the end.

This quickening impulse cannot be derived from books. The soul can only receive impulses from another soul, and from nothing else. We may study books all our lives, we may become very intellectual, but in the end we find that we have not developed at all spiritually. It is not true that a high order of intellectual development always goes hand in hand with a proportionate development of the spiritual side in Man. In studying books we are sometimes deluded into thinking that thereby we are being spiritually helped ; but if we analyse the effect of the study of books on ourselves, we shall find that at the utmost it is only our intellect that derives profit from such studies, and not our inner spirit. This inadequacy of books to quicken spiritual growth is the reason why, although almost every one of us can *speak* most wonderfully on spiritual matters, when it comes to action and the living of a truly spiritual life, we find ourselves so awfully deficient. To quicken the spirit, the impulse must come from another soul.

The person from whose soul such impulse comes is called the Guru—the teacher ; and the person to whose soul the impulse is conveyed is called the Shishya—the student. To convey such an impulse to any soul, in the first place, the soul from which it proceeds must possess the power of transmitting it, as it were, to another ; and in the second place, the soul to which it is transmitted must be fit to receive it. The seed must be a living seed, and the field must be ready ploughed ; and when both these conditions are fulfilled, a wonderful growth of genuine religion takes place. "The true preacher of religion has to be of wonderful capabilities, and clever shall his hearer be"—आश्चर्यो वक्ता कुशलोऽस्य लब्धा ; and when both of these are really wonderful and extraordinary, then will a splendid spiritual awakening result, and not otherwise. Such alone are the real teachers, and such alone are also the real students, the real aspirants. All others are only playing with spirituality. They have just a little curiosity awakened, just a little intellectual aspiration kindled in them, but are merely standing on the outward fringe of the horizon of religion. There is no doubt some value even in that, as it may in course of time result in the awakening of a real thirst for religion ; and it is a mysterious law of nature that as soon as the field is ready, the seed *must* and does come ; as soon as the soul earnestly desires to have religion, the transmitter of the religious force *must* and does appear to help that soul. When the power that attracts the light of religion in the receiving soul is full and strong, the power which answers to that attraction and sends in light does come as a matter of course.

There are, however, certain great dangers in the way. There is, for instance, the danger to the receiving soul of its mistaking momentary emotions for real religious yearning. We may study that in ourselves. Many a time in our lives, somebody dies whom we loved ; we receive a blow ; we feel that the world is slipping between our fingers, that we want something surer and higher, and that we must become religious. In a few days that wave of feeling has passed away, and we are left stranded just where we were before. We are all of us often mistaking

such impulses for real thirst after religion ; but as long as
these momentary emotions are thus mistaken, that continuous, real craving of the soul for religion will not come,
and we shall not find the true transmitter of spirituality
into our nature. So whenever we are tempted to complain of our search after the truth that we desire so much,
proving vain, instead of so complaining, our first duty
ought to be to look into our own souls and find whether
the craving in the heart is real. Then in the vast majority
of cases it would be discovered that we were not fit for
receiving the truth, that there was no real thirst for
spirituality.

There are still greater dangers in regard to the *transmitter*, the Guru. There are many who, though immersed
in ignorance, yet, in the pride of their hearts, fancy they
know everything, and not only do not stop there, but offer
to take others on their shoulders ; and thus the blind leading the blind, both fall into the ditch. अविद्यायामन्तरे वर्तमानाः
स्वयं धीराः पण्डितम्मन्यमानाः। दन्द्रम्यमाणाः परियन्ति मूढा अन्धेनैव
नीयमाना यथान्धाः ॥ —"Fools dwelling in darkness, wise in
their own conceit, and puffed up with vain knowledge, go
round and round staggering to and fro, like blind men led
by the blind."—(Katha Up., I. ii. 5). The world is full of
these. Every one wants to be a teacher, every beggar
wants to make a gift of a million dollars! Just as these
beggars are ridiculous, so are these teachers.

QUALIFICATIONS OF THE ASPIRANT AND THE TEACHER

How are we to know a teacher, then? The sun
requires no torch to make him visible, we need not light a
candle in order to see him. When the sun rises, we instinctively become aware of the fact, and when a teacher of
men comes to help us, the soul will instinctively know that
truth has already begun to shine upon it. Truth stands on
its own evidence, it does not require any other testimony

to prove it true, it is self-effulgent. It penetrates into the innermost corners of our nature, and in its presence the whole universe stands up and says, "This is truth." The teachers whose wisdom and truth shine like the light of the sun are the very greatest the world has known, and they are worshipped as God by the major portion of mankind. But we may get help from comparatively lesser ones also ; only we ourselves do not possess intuition enough to judge properly of the man from whom we receive teaching and guidance ; so there ought to be certain tests, certain conditions, for the teacher to satisfy, as there are also for the taught.

The conditions necessary for the taught are purity, a real thirst after knowledge, and perseverance. No impure soul can be really religious. Purity in thought, speech, and act is absolutely necessary for any one to be religious. As to the thirst after knowledge, it is an old law that we all get whatever we want. None of us can get anything other than what we fix our hearts upon. To pant for religion truly is a very difficult thing, not at all so easy as we generally imagine. Hearing religious talks or reading religious books is no proof yet of a real want felt in the heart ; there must be a continuous struggle, a constant fight, an unremitting grappling with our lower nature, till the higher want is actually felt and the victory is achieved. It is not a question of one or two days, of years, or of lives ; the struggle may have to go on for hundreds of lifetimes. The success sometimes may come immediately, but we must be ready to wait patiently even for what may look like an infinite length of time. The student who sets out with such a spirit of perseverance will surely find success and realisation at last.

In regard to the teacher, we must see that he knows the spirit of the scriptures. The whole world reads Bibles, Vedas, and Korans ; but they are all only words, syntax, etymology, philology, the dry bones of religion. The

teacher who deals too much in words and allows the mind
to be carried away by the force of words loses the spirit.
It is the knowledge of the *spirit* of the scriptures alone
that constitutes the true religious teacher. The network
of the words of the scriptures is like a huge forest in which
the human mind often loses itself and finds no way out.
शब्दजालं महारण्यं चित्तभ्रमणकारणम् ।—"The network of words is
a big forest ; it is the cause of a curious wandering of
the mind." "The various methods of joining words, the
various methods of speaking in beautiful language, the
various methods of explaining the diction of the scriptures
are only for the disputations and enjoyment of the learned,
they do not conduce to the development of spiritual perception"—वाग्वैखरी शब्दझरी शास्त्रव्याख्यानकौशलम् । वैदुष्यं विदुषां
तद्वत् भुक्तये न तु मुक्तये ॥ Those who employ such methods to
impart religion to others are only desirous to show off
their learning, so that the world may praise them as
great scholars. You will find that no one of the great
teachers of the world ever went into these various
explanations of the text ; there is with them no attempt
at "text-torturing", no eternal playing upon the meaning
of words and their roots. Yet they nobly taught, while
others who have nothing to teach have taken up a word
sometimes and written a three-volume book on its origin,
on the man who used it first, and on what that man was
accustomed to eat, and how long he slept, and so on.

Bhagavân Ramakrishna used to tell a story of some
men who went into a mango orchard and busied themselves in counting the leaves, the twigs, and the branches,
examining their colour, comparing their size, and noting
down everything most carefully, and then got up a learned
discussion on each of these topics, which were undoubt-
edly highly interesting to them. But one of them, more
sensible than the others, did not care for all these things,
and instead thereof, began to eat the mango fruit. And
was he not wise? So leave this counting of leaves and

twigs and note-taking to others. This kind of work has its
proper place, but not here in the spiritual domain. You
never see a strong spiritual man among these "leaf-
counters". Religion, the highest aim, the highest glory of
man, does not require so much labour. If you want to
be a Bhakta, it is not at all necessary for you to know
whether Krishna was born in Mathurâ or in Vraja, what
he was doing, or just the exact date on which he pronounced the teachings of the Gitâ. You only require to
feel the craving for the beautiful lessons of duty and love
in the Gita. All the other particulars about it and its
author are for the enjoyment of the learned. Let them
have what they desire. Say "Shântih, Shântih" to their
learned controversies, and let *us* "eat the mangoes".

The second condition necessary in the teacher is—
sinlessness. The question is often asked, "Why should
we look into the character and personality of a teacher?
We have only to judge of what he says, and take that up."
This is not right. If a man wants to teach me something
of dynamics, or chemistry, or any other physical science,
he may be anything he likes, because what the physical
sciences require is merely an intellectual equipment; but
in the spiritual sciences it is impossible from first to last
that there can be any spiritual light in the soul that is
impure. What religion can an impure man teach? The
sine qua non of acquiring spiritual truth for one's self or
for imparting it to others is the purity of heart and soul.
A vision of God or a glimpse of the beyond never comes
until the soul is pure. Hence with the teacher of religion
we must see first what he *is*, and then what he says. He
must be perfectly pure, and then alone comes the value of
his words, because he is only then the true "transmitter".
What can he transmit if he has not spiritual power
in himself? There must be the worthy vibration of
spirituality in the mind of the teacher, so that it may be
sympathetically conveyed to the mind of the taught. The

function of the teacher is indeed an affair of the trans-
ference of something, and not one of mere stimulation
of the existing intellectual or other faculties in the
taught. Something real and appreciable as an influence
comes from the teacher and goes to the taught. Therefore the teacher must be pure.

The third condition is in regard to the motive. The
teacher must not teach with any ulterior selfish motive—
for money, name, or fame ; his work must be simply
out of love, out of. pure love for mankind at large. The
only medium through which spiritual force can be transmitted is love. Any selfish motive, such as the desire for
gain or for name, will immediately destroy this conveying
medium. God is love, and only he who has known God
as love can be a teacher of godliness and God to man.

When you see that in your teacher these conditions
are all fulfilled, you are safe ; if they are not, it is unsafe
to allow yourself to be taught by him, for there is the great
danger that, if he cannot convey goodness to your heart,
he may convey wickedness. This danger must by all
means be guarded against. श्रोत्रियोऽवृजिनोऽकामहतो यो ब्रह्मवित्तमः
—"He who is learned in the scriptures, sinless, un-
polluted by lust, and is the greatest knower of the
Brahman" is the real teacher.

From what has been said, it naturally follows that we
cannot be taught to love, appreciate, and assimilate
religion everywhere and by everybody. The "books in the
running brooks, sermons in stones, and good in every
thing" is all very true as a poetical figure ; but nothing
can impart to a man a single grain of truth unless he has
the undeveloped germs of it in himself. To whom do the
stones and brooks preach sermons? To the human soul,
the lotus of whose inner holy shrine is already quick with
life. And the light which causes the beautiful opening
out of this lotus comes always from the good and wise
teacher. When the heart has thus been opened, it

becomes fit to receive teaching from the stones or the brooks, the stars, or the sun, or the moon, or from any thing which has its existence in our divine universe; but the unopened heart will see in them nothing but mere stones or mere brooks. A blind man may go to a museum, but he will not profit by it in any way; his eyes must be opened first, and then alone he will be able to learn what the things in the museum can teach.

This eye-opener of the aspirant after religion is the teacher. With the teacher, therefore, our relationship is the same as that between an ancestor and his descendant. Without faith, humility, submission, and veneration in our hearts towards our religious teacher, there cannot be any growth of religion in us; and it is a significant fact that, where this kind of relation between the teacher and the taught prevails, there alone gigantic spiritual men are growing; while in those countries which have neglected to keep up this kind of relation the religious teacher has become a mere lecturer, the teacher expecting his five dollars and the person taught expecting his brain to be filled with the teacher's words, and each going his own way after this much has been done. Under such circumstances spirituality becomes almost an unknown quantity. There is none to transmit it and none to have it transmitted to. Religion with such people becomes business; they think they can obtain it with their dollars. Would to God that religion could be obtained so easily! But unfortunately it cannot be.

Religion, which is the highest knowledge and the highest wisdom, cannot be bought, nor can it be acquired from books. You may thrust your head into all the corners of the world, you may explore the Himalayas, the Alps, and the Caucasus, you may sound the bottom of the sea and pry into every nook of Tibet and the desert of Gobi, you will not find it anywhere until your heart is ready for receiving it and your teacher has come. And when that

divinely appointed teacher comes, serve him with childlike confidence and simplicity, freely open your heart to
his influence, and see in him God manifested. Those who
come to seek truth with such a spirit of love and veneration, to them the Lord of Truth reveals the most wonderful
things regarding truth, goodness, and beauty.

INCARNATE TEACHERS AND INCARNATION

Wherever His name is spoken, that very place is
holy. How much more so is the man who speaks His
name, and with what veneration ought we to approach
that man out of whom comes to us spiritual truth! Such
great teachers of spiritual truth are indeed very few in
number in this world, but the world is never altogether
without them. They are always the fairest flowers of
human life—अहेतुकदयासिन्धुः —"the ocean of mercy without
any motive". आचार्यं मां विजानीयात् —"Know the Guru to be
Me", says Shri Krishna in the *Bhagavata*. The moment
the world is absolutely bereft of these, it becomes a hideous
hell and hastens on to its destruction.

Higher and nobler than all ordinary ones are another
set of teachers, the Avatâras of Ishvara, in the world.
They can transmit spirituality with a touch, even with a
mere wish. The lowest and the most degraded characters
become in one second saints at their command. They are
the Teachers of all teachers, the highest manifestations
of God through man. We cannot see God except through
them. We cannot help worshipping them; and indeed
they are the only ones whom we are bound to worship.

No man can really see God except through these
human manifestations. If we try to see God otherwise,
we make for ourselves a hideous caricature of Him and
believe the caricature to be no worse than the original.

There is a story of an ignorant man who was asked to make an image of the God Shiva, and who, after days of hard struggle, manufactured only the image of a monkey. So whenever we try to think of God as He is in His absolute perfection, we invariably meet with the most miserable failure, because as long as we are men, we cannot conceive Him as anything higher than man. The time will come when we shall transcend our human nature and know Him as He is; but as long as we are men, we must worship Him in man and as man. Talk as you may, try as you may, you cannot think of God except as a man. You may deliver great intellectual discourses on God and on all things under the sun, become great rationalists and prove to your satisfaction that all these accounts of the Avataras of God as man are nonsense. But let us come for a moment to practical common sense. What is there behind this kind of remarkable intellect? Zero, nothing, simply so much froth. When next you hear a man delivering a great intellectual lecture against this worship of the Avataras of God, get hold of him and ask what *his* idea of God is, what *he* understands by "omnipotence", "omnipresence", and all similar terms, beyond the spelling of the words. He really means nothing by them; he cannot formulate as their meaning any idea unaffected by his own human nature; he is no better off in this matter than the man in the street who has not read a single book. That man in the street, however, is quiet and does not disturb the peace of the world, while this big talker creates disturbance and misery among mankind. Religion is, after all, realisation, and we must make the sharpest distinction between talk and intuitive experience. What we experience in the depths of our souls is realisation. Nothing indeed is so uncommon as common sense in regard to this matter.

By our present constitution we are limited and bound to see God as man. If, for instance, the buffaloes want to worship God, they will, in keeping with their own nature, see Him as a huge buffalo; if a fish wants to worship God, it will have to form an idea of Him as a big fish ; and man has to think of Him as man. And these various conceptions are not due to morbidly active imagination. Man, the buffalo,· and the fish all may be supposed to represent so many different vessels, so to say. All these vessels go to the sea of God to get filled with water, each according to its own shape and capacity; in the man the water takes the shape of man, in the buffalo, the shape of a buffalo, and in the fish, the shape of a fish. In each of these vessels there is the same water of the sea of God. When men see Him, they see Him as man, and the animals, if they have any conception of God at all, must see Him as animal, each according to its own ideal. So we cannot help seeing God as man, and, therefore, we are bound to worship Him as man. There is no other way.

Two kinds of men do not worship God as man—the human brute who has no religion, and the Paramahamsa who has risen beyond all the weaknesses of humanity and has transcended the limits of his own human nature. To him all nature has become his own Self. He alone can worship God as He is. Here, too, as in all other cases, the two extremes meet. The extreme of ignorance and the other extreme of knowledge—neither of these go through acts of worship. The human brute does not worship because of his ignorance, and the Jivanmuktas (free souls) do not worship because they have realised God in themselves. Being between these two poles of existence, if any one tells you that he is not going to worship God as man, take kindly care of that man; he is, not to use any harsher term, an irresponsible talker; his religion is for unsound and empty brains.

God understands human failings and becomes man to do good to humanity: यदा यदा हि धर्मस्य ग्लानिर्भवति भारत । अभ्युत्थानमधर्मस्य तदात्मानं सृजाम्यहम् ॥ परित्राणाय साधूनां विनाशाय च

III—5

दुष्कृताम्। धर्मसंस्थापनार्थाय संभवामि युगे युगे ॥—"Whenever virtue subsides and wickedness prevails, I manifest Myself. To establish virtue, to destroy evil, to save the good I come from Yuga (age) to Yuga." अवजानन्ति मां मूढा मानुषीं तनुमाश्रितम् । परं भावमजानन्तो मम भूतमहेश्वरम् ॥—"Fools deride Me who have assumed the human form, without knowing My real nature as the Lord of the universe." Such is Shri Krishna's declaration in the Gita on Incarnation. "When a huge tidal wave comes," says Bhagavan Shri Ramakrishna, "all the little brooks and ditches become full to the brim without any effort or consciousness on their own part; so when an Incarnation comes, a tidal wave of spirituality breaks upon the world, and people feel spirituality almost full in the air."

THE MANTRA: OM: WORD AND WISDOM

But we are now considering not these Mahâ-purushas, the great Incarnations, but only the Siddha-Gurus (teachers who have attained the goal); they, as a rule, have to convey the germs of spiritual wisdom to the disciple by means of words (Mantras) to be meditated upon. What are these Mantras? The whole of this universe has, according to Indian philosophy, both name and form (Nâma-Rupa) as its conditions of manifestation. In the human microcosm, there cannot be a single wave in the mind-stuff (Chitta-vritti) unconditioned by name and form. If it be true that nature is built throughout on the same plan, this kind of conditioning by name and form must also be the plan of the building of the whole of the cosmos. यथा एकेन मृत्पिण्डेन सर्वं मृन्मयं विज्ञातं स्यात्—"As one lump of clay being known, all things of clay are known", so the knowledge of the microcosm must lead to the knowledge of the macrocosm. Now form is the outer crust, of which the name or the idea is the inner essence or kernel. The body is the form, and the mind or the Antahkarana is the name, and sound-symbols are universally associated with Nâma (name) in all beings having the power of speech. In the individual man the thought-waves rising in the limited Mahat or Chitta (mind-stuff), must manifest themselves, first as *words*, and then as the more concrete *forms*.

In the universe, Brahmâ or Hiranyagarbha or the cosmic Mahat first manifested himself as name, and then as form, i.e. as this universe. All this expressed sensible universe is the form, behind which stands the eternal inexpressible Sphota, the manifester as *Logos* or Word. This eternal Sphota, the essential eternal material of all ideas or names, is the power through which the Lord creates the universe ; nay, the Lord first becomes conditioned as the Sphota, and then evolves Himself out as the yet more concrete sensible universe. This Sphota has one word as its only possible symbol, and this is the ॐ (Om). And as by no possible means of analysis can we separate the word from the idea, this Om and the eternal Sphota are inseparable ; and, therefore, it is out of this holiest of all holy words, the mother of all names and forms, the eternal Om, that the whole universe may be supposed to have been created. But it may be said that, although thought and word are inseparable, yet as there may be various word-symbols for the same thought, it is not necessary that this particular word Om should be the word representative of the thought, out of which the universe has become manifested. To this objection we reply that this Om is the only possible symbol which covers the whole ground, and there is none other like it. The Sphota is the material of all words, yet it is not any definite word in its fully formed state. That is to say, if all the peculiarities which distinguish one word from another be removed, then what remains will be the Sphota ; therefore this Sphota is called the Nâda-Brahma, the *Sound-Brahman*.

Now, as every word-symbol, intended to express the inexpressible Sphota, will so particularise it that it will no longer be the Sphota, that symbol which particularises it the least and at the same time most approximately expresses its nature, will be the truest symbol thereof ; and this is the Om, and the Om only; because these three letters अ उ म (A.U.M.), pronounced in combination as Om, may well be the generalised symbol of all possible sounds. The letter A is the least differentiated of all sounds, therefore Krishna says in the Gita अक्षराणां अकारोऽस्मि—"I am A among the letters". Again, all articulate sounds are produced in the space within the mouth beginning with the root of the tongue and ending in the lips—the throat sound is A, and M is the last lip sound, and the U exactly represents the rolling forward of the impulse which begins at the root of the tongue till it ends in the lips. If properly pronounced, this Om will represent the whole phenomenon of sound-production, and no other word can do this; and this, therefore, is the fittest symbol of the Sphota, which is the real meaning of the Om. And as the symbol can never be separated from the thing signified, the Om and the Sphota are one. And as the Sphota, being the finer side of the manifested universe, is nearer to God, and is indeed that first manifestation of divine wisdom, this Om is truly symbolic of God. Again, just as the "One only" Brahman, the Akhanda-Sachchidânanda, the undivided Existence-Knowledge-Bliss, can be conceived by imperfect human souls only from particular standpoints and associated with particular qualities, so this universe, His body, has also to be thought of along the line of the thinker's mind.

This direction of the worshipper's mind is guided by its prevailing elements or Tattvas. The result is that the same God will be seen in various manifestations as the possessor of various predominant qualities, and the same universe will appear as full of manifold forms. Even as in the case of the least differentiated and the most universal symbol Om, thought and sound-symbol are seen to be inseparably associated with each other, so also this law of their inseparable association applies to the many differentiated views of God and the universe: each of them therefore must have a particular word-symbol to express it. These word-symbols, evolved out of the deepest spiritual perception of sages, symbolise and express, as nearly as possible, the particular view of God and the universe they stand for. And as the Om represents the Akhanda, the undifferentiated Brahman, the others represent the Khanda or the differentiated views of the same Being ; and they are all helpful to divine meditation and the acquisition of true knowledge.

WORSHIP OF SUBSTITUTES AND IMAGES

The next points to be considered are the worship of Pratikas or of things more or less satisfactory as substitutes for God, and the worship of Pratimâs or images. What is the worship of God through a Pratika? It is अब्रह्मणि ब्रह्मदृष्ट्यासन्धानम् —"Joining the mind with devotion to that which is not Brahman, taking it to be Brahman"—says Bhagavân Râmânuja. "Worship the mind as Brahman, this is internal; and the Âkâsha as Brahman, this is with regard to the Devas", says Shankara. The mind is an internal Pratika, the Akasha is an external one; and both have to be worshipped as substitutes of God. He continues, "Similarly—'the Sun is Brahman, this is the command', 'He who worships Name as Brahman'—in all such passages the doubt arises as to the worship of Pratikas." The word Pratika means going towards; and worshipping a Pratika is worshipping something as a substitute which is, in some one or more respects, like Brahman more and more, but is not Brahman. Along with the Pratikas mentioned in the Shrutis there are various others to be found in the Purânas and the Tantras. In this kind of Pratika-worship may be included all the various forms of Pitri-worship and Deva-worship.

Now worshipping Ishvara and Him alone is Bhakti; the worship of anything else—Deva, or Pitri, or any other being—cannot be Bhakti. The various kinds of worship of the various Devas are all to be included in ritualistic Karma, which gives to the worshipper only a particular result in the form of some celestial enjoyment, but can neither give rise to Bhakti nor lead to Mukti. One thing, therefore, has to be carefully borne in mind. If, as it may happen in some cases, the highly philosophic ideal, the supreme Brahman, is dragged down by Pratika-worship to the level of the Pratika, and the Pratika itself is taken to be the Atman of the worshipper or his Antar-yâmin (Inner Ruler), the worshipper gets entirely misled, as no Pratika can really be the Atman of the worshipper.

But where Brahman Himself is the object of worship, and the Pratika stands only as a substitute or a suggestion thereof, that is to say, where, through the Pratika the omnipresent Brahman is worshipped—the Pratika itself being idealised into the cause of all, Brahman—the worship is positively beneficial; nay, it is absolutely necessary for all mankind until they have all got beyond the primary or preparatory state of the mind in regard to worship. When, therefore, any gods or other beings are worshipped in and for themselves, such worship is only a ritualistic Karma; and as a Vidyâ (science) it gives us only the fruit belonging to that particular Vidya; but when the Devas or any other beings are looked upon as Brahman and worshipped, the result obtained is the same as by the worshipping of Ishvara. This explains how, in many cases, both in the Shrutis and the Smritis, a god, or a sage, or some other extraordinary being is taken up and lifted, as it were, out of his own nature and idealised into Brahman, and is then worshipped. Says the Advaitin, "Is not everything Brahman when the name and the form have been removed from it?" "Is not He, the Lord, the innermost Self of every one?" says the Vishishtâdvaitin. फलम् आदित्याद्युपासनेषु ब्रह्मैव दास्यति सर्वाध्यक्षत्वात् —"The fruition of even the worship of Adityas etc. Brahman Himself bestows, because He is the Ruler of all." Says Shankara in his *Brahma-Sutra-Bhâsya*— ईदृशं चात्र ब्रह्मण उपास्यत्वं यतः प्रतीकेषु तद्दृष्ट्याध्यारोपणं प्रतिमादिषु इव विष्ण्वादीनाम् । "Here in this way does Brahman become the object of worship, because He, as Brahman, is superimposed on the Pratikas, just as Vishnu etc. are superimposed upon images etc."

The same ideas apply to the worship of the Pratimas as to that of the Pratikas; that is to say, if the image stands for a god or a saint, the worship is not the result of Bhakti, and does not lead to liberation; but if it stands for the one God, the worship thereof will bring both Bhakti and Mukti. Of the principal religions of the world we see Vedantism, Buddhism, and certain forms of Christianity freely using images; only two religions, Mohammedanism and Protestantism, refuse such help. Yet the Mohammedans use the grave of their saints and martyrs almost in the place of images; and the Protestants, in rejecting all concrete helps to religion, are drifting away every year farther and farther from spirituality till at present there is scarcely any difference between the advanced Protestants and the followers of August Comte, or agnostics who preach ethics alone. Again, in Christianity and Mohammedanism whatever exists of image worship is made to fall under that category in which the Pratika or the Pratima is worshipped in itself, but not as a "help to the vision" (Drishtisaukaryam) of God; therefore it is at best only of the nature of ritualistic Karmas and cannot produce either Bhakti or Mukti. In this form of image-worship, the allegiance of the soul is given to other things than Ishvara, and, therefore, such use of images, or graves, or temples, or tombs, is real idolatry; it is in itself neither sinful nor wicked—it is a rite—a Karma, and worshippers must and will get the fruit thereof.

THE CHOSEN IDEAL

The next thing to be considered is what we know as Ishta-Nishthâ. One who aspires to be a Bhakta must know that "so many opinions are so many ways". He must know that all the various sects of the various religions are the various manifestations of the glory of the same Lord. "They call You by so many names; they divide You, as it were, by different names, yet in each one of these is to be found Your omnipotence. . . . You reach the worshipper through all of these, neither is there any special time so long as the soul has intense love for You. You are so easy of approach; it is my misfortune that I cannot love You." Not only this, the Bhakta must take care not to hate, nor even to criticise those radiant sons of light who are the founders of various sects; he must not even hear them spoken ill of. Very few indeed are those who are at once the possessors of an extensive sympathy and power of appreciation, as well as an intensity of love. We find, as a rule, that liberal and sympathetic sects lose the intensity of religious feeling, and in their hands, religion is apt to degenerate into a kind of politico-social club life. On the other hand, intensely narrow sectaries, whilst displaying a very commendable love of their own ideals, are seen to have acquired every particle of that love by hating every one who is not of exactly the same opinions as themselves. Would to God that this world was full of men who were as intense in their love as world-wide in their sympathies! But such are only few and far between. Yet we know that it is practicable to educate large numbers of human beings into the ideal of a wonderful blending of both the width and the intensity of love; and the way to do that is by this path of the Istha-Nishtha or "steadfast devotion to the chosen ideal". Every sect of every religion presents only one ideal of its own to mankind, but the eternal Vedantic religion opens to mankind an infinite number of doors for ingress into the inner shrine of divinity, and places before humanity an almost inexhaustible array of ideals, there being in each of them a manifestation of the Eternal One. With the kindest solicitude, the Vedanta points out to aspiring men and women the numerous roads, hewn out of the solid rock of the realities of human life, by the glorious sons, or human manifestations, of God, in the past and in the present, and stands with outstretched arms to welcome all—to welcome even those that are yet to be—to that Home of Truth and that Ocean of Bliss, wherein the human soul, liberated from the net of Mâyâ, may transport itself with perfect freedom and with eternal joy.

Bhakti-Yoga, therefore, lays on us the imperative command not to hate or deny any one of the various paths that lead to salvation. Yet the growing plant must be hedged round to protect it until it has grown into a tree. The tender plant of spirituality will die if exposed too early to the action of a constant change of ideas and ideals. Many people, in the name of what may be called religious liberalism, may be seen feeding their idle curiosity with a continuous succession of different ideals. With them, hearing new things grows into a kind of disease, a sort of religious drink-mania. They want to hear new things just by way of getting a temporary nervous excitement, and when one such exciting influence has had its effect on them, they are ready for another. Religion is with these people a sort of intellectual opium-eating, and there it ends. "There is another sort of man", says Bhagavan Ramakrishna, "who is like the pearl-oyster of the story. The pearl-oyster leaves its bed at the bottom of the sea, and comes up to the surface to catch the rain-water when the star Svâti is in the ascendant. It floats about on the surface of the sea with its shell wide open, until it has succeeded in catching a drop of the rain-water, and then it dives deep down to its sea-bed, and there rests until it has succeeded in fashioning a beautiful pearl out of that rain-drop."

This is indeed the most poetical and forcible way in which the theory of Ishta-Nishtha has ever been put. This Eka-Nishtha or devotion to one ideal is absolutely necessary for the beginner in the practice of religious devotion. He must say with Hanuman in the Râmâyana, "Though I know that the Lord of Shri and the Lord of Jânaki are both manifestations of the same Supreme Being, yet my all in all is the lotus-eyed Râma." Or, as was said by the sage Tulasidâsa, he must say, "Take the sweetness of all, sit with all, take the name of all, say yea, yea, but keep your seat firm." Then, if the devotional aspirant is sincere, out of this little seed will come a gigantic tree like the Indian banyan, sending out branch after branch and root after root to all sides, till it covers the entire field of religion. Thus will the true devotee realise that He who was his own ideal in life is worshipped in all ideals by all sects, under all names, and through all forms.

THE METHOD AND THE MEANS

In regard to the method and the means of Bhakti-Yoga we read in the commentary of Bhagavan Ramanuja on the *Vedanta-Sutras*: "The attaining of That comes through discrimination, controlling the passions, practice, sacrificial work, purity, strength, and suppression of excessive joy." Viveka or discrimination is, according to Ramanuja, discriminating, among other things, the pure food from the impure. According to him, food becomes impure from three causes:. (1) by the nature of the food itself, as in the case of garlic etc.; (2) owing to its coming from wicked and accursed persons; and (3) from physical impurities, such as dirt, or hair, etc. The Shrutis say, "When the food is pure, the Sattva element gets purified, and the memory becomes unwavering", and Ramanuja quotes this from the Chhândogya Upanishad.

The question of food has always been one of the most vital with the Bhaktas. Apart from the extravagance into which some of the Bhakti sects have run, there is a great truth underlying this question of food. We must remember that, according to the Sankhya philosophy, the Sattva, Rajas, and Tamas, which in the state of homogeneous equilibrium form the Prakriti, and in the heterogeneous disturbed condition form the universe—are both the substance and the quality of Prakriti. As such they are the materials out of which every human form has been manufactured, and the predominance of the Sattva material is what is absolutely necessary for spiritual development. The materials which we receive through our food into our body-structure go a great way to determine our mental constitution; therefore the food we eat has to be particularly taken care of. However, in this matter, as in others, the fanaticism into which the disciples invariably fall is not to be laid at the door of the masters.

And this discrimination of food is, after all, of secondary importance. The very same passage quoted above is explained by Shankara in his Bhâshya on the Upanishads in a different way by giving an entirely different meaning to the word Âhâra, translated generally as food. According to him, "That which is gathered in is Ahara. The knowledge of the sensations, such as sound etc., is gathered in for the enjoyment of the enjoyer (self); the purification of the knowledge which gathers in the perception of the senses is the purifying of the food (Ahara). The word 'purification-of-food' means the acquiring of the knowledge of sensations untouched by the defects of attachment, aversion, and delusion ; such is the meaning. Therefore such knowledge or Ahara being purified, the Sattva material of the possessor of it—the internal organ—will become purified, and the Sattva being purified, an unbroken memory of the Infinite One, who has been known in His real nature from scriptures, will result."

These two explanations are apparently conflicting, yet both are true and necessary. The manipulating and controlling of what may be called the finer body, viz the mind, are no doubt higher functions than the controlling of the grosser body of flesh. But the control of the grosser is absolutely necessary to enable one to arrive at the control of the finer. The beginner, therefore, must pay particular attention to all such dietetic rules as have come down from the line of his accredited teachers ; but the extravagant, meaningless fanaticism, which has driven religion entirely to the kitchen, as may be noticed in the case of many of our sects, without any hope of the noble truth of that religion ever coming out to the sunlight of spirituality, is a peculiar sort of pure and simple materialism. It is neither Jnâna, nor Bhakti, nor Karma ; it is a special kind of lunacy, and those who pin their souls to it are more likely to go to lunatic asylums than to Brahmaloka. So it stands to reason that discrimination in the choice of food is necessary for the attainment of this higher state of mental composition which cannot be easily obtained otherwise.

Controlling the passions is the next thing to be attended to. To restrain the Indriyas (organs) from going towards the objects of the senses, to control them and bring them under the guidance of the will, is the very central virtue in religious culture. Then comes the practice of self-restraint and self-denial. All the immense possibilities of divine realisation in the soul cannot get actualised without struggle and without such practice on the part of the aspiring devotee. "The mind must always think of the Lord." It is very hard at first to compel the mind to think of the Lord always, but with every new effort the power to do so grows stronger in us. "By practice, O son of Kunti, and by non-attachment is it attained", says Shri Krishna in the Gita. And then as to sacrificial work, it is understood that the five great sacrifices[1] (Pancha-mahâyajna) have to be performed as usual.

Purity is absolutely the basic work, the bed-rock upon which the whole Bhakti-building rests. Cleansing the external body and discriminating the food are both easy, but without internal cleanliness and purity, these external observances are of no value whatsoever. In the list of qualities conducive to purity, as given by Ramanuja, there are enumerated, Satya, truthfulness; Ârjava, sincerity; Dayâ, doing good to others without any gain to one's self; Ahimsâ, not injuring others by thought, word, or deed; Anabhidhyâ, not coveting others' goods. not thinking vain thoughts, and not brooding over injuries received from another. In this list, the one idea that deserves special notice is Ahimsa, non-injury to others. This duty of non-injury is, so to speak, obligatory on us in relation to all beings. As with some, it does not simply mean the non-injuring of human beings and mercilessness towards the lower animals; nor, as with some others, does it mean the protecting of cats and dogs and feeding of ants with sugar—with liberty to injure brother-man in every horrible way! It is remarkable that almost every good idea in this world can be carried to a disgusting extreme. A good practice carried to an extreme and worked in accordance with the letter of the law becomes a positive evil. The stinking monks of certain religious sects, who do not bathe lest the vermin on their bodies should be killed, never think of the discomfort and disease they bring to their fellow human beings. They do not, however, belong to the religion of the Vedas!

The test of Ahimsa is absence of jealousy. Any man may do a good deed or make a good gift on the spur of

---

[1] To gods, sages, manes, guests, and all creatures.

the moment or under the pressure of some superstition or
priestcraft; but the real lover of mankind is he who is
jealous of none. The so-called great men of the world may
all be seen to become jealous of each other for a small
name, for a little fame, and for a few bits of gold. So
long as this jealousy exists in a heart, it is far away from
the perfection of Ahimsa. The cow does not eat meat, nor
does the sheep. Are they great Yogis, great non-injurers
(Ahimsakas)? Any fool may abstain from eating this or
that ; surely that gives him no more distinction than to
herbivorous animals. The man who will mercilessly cheat
widows and orphans and do the vilest deeds for money is
worse than any brute even if he lives entirely on grass.
The man whose heart never cherishes even the thought
of injury to any one, who rejoices at the prosperity of
even his greatest enemy, that man is the Bhakta, he is
the Yogi, he is the Guru of all, even though he lives
every day of his life on the flesh of swine. Therefore we
must always remember that external practices have value
only as helps to develop internal purity. It is better to
have internal purity alone when minute attention to
external observances is not practicable. But woe unto
the man and woe unto the nation that forgets the real,
internal, spiritual essentials of religion and mechanically
clutches with death-like grasp at all external forms and
never lets them go. The forms have value only so far as
they are expressions of the life within. If they have ceased
to express life, crush them out without mercy.

The next means to the attainment of Bhakti-Yoga is
strength (Anavasâda). "This Atman is not to be attained
by the weak", says the Shruti. Both physical weakness
and mental weakness are meant here. "The strong, the
hardy" are the only fit students. What can puny, little,
decrepit things do? They will break to pieces whenever
the mysterious forces of the body and mind are even
slightly awakened by the practice of any of the Yogas. It

is "the young, the healthy, the strong" that can score success. Physical strength, therefore, is absolutely necessary. It is the strong body alone that can bear the shock of reaction resulting from the attempt to control the organs. He who wants to become a Bhakta must be strong, must be healthy. When the miserably weak attempt any of the Yogas, they are likely to get some incurable malady, or they weaken their minds. Voluntarily weakening the body is really no prescription for spiritual enlightenment.

The mentally weak also cannot succeed in attaining the Atman. The person who aspires to be a Bhakta must be cheerful. In the Western world the idea of a religious man is that he never smiles, that a dark cloud must always hang over his face, which, again, must be long-drawn with the jaws almost collapsed. People with emaciated bodies and long faces are fit subjects for the physician, they are not Yogis. It is the cheerful mind that is persevering. It is the strong mind that hews its way through a thousand difficulties. And this, the hardest task of all, the cutting of our way out of the net of Maya, is the work reserved only for giant wills.

Yet at the same time excessive mirth should be avoided (Anuddharsha). Excessive mirth makes us unfit for serious thought. It also fritters away the energies of the mind in vain. The stronger the will, the less the yielding to the sway of the emotions. Excessive hilarity is quite as objectionable as too much of sad seriousness, and all religious realisation is possible only when the mind is in a steady, peaceful condition of harmonious equilibrium.

It is thus that one may begin to learn how to love the Lord.

PARA-BHAKTI OR SUPREME DEVOTION

THE PREPARATORY RENUNCIATION

We have now finished the consideration of what may be called the preparatory Bhakti, and are entering on the study of the Parâ-Bhakti or supreme devotion. We have to speak of a preparation to the practice of this Para-Bhakti. All such preparations are intended only for the purification of the soul. The repetition of names, the rituals, the forms, and the symbols, all these various things are for the purification of the soul. The greatest purifier among all such things, a purifier without which no one can enter the regions of this higher devotion (Para-Bhakti), is renunciation. This frightens many; yet, without it, there cannot be any spiritual growth. In all our Yogas this renunciation is necessary. This is the stepping-stone and the real centre and the real heart of all spiritual culture—renunciation. This is religion—renunciation.

When the human soul draws back from the things of the world and tries to go into deeper things; when man, the spirit which has here somehow become concretised and materialised, understands that he is thereby going to be destroyed and to be reduced almost into mere matter, and turns his face away from matter—then begins renunciation, then begins real spiritual growth. The Karma-Yogi's renunciation is in the shape of giving up all the fruits of his action; he is not attached to the results of his labour; he does not care for any reward here or hereafter. The Râja-Yogi knows that the whole of nature is intended for the soul to acquire experience, and that the result of all the experiences of the soul is for it to become aware of its eternal separateness from nature. The human soul has to understand and realise that it has been spirit, and not matter, through eternity, and that this conjunction of it with matter is and can be only for a time. The Raja-Yogi learns the lesson of renunciation through his own experience of nature. The Jnâna-Yogi has the harshest of all renunciations to go through, as he has to realise from the very first that the whole of this solid-looking nature is all an illusion. He has to understand that all that is any kind of manifestation of power in nature belongs to the soul, and not to nature. He has to know from the very start that all knowledge and all experience are in the soul and not in nature; so he has at once and by the sheer force of rational conviction to tear himself away from all bondage to nature. He lets nature and all that belongs to her go, he lets them vanish and tries to stand alone!

Of all renunciations, the most natural, so to say, is that of the Bhakti-Yogi. Here there is no violence, nothing to give up, nothing to tear off, as it were, from ourselves, nothing from which we have violently to separate ourselves. The Bhakta's renunciation is easy, smooth flowing, and as natural as the things around us. We see the manifestation of this sort of renunciation, although more or less in the form of caricatures, every day around us. A man begins to love a woman; after a while he loves another, and the first woman he lets go. She drops out of his mind smoothly, gently, without his feeling the want of her at all. A woman loves a man ; she then begins to love another man, and the first one drops off from her mind quite naturally. A man loves his own city, then he begins to love his country, and the intense love for his little city drops off smoothly, naturally. Again, a man learns to love the whole world; his love for his country, his intense, fanatical patriotism drops off without hurting him, without any manifestation of violence. An uncultured man loves the pleasures of the senses intensely ; as he becomes cultured, he begins to love intellectual pleasures, and his sense-enjoyments become less and less. No man can enjoy a meal with the same gusto or pleasure as a dog or a wolf, but those pleasures which a man gets from intellectual experiences and achievements, the dog can never enjoy. At first, pleasure is in association with the lowest senses ; but as soon as an animal reaches a higher plane of existence, the lower kind of pleasures becomes less intense. In human society, the nearer the man is to the animal, the stronger is his pleasure in the senses; and the higher and the more cultured the man is, the greater is his pleasure in intellectual and such other finer pursuits. So when a man gets even higher than the plane of the intellect, higher than that of mere thought, when he gets to the plane of spirituality and of divine inspiration, he finds there a state of bliss, compared with which all the pleasures of the senses, or even of the intellect, are as nothing. When the moon shines brightly, all the stars become dim ; and when the sun shines, the moon herself becomes dim. The renunciation necessary for the attainment of Bhakti is not obtained by killing anything, but just comes in as naturally as in the presence of an increasingly stronger light, the less intense ones become dimmer and dimmer until they vanish away completely. So this love of the pleasures of the senses and of the intellect is all made dim and thrown aside and cast into the shade by the love of God Himself.

That love of God grows and assumes a form which is called Para-Bhakti or supreme devotion. Forms vanish, rituals fly away, books are superseded ; images, temples, churches, religions and sects, countries and nationalities —all these little limitations and bondages fall off by their own nature from him who knows this love of God. Nothing remains to bind him or fetter his freedom. A ship, all of a sudden, comes near a magnetic rock, and its iron bolts and bars are all attracted and drawn out, and the planks get loosened and freely float on the water. Divine grace thus loosens the binding bolts and bars of the soul, and it becomes free. So in this renunciation auxiliary to devotion, there is no harshness, no dryness, no struggle, nor repression nor suppression. The Bhakta has not to suppress any single one of his emotions, he only strives to intensify them and direct them to God.

THE BHAKTA'S RENUNCIATION RESULTS FROM LOVE

We see love everywhere in nature. Whatever in society is good and great and sublime is the working out of that love ; whatever in society is very bad, nay diabolical, is also the ill-directed working out of the same emotion of love. It is this same emotion that gives us the pure and holy conjugal love between husband and wife as well as the sort of love which goes to satisfy the lowest forms of animal passion. The emotion is the same, but its manifestation is different in different cases. It is the same feeling of love, well or ill directed, that impels one man to do good and to give all he has to the poor, while it makes another man cut the throats of his brethren and take away all their possessions. The former loves others as much as the latter loves himself. The direction of the love is bad in the case of the latter, but it is right and proper in the other case. The same fire that cooks a meal for us may burn a child, and it is no fault of the fire if it does so; the difference lies in the way in which it is used. Therefore love, the intense longing for association, the strong desire on the part of two to become one—and it may be, after all, of all to become merged in one—is being manifested everywhere in higher or lower forms as the case may be.

Bhakti-Yoga is the science of higher love. It shows us how to direct it ; it shows us how to control it, how to manage it, how to use it, how to give it a new aim, as it were, and from it obtain the highest and most

glorious results, that is, how to make it lead us to spiritual
blessedness. Bhakti-Yoga does not say, "Give up"; it only
says, "Love; love the Highest!"—and everything low
naturally falls off from him, the object of whose love is
the Highest.

"I cannot tell anything about Thee except that Thou
art my love. Thou art beautiful, Oh, Thou art beautiful!
Thou art beauty itself." What is after all really required
of us in this Yoga is that our thirst after the beautiful
should be directed to God. What is the beauty in the
human face, in the sky, in the stars, and in the moon? It
is only the partial apprehension of the real all-embracing
Divine Beauty. "He shining, everything shines. It is
through His light that all things shine." Take this high
position of Bhakti which makes you forget at once all
your little personalities. Take yourself away from all the
world's little selfish clingings. Do not look upon humanity
as the centre of all your human and higher interests.
Stand as a witness, as a student, and observe the phenomena of nature. Have the feeling of personal non-
attachment with regard to man, and see how this mighty
feeling of love is working itself out in the world. Sometimes a little friction is produced, but that is only in the
course of the struggle to attain the higher real love.
Sometimes there is a little fight or a little fall; but it is
all only by the way. Stand aside, and freely let these
frictions come. You feel the frictions only when you are
in the current of the world, but when you are outside of
it simply as a witness and as a student, you will be able
to see that there are millions and millions of channels
in which God is manifesting Himself as Love.

"Wherever there is any bliss, even though in the most
sensual of things, there is a spark of that Eternal Bliss
which is the Lord Himself." Even in the lowest kinds of
attraction there is the germ of divine love. One of the
names of the Lord in Sanskrit is Hari, and this means

that He attracts all things to Himself. His is in fact the only attraction worthy of human hearts. Who can attract a soul really? Only He! Do you think dead matter can truly attract the soul? It never did, and never will. When you see a man going after a beautiful face, do you think that it is the handful of arranged material molecules which really attracts the man? Not at all. Behind those material particles there must be and is the play of divine influence and divine love. The ignorant man does not know it, but yet, consciously or unconsciously, he is attracted by it and it alone. So even the lowest forms of attraction derive their power from God Himself. "None, O beloved, ever loved the husband for the husband's sake; it is the Âtman, the Lord who is within, for whose sake the husband is loved." Loving wives may know this or they may not; it is true all the same. "None, O beloved, ever loved the wife for the wife's sake, but it is the Self in the wife that is loved." Similarly, no one loves a child or anything else in the world except on account of Him who is within. The Lord is the great magnet, and we are all like iron filings; we are being constantly attracted by Him, and all of us are struggling to reach Him. All this struggling of ours in this world is surely not intended for selfish ends. Fools do not know what they are doing: the work of their life is, after all, to approach the great magnet. All the tremendous struggling and fighting in life is intended to make us go to Him ultimately and be one with Him.

The Bhakti-Yogi, however, knows the meaning of life's struggles; he understands it. He has passed through a long series of these struggles and knows what they mean and earnestly desires to be free from the friction thereof; he wants to avoid the clash and go direct to the centre of all attraction, the great Hari. This is the renunciation of the Bhakta. This mighty attraction in the direction of God makes all other attractions vanish for him.

This mighty infinite love of God which enters his heart leaves no place for any other love to live there. How can it be otherwise? Bhakti fills his heart with the divine waters of the ocean of love, which is God Himself; there is no place there for little loves. That is to say, the Bhakta's renunciation is that Vairâgya or non-attachment for all things that are not God which results from Anurâga or great attachment to God.

This is the ideal preparation for the attainment of the supreme Bhakti. When this renunciation comes, the gate opens for the soul to pass through and reach the lofty regions of supreme devotion or Para-Bhakti. Then it is that we begin to understand what Para-Bhakti is; and the man who has entered into the inner shrine of the Para-Bhakti alone has the right to say that all forms and symbols are useless to him as aids to religious realisation. He alone has attained that supreme state of love commonly called the brotherhood of man; the rest only talk. He sees no distinctions; the mighty ocean of love has entered into him, and he sees not man in man, but beholds his Beloved everywhere. Through every face shines to him his Hari. The light in the sun or the moon is all His manifestation. Wherever there is beauty or sublimity, to him it is all His. Such Bhaktas are still living; the world is never without them. Such, though bitten by a serpent, only say that a messenger came to them from their Beloved. Such men alone have the right to talk of universal brotherhood. They feel no resentment; their minds never react in the form of hatred or jealousy. The external, the sensuous, has vanished from them for ever. How can they be angry, when, through their love, they are always able to see the Reality behind the scenes?

THE NATURALNESS OF BHAKTI-YOGA AND ITS CENTRAL SECRET

"Those who with constant attention always worship You, and those who worship the Undifferentiated, the Absolute, of these who are the greatest Yogis?"—Arjuna asked of Shri Krishna. The answer was: "Those who concentrating their minds on Me worship Me with eternal constancy and are endowed with the highest faith, they are My best worshippers, they are the greatest Yogis. Those that worship the Absolute, the Indescribable, the Undifferentiated, the Omnipresent, the Unthinkable, the All-comprehending, the Immovable, and the Eternal, by controlling the play of their organs and having the conviction of sameness in regard to all things, they also, being engaged in doing good to all beings, come to Me alone. But to those whose minds have been devoted to the unmanifested Absolute, the difficulty of the struggle along the way is much greater, for it is indeed with great difficulty that the path of the unmanifested Absolute is trodden by any embodied being. Those who, having offered up all their work unto Me, with entire reliance on Me, meditate on Me and worship Me without any attachment to anything else—them, I soon lift up from the ocean of ever-recurring births and deaths, as their mind is wholly attached to Me" (Gita, XII).

Jnâna-Yoga and Bhakti-Yoga are both referred to here. Both may be said to have been defined in the above passage. Jnana-Yoga is grand; it is high philosophy; and almost every human being thinks, curiously enough, that he can surely do everything required of him by philosophy; but it is really very difficult to live truly the life of philosophy. We are often apt to run into great dangers in trying to guide our life by philosophy. This world may be said to be divided between persons of demoniacal nature who think the care-taking of the body

to be the be-all and the end-all of existence, and persons
of godly nature who realise that the body is simply a
means to an end, an instrument intended for the culture
of the soul. The devil can and indeed does cite the
scriptures for his own purpose; and thus the way of
knowledge appears to offer justification to what the bad
man does, as much as it offers inducements to what the
good man does. This is the great danger in Jnana-Yoga.
But Bhakti-Yoga is natural, sweet, and gentle; the
Bhakta does not take such high flights as the Jnana-
Yogi, and, therefore, he is not apt to have such big falls.
Until the bondages of the soul pass away, it cannot of
course be free, whatever may be the nature of the path
that the religious man takes.

Here is a passage showing how, in the case of one of
the blessed Gopis, the soul-binding chains of both merit
and demerit were broken. "The intense pleasure in meditating on God took away the binding effects of her good
deeds. Then her intense misery of soul in not attaining
unto Him washed off all her sinful propensities; and then
she became free."—तच्चिन्ताविपुलाह्लादक्षीणपुण्यचया तथा । तदप्राप्ति
महदुःखविलीनाशेषपातका ॥ निरुच्छ्वासतया मुक्ति गतान्या गोपकन्यका ॥
(Vishnu-Purâna). In Bhakti-Yoga the central secret is,
therefore, to know that the various passions and feelings and emotions in the human heart are not wrong in
themselves; only they have to be carefully controlled
and given a higher and higher direction, until they attain
the very highest condition of excellence. The highest
direction is that which takes us to God; every other direction is lower. We find that pleasures and pains are very
common and oft-recurring feelings in our lives. When
a man feels pain because he has not wealth or some
such worldly thing, he is giving a wrong direction to the
feeling. Still pain has its uses. Let a man feel pain that
he has not reached the Highest, that he has not reached
God, and that pain will be to his salvation. When you

become glad that you have a handful of coins, it is a wrong direction given to the faculty of joy ; it should be given a higher direction, it must be made to serve the Highest Ideal. Pleasure in that kind of ideal must surely be our highest joy. This same thing is true of all our other feelings. The Bhakta says that not one of them is wrong, he gets hold of them all and points them unfailingly towards God.

THE FORMS OF LOVE-MANIFESTATION

Here are some of the forms in which love manifests itself. First there is reverence. Why do people show reverence to temples and holy places? Because He is worshipped there, and His presence is associated with all such places. Why do people in every country pay reverence to teachers of religion? It is natural for the human heart to do so, because all such teachers preach the Lord At bottom, reverence is a growth out of love ; we can none of us revere him whom we do not love. Then comes Priti—pleasure in God. What an immense pleasure men take in the objects of the senses. They go anywhere, run through any danger, to get the thing which they love, the thing which their senses like. What is wanted of the Bhakta is this very kind of intense love which has, however, to be directed to God. Then there is the sweetest of pains, Viraha, the intense misery due to the absence of the beloved. When a man feels intense misery because he has not attained to God, has not known that which is the only thing worthy to be known, and becomes in consequence very dissatisfied and almost mad—then there is Viraha ; and this state of the mind makes him feel disturbed in the presence of anything other than the beloved (Ekarativichikitsâ). In earthly love we see how often this Viraha comes. Again, when men are really and intensely in love with women or women with men,

they feel a kind of natural annoyance in the presence
of all those whom they do not love. Exactly the same
state of impatience in regard to things that are not loved
comes to the mind when Para-Bhakti holds sway over
it ; even to talk about things other than God becomes
distasteful then. "Think of Him, think of Him alone,
and give up all other vain words"— अन्या   वाचो   विमुंचथ ।
Those who talk of Him alone, the Bhakta finds to be
friendly to him ; while those who talk of anything else
appear to him to be unfriendly. A still higher stage of
love is reached when life itself is maintained for the sake
of the one Ideal of Love, when life itself is considered
beautiful and worth living only on account of that Love
(तदर्थप्राणसं'स्थानं). Without it, such a life would not remain
even for a moment. Life is sweet, because it thinks
of the Beloved. Tadiyatâ (*His-ness*) comes when a
man becomes perfect according to Bhakti—when he
has become blessed, when he has attained God, when
he has touched the feet of God, as it were. Then his
whole nature is purified and completely changed. All his
purpose in life then becomes fulfilled. Yet many such
Bhaktas live on just to worship Him. That is the bliss,
the only pleasure in life which they will not give up.
"O king, such is the blessed quality of Hari that even
those who have become satisfied with everything, all the
knots of whose hearts have been cut asunder, even they
love the Lord for love's sake"—the Lord "Whom all
the gods worship—all the lovers of liberation, and all
the knowers of the Brahman"—यं सर्वे देवा नमन्ति मुमुक्षवो
ब्रह्मवादिनश्चेति (*Nri. Tap. Up.*). Such is the power of love.
When a man has forgotten himself altogether, and does
not feel that anything belongs to him, then he acquires
the state of Tadiyata ; everything is sacred to him,
because it belongs to the Beloved. Even in regard to
earthly love, the lover thinks that everything belonging
to his beloved is sacred and so dear to him. He loves

even a piece of cloth belonging to the darling of his heart. In the same way, when a person loves the Lord, the whole universe becomes dear to him, because it is all His.

UNIVERSAL LOVE AND HOW IT LEADS TO SELF-SURRENDER

How can we love the Vyashti, the particular, without first loving the Samashti, the universal? God is the Samashti, the generalised and the abstract universal whole ; and the universe that we see is the Vyashti, the particularised thing. To love the whole universe is possible only by way of loving the Samashti—the universal —which is, as it were, the one unity in which are to be found millions and millions of smaller unities. The philosophers of India do not stop at the particulars ; they cast a hurried glance at the particulars and immediately start to find the generalised forms which will include all the particulars. The search after the universal is the one search of Indian philosophy and religion. The Jnâni aims at the wholeness of things, at that one absolute and generalised Being, knowing which he knows everything. The Bhakta wishes to realise that one generalised abstract Person, in loving whom he loves the whole universe. The Yogi wishes to have possession of that one generalised form of power, by controlling which he controls this whole universe. The Indian mind, throughout its history, has been directed to this kind of singular search after the universal in everything—in science, in psychology, in love, in philosophy. So the conclusion to which the Bhakta comes is that, if you go on merely loving one person after another, you may go on loving them so for an infinite length of time, without being in the least able to love the world as a whole. When, at last, the central idea is, however, arrived at that the sum total of all

love is God, that the sum total of the aspirations of all the
souls in the universe, whether they be free, or bound, or
struggling towards liberation, is God, then alone it becomes
possible for any one to put forth universal love. God is
the Samashti, and this visible universe is God differentiated
and made manifest. If we love this sum total, we love
everything. Loving the world and doing it good will all
come easily then ; we have to obtain this power only by
loving God first; otherwise it is no joke to do good to the
world. "Everything is His and He is my Lover; I love
Him," says the Bhakta. In this way everything becomes
sacred to the Bhakta, because all things are His. All are
His children, His body, His manifestation. How then may
we hurt any one? How then may we not love any one?
With the love of God will come, as a sure effect, the love
of every one in the universe. The nearer we approach
God, the more do we begin to see that all things are in
Him. When the soul succeeds in appropriating the bliss of
this supreme love, it also begins to see Him in everything.
Our heart will thus become an eternal fountain of love.
And when we reach even higher states of this love, all the
little differences between the things of the world are
entirely lost ; man is seen no more as man, but only as
God ; the animal is seen no more as animal, but as God ;
even the tiger is no more a tiger, but a manifestation of
God. Thus in this intense state of Bhakti, worship is
offered to every one, to every life, and to every being.
एवं सर्वेषु भूतेषु भक्तिरव्यभिचारिणी । कर्तव्या पण्डितैर्ज्ञात्वा सर्वभूतमयं
हरिम् ॥ —"Knowing that Hari, the Lord, is in every being,
the wise have thus to manifest unswerving love towards
all beings."

As a result of this kind of intense all-absorbing love,
comes the feeling of perfect self-surrender, the conviction
that nothing that happens is against us, Aprâtikulya. Then
the loving soul is able to say, if pain comes, "Welcome
pain." If misery comes, it will say, "Welcome misery,

you are also from the Beloved." If a serpent comes, it will say, "Welcome serpent." If death comes, such a Bhakta will welcome it with a smile. "Blessed am I that they all come to me ; they are all welcome." The Bhakta in this state of perfect resignation, arising out of intense love to God and to all that are His, ceases to distinguish between pleasure and pain in so far as they affect him. He does not know what it is to complain of pain or misery ; and this kind of uncomplaining resignation to the will of God, who is all love, is indeed a worthier acquisition than all the glory of grand and heroic performances.

To the vast majority of mankind, the body is everything ; the body is all the universe to them ; bodily enjoyment is their all in all. This demon of the worship of the body and of the things of the body has entered into us all. We may indulge in tall talk and take very high flights, but we are like vultures all the same ; our mind is directed to the piece of carrion down below. Why should our body be saved, say, from the tiger? Why may we not give it over to the tiger? The tiger will thereby be pleased, and that is not altogether so very far from self-sacrifice and worship. Can you reach the realisation of such an idea in which all sense of self is completely lost? It is a very dizzy height on the pinnacle of the religion of love, and few in this world have ever climbed up to it ; but until a man reaches that highest point of ever-ready and ever-willing self-sacrifice, he cannot become a perfect Bhakta. We may all manage to maintain our bodies more or less satisfactorily and for longer or shorter intervals of time. Nevertheless, our bodies have to go ; there is no permanence about them Blessed are they whose bodies get destroyed in the service of others. "Wealth, and even life itself, the sage always holds ready for the service of others. In this world, there being one thing certain, viz death, it is far better that this body dies in a good cause than in a bad one." We may drag

our life on for fifty years or a hundred years; but after
that, what is it that happens? Everything that is the result
of combination must get dissolved and die. There must and
will come a time for it to be decomposed. Jesus and
Buddha and Mohammed are all dead; all the great
Prophets and Teachers of the world are dead.

"In this evanescent world, where everything is falling
to pieces, we have to make the highest use of what time
we have," says the Bhakta; and really the highest use of
life is to hold it at the service of all beings. It is the horrible body-idea that breeds all the selfishness in the world,
just this one delusion that we are wholly the body we
own, and that we must by all possible means try our
very best to preserve and to please it. If you know that
you are positively other than your body, you have then
none to fight with or struggle against; you are dead to all
ideas of selfishness. So the Bhakta declares that we have to
hold ourselves as if we are altogether dead to all the
things of the world; and that is indeed self-surrender.
Let things come as they may. This is the meaning of
"Thy will be done"—not going about fighting and struggling and thinking all the while that God wills all our
own weaknesses and worldly ambitions. It may be that
good comes even out of our selfish struggles; that is,
however, God's look-out. The perfected Bhakta's idea
must be never to will and work for himself. "Lord, they
build high temples in Your name; they make large gifts in
Your name; I am poor; I have nothing; so I take this body
of mine and place it at Your feet. Do not give me up, O
Lord." Such is the prayer proceeding out of the depths of
the Bhakta's heart. To him who has experienced it, this
eternal sacrifice of the self unto the Beloved Lord is
higher by far than all wealth and power, than even all
soaring thoughts of renown and enjoyment. The peace of
the Bhakta's calm resignation is a peace that passeth
all understanding and is of incomparable value. His

Apratikulya is a state of the mind in which it has no interests and naturally knows nothing that is opposed to it. In this state of sublime resignation everything in the shape of attachment goes away completely, except that one all-absorbing love to Him in whom all things live and move and have their being. This attachment of love to God is indeed one that does not bind the soul but effectively breaks all its bondages.

THE HIGHER KNOWLEDGE AND THE HIGHER LOVE ARE ONE TO THE TRUE LOVER

The Upanishads distinguish between a higher knowledge and a lower knowledge ; and to the Bhakta there is really no difference between this higher knowledge and his higher love (Parâ-Bhakti). The Mundaka Upanishad says:

द्वे विद्ये वेदितव्ये इति ह स्म यद्ब्रह्मविदो वदन्ति । परा चैवापरा च ॥
तत्रापरा ऋग्वेदो यजुर्वेदः सामवेदोऽथर्ववेदः शिक्षा कल्पो व्याकरणं निरुक्तं
छन्दो ज्योतिषमिति । अथ परा यया तदक्षरमधिगम्यते ॥ —"The knowers of the Brahman declare that there are two kinds of knowledge worthy to be known, namely, the Higher (Parâ) and the lower (Aparâ). Of these the lower (knowledge) consists of the Rig-Veda, the Yajur-Veda, the Sâma-Veda, the Atharva-Veda, the Shikshâ (or the science dealing with pronunciation and accent), the Kalpa (or the sacrificial liturgy), grammar, the Nirukta (or the science dealing with etymology and the meaning of words), prosody, and astronomy ; and the higher (knowledge) is that by which that Unchangeable is known."

The higher knowledge is thus clearly shown to be the knowledge of the Brahman ; and the *Devi-Bhâgavata* gives us the following definition of the higher love (Para-Bhakti): "As oil poured from one vessel to another falls in an unbroken line, so, when the mind in an unbroken stream thinks of the Lord, we have what is called Para-Bhakti or supreme love." This kind of undisturbed and ever-steady direction of the mind and the heart to the Lord with an inseparable attachment is indeed the highest manifestation of man's love to God. All other forms of Bhakti are only preparatory to the attainment of this highest form thereof, viz the Para-Bhakti which is also known as the love that comes after attachment (Râgânugâ). When this supreme love once comes into the heart of man, his mind will continuously think of God and remember nothing else. He will give no room in himself to thoughts other than those of God, and his soul will be unconquerably pure and will alone break all the bonds of mind and matter and become serenely free. He alone can worship the Lord in his own heart; to him forms, symbols, books, and doctrines are all unnecessary and are incapable of proving serviceable in any way. It is not easy to love the Lord thus. Ordinarily human love is seen to flourish only in places where it is returned; where love is not returned for love, cold indifference is the natural result. There are, however, rare instances in which we may notice love exhibiting itself even where there is no return of love. We may compare this kind of love, for purposes of illustration, to the love of the moth for the fire ; the insect loves the fire, falls into it, and dies. It is indeed in the nature of this insect to love so. To love because it is the nature of love to love is undeniably the highest and the most unselfish manifestation of love that may be seen in the world. Such love, working itself out on the plane of spirituality, necessarily leads to the attainment of Para-Bhakti.

THE TRIANGLE OF LOVE

We may represent love as a triangle, each of the angles of which corresponds to one of its inseparable characteristics. There can be no triangle without all its three angles ; and there can be no true love without its three following characteristics. The first angle of our triangle of love is that love knows no bargaining. Wherever there is any seeking for something in return, there can be no real love ; it becomes a mere matter of shop-keeping. As long as there is in us any idea of deriving this or that favour from God in return for our respect and allegiance to Him, so long there can be no true love growing in our hearts. Those who worship God because they wish Him to bestow favours on them are sure not to worship Him if those favours are not forthcoming. The Bhakta loves the Lord because He is lovable ; there is no other motive originating or directing this divine emotion of the true devotee.

We have heard it said that a great king once went into a forest and there met a sage. He talked with the sage a little and was very much pleased with his purity and wisdom. The king then wanted the sage to oblige him by receiving a present from him. The sage refused to do so, saying, "The fruits of the forest are enough food for me ; the pure streams of water flowing down from the mountains give enough drink for me; the barks of the trees supply me with enough covering; and the caves of the mountains form my home. Why should I take any present from you or from anybody?" The king said, "Just to benefit me, sir, please take something from my hands and please come with me to the city and to my palace." After much persuasion, the sage at last consented to do as the king desired and went with him to his palace. Before offering the gift to the sage, the king repeated his prayers, saying, "Lord, give me more children; Lord, give me more wealth; Lord, give me more territory; Lord, keep my body in better health", and so on. Before the king finished saying his prayer, the sage had got up and walked away from the room quietly. At this the king became perplexed and began to follow him, crying aloud, "Sir, you are going away, you have not received my gifts." The sage turned round to him and said, "I do not beg of beggars. You are yourself nothing but a beggar, and how can you give me anything? I am no fool to think of taking anything from a beggar like you. Go away, do not follow me."

There is well brought out the distinction between mere beggars and the real lovers of God. Begging is not the language of love. To worship God even for the sake of salvation or any other rewards equally degenerate. Love knows no reward. Love is always for love's sake. The Bhakta loves because he cannot help loving. When you see a beautiful scenery and fall in love with it, you do not demand anything in the way of favour from the scenery, nor does the scenery demand anything from you. Yet the vision thereof brings you to a blissful state of the mind; it tones down all the friction in your soul, it makes you calm, almost raises you, for the time being, beyond your mortal nature and places you in a condition of quite divine ecstasy. This nature of real love is the first angle of our triangle. Ask not anything in return for your love; let your position be always that of the giver; give your love unto God, but do not ask anything in return even from Him.

The second angle of the triangle of love is that love knows no fear. Those that love God through fear are the lowest of human beings, quite undeveloped as men. They worship God from fear of punishment. He is a great Being to them, with a whip in one hand and the sceptre in the other; if they do not obey Him, they are afraid they will be whipped. It is a degradation to worship God through fear of punishment; such worship is, if worship at all, the crudest form of the worship of love. So long as there is any fear in the heart, how can there be love also? Love conquers naturally all fear. Think of a young mother in the street and a dog barking at her; she is frightened and flies into nearest house. But suppose the next day she is in the street with her child, and a lion springs upon the child. Where will be her position now? Of course, in the very mouth of the lion, protecting her child. Love conquers all fear. Fear comes from the selfish idea of cutting one's self off from the universe. The smaller and the more selfish I make myself, the more is my fear. If a man thinks he is a little nothing, fear will surely come upon him. And the less you think of yourself as an insignificant person, the less fear there will be for you. So long as there is the least spark of fear in you there can be no love there. Love and fear are incompatible; God is never to be feared by those who love Him. The commandment, "Do not take the name of the Lord thy God in vain", the true lover of God laughs at. How can there be any blasphemy in the religion of love? The more you take the name of the Lord, the better for you, in whatever way you may do it. You are only repeating His name because you love Him.

The third angle of the love-triangle is that love knows no rival, for in it is always embodied the lover's highest ideal. True love never comes until the object of our love becomes to us our highest ideal. It may be that in many cases human love is misdirected and misplaced, but to the person who loves, the thing he loves is always his own highest idea. One may see his ideal in the vilest of beings, and another in the highest of beings; nevertheless, in every case it is the ideal alone that can be truly and intensely loved. The highest ideal of every man is called God. Ignorant or wise, saint or sinner, man or woman, educated or uneducated, cultivated or uncultivated, to every human being the highest ideal is God. The synthesis of all the highest ideals of beauty, of sublimity, and of power gives us the completest conception of the loving and lovable God.

These ideals exist in some shape or other in every mind naturally; they form a part and parcel of all our minds. All the active manifestations of human nature are struggles of those ideals to become realised in practical life. All the various movements that we see around us in society are caused by the various ideals in various souls trying to come out and become concretised; what is inside presses on to come outside. This perennially dominant influence of the ideal is the one force, the one motive power, that may be seen to be constantly working in the midst of mankind. It may be after hundreds of births, after struggling through thousands of years, that man finds that it is vain to try to make the inner ideal mould completely the external conditions and square well with them; after realising this he no more tries to project his own ideal on the outside world, but worships the ideal itself as ideal from the highest standpoint of love. This ideally perfect ideal embraces all lower ideals. Every one admits the truth of the saying that a lover sees Helen's beauty on an Ethiop's brow. The man who is standing aside as a looker-on sees that love is here misplaced, but the lover sees his Helen all the same and does not see the Ethiop at all. Helen or Ethiop, the objects of our love are really the centres round which our ideals become crystallised. What is it that the world commonly worships? Not certainly this all-embracing, ideally perfect ideal of the supreme devotee and lover. That ideal which men and women commonly worship is what is in themselves; every person projects his or her own ideal on the outside world and kneels before it. That is why we find that men who are cruel and blood-thirsty conceive of a blood-thirsty God, because they can only love their own highest ideal. That is why good men have a very high ideal of God, and their ideal is indeed so very different from that of others.

THE GOD OF LOVE IS HIS OWN PROOF

What is the ideal of the lover who has quite passed beyond the idea of selfishness, of bartering and bargaining, and who knows no fear? Even to the great God such a man will say, "I will give You my all, and I do not want anything from You; indeed there is nothing that I can call my own." When a man has acquired this conviction, his ideal becomes one of perfect love, one of perfect fearlessness of love. The highest ideal of such a person has no narrowness of particularity about it; it is love universal, love without limits and bonds, love itself, absolute love. This grand ideal of the religion of love is worshipped and lovèd absolutely as such without the aid of any symbols or suggestions. This is the highest form of Para-Bhakti—the worship of such an all-comprehending ideal as the ideal; all the other forms of Bhakti are only stages on the way to reach it.

All our failures and all our successes in following the religion of love are on the road to the realisation of that one ideal. Object after object is taken up, and the inner ideal is successively projected on them all; and all such external objects are found inadequate as exponents of the ever-expanding inner ideal and are naturally rejected one after another. At last the aspirant begins to think that it is vain to try to realise the ideal in external objects, that all external objects are as nothing when compared with the ideal itself; and, in course of time, he acquires the power of realising the highest and the most generalised abstract ideal entirely as an abstraction that is to him quite alive and real. When the devotee has reached this point, he is no more impelled to ask whether God can be demonstrated or not, whether He is omnipotent and omniscient or not. To him He is only the God of Love; He is the highest ideal of love, and that is sufficient for all his purposes. He, as love, is self-evident. It requires no proofs to demonstrate the existence of the beloved to the lover. The magistrate-Gods of other forms of religion may require a good deal of proof to prove Them, but the Bhakta does not and cannot think of such Gods at all. To him God exists entirely as love. "None, O beloved, loves the husband for the husband's sake, but it is for the sake of the Self who is in the husband that the husband is loved; none, O beloved, loves the wife for the wife's sake, but it is for the sake of the Self who is in the wife that the wife is loved."

It is said by some that selfishness is the only motive power in regard to all human activities. That also is love lowered by being particularised. When I think of myself as comprehending the Universal, there can surely be no selfishness in me; but when I, by mistake, think that I am a little something, my love becomes particularised and narrowed. The mistake consists in making the sphere of love narrow and contracted. All things in the universe are of divine origin and deserve to be loved ; it has, however, to be borne in mind that the love of the whole includes the love of the parts. This whole is the God of the Bhaktas, and all the other Gods, Fathers in Heaven, or Rulers, or Creators, and all theories and doctrines and books have no purpose and no meaning for them, seeing that they have through their supreme love and devotion risen above those things altogether. When the heart is purified and cleansed and filled to the brim with the divine nectar of love, all other ideas of God become simply puerile and are rejected as being inadequate or unworthy. Such is indeed the power of Para-Bhakti or Supreme Love; and the perfected Bhakta no more goes to see God in temples and churches; he knows no place where he will not find Him. He finds Him in the temple as well as out of the temple, he finds Him in the saint's saintliness as well as in the wicked man's wickedness, because he has Him already seated in glory in his own heart as the one Almighty inextinguishable Light of Love which is ever shining and eternally present.

HUMAN REPRESENTATIONS OF THE DIVINE IDEAL OF LOVE

It is impossible to express the nature of this supreme and absolute ideal of love in human language. Even the highest flight of human imagination is incapable of comprehending it in all its infinite perfection and beauty. Nevertheless, the followers of the religion of love, in its higher as well as its lower forms, in all countries, have all along had to use the inadequate human language to comprehend and to define their own ideal of love. Nay more, human love itself, in all its varied forms has been made to typify this inexpressible divine love. Man can think of divine things only in his own human way; to us the Absolute can be expressed only in our relative language. The whole universe is to us a writing of the Infinite in the language of the finite. Therefore Bhaktas make use of all the common terms associated with the common love of humanity in relation to God and His worship through love.

Some of the great writers on Para-Bhakti have tried to understand and experience this divine love in so many different ways. The lowest form in which this love is apprehended is what they call the peaceful—the Shânta. When a man worships God without the fire of love in him, without its madness in his brain, when his love is just the calm commonplace love, a little higher than mere forms and ceremonies and symbols, but not at all characterised by the madness of intensely active love, it is said to be Shanta. We see some people in the world who like to move on slowly, and others who come and go like the whirlwind. The Shânta-Bhakta is calm, peaceful, gentle.

The next higher type is that of Dâsya, i.e. servant-
ship; it comes when a man thinks he is the servant of the
Lord. The attachment of the faithful servant unto the
master is his ideal.

The next type of love is Sakhya, friendship—"Thou
art our beloved friend." Just as a man opens his heart
to his friend and knows that the friend will never chide
him for his faults but will always try to help him, just
as there is the idea of equality between him and his
friend, so equal love flows in and out between the worshipper and his friendly God. Thus God becomes our
friend, the friend who is near, the friend to whom we
may freely tell all the tales of our lives. The innermost secrets of our hearts we may place before Him with
the great assurance of safety and support. He is the friend
whom the devotee accepts as an equal. God is viewed
here as our playmate. We may well say that we are
all playing in this universe. Just as children play their
games, just as the most glorious kings and emperors play
their own games, so is the Beloved Lord Himself in
sport with this universe. He is perfect; He does not
want anything. Why should He create? Activity is always
with us for the fulfilment of a certain want, and want
always presupposes imperfection. God is perfect; He
has no wants. Why should He go on with this work
of an ever-active creation? What purpose has He in
view? The stories about God creating this world for
some end or other that we imagine are good as stories,
but not otherwise. It is all really in sport; the universe
is His play going on. The whole universe must after all
be a big piece of pleasing fun to Him. If you are poor,
enjoy that as fun; if you are rich, enjoy the fun of being
rich; if dangers come, it is also good fun; if happiness
comes, there is more good fun. The world is just a
playground, and we are here having good fun, having a
game; and God is with us playing all the while, and we are

with Him playing. God is our eternal playmate. How beauti-
fully He is playing! The play is finished when the cycle
comes to an end. There is rest for a shorter or longer
time; again all come out and play. It is only when you
forget that it is all play and that you are also helping in
the play, it is only then that misery and sorrows come. Then
the heart becomes heavy, then the world weighs upon
you with tremendous power. But as soon as you give
up the serious idea of reality as the characteristic of
the changing incidents of the three minutes of life and
know it to be but a stage on which we are playing, helping Him to play, at once misery ceases for you. He
plays in every atom; He is playing when He is building
up earths, and suns, and moons; He is playing with the
human heart, with animals, with plants. We are His
chessmen; He puts the chessmen on the board and shakes
them up. He arranges us first in one way and then
in another, and we are consciously or unconsciously helping in His play. And, oh, bliss! we are His playmates!

The next is what is known as Vâtsalya, loving God
not as our Father but as our Child. This may look
peculiar, but it is a discipline to enable us to detach
all ideas of power from the concept of God. The idea
of power brings with it awe. There should be no awe
in love. The ideas of reverence and obedience are necessary for the formation of character; but when character
is formed, when the lover has tasted the calm, peaceful love and tasted also a little of its intense madness,
then he need talk no more of ethics and discipline.
To conceive God as mighty, majestic, and glorious, as
the Lord of the universe, or as the God of gods, the lover
says he does not care. It is to avoid this association
with God of the fear-creating sense of power that he
worships God as his own child. The mother and the
father are not moved by awe in relation to the child; they
cannot have any reverence for the child. They cannot think

of asking any favour from the child. The child's position is always that of the receiver, and out of love for
the child the parents will give up their bodies a hundred
times over. A thousand lives they will sacrifice for that
one child of theirs, and, therefore, God is loved as a child.
This idea of loving God as a child comes into existence and
grows naturally among those religious sects which believe in the incarnation of God. For the Mohammedans
it is impossible to have this idea of God as a child; they
will shrink from it with a kind of horror. But the
Christian and the Hindu can realise it easily, because
they have the baby Jesus and the baby Krishna. The
women in India often look upon themselves as Krishna's
mother ; Christian mothers also may take up the idea
that they are Christ's mothers, and it will bring to the
West the knowledge of God's Divine Motherhood which
they so much need. The superstitions of awe and reverence in relation to God are deeply rooted in the heart
of our hearts, and it takes long years to sink entirely in
love our ideas of reverence and veneration, of awe and
majesty and glory with regard to God.

There is one more human representation of the divine
ideal of love. It is known as Madhura, sweet, and is the
highest of all such representations. It is indeed based
on the highest manifestation of love in this world, and
this love is also the strongest known to man. What love
shakes the whole nature of man, what love runs through
every atom of his being—makes him mad, makes him
forget his own nature, transforms him, makes him either
a God or a demon—as the love between man and woman? In this sweet representation of divine love God is
our husband. We are all women; there are no men in
this world; there is but One man, and this is He, our Beloved. All that love which man gives to woman, or woman
to man, has here to be given up to the Lord.

All the different kinds of love which we see in the

world, and with which we are more or less playing merely, have God as the one goal; but unfortunately, man does
not know the infinite ocean into which this mighty river
of love is constantly flowing, and so, foolishly, he often
tries to direct it to little dolls of human beings. The
tremendous love for the child that is in human nature is
not for the little doll of a child; if you bestow it blindly
and exclusively on the child, you will suffer in consequence.
But through such suffering will come the awakening
by which you are sure to find out that the love
which is in you, if it is given to any human being, will
sooner or later bring pain and sorrow as the result. Our
love must, therefore, be given to the Highest One who
never dies and never changes, to Him in the ocean of whose
love there · is neither ebb nor flow. Love must get to
its right destination, it must go unto Him who is really the
infinite ocean of love. All rivers flow into the ocean. Even
the drop of water coming down from the mountain side
cannot stop its course after reaching a brook or a river,
however big it may be; at last even that drop somehow does find its way to the ocean. God is the one
goal of all our passions and emotions. If you want to
be angry, be angry with Him. Chide your Beloved, chide
your Friend. Whom else can you safely chide? Mortal
man will not patiently put up with your anger; there will
be a reaction. If you are angry with me I am sure
quickly to react, because I cannot patiently put up with
your anger. Say unto the Beloved, "Why do You not come
to me; why do You leave me thus alone?" Where is there
any enjoyment but in Him? What enjoyment can there
be in little clods of earth? It is the crystallised essence
of infinite enjoyment that we have to seek, and that
is in God. Let all our passions and emotions go up
unto Him. They are meant for Him, for if they miss their
mark and go lower, they become vile; and when they
go straight to the mark, to the Lord, even the lowest of

them becomes transfigured. All the energies of the human body and mind, howsoever they may express themselves, have the Lord as their one goal, as their Ekâyana. All loves and all passions of the human heart must go to God. He is the Beloved. Whom else can this heart love? He is the most beautiful, the most sublime, He is beauty itself, sublimity itself. Who in this universe is more beautiful than He? Who in this universe is more fit to become the husband than He? Who in this universe is fitter to be loved than He? So let Him be the husband, let Him be the Beloved.

Often it so happens that divine lovers who sing of this divine love accept the language of human love in all its aspects as adequate to describe it. Fools do not understand this ; they never will. They look at it only with the physical eye. They do not understand the mad throes of this spiritual love. How can they? "For one kiss of Thy lips, O Beloved! One who has been kissed by Thee, has his thirst for Thee increasing for ever, all his sorrows vanish, and he forgets all things except Thee alone." Aspire after that kiss of the Beloved, that touch of His lips which makes the Bhakta mad, which makes of man a god. To him, who has been blessed with such a kiss, the whole of nature changes, worlds vanish, suns and moons die out, and the universe itself melts away into that one infinite ocean of love. That is the perfection of the madness of love.

Ay, the true spiritual lover does not rest even there ; even the love of husband and wife is not mad enough for him. The Bhaktas take up also the idea of illegitimate love, because it is so strong; the impropriety of it is not at all the thing they have in view. The nature of this love is such that the more obstructions there are for its free play, the more passionate it becomes. The love between husband and wife is smooth, there are no obstructions there. So the Bhaktas take up the idea of a girl who is in love with her own beloved, and her mother or father or husband objects to such love ; and the more anybody obstructs the course of her love, so much the more is her love tending to grow in strength. Human language cannot describe how Krishna in the groves of Vrindâ was madly loved, how at the sound of his voice the ever-blessed Gopis rushed out to meet him, forgetting everything, forgetting this world and its ties, its duties, its joys, and its sorrows. Man, O man, you speak of divine love and at the same time are able to attend to all the vanities of this world—are you sincere? "Where Râma is, there is no room for any desire—where desire is, there is no room for Rama; these never coexist—like light and darkness they are never together."

CONCLUSION

When this highest ideal of love is reached, philosophy is thrown away; who will then care for it? Freedom, Salvation, Nirvâna—all are thrown away; who cares to become free while in the enjoyment of divine love? "Lord, I do not want wealth, nor friends, nor beauty, nor learning, nor even freedom; let me be born again and again, and be Thou ever my Love. Be Thou ever and ever my Love." "Who cares to become sugar?" says the Bhakta, "I want to taste sugar." Who will then desire to become free and one with God? "I may know that I am He; yet will I take myself away from Him and become different, so that I may enjoy the Beloved." That is what the Bhakta says. Love for love's sake is his highest enjoyment. Who will not be bound hand and foot a thousand times over to enjoy the Beloved? No Bhakta cares for anything except love, except to love and to be loved. His unworldly love is like the tide rushing up the river; this lover goes up the river against the current. The world calls him mad. I know one whom the world used to call mad, and this was his answer: "My friends, the whole world is a lunatic asylum. Some are mad after worldly love, some after name, some after fame, some after money, some after salvation and going to heaven. In this big lunatic asylum I am also mad, I am mad after God. If you are mad after money, I am mad after God. You are mad; so am I. I think my madness is after all the best." The true Bhakta's love is this burning madness before which everything else vanishes for him. The whole universe is to him full of love and love alone; that is how it seems to the lover. So when a man has this love in him, he becomes eternally blessed, eternally happy. This blessed madness of divine love alone can cure for ever the disease of the world that is in us. With desire, selfishness has vanished. He has drawn near to God, he has thrown off all those vain desires of which he was full before.

We all have to begin as dualists in the religion of love. God is to us a separate Being, and we feel ourselves to be separate beings also. Love then comes in the middle, and man begins to approach God, and God also comes nearer and nearer to man. Man takes up all the various relationships of life, as father, as mother, as son, as friend, as master, as lover, and projects them on his ideal of love, on his God. To him God exists as all these, and the last point of his progress is reached when he feels that he has become absolutely merged in the object of his worship. We all begin with love for ourselves, and the unfair claims of the little self make even love selfish. At last, however, comes the full blaze of light, in which this little self is seen to have become one with the Infinite. Man himself is transfigured in the presence of this Light of Love, and he realises at last the beautiful and inspiring truth that Love, the Lover, and the Beloved are One.

LECTURES FROM
COLOMBO TO ALMORA

FIRST PUBLIC LECTURE IN THE EAST

(Delivered in Colombo)

After his memorable work in the West, Swami Vivekananda landed at Colombo on the afternoon of January 15, 1897, and was given a right royal reception by the Hindu community there. The following address of welcome was then presented to him:

SRIMAT VIVEKANANDA SWAMI

REVERED SIR,

In pursuance of a resolution passed at a public meeting of the Hindus of the city of Colombo, we beg to offer you a hearty welcome to this Island. We deem it a privilege to be the first to welcome you on your return home from your great mission in the West.

We have watched with joy and thankfulness the success with which the mission has, under God's blessing, been crowned. You have proclaimed to the nations of Europe and America the Hindu ideal of a universal religion, harmonising all creeds, providing spiritual food for each soul according to its needs, and lovingly drawing it unto God. You have preached the Truth and the Way, taught from remote ages by a succession of Masters whose blessed feet have walked and sanctified the soil of India, and whose gracious presence and inspiration have made her, through all her vicissitudes, the Light of the World.

To the inspiration of such a Master, Shri Ramakrishna Paramahamsa Deva, and to your self-sacrificing zeal, Western nations owe the priceless boon of being placed in living contact with the spiritual genius of India, while to many of our own countrymen, delivered from the glamour of Western civilisation, the value of our glorious heritage has been brought home.

III—8

By your noble work and example you have laid humanity under an obligation difficult to repay, and you have shed fresh lustre upon our Motherland. We pray that the grace of God may continue to prosper you and your work, and

We remain, Revered Sir,
Yours faithfully,
for and on behalf of the Hindus of Colombo,
P. COOMARA SWAMY,
Member of the Legislative Council of Ceylon,
Chairman of the Meeting.
A. KULAVEERASINGHAM, *Secretary.*

Colombo, January, 1897.

The Swami gave a brief reply, expressing his appreciation of the kind welcome he had received. He took advantage of the opportunity to point out that the demonstration had not been made in honour of a great politician, or a great soldier, or a millionaire, but of a begging Sannyâsin, showing the tendency of the Hindu mind towards religion. He urged the necessity of keeping religion as the backbone of the national life if the nation were to live, and disclaimed any personal character for the welcome he had received, but insisted upon its being the recognition of a principle.

On the evening of the 16th the Swami gave the following public lecture in the Floral Hall:

What little work has been done by me has not been from any inherent power that resides in me, but from the cheers, the goodwill, the blessings that have followed my path in the West from this our very beloved, most sacred, dear Motherland. Some good has been done, no doubt, in the West, but specially to myself; for what before was the result of an emotional nature, perhaps, has gained the certainty of conviction and attained the power and strength of demonstration. Formerly I thought as every

Hindu thinks, and as the Hon. President has just pointed
out to you, that this is the Punya Bhumi, the land of
Karma. Today I stand here and say, with the conviction
of truth, that it is so. If there is any land on this earth that
can lay claim to be the blessed Punya Bhumi, to be the
land to which all souls on this earth must come to account
for Karma, the land to which every soul that is wending
its way Godward must come to attain its last home, the
land where humanity has attained its highest towards
gentleness, towards generosity, towards purity, towards
calmness, above all, the land of introspection and of
spirituality—it is India. Hence have started the founders
of religions from the most ancient times, deluging the
earth again and again with the pure and perennial waters
of spiritual truth. Hence have proceeded the tidal waves
of philosophy that have covered the earth, East or West,
North or South, and hence again must start the wave
which is going to spiritualise the material civilisation of
the world. Here is the life-giving water with which must
be quenched the burning fire of materialism which is
burning the core of the hearts of millions in other lands.
Believe me, my friends, this is going to be.

So much I have seen, and so far those of you who are
students of the history of races are already aware of this
fact. The debt which the world owes to our Motherland
is immense. Taking country with country, there is not one
race on this earth to which the world owes so much as to
the patient Hindu, the mild Hindu. "The mild Hindu"
sometimes is used as an expression of reproach; but if
ever a reproach concealed a wonderful truth, it is in the
term, "the mild Hindu", who has always been the blessed
child of God. Civilisations have arisen in other parts of
the world. In ancient times and in modern times, great
ideas have emanated from strong and great races. In
ancient and in modern times, wonderful ideas have been
carried forward from one race to another. In ancient and

in modern times, seeds of great truth and power have
been cast abroad by the advancing tides of national life ;
but mark you, my friends, it has been always with the
blast of war trumpets and with the march of embattled
cohorts. Each idea had to be soaked in a deluge of
blood. Each idea had to wade through the blood of
millions of our fellow-beings. Each word of power had
to be followed by the groans of millions, by the wails of
orphans, by the tears of widows. This, in the main, other
nations have taught; but India has for thousands of
years peacefully existed. Here activity prevailed when
even Greece did not exist, when Rome was not thought
of, when the very fathers of the modern Europeans lived
in the forests and painted themselves blue. Even earlier,
when history has no record, and tradition dares not peer
into the gloom of that intense past, even from then until
now, ideas after ideas have marched out from her, but
every word has been spoken with a blessing behind it
and peace before it. We, of all nations of the world, have
never been a conquering race, and that blessing is on our
head, and therefore we live.

There was a time when at the sound of the march of
big Greek battalions the earth trembled. Vanished from
off the face of the earth, with not even a tale left behind
to tell, gone is that ancient land of the Greeks. There
was a time when the Roman Eagle floated over everything worth having in this world; everywhere Rome's
power was felt and pressed on the head of humanity; the
earth trembled at the name of Rome. But the Capitoline
Hill is a mass of ruins, the spider weaves its web where
the Caesars ruled. There have been other nations equally
glorious that have come and gone, living a few hours of
exultant and exuberant dominance and of a wicked
national life, and then vanishing like ripples on the face
of the waters. Thus have these nations made their mark
on the face of humanity. But we live, and if Manu came

back today he would not be bewildered, and would not find himself in a foreign land. The same laws are here, laws adjusted and thought out through thousands and thousands of years; customs, the outcome of the acumen of ages and the experience of centuries, that seem to be eternal; and as the days go by, as blow after blow of misfortune has been delivered upon them, such blows seem to have served one purpose only, that of making them stronger and more constant. And to find the centre of all this, the heart from which the blood flows, the mainspring of the national life, believe me when I say after my experience of the world, that it is here.

To the other nations of the world, religion is one among the many occupations of life. There is politics, there are the enjoyments of social life, there is all that wealth can buy or power can bring, there is all that the senses can enjoy; and among all these various occupations of life and all this searching after something which can give yet a little more whetting to the cloyed senses— among all these, there is perhaps a little bit of religion. But here, in India, religion is the one and the only occupation of life. How many of you know that there has been a Sino-Japanese War? Very few of you, if any. That there are tremendous political movements and socialistic movements trying to transform Western society, how many of you know? Very few indeed, if any. But that there was a Parliament of Religions in America, and that there was a Hindu Sannyâsin sent over there, I am astonished to find that even the cooly knows of it. That shows the way the wind blows, where the national life is. I used to read books written by globe-trotting travellers, especially foreigners, who deplored the ignorance of the Eastern masses, but I found out that it was partly true and at the same time partly untrue. If you ask a plough-man in England, or America, or France, or Germany to what party he belongs, he can tell you whether he belongs to the Radicals or the Conservatives, and for whom he is going to vote. In America he will say whether he is Republican or Democrat, and he even knows something about the silver question. But if you ask him about his religion, he will tell you that he goes to church and belongs to a certain denomination. That is all he knows, and he thinks it is sufficient.

Now, when we come to India, if you ask one of our ploughmen, "Do you know anything about politics?" He will reply, "What is that?" He does not understand the socialistic movements, the relation between capital and labour, and all that ; he has never heard of such things in his life, he works hard and earns his bread. But you ask, "What is your religion?" he replies, "Look here, my friend, I have marked it on my forehead." He can give you a good hint or two on questions of religion. That has been my experience. That is our nation's life.

Individuals have each their own peculiarities, and each man has his own method of growth, his own life marked out for him by the infinite past life, by all his past Karma as we Hindus say. Into this world he comes with all the past on him, the infinite past ushers the present, and the way in which we use the present is going to make the future. Thus everyone born into this world has a bent, a direction towards which he must go, through which he must live, and what is true of the individual is equally true of the race. Each race, similarly, has a peculiar bent, each race has a peculiar raison d'être, each race has a peculiar mission to fulfil in the life of the world. Each race has to make its own result, to fulfil its own mission. Political greatness or military power is never the mission of our race ; it never was, and, mark my words, it never will be. But there has been the other mission given to us, which is to conserve, to preserve, to accumulate, as it were, into a dynamo, all the spiritual energy of the race, and that concentrated energy is to pour forth in a deluge on the world whenever circumstances are propitious. Let the Persian or the Greek, the Roman, the Arab, or the Englishman march his battalions, conquer the world, and link the different nations together, and the philosophy and spirituality of India is ever ready to flow along the new-made channels into the veins of the nations of the world. The Hindu's calm brain must pour out its own quota to give to the sum total of human progress. India's gift to the world is the light spiritual.

Thus, in the past, we read in history that whenever there arose a great conquering nation uniting the different races of the world, binding India with the other races, taking her out, as it were, from her loneliness and from her aloofness from the rest of the world into which she again and again cast herself, that whenever such a state has been brought about, the result has been the flooding of the world with Indian spiritual ideas. At the beginning of this century, Schopenhauer, the great German philosopher, studying from a not very clear translation of the Vedas made from an old translation into Persian and thence by a young Frenchman into Latin, says, "In the whole world there is no study so beneficial and so elevating as that of the Upanishads. It has been the solace of my life, it will be the solace of my death." This great German sage foretold that "The world is about to see a revolution in thought more extensive and more powerful than that which was witnessed by the Renaissance of Greek Literature", and today his predictions are coming to pass. Those who keep their eyes open, those who understand the workings in the minds of different nations of the West, those who are thinkers and study the different nations, will find the immense change that has been produced in the tone, the procedure, in the methods, and in the literature of the world by this slow, never-ceasing permeation of Indian thought.

But there is another peculiarity, as I have already

hinted to you. We never preached our thoughts with fire and sword. If there is one word in the English language to represent the gift of India to the world, if there is one word in the English language to express the effect which the literature of India produces upon mankind, it is this one word, "fascination". It is the opposite of anything that takes you suddenly; it throws on you, as it were, a charm imperceptibly. To many, Indian thought, Indian manners, Indian customs, Indian philosophy, Indian literature are repulsive at the first sight; but let them persevere, let them read, let them become familiar with the great principles underlying these ideas, and it is ninety-nine to one that the charm will come over them, and fascination will be the result. Slow and silent, as the gentle dew that falls in the morning, unseen and unheard yet producing a most tremendous result, has been the work of the calm, patient, all-suffering spiritual race upon the world of thought.

Once more history is going to repeat itself. For today, under the blasting light of modern science, when old and apparently strong and invulnerable beliefs have been shattered to their very foundations, when special claims laid to the allegiance of mankind by different sects have been all blown into atoms and have vanished into air, when the sledge-hammer blows of modern antiquarian researches are pulverising like masses of porcelain all sorts of antiquated orthodoxies, when religion in the West is only in the hands of the ignorant and the knowing ones look down with scorn upon anything belonging to religion, here comes to the fore the philosophy of India, which displays the highest religious aspirations of the Indian mind, where the grandest philosophical facts have been the practical spirituality of the people. This naturally is coming to the rescue, the idea of the oneness of all, the Infinite, the idea of the Impersonal, the wonderful idea of the eternal soul of man, of the unbroken continuity in the

march of beings, and the infinity of the universe. The old
sects looked upon the world as a little mud-puddle and
thought that time began but the other day. It was there in
our old books, and only there that the grand idea of the
infinite range of time, space, and causation, and above
all, the infinite glory of the spirit of man governed all
the search for religion. When the modern tremendous
theories of evolution and conservation of energy and
so forth are dealing death blows to all sorts of crude
theologies, what can hold any more the allegiance of
cultured humanity but the most wonderful, convincing,
broadening, and ennobling ideas that can be found only
in that most marvellous product of the soul of man, the
wonderful voice of God, the Vedanta?

At the same time, I must remark that what I mean
by our religion working upon the nations outside of India
comprises only the principles, the background, the
foundation upon which that religion is built. The detailed
workings, the minute points which have been worked out
through centuries of social necessity, little ratiocinations
about manners and customs and social well-being, do not
rightly find a place in the category of religion. We know
that in our books a clear distinction is made between two
sets of truths. The one set is that which abides for ever,
being built upon the nature of man, the nature of the soul,
the soul's relation to God, the nature of God, perfection,
and so on ; there are also the principles of cosmology, of
the infinitude of creation, or more correctly speaking—
projection, the wonderful law of cyclical procession, and
so on—these are the eternal principles founded upon the
universal laws in nature. The other set comprises the
minor laws which guided the working of our everyday life.
They belong more properly to the Purânas, to the Smritis,
and not to the Shrutis. These have nothing to do with
the other principles. Even in our own nation these minor
laws have been changing all the time. Customs of one

age, of one Yuga, have not been the customs of another, and as Yuga comes after Yuga, they will still have to change. Great Rishis will appear and lead us to customs and manners that are suited to new environments.

The great principles underlying all this wonderful, infinite, ennobling, expansive view of man and God and the world have been produced in India. In India alone man has not stood up to fight for a little tribal God, saying "My God is true and yours is not true; let us have a good fight over it." It was only here that such ideas did not occur as fighting for little gods. These great underlying principles, being based upon the eternal nature of man, are as potent today for working for the good of the human race as they were thousands of years ago, and they will remain so, so long as this earth remains, so long as the law of Karma remains, so long as we are born as individuals and have to work out our own destiny by our individual power.

And above all, what India has to give to the world is this. If we watch the growth and development of religions in different races, we shall always find this that each tribe at the beginning has a god of its own. If the tribes are allied to each other, these gods will have a generic name, as for example, all the Babylonian gods had. When the Babylonians were divided into many races, they had the generic name of Baal, just as the Jewish races had different gods with the common name of Moloch; and at the same time you will find that one of these tribes becomes superior to the rest, and lays claim to its own king as the king over all. Therefrom it naturally follows that it also wants to preserve its own god as the god of all the races. Baal-Merodach, said the Babylonians, was the greatest god; all the others were inferior. Moloch-Yahveh was the superior over all other Molochs. And these questions had to be decided by the fortunes of battle. The same struggle was here also. In India the same competing gods had been struggling with each other for supremacy, but the great good fortune of this country and of the world was that there came out in the midst of the din and confusion a voice which declared एकं सद्विप्रा बहुधा वदन्ति—"That which exists is One; sages call It by various names." It is not that Shiva is superior to Vishnu, not that Vishnu is everything and Shiva is nothing, but it is the same one whom you call either Shiva, or Vishnu, or by a hundred other names. The names are different, but it is the same one. The whole history of India you may read in these few words. The whole history has been a repetition in massive language, with tremendous power, of that one central doctrine. It was repeated in the land till it had entered into the blood of the nation, till it began to tingle with every drop of blood that flowed in its veins, till it became one with the life, part and parcel of the material of which it was composed ; and thus the land was transmuted into the most wonderful land of toleration, giving the right to welcome the various religions as well as all sects into the old mother-country.

And herein is the explanation of the most remarkable phenomenon that is only witnessed here—all the various sects, apparently hopelessly contradictory, yet living in such harmony. You may be a dualist, and I may be a monist. You may believe that you are the eternal servant of God, and I may declare that I am one with God Himself ; yet both of us are good Hindus. How is that possible ? Read then एकं सद्विप्रा बहुधा वदन्ति—"That which exists is One ; sages call It by various names." Above all others, my countrymen, this is the one grand truth that we have to teach to the world. Even the most educated people of other countries turn up their noses at an angle of forty-five degrees and call our religion idolatry. I have seen that ; and they never stopped to think what a mass of superstition there was in their own heads. It is still so everywhere, this tremendous sectar-

ianism, the low narrowness of the mind. The thing
which a man has is the only thing worth having; the only
life worth living is his own little life of dollar-worship and
mammon-worship; the only little possession worth having
is his own property, and nothing else. If he can manufacture a little clay nonsense or invent a machine, that is
to be admired beyond the greatest possessions. That is
the case over the whole world in spite of education and
learning. But education has yet to be in the world, and
civilisation—civilisation has begun nowhere yet. Ninety-
nine decimal nine per cent of the human race are more
or less savages even now. We may read of these things
in books, and we hear of toleration in religion and all
that, but very little of it is there yet in the world; take
my experience for that. Ninety-nine per cent do not even
think of it. There is tremendous religious persecution
yet in every country in which I have been, and the same
old objections are raised against learning anything new.
The little toleration that is in the world, the little sympathy
that is yet in the world for religious thought, is practically
here in the land of the Aryas, and nowhere else. It is
here that Indians build temples for Mohammedans and
Christians; nowhere else. If you go to other countries
and ask Mohammedans or people of other religions to
build a temple for you, see how they will help. They will
instead try to break down your temple and you too if
they can. The one great lesson, therefore, that the world
wants most, that the world has yet to learn from India,
is the idea not only of toleration, but of sympathy. Well
has it been said in the *Mahimnah-stotra*: "As the different
rivers, taking their start from different mountains, running
straight or crooked, at last come unto the ocean, so,
O Shiva, the different paths which men take through
different tendencies, various though they appear, crooked
or straight, all lead unto Thee." Though they may take
various roads, all are on the way. Some may run a little

crooked, others may run straight, but at last they will all come unto the Lord, the One. Then and then alone, is your Bhakti of Shiva complete when you not only see Him in the Linga, but you see Him everywhere. He is the sage, he is the lover of Hari who sees Hari in everything and in everyone. If you are a real lover of Shiva, you must see Him in everything and in everyone. You must see that every worship is given unto Him whatever may be the name or the form; that all knees bending towards the Caaba, or kneeling in a Christian church, or in a Buddhist temple are kneeling to Him whether they know it or not, whether they are conscious of it or not; that in whatever name or form they are offered, all these flowers are laid at His feet; for He is the one Lord of all, the one Soul of all souls. He knows infinitely better what this world wants than you or I. It is impossible that all difference can cease; it must exist; without variation life must cease. It is this clash, the differentiation of thought that makes for light, for motion, for everything. Differentiation, infinitely contradictory, must remain, but it is not necessary that we should hate each other therefore; it is not necessary therefore that we should fight each other.

Therefore we have again to learn the one central truth that was preached only here in our Motherland, and that has to be preached once more from India. Why? Because not only is it in our books, but it runs through every phase of our national literature and is in the national life. Here and here alone is it practised every day, and any man whose eyes are open can see that it is practised here and here alone. Thus we have to teach religion. There are other and higher lessons that India can teach, but they are only for the learned. The lessons of mildness, gentleness, forbearance, toleration, sympathy, and brotherhood, everyone may learn, whether man, woman, or child, learned or unlearned, without respect of race, caste, or creed. "They call Thee by various names; Thou art One."

VEDANTISM

The following address of welcome from the Hindus
of Jaffna was presented to Swami Vivekananda:

SRIMAT VIVEKANANDA SWAMI

REVERED SIR,

We, the inhabitants of Jaffna professing the Hindu
religion, desire to offer you a most hearty welcome to our
land, the chief centre of Hinduism in Ceylon, and to
express our thankfulness for your kind acceptance of our
invitation to visit this part of Lanka.

Our ancestors settled here from Southern India, more
than two thousand years ago, and brought with them their
religion, which was patronised by the Tamil kings of
Jaffna; but when their government was displaced by that
of the Portuguese and the Dutch, the observance of religious rites was interfered with, public religious worship
was prohibited, and the Sacred Temples, including two of
the most far-famed Shrines, were razed to the ground by
the cruel hand of persecution. In spite of the persistent
attempts of these nations to force upon our forefathers the
Christian religion, they clung to their old faith firmly, and
have transmitted it to us as the noblest of our heritages.
Now under the rule of Great Britain, not only has there
been a great and intelligent revival, but the sacred edifices
have been, and are being, restored.

We take this opportunity to express our deep-felt
gratitude for your noble and disinterested labours in the
cause of our religion in carrying the light of truth, as
revealed in the Vedas, to the Parliament of Religions, in
disseminating the truths of the Divine Philosophy of India
in America and England, and in making the Western world

acquainted with the truths of Hinduism and thereby bringing the West in closer touch with the East. We also express our thankfulness to you for initiating a movement for the revival of our ancient religion in this materialistic age when there is a decadence of faith and a disregard for search after spiritual truth.

We cannot adequately express our indebtedness to you for making the people of the West know the catholicity of our religion and for impressing upon the minds of the savants of the West the truth that there are more things in the Philosophy of the Hindus than are dreamt of in the Philosophy of the West.

We need hardly assure you that we have been carefully watching the progress of your Mission in the West and always heartily rejoicing at your devotedness and successful labours in the field of religion. The appreciative references made by the press in the great centres of intellectual activity, moral growth, and religious inquiry in the West, to you and to your valuable contributions to our religious literature, bear eloquent testimony to your noble and magnificent efforts.

We beg to express our heartfelt gratification at your visit to our land and to hope that we, who, in common with you, look to the Vedas as the foundation of all true spiritual knowledge, may have many more occasions of seeing you in our midst.

May God, who has hitherto crowned your noble work with conspicuous success, spare you long, giving you vigour and strength to continue your noble Mission.

We remain, Revered Sir,

Yours faithfully,

. . .

for and on behalf of the HINDUS OF JAFFNA.

An eloquent reply was given, and on the following evening the Swami lectured on *Vedantism*, a report of which is here appended:

The subject is very large and the time is short; a full analysis of the religion of the Hindus is impossible in one lecture. I will, therefore, present before you the salient points of our religion in as simple language as I can. The word Hindu, by which it is the fashion nowadays to style ourselves, has lost all its meaning, for this word merely meant those who lived on the other side of the river Indus (in Sanskrit, Sindhu). This name was murdered into Hindu by the ancient Persians, and all people living on the other side of the river Sindhu were called by them Hindus. Thus this word has come down to us; and during the Mohammedan rule we took up the word ourselves. There may not be any harm in using the word of course; but, as I have said, it has lost its significance, for you may mark that all the people who live on this side of the Indus in modern times do not follow the same religion as they did in ancient times. The word, therefore, covers not only Hindus proper, but Mohammedans, Christians, Jains, and other people who live in India. I therefore, would not use the word Hindu. What word should we use then? The other words which alone we can use are either the Vaidikas, followers of the Vedas, or better still, the Vedantists, followers of the Vedanta. Most of the great religions of the world owe allegiance to certain books which they believe are the words of God or some other supernatural beings, and which are the basis of their religion. Now of all these books, according to the modern savants of the West, the oldest are the Vedas of the Hindus. A little understanding, therefore, is necessary about the Vedas.

This mass of writing called the Vedas is not the utterance of persons. Its date has never been fixed, can never be fixed, and, according to us, the Vedas are eternal. There is one salient point which I want you to remember, that all the other religions of the world claim their authority as being delivered by a Personal God or a number of personal beings, angels, or special messengers of God, unto certain persons; while the claim of the Hindus is that the Vedas do not owe their authority to anybody, they are themselves the authority, being eternal—the knowledge of God. They were never written, never created, they have existed throughout time ; just as creation is infinite and eternal, without beginning and without end, so is the knowledge of God without beginning and without end. And this knowledge is what is meant by the Vedas (*Vid* to know). The mass of knowledge called the Vedanta was discovered by personages called Rishis, and the Rishi is defined as a Mantra-drashtâ, a seer of thought; not that the thought was his own. Whenever you hear that a certain passage of the Vedas came from a certain Rishi, never think that he wrote it or created it out of his mind ; he was the seer of the thought which already existed ; it existed in the universe eternally. This sage was the discoverer ; the Rishis were spiritual discoverers.

This mass of writing, the Vedas, is divided principally into two parts, the Karma Kânda and the Jnâna Kânda —the work portion and the knowledge portion, the ceremonial and the spiritual. The work portion consists of various sacrifices ; most of them of late have been given up as not practicable under present circumstances, but others remain to the present day in some shape or other. The main ideas of the Karma Kanda, which consists of the duties of man, the duties of the student, of the householder, of the recluse, and the various duties of the different stations of life, are followed more or less down to the present day. But the spiritual portion of our religion is in the second part, the Jnana Kanda, the Vedanta, the end of the Vedas, the gist, the goal of the Vedas. The essence of the knowledge of the Vedas was called by the name of Vedanta, which comprises the Upanishads ; and all the sects of India—Dualists, Qualified-Monists, Monists, or the Shaivites. Vaishnavites, Shâktas, Sauras,

Gânapatyas, each one that dares to come within the fold
of Hinduism—must acknowledge the Upanishads of the
Vedas. They can have their own interpretations and can
interpret them in their own way, but they must obey
the authority. That is why we want to use the word
Vedantist instead of Hindu. All the philosophers of India
who are orthodox have to acknowledge the authority of
the Vedanta ; and all our present-day religions, however
crude some of them may appear to be, however inexpli-
cable some of their purposes may seem, one who understands them and studies them can trace them back to
the ideas of the Upanishads. So deeply have these
Upanishads sunk into our race that those of you who study
the symbology of the crudest religion of the Hindus will
be astonished to find sometimes figurative expressions of
the Upanishads—the Upanishads become symbolised after
a time into figures and so forth. Great spiritual and
philosophical ideas in the Upanishads are today with us,
converted into household worship in the form of symbols.
Thus the various symbols now used by us, all come from
the Vedanta, because in the Vedanta they are used as
figures, and these ideas spread among the nation and
permeated it throughout until they became part of their
everyday life as symbols.

Next to the Vedanta come the Smritis. These also
are books written by sages, but the authority of the
Smritis is subordinate to that of the Vedanta, because they
stand in the same relation with us as the scriptures of the
other religions stand with regard to them. We admit that
the Smritis have been written by particular sages ; in that
sense they are the same as the scriptures of other religions,
but these Smritis are not final authority. If there is anything in a Smriti which contradicts the Vedanta, the Smriti
is to be rejected—its authority is gone. These Smritis,
we see again, have varied from time to time. We read that
such and such Smriti should have authority in the Satya

Yuga, such and such in the Tretâ Yuga, some in the Dwâpara Yuga, and some in the Kali Yuga, and so on. As essential conditions changed, as various circumstances came to have their influence on the race, manners and customs had to be changed, and these Smritis, as mainly regulating the manners and customs of the nation, had also to be changed from time to time. This is a point I specially ask you to remember. The principles of religion that are in the Vedanta are unchangeable. Why ? Because they are all built upon the eternal principles that are in man and nature ; they can never change. Ideas about the soul, going to heaven, and so on can never change ; they were the same thousands of years ago, they are the same today, they will be the same millions of years hence. But those religious practices which are based entirely upon our social position and correlation must change with the changes in society. Such an order, therefore, would be good and true at a certain period and not at another. We find accordingly that a certain food is allowed at one time and not another, because the food was suitable for that time ; but climate and other things changed, various other circumstances required to be met, so the Smriti changed the food and other things. Thus it naturally follows that if in modern times our society requires changes to be made, they must be met, and sages will come and show us the way how to meet them ; but not one jot of the principles of our religion will be changed ; they will remain intact.

Then there are the Purânas. पुराणं पञ्चलक्षणम् —which means, the Puranas are of five characteristics—that which treats of history, of cosmology, with various symbological illustration of philosophical principles, and so forth. These were written to popularise the religion of the Vedas. The language in which the Vedas are written is very ancient, and even among scholars very few can trace the date of these books. The Puranas

were written in the language of the people of that time,
what we call modern Sanskrit. They were then meant not
for scholars, but for the ordinary people ; and ordinary
people cannot understand philosophy. Such things were
given unto them in concrete form, by means of the lives of
saints and kings and great men and historical events that
happened to the race etc. The sages made use of these
things to illustrate the eternal principles of religion.
There are still other books, the Tantras. These are
very much like Puranas in some respects, and in some of
them there is an attempt to revive the old sacrificial ideas
of the Karma Kanda.

All these books constitute the scriptures of the
Hindus. When there is such a mass of sacred books in a
nation and a race which has devoted the greatest part of
its energies to the thought of philosophy and spirituality
(nobody knows for how many thousands of years), it is
quite natural that there should be so many sects; indeed
it is a wonder that there are not thousands more. These
sects differ very much from each other in certain points.
We shall not have time to understand the differences between these sects and all the spiritual details about them ;
therefore I shall take up the common grounds, the essential
principles of all these sects which every Hindu must
believe.

The first is the question of creation, that this
nature, Prakriti, Mâyâ is infinite, without beginning. It is
not that this world was created the other day, not that a
God came and created the world and since that time has
been sleeping; for that cannot be. The creative energy
is still going on. God is eternally creating—is never at rest.
Remember the passage in the Gita where Krishna says,
"If I remain at rest for one moment, this universe will be
destroyed." If that creative energy which is working all
around us, day and night, stops for a second, the whole
thing falls to the ground. There never was a time when

that energy did not work throughout the universe, but
there is the law of cycles, Pralaya. Our Sanskrit word for
creation, properly translated, should be *projection* and *not
creation*. For the word creation in the English language
has unhappily got that fearful, that most crude idea of
something coming out of nothing, creation out of non-
entity, non-existence becoming existence, which, of course,
I would not insult you by asking you to believe. Our
word, therefore, is projection. The whole of this nature
exists, it becomes finer, subsides ; and then after a period
of rest, as it were, the whole thing is again projected forward, and the same combination, the same evolution, the
same manifestations appear and remain playing, as
it were, for a certain time, only again to break into pieces,
to become finer and finer, until the whole thing subsides,
and again comes out. Thus it goes on backwards and for-
wards with a wave-like motion throughout eternity.
Time, space, and causation are all within this nature.
To say, therefore, that it had a beginning is utter
nonsense. No question can occur as to its beginning
or its end. Therefore wherever in our scriptures the words
beginning and end are used, you must remember that it
means the beginning and the end of one particular cycle ;
no more than that.

What makes this creation ? God. What do I mean by
the use of the English word God ? Certainly not the word
as ordinarily used in English—a good deal of difference.
There is no other suitable word in English. I would
rather confine myself to the Sanskrit word Brahman. He
is the general cause of all these manifestations. What
is this Brahman ? He is eternal, eternally pure, eternally
awake, the almighty, the all-knowing, the all-merciful, the
omnipresent, the formless, the partless. He creates this
universe. If he is always creating and holding up this
universe, two difficulties arise. We see that there is
partiality in the universe. One person is born happy, and

another unhappy; one is rich, and another is poor; this shows partiality. Then there is cruelty also, for here the very condition of life is death. One animal tears another to pieces, and every man tries to get the better of his own brother. This competition, cruelty, horror, and sighs rending hearts day and night is the state of things in this world of ours. If this be the creation of a God, that God is worse than cruel, worse than any devil that man ever imagined. Ay! says the Vedanta, it is not the fault of God that this partiality exists, that this competition exists. Who makes it ? We ourselves. There is a cloud shedding its rain on all fields alike. But it is only the field that is well cultivated, which gets the advantage of the shower; another field, which has not been tilled or taken care of cannot get that advantage. It is not the fault of the cloud. The mercy of God is eternal and unchangeable; it is we that make the differentiation. But how can this difference of some being born happy and some unhappy be explained? They do nothing to make out that difference! Not in this life, but they did in their last birth and the difference is explained by this action in the previous life.

We now come to the second principle on which we all agree, not only all Hindus, but all Buddhists and all Jains. We all agree that life is eternal. It is not that it has sprung out of nothing, for that cannot be. Such a life would not be worth having. Everything that has a beginning in time must end in time. If life began but yesterday, it must end tomorrow, and annihilation is the result. Life must have been existing. It does not now require much acumen to see that, for all the sciences of modern times have been coming round to our help, illustrating from the material world the principles embodied in our scriptures. You know it already that each one of us is the effect of the infinite past; the child is ushered into the world not as something flashing from the hands of nature, as poets delight so much to depict, but he has the burden of an infinite past ; for good or evil he comes to work out his own past deeds. That makes the differentiation. This is the law of Karma. Each one of us is the maker of his own fate. This law knocks on the head at once all doctrines of predestination and fate and gives us the only means of reconciliation between God and man. We, we, and none else, are responsible for what we suffer. We are the effects, and we are the causes. We are free therefore. If I am unhappy, it has been of my own making, and that very thing shows that I can be happy if I will. If I am impure, that is also of my own making, and that very thing shows that I can be pure if I will. The human will stands beyond all circumstance. Before it—the strong, gigantic, infinite will and freedom in man—all the powers, even of nature, must bow down, succumb, and become its servants. This is the result of the law of Karma.

The next question, of course, naturally would be: What is the soul ? We cannot understand God in our scriptures without knowing the soul. There have been attempts in India, and outside of India too, to catch a glimpse of the beyond by studying external nature ; and we all know what an awful failure has been the result. Instead of giving us a glimpse of the beyond, the more we study the material world, the more we tend to become materialised. The more we handle the material world, even the little spirituality which we possessed before vanishes. Therefore that is not the way to spirituality, to knowledge of the Highest ; but it must come through the heart, the human soul. The external workings do not teach us anything about the beyond, about the Infinite, it is only the internal that can do so. Through soul, there-fore, the analysis of the human soul alone, can we under-stand God. There are differences of opinion as to the nature of the human soul among the various sects in India, but there are certain points of agreement. We all agree that souls are without beginning and without end, and immortal by their very nature ; also that all powers, blessing, purity, omnipresence, omniscience are buried in each soul. That is a grand idea we ought to remember. In every man and in every animal, however weak or wicked, great or small, resides the same omnipresent, omniscient soul. The difference is not in the soul, but in the manifestation. Between me and the smallest animal, the difference is only in manifestation, but as a principle he is the same as I am, he is my brother, he has the same soul as I have. This is the greatest principle that India has preached. The talk of the brotherhood of man becomes in India the brotherhood of universal life, of animals, and of all life down to the little ants—all these are our bodies. Even as our scripture says, "Thus the sage, knowing that the same Lord inhabits all bodies, will worship every body as such." That is why in India there have been such merciful ideas about the poor, about animals, about everybody, and everything else. This is one of the common grounds about our ideas of the soul.

Naturally, we come to the idea of God. One thing more about the soul. Those who study the English language are often deluded by the words, soul and mind. Our Âtman and soul are entirely different things. What we call Manas, the mind, the Western people call soul. The West never had the idea of soul until they got it through Sanskrit philosophy, some twenty years ago. The body is here, beyond that is the mind, yet the mind is not the Âtman ; it is the fine body, the Sukshma Sharira, made of fine particles, which goes from birth to death, and so on ; but behind the mind is the Atman, the soul, the Self of man. It cannot be translated by the word soul or mind, so we have to use the word Atman, or, as Western philosophers have designated it, by the word Self. Whatever word you use, you must keep it clear in your mind that the Atman is separate from the mind, as well as from the body, and that this Atman goes through birth and death, accompanied by the mind, the Sukshma Sharira. And when the time comes that it has attained to all knowledge and manifested itself to perfection, then this going from birth to death ceases for it. Then it is at liberty either to keep that mind, the Sukshma Sharira, or to let it go for ever, and remain independent and free throughout all eternity. The goal of the soul is freedom. That is one peculiarity of our religion. We also have heavens and hells too ; but these are not infinite, for in the very nature of things they cannot be. If there were any heavens, they would be only repetitions of this world of ours on a bigger scale, with a little more happiness and a little more enjoyment, but that is all the worse for the soul. There are many of these heavens. Persons who do good works here with the thought of reward, when they die, are born again as gods in one of these heavens, as Indra and others. These gods are the names of certain states. They also had been men, and by good work they have become gods ; and those different names that you read of, such as Indra and so on, are not the names of the same person. There will be thousands of Indras. Nahusha was a great king, and when he died, he became Indra. It is a position ; one soul becomes high and takes the Indra position and remains in it only a certain time ; he then dies and is born again as man. But the human body is the highest of all. Some of the gods may try to go higher and give up all ideas of enjoyment in heavens ; but, as in this world, wealth and position and enjoyment delude the vast majority, so do most of the gods become deluded also, and after working out their good Karma, they fall down and become human beings again. This earth, therefore, is the Karma Bhumi; it is this earth from which we attain to liberation. So even these heavens are not worth attaining to.

What is then worth having ? Mukti, freedom. Even in the highest of heavens, says our scripture, you are a slave ; what matters it if you are a king for twenty thousand years ? So long as you have a body, so long as you are a slave to happiness, so long as time works on you, space works on you, you are a slave. The idea, therefore, is to be free of external and internal nature. Nature must fall at your feet, and you must trample on it and be free and glorious by going beyond. No more is there life ; therefore no more is there death. No more enjoyment ; therefore no more misery. It is bliss unspeakable, indestructible, beyond everything. What we call happiness and good here are but particles of that eternal Bliss. And this eternal Bliss is our goal.

The soul is also sexless ; we cannot say of the Atman that it is a man or a woman. Sex belongs to the body alone. All such ideas, therefore, as man or woman, are a delusion when spoken with regard to the Self, and are only proper when spoken of the body. So are the ideas of age. It never ages; the ancient One is always the same. How did It come down to earth ? There is but one answer to that in our scriptures. Ignorance is the cause of all this bondage. It is through ignorance that we have become bound ; knowledge will cure it by taking us to the other side. How will that knowledge come ? Through love, Bhakti : by the worship of God, by loving all beings as the temples of God. He resides within them. Thus, with that intense love will come knowledge, and ignorance will disappear, the bonds will break, and the soul will be free.

There are two ideas of God in our scriptures—the one, the personal ; and the other, the impersonal. The idea of the Personal God is that He is the omnipresent creator, preserver, and destroyer of everything, the eternal Father and Mother of the universe, but One who is eternally separate from us and from all souls ; and liberation consists in coming near to Him and living in Him. Then there is the other idea of the Impersonal, where all those adjectives are taken away as superfluous, as illogical and there remains an impersonal, omnipresent Being

who cannot be called a knowing being, because knowledge
only belongs to the human mind. He cannot be called a
thinking being, because that is a process of the weak only.
He cannot be called a reasoning being, because reasoning is a sign of weakness. He cannot be called a creating
being, because none creates except in bondage. What bondage has He ? None works except for the fulfilment of
desires; what desires has He? None works except it be to
supply some wants; what wants has He? In the Vedas it
is not the word "He" that is used, but "It", for "He" would
make an invidious distinction, as if God were a man. "It",
the impersonal, is used, and this impersonal "It" is
preached. This system is called the Advaita.

And what are our relations with this Impersonal
Being ?—that we are He. We and He are one. Every
one is but a manifestation of that Impersonal, the basis
of all being, and misery consists in thinking of ourselves
as different from this Infinite, Impersonal Being ; and
liberation consists in knowing our unity with this wonderful Impersonality. These, in short, are the two ideas of
God that we find in our scriptures.

Some remarks ought to be made here. It is only
through the idea of the Impersonal God that you can
have any system of ethics. In every nation the truth has
been preached from the most ancient times—love your
fellow-beings as yourselves—I mean, love human beings
as yourselves. In India it has been preached, "love all
beings as yourselves" ; we make no distinction between
men and animals. But no reason was forthcoming, no one
knew why it would be good to love other beings as
ourselves. And the reason, why, is there in the idea of
the Impersonal God ; you understand it when you learn
that the whole world is one—the oneness of the universe—
the solidarity of all life—that in hurting any one I am
hurting myself, in loving any one I am loving myself.
Hence we understand why it is that we ought not to hurt

others. The reason for ethics, therefore, can only be had from this ideal of the Impersonal God. Then there is the question of the position of the Personal God in it. I understand the wonderful flow of love that comes from the idea of a Personal God, I thoroughly appreciate the power and potency of Bhakti on men to suit the needs of different times. What we now want in our country, however, is not so much of weeping, but a little strength. What a mine of strength is in this Impersonal God, when all superstitions have been thrown overboard, and man stands on his feet with the knowledge—I am the Impersonal Being of the world! What can make me afraid ? I care not even for nature's laws. Death is a joke to me. Man stands on the glory of his own soul, the infinite, the eternal, the deathless—that soul which no instruments can pierce, which no air can dry, nor fire burn, no water melt, the infinite, the birthless, the deathless, without beginning and without end, before whose magnitude the suns and moons and all their systems appear like drops in the ocean, before whose glory space melts away into nothingness and time vanishes into non-existence. This glorious soul we must believe in. Out of that will come power. Whatever you think, that you will be. If you think yourselves weak, weak you will be ; if you think yourselves strong, strong you will be ; if you think yourselves impure, impure you will be ; if you think yourselves pure, pure you will be. This teaches us not to think ourselves as weak, but as strong, omnipotent, omniscient. No matter that I have not expressed it yet, it is in me. All knowledge is in me, all power, all purity, and all freedom. Why cannot I express this knowledge ? Because I do not believe in it. Let me believe in it, and it must and will come out. This is what the idea of the Impersonal teaches. Make your children strong from their very childhood ; teach them not weakness, nor forms, but make them strong ; let them stand on their feet—bold, all-conquering, all-suffering ; and first of all, let them learn of the glory of the soul. That you get alone in the Vedanta—and there alone. It has ideas of love and worship and other things which we have in other religions, and more besides ; but this idea of the soul is the life-giving thought, the most wonderful. There and there alone is the great thought that is going to revolutionise the world and reconcile the knowledge of the material world with religion.

Thus I have tried to bring before you the salient points of our religion—the principles. I have only to say a few words about the practice and the application. As we have seen, under the circumstances existing in India, naturally many sects must appear. As a fact, we find that there are so many sects in India, and at the same time we know this mysterious fact that these sects do not quarrel with each other. The Shaivite does not say that every Vaishnavite is going to be damned, nor the Vaishnavite that every Shaivite will be damned. The Shaivite says, this is my path, and you have yours ; at the end we must come together. They all know that in India. This is the theory of Ishta. It has been recognised in the most ancient times that there are various forms of worshipping God. It is also recognised that different natures require different methods. Your method of coming to God may not be my method, possibly it might hurt me. Such an idea as that there is but one way for everybody is injurious, meaningless, and entirely to be avoided. Woe unto the world when everyone is of the same religious opinion and takes to the same path. Then all religions and all thought will be destroyed. Variety is the very soul of life. When it dies out entirely, creation will die. When this variation in thought is kept up, we must exist ; and we need not quarrel because of that variety. Your way is very good for you, but not for me. My way is good for me, but not for you. My way is called in Sanskrit, my "Ishta". Mind you, we have no quarrel with any religion in the world. We have each our Ishta. But when we see men coming and saying, "This is the only way", and trying to force it on us in India, we have a word to say ; we laugh at them. For such people who want to destroy their brothers because they seem to follow a different path towards God—for them to talk of love is absurd. Their love does not count for much. How can they preach of love who cannot bear another man to follow a different path from their own ? If that is love, what is hatred? We have no quarrel with any religion in the world, whether it teaches men to worship Christ, Buddha, or Mohammed, or any other prophet. "Welcome, my brother," the Hindu says, "I am going to help you ; but you must allow me to follow my way too. That is my Ishta. Your way is very good, no doubt ; but it may be dangerous for me. My own experience tells me what food is good for me, and no army of doctors can tell me that. So I know from my own experience what path is the best for me." That is the goal, the Ishta, and, therefore, we say that if a temple, or a symbol, or an image helps you to realise the Divinity within, you are welcome to it. Have two hundred images if you like. If certain forms and formularies help you to realise the Divine, God speed you ; have, by all means, whatever forms, and whatever temples, and whatever ceremonies you want to bring you nearer to God. But do not quarrel about them ; the moment you quarrel, you are not going Godward, you are going backward, towards the brutes.

These are a few ideas in our religion. It is one of inclusion of every one, exclusion of none. Though our castes and our institutions are apparently linked with our religion, they are not so. These institutions have been necessary to protect us as a nation, and when this necessity for self-preservation will no more exist, they will die a natural death. But the older I grow, the better I seem to think of these time-honoured institutions of India. There was a time when I used to think that many of them were useless and worthless ; but the older I grew, the more I seem to feel a diffidence in cursing any one of them, for each one of them is the embodiment of the experience of centuries. A child of but yesterday, destined to die the day after tomorrow, comes to me and asks me to change all my plans ; and if I hear the advice of that baby and change all my surroundings according to his ideas, I myself should be a fool, and no one else. Much of the advice that is coming to us from different countries is similar to this. Tell these wiseacres: "I will hear you when you have made a stable society yourselves. You cannot hold on to one idea for two days, you quarrel and fail ; you are born like moths in the spring and die like them in five minutes. You come up like bubbles and burst like bubbles too. First form a stable society like ours. First make laws and institutions that remain undiminished in their power through scores of centuries. Then will be the time to talk on the subject with you, but till then, my friend, you are only a giddy child."

I have finished what I had to say about our religion. I will end by reminding you of the one pressing necessity of the day. Praise be to Vyâsa, the great author of the Mahâbhârata, that in this Kali Yuga there is one great work. The Tapas and the other hard Yogas that were practised in other Yugas do not work now. What is needed in this Yuga is giving, helping others. What is meant by Dâna? The highest of gifts is the giving of spiritual knowledge, the next is the giving of secular knowledge, and the next is the saving of life, the last is giving food and drink. He who gives spiritual knowledge, saves the soul from many and many a birth. He who gives secular knowledge opens the eyes of human beings towards spiritual knowledge, and far below these rank all other gifts, even the saving of life. Therefore it is necessary that you learn this and note that all other kinds of work are of much less value than that of imparting spiritual knowledge. The highest and greatest help is that given in the dissemination of spiritual knowledge. There is an eternal fountain of spirituality in our scriptures, and nowhere on earth, except in this land of renunciation, do we find such noble examples of practical spirituality. I have had a little experience of the world. Believe me, there is much talking in other lands; but the practical man of religion, who has carried it into his life, is here and here alone. Talking is not religion; parrots may talk, machines may talk nowadays. But show me the life of renunciation, of spirituality, of all-suffering, of love infinite. This kind of life indicates a spiritual man. With such ideas and such noble practical examples in our country, it would be a great pity if the treasures in the brains and hearts of all these great Yogis were not brought out to become the common property of every one, rich and poor, high and low; not only in India, but they must be thrown broadcast all over the world. This is one of our greatest duties, and you will find that the more you work to help others, the more you help yourselves. The one vital duty incumbent on you, if you really love your religion, if you really love your country, is that you must struggle hard to be up and doing, with this one great idea of bringing out the treasures from your closed books and delivering them over to their rightful heirs.

And above all, one thing is necessary. Ay, for ages we have been saturated with awful jealousy; we are always getting jealous of each other. Why has this man a little precedence, and not I? Even in the worship of God we want precedence, to such a state of slavery have we come. This is to be avoided. If there is any crying sin in India at this time it is this slavery. Every one wants to command, and no one wants to obey; and this is owing to the absence of that wonderful Brahmacharya system of yore. First, learn to obey. The command will come by itself. Always first learn to be a servant, and then you will be fit to be a master. Avoid this jealousy, and you will do great works that have yet to be done. Our ancestors did most wonderful works, and we look back upon their work with veneration and pride. But we also are going to do great deeds, and let others look back with blessings and pride upon us as their ancestors. With the blessing of the Lord every one here will yet do such deeds that will eclipse those of our ancestors, great and glorious as they may have been.

REPLY TO THE ADDRESS OF WELCOME
AT PAMBAN

On the arrival of Swami Vivekananda at Pamban, he was met by His Highness the Raja of Ramnad, who accorded him a hearty welcome. Preparations had been made at the landing wharf for a formal reception; and here, under a pandal which had been decorated with great taste, the following address on behalf of the Pamban people was read:

MAY IT PLEASE YOUR HOLINESS,

We greatly rejoice to welcome Your Holiness with hearts full of deepest gratitude and highest veneration—gratitude for having so readily and graciously consented to pay us a flying visit in spite of the numerous calls on you, and veneration for the many noble and excellent qualities that you possess and for the great work you have so nobly undertaken to do, and which you have been discharging with conspicuous ability, utmost zeal, and earnestness.

We truly rejoice to see that the efforts of Your Holiness in sowing the seeds of Hindu philosophy in the cultured minds of the great Western nations are being crowned with so much success that we already see all around the bright and cheerful aspect of the bearing of excellent fruits in great abundance, and most humbly pray that Your Holiness will, during your sojourn in Âryâvarta, be graciously pleased to exert yourself even a little more than you did in the West to awaken the minds of your brethren in this our motherland from their dreary life-long slumber and make them recall to their minds the long-forgotten gospel of truth.

Our hearts are so full of the sincerest affection, greatest

reverence, and highest admiration for Your Holiness—our great spiritual leader, that we verily find it impossible to adequately express our feelings, and, therefore, beg to conclude with an earnest and united prayer to the merciful Providence to bless Your Holiness with a long life of usefulness and to grant you everything that may tend to bring about the long-lost feelings of universal brotherhood.

The Raja added to this a brief personal welcome, which was remarkable for its depth of feeling, and then the Swami replied to the following effect:

Our sacred motherland is a land of religion and philosophy—the birthplace of spiritual giants—the land of renunciation, where and where alone, from the most ancient to the most modern times, there has been the highest ideal of life open to man.

I have been in the countries of the West—have travelled through many lands of many races; and each race and each nation appears to me to have a particular ideal—a prominent ideal running through its whole life; and this ideal is the backbone of the national life. Not politics nor military power, not commercial supremacy nor mechanical genius furnishes India with that backbone, but religion; and religion alone is all that we have and mean to have. Spirituality has been always in India.

Great indeed are the manifestations of muscular power, and marvellous the manifestations of intellect expressing themselves through machines by the appliances of science; yet none of these is more potent than the influence which spirit exerts upon the world.

The history of our race shows that India has always been most active. Today we are taught by men who ought to know better that the Hindu is mild and passive; and this has become a sort of proverb with the people of other lands. I discard the idea that India was ever passive. Nowhere has activity been more pronounced than in this blessed land of ours, and the great proof of this activity is that our most ancient and magnanimous race still lives, and at every decade in its glorious career seems to take on fresh youth—undying and imperishable. This activity manifests here in religion. But it is a peculiar fact in human nature that it judges others according to its own standard of activity. Take, for instance, a shoemaker. He understands only shoemaking and thinks there is nothing in this life except the manufacturing of shoes. A bricklayer understands nothing but bricklaying and proves this alone in his life from day to day. And there is another reason which explains this. When the vibrations of light are very intense, we do not see them, because we are so constituted that we cannot go beyond our own plane of vision. But the Yogi with his spiritual introspection is able to see through the materialistic veil of the vulgar crowds.

The eyes of the whole world are now turned towards this land of India for spiritual food ; and India has to provide it for all the races. Here alone is the best ideal for mankind ; and Western scholars are now striving to understand this ideal which is enshrined in our Sanskrit literature and philosophy, and which has been the characteristic of India all through the ages.

Since the dawn of history, no missionary went out of India to propagate the Hindu doctrines and dogmas; but now a wonderful change is coming over us. Shri Bhagavân Krishna says, "Whenever virtue subsides and immorality prevails, then I come again and again to help the world." Religious researches disclose to us the fact that there is not a country possessing a good ethical code but has borrowed something of it from us, and there is not one religion possessing good ideas of the immortality of the soul but has derived it directly or indirectly from us.

There never was a time in the world's history when there was so much robbery, and high-handedness, and

tyranny of the strong over the weak, as at this latter end
of the nineteenth century. Everybody should know that
there is no salvation except through the conquering of
desires, and that no man is free who is subject to the
bondage of matter. This great truth all nations are slowly
coming to understand and appreciate. As soon as the
disciple is in a position to grasp this truth, the words of
the Guru come to his help. The Lord sends help to His
own children in His infinite mercy which never ceaseth
and is ever flowing in all creeds. Our Lord is the Lord
of all religions. This idea belongs to India alone; and I
challenge any one of you to find it in any other scripture
of the world.

We Hindus have now been placed, under God's
providence, in a very critical and responsible position. The
nations of the West are coming to us for spiritual help. A
great moral obligation rests on the sons of India to fully
equip themselves for the work of enlightening the world
on the problems of human existence. One thing we may
note, that whereas you will find that good and great men
of other countries take pride in tracing back their descent
to some robber-baron who lived in a mountain fortress and
emerged from time to time to plunder passing wayfarers,
we Hindus, on the other hand, take pride in being the descendants of Rishis and sages who lived on roots and fruits
in mountains and caves, meditating on the Supreme.
We may be degraded and degenerated now ; but however degraded and degenerated we may be, we can
become great if only we begin to work in right earnest on
behalf of our religion.

Accept my · hearty thanks for the kind and cordial
reception you have given me. It is impossible for me to
express my gratitude to H. H. the Raja of Ramnad for his
love towards me. If any good work has been done by
me and through me, India owes much to this good man,
for it was he who conceived the idea of my going to

Chicago, and it was he who put that idea into my head and persistently urged me on to accomplish it. Standing beside me, he with all his old enthusiasm is still expecting me to do more and more work. I wish there were half a dozen more such Rajas to take interest in our dear motherland and work for her amelioration in the spiritual line.

ADDRESS AT THE RAMESWARAM TEMPLE ON REAL WORSHIP

A visit was subsequently paid to the Rameswaram Temple, where the Swami was asked to address a few words to the people who had assembled there. This he did in the following terms:

It is in love that religion exists and not in ceremony, in the pure and sincere love in the heart. Unless a man is pure in body and mind, his coming into a temple and worshipping Shiva is useless. The prayers of those that are pure in mind and body will be answered by Shiva, and those that are impure and yet try to teach religion to others will fail in the end. External worship is only a symbol of internal worship; but internal worship and purity are the real things. Without them, external worship would be of no avail. Therefore you must all try to remember this.

People have become so degraded in this Kali Yuga that they think they can do anything, and then they can go to a holy place, and their sins will be forgiven. If a man goes with an impure mind into a temple, he adds to the sins that he had already, and goes home a worse man than when he left it. Tirtha (place of pilgrimage) is a place which is full of holy things and holy men. But if holy people live in a certain place, and if there is no temple there, even that is a Tirtha. If unholy people live in a place where there may be a hundred temples, the Tirtha has vanished from that place. And it is most difficult to live in a Tirtha; for if sin is committed in any ordinary place it can easily be removed, but sin committed in a Tirtha cannot be removed. This is the gist of all worship—to be pure and to do good to others.

He who sees Shiva in the poor, in the weak, and in the
diseased, really worships Shiva ; and if he sees Shiva only
in the image, his worship is but preliminary. He who
has served and helped one poor man seeing Shiva in him,
without thinking of his caste, or creed, or race, or anything, with him Shiva is more pleased than with the man
who sees Him only in temples.

A rich man had a garden and two gardeners. One of
these gardeners was very lazy and did not work ; but when
the owner came to the garden, the lazy man would get
up and fold his arms and say, "How beautiful is the face
of my master", and dance before him. The other gardener
would not talk much, but would work hard, and produce
all sorts of fruits and vegetables which he would carry on
his head to his master who lived a long way off. Of
these two gardeners, which would be the more beloved
of his master ? Shiva is that master, and this world is
His garden, and there are two sorts of gardeners here ;
the one who is lazy, hypocritical, and does nothing, only
talking about Shiva's beautiful eyes and nose and other
features ; and the other, who is taking care of Shiva's
children, all those that are poor and weak, all animals,
and all His creation. Which of these would be the
more beloved of Shiva? Certainly he that serves His
children. He who wants to serve the father must serve
the children first. He who wants to serve Shiva must
serve His children—must serve all creatures in this world
first. It is said in the Shâstra that those who serve the
servants of God are His greatest servants. So you will
bear this in mind.

Let me tell you again that you must be pure and
help any one who comes to you, as much as lies in your
power. And this is good Karma. By the power of this,
the heart becomes pure (Chitta-shuddhi), and then Shiva
who is residing in every one will become manifest. He
is always in the heart of every one. If there is dirt and

dust on a mirror, we cannot see our image. So ignorance
and wickedness are the dirt and dust that are on the
mirror of our hearts. Selfishness is the chief sin, thinking
of ourselves first. He who thinks, "I will eat first, I will
have more money than others, and I will possess everything", he who thinks, "I will get to heaven before others,
I will get Mukti before others" is the selfish man.
The unselfish man says, "I will be last, I do not care
to go to heaven, I will even go to hell if by doing
so I can help my brothers." This unselfishness is the
test of religion. He who has more of this unselfishness
is more spiritual and nearer to Shiva. Whether he is
learned or ignorant, he is nearer to Shiva than anybody
else, whether he knows it or not. And if a man is selfish,
even though he has visited all the temples, seen all the
places of pilgrimage, and painted himself like a leopard.
he is still further off from Shiva.

REPLY TO THE ADDRESS OF WELCOME
AT RAMNAD

At Ramnad the following address was presented to Swami Vivekananda by the Raja:

His Most Holiness,

Sri Paramahamsa, Yati-Râja, Digvijaya-Kolâhala, Sarvamata-Sampratipanna, Parama-Yogeeswara, Srimat Bhagavân Sree Ramakrishna Paramahamsa Karakamala-Sanjâta, Râjâdhirâja-Sevita, SREE VIVEKANANDA SWAMI, MAY IT PLEASE YOUR HOLINESS,

We, the inhabitants of this ancient and historic Samsthânam of Sethu Bandha Rameswaram, otherwise known as Râmanâthapuram or Ramnad, beg, most cordially, to welcome you to this, our motherland. We deem it a very rare privilege to be the first to pay your Holiness our heartfelt homage on your landing in India, and that, on the shores sanctified by the footsteps of that great Hero and our revered Lord—Sree Bhagavân Râmachandra.

We have watched with feelings of genuine pride and pleasure the unprecedented success which has crowned your laudable efforts in bringing home to the master-minds of the West the intrinsic merits and excellence of our time-honoured and noble religion. You have with an eloquence that is unsurpassed and in language plain and unmistakable, proclaimed to and convinced the cultured audiences in Europe and America that Hinduism fulfils all the requirements of the ideal of a universal religion and adapts itself to the temperament and needs of men and women of all races and creeds. Animated purely by a disinterested impulse, influenced by the best of motives and at considerable self-sacrifice, Your Holiness has crossed boundless seas and oceans to convey the message of truth and peace, and to plant the flag of India's spiritual

triumph and glory in the rich soil of Europe and America.
Your Holiness has, both by precept and practice, shown
the feasibility and importance of universal brotherhood.
Above all, your labours in the West have indirectly and
to a great extent tended to awaken the apathetic sons
and daughters of India to a sense of the greatness and
glory of their ancestral faith, and to create in them a
genuine interest in the study and observance of their dear
and priceless religion.

We feel we cannot adequately convey in words our
feelings of gratitude and thankfulness to your Holiness
for your philanthropic labours towards the spiritual regeneration of the East and the West. We cannot close
this address without referring to the great kindness which
your Holiness has always extended to our Raja, who is
one of your devoted disciples, and the honour and pride
he feels by this gracious act of your Holiness in landing
first on his territory is indescribable.

In conclusion, we pray to the Almighty to bless your
Holiness with long life, and health, and strength to enable
you to carry on the good work that has been so ably
inaugurated by you.

> With respects and love,
> We beg to subscribe ourselves,
> Your Holiness' most devoted and obedient
> RAMNAD,   DISCIPLES and SERVANTS.
> *25th January, 1897.*

The Swami's reply follows *in extenso*:
The longest night seems to be passing away, the
sorest trouble seems to be coming to an end at last, the
seeming corpse appears to be awaking and a voice is
coming to us—away back where history and even tradition fails to peep into the gloom of the past, coming down
from there, reflected as it were from peak to peak of the
infinite Himalaya of knowledge, and of love, and of work,

India, this motherland of ours—a voice is coming unto us, gentle, firm, and yet unmistakable in its utterances, and is gaining volume as days pass by, and behold, the sleeper is awakening! Like a breeze from the Himalayas, it is bringing life into the almost dead bones and muscles, the lethargy is passing away, and only the blind cannot see, or the perverted will not see, that she is awakening, this motherland of ours, from her deep long sleep. None can resist her any more ; never is she going to sleep any more ; no outward powers can hold her back any more ; for the infinite giant is rising to her feet.

Your Highness and gentlemen of Ramnad, accept my heartleft thanks for the cordiality and kindness with which you have received me. I feel that you are cordial and kind, for heart speaks unto heart better than any language of the mouth ; spirit speaks unto spirit in silence, and yet in most unmistakable language, and I feel it in my heart of hearts. Your Highness of Ramnad, if there has been any work done by my humble self in the cause of our religion and our motherland in the Western countries, if any little work has been done in rousing the sympathies of our own people by drawing their attention to the inestimable jewels that, they know not, are lying deep buried about their own home—if, instead of dying of thirst and drinking dirty ditch water elsewhere out of the blindness of ignorance, they are being called to go and drink from the eternal fountain which is flowing perennially by their own home—if anything has been done to rouse our people towards action, to make them understand that in everything, religion and religion alone is the life of India, and when that goes India will die, in spite of politics, in spite of social reforms, in spite of Kubera's wealth poured upon the head of every one of her children—if anything has been done towards this end, India and every country where any work has been done owe much of it to you, Raja of Ramnad. For it was you who gave me the idea first, and it was you who persistently urged me on towards the work. You, as it were, intuitively understood what was going to be, and took me by the hand, helped me all along, and have never ceased to encourage me. Well is it, therefore, that you should be the first to rejoice at my success, and meet it is that I should first land in your territory on my return to India.

Great works are to be done, wonderful powers have to be worked out, we have to teach other nations many things, as has been said already by your Highness. This is the motherland of philosophy, of spirituality, and of ethics, of sweetness, gentleness, and love. These still exist, and my experience of the world leads me to stand on firm ground and make the bold statement that India is still the first and foremost of all the nations of the world in these respects. Look at this little phenomenon. There have been immense political changes within the last four or five years. Gigantic organisations undertaking to sub-vert the whole of existing institutions in different countries and meeting with a certain amount of success have been working all over the Western world. Ask our people if they have heard anything about them. They have heard not a word about them. But that there was a Parliament of Religions in Chicago, and that there was a Sannyâsin sent over from India to that Parliament, and that he was very well received and since that time has been working in the West, the poorest beggar has known. I have heard it said that our masses are dense, that they do not want any education, and that they do not care for any informa-tion. I had at one time a foolish leaning towards that opinion myself, but I find experience is a far more glorious teacher than any amount of speculation, or any amount of books written by globe-trotters and hasty observers. This experience teaches me that they are not dense, that they are not slow, that they are as eager and thirsty for information as any race under the sun ; but then each nation has its own part to play, and naturally, each nation has its own peculiarity and individuality with which it is born. Each represents, as it were, one peculiar note in this harmony of nations, and this is its very life, its vitality. In it is the backbone, the foundation, and the bed-rock of the national life, and here in this blessed land, the foundation, the backbone, the life-centre is religion and religion alone. Let others talk of politics, of the glory of acquisition of immense wealth poured in by trade, of the power and spread of commercialism, of the glorious fountain of physical liberty; but these the Hindu mind does not understand and does not want to understand. Touch him on spirituality, on religion, on God, on the soul, on the Infinite, on spiritual freedom, and I assure you, the lowest peasant in India is better informed on these subjects than many a so-called philosopher in other lands. I have said, gentlemen, that we have yet something to teach to the world. This is the very reason, the *raison d'être*, that this nation has lived on, in spite of hundreds of years of persecution, in spite of nearly a thousand year of foreign rule and foreign oppression. This nation still lives ; the *raison d'être* is it still holds to God, to the treasure-house of religion and spirituality.

In this land are, still, religion and spirituality, the fountains which will have to overflow and flood the world to bring in new life and new vitality to the Western and other nations, which are now almost borne down, half-killed, and degraded by political ambitions and social scheming. From out of many voices, consonant and dissentient, from out of the medley of sounds filling the Indian atmosphere, rises up supreme, striking, and full, one note, and that is renunciation. Give up! That is the watchword of the Indian religions. This world is a delusion of two days. The present life is of five minutes. Beyond is the Infinite, beyond this world of delusion ; let us seek that. This continent is illumined with brave and

gigantic minds and intelligences which even think of this
so-called infinite universe as only a mud-puddle ; beyond
and still beyond they go. Time, even infinite time, is to
them but non-existence. Beyond and beyond time they
go. Space is nothing to them; beyond that they want to
go, and this going beyond the phenomenal is the very
soul of religion. The characteristic of my nation is this
transcendentalism, this struggle to go beyond, this daring
to tear the veil off the face of nature and have at any
risk, at any price, a glimpse of the beyond. That is our
ideal, but of course all the people in a country cannot give
up entirely. Do you want to enthuse them, then here is
the way to do so. Your talks of politics, of social regeneration, your talks of money-making and commercialism—
all these will roll off like water from a duck's back. This
spirituality, then, is what you have to teach the world.
Have we to learn anything else, have we to learn anything
from the world ? We have, perhaps, to gain a little in
material knowledge, in the power of organisation, in the
ability to handle powers, organising powers, in bringing
the best results out of the smallest of causes. This perhaps
to a certain extent we may learn from the West. But if
any one preaches in India the ideal of eating and drinking
and making merry, if any one wants to apotheosise the
material world into a God, that man is a liar ; he has no
place in this holy land, the Indian mind does not want to
listen to him. Ay, in spite of the sparkle and glitter of
Western civilisation, in spite of all its polish and its marvellous manifestation of power, standing upon this platform, I tell them to their face that it is all vain. It is
vanity of vanities. God alone lives. The soul alone lives.
Spirituality alone lives. Hold on to that.

Yet, perhaps, some sort of materialism, toned down
to our own requirements, would be a blessing to many of
our brothers who are not yet ripe for the highest truths.
This is the mistake made in every country and in every

society, and it is a greatly regrettable thing that in India, where it was always understood, the same mistake of forcing the highest truths on people who are not ready for them has been made of late. My method need not be yours. The Sannyasin, as you all know, is the ideal of the Hindu's life, and every one by our Shâstrâs is compelled to give up. Every Hindu who has tasted the fruits of this world must give up in the latter part of his life, and he who does not is not a Hindu and has no more right to call himself a Hindu. We know that this is the ideal—to give up after seeing and experiencing the vanity of things. Having found out that the heart of the material world is a mere hollow, containing only ashes, give it up and go back. The mind is circling forward, as it were, towards the senses, and that mind has to circle backwards ; the Pravritti has to stop and the Nivritti has to begin. That is the ideal. But that ideal can only be realised after a certain amount of experience. We cannot teach the child the truth of renunciation; the child is a born optimist ; his whole life is in his senses; his whole life is one mass of sense-enjoyment. So there are childlike men in every society who require a certain amount of experience, of enjoyment, to see through the vanity of it, and then renunciation will come to them. There has been ample provision made for them in our Books ; but unfortunately, in later times, there has been a tendency to bind every one down by the same laws as those by which the Sannyasin is bound, and that is a great mistake. But for that a good deal of the poverty and the misery that you see in India need not have been. A poor man's life is hemmed in and bound down by tremendous spiritual and ethical laws for which he has no use. Hands off! Let the poor fellow enjoy himself a little, and then he will raise himself up, and renunciation will come to him of itself Perhaps in this line, we can be taught something by the Western people ; but we must be very cautious in

learning these things. I am sorry to say that most of the
examples one meets nowadays of men who have imbibed
the Western ideas are more or less failures.

There are two great obstacles on our path in India,
the Scylla of old orthodoxy and the Charybdis of modern
European civilisation. Of these two, I vote for the old
orthodoxy, and not for the Europeanised system; for the
old orthodox man may be ignorant, he may be crude,
but he is a man, he has a faith, he has strength, he stands
on his own feet; while the Europeanised man has no
backbone, he is a mass of heterogeneous ideas picked up
at random from every source—and these ideas are un-
assimilated, undigested, unharmonised. He does not
stand on his own feet, and his head is turning round and
round. Where is the motive power of his work ?—in a
few patronising pats from the English people. His schemes
of reforms, his vehement vituperations against the evils
of certain social customs, have, as the mainspring, some
European patronage. Why are some of our customs called
evils? Because the Europeans say so. That is about the
reason he gives. I would not submit to that. Stand and
die in your own strength, if there is any sin in the world,
it is weakness; avoid all weakness, for weakness is sin,
weakness is death. These unbalanced creatures are not
yet formed into distinct personalities; what are we to call
them—men, women, or animals? While those old orthodox
people were staunch and were men. There are still some
excellent examples, and the one I want to present before
you now is your Raja of Ramnad. Here you have a
man than whom there is no more zealous a Hindu
throughout the length and breadth of this land; here
you have a prince than whom there is no prince in this
land better informed in all affairs, both oriental and
occidental, who takes from every nation whatever he can
that is good. "Learn good knowledge with all devotion
from the lowest caste. Learn the way to freedom, even

if it comes from a Pariah, by serving him. If a woman is
a jewel, take her in marriage even if she comes from a
low family of the lowest caste." Such is the law laid
down by our great and peerless legislator, the divine
Manu. This is true. Stand on your own feet, and assimilate what you can; learn from every nation, take what
is of use to you. But remember that as Hindus everything else must be subordinated to our own national ideals.
Each man has a mission in life, which is the result of all
his infinite past Karma. Each of you was born with a
splendid heritage, which is the whole of the infinite past
life of your glorious nation. Millions of your ancestors are
watching, as it were, every action of yours, so be alert.
And what is the mission with which every Hindu child
is born ? Have you not read the proud declaration of
Manu regarding the Brâhmin where he says that the
birth of the Brahmin is "for the protection of the
treasury of religion"? I should say that *that* is the mission
not only of the Brahmin, but of every child, whether boy
or girl, who is born in this blessed land "for the protection of the treasury of religion". And every other
problem in life must be subordinated to that one principal
theme. That is also the law of harmony in music. There
may be a nation whose theme of life is political supremacy; religion and everything else must become subordinate to that one great theme of its life. But here is
another nation whose great theme of life is spirituality
and renunciation, whose one watchword is that this
world is all vanity and a delusion of three days, and
everything else, whether science or knowledge, enjoyment or powers, wealth, name, or fame, must be subordinated to that one theme. The secret of a true Hindu's
character lies in the subordination of his knowledge of
European sciences and learning, of his wealth, position,
and name, to that one principal theme which is inborn in
every Hindu child—the spirituality and purity of the race.

Therefore between these two, the case of the orthodox
man who has the whole of that life-spring of the race,
spirituality, and the other man whose hands are full of
Western imitation-jewels but has no hold on the life-
giving principle, spirituality—of these, I do not doubt
that every one here will agree that we should choose the
first, the orthodox, because there is some hope in him—
he has the national theme, something to hold to; so he
will live, but the other will die. Just as in the case of
individuals, if the principle of life is undisturbed, if the
principal function of that individual life is present, any
injuries received as regards other functions are not
serious, do not kill the individual, so, as long as this
principal function of our life is not disturbed, nothing can
destroy our nation. But mark you, if you give up that
spirituality, leaving it aside to go after the materialising
civilisationof the West, the result will be that in three
generations you will be an extinct race ; because the
backbone of the nation will be broken, the foundation
upon which the national edifice has been built will be
undermined, and the result will be annihilation all round.

Therefore, my friends, the way out is that first and
foremost we must keep a firm hold on spirituality—that
inestimable gift handed down to us by our ancient forefathers. Did you ever hear of a country where the greatest
kings tried to trace their descent not to kings, not to
robber-barons living in old castles who plundered poor
travellers, but to semi-naked sages who lived in the forest?
Did you ever hear of such a land? This is the land. In
other countries great priests try to trace their descent to
some king, but here the greatest kings would trace their
descent to some ancient priest. Therefore, whether you
believe in spirituality or not, for the sake of the national
life, you have to get a hold on spirituality and keep to it.
Then stretch the other hand out and gain all you can
from other races, but everything must be subordinated to

that one ideal of life ; and out of that a wonderful, glorious, future India will come—I am sure it is coming— a greater India than ever was. Sages will spring up greater than all the ancient sages ; and your ancestors will not only be satisfied, but I am sure, they will be proud from their positions in other worlds to look down upon their descendants, so glorious, and so great.

Let us all work hard, my brethren ; this is no time for sleep. On our work depends the coming of the India of the future. She is there ready waiting. She is only sleeping. Arise and awake and see her seated here on her eternal throne, rejuvenated, more glorious than she ever was—this motherland of ours. The idea of God was nowhere else ever so fully developed as in this mother-land of ours, for the same idea of God never existed any-where else. Perhaps you are astonished at my assertion ; but show me any idea of God from any other scripture equal to ours; they have only clan-Gods, the God of the Jews, the God of the Arabs, and of such and such a race, and their God is fighting the Gods of the other races. But the idea of that beneficent, most merciful God, our father, our mother, our friend, the friend of our friends, the soul of our souls, is here and here alone. And may He who is the Shiva of the Shaivites, the Vishnu of the Vaishnavites, the Karma of the Karmis, the Buddha of the Buddhists, the Jina of the Jains, the Jehovah of the Christians and the Jews, the Allah of the Mohammedans, the Lord of every sect, the Brahman of the Vedantists, He the all-pervading, whose glory has been known only in this land—may He bless us, may He help us, may He give strength unto us, energy unto us, to carry this idea into practice. May that which we have listened to and studied become food to us, may it become strength in us, may it become energy in us to help each other ; may we, the teacher and the taught, not be jealous of each other! Peace, peace, peace, in the name of Hari!

REPLY TO THE ADDRESS OF WELCOME AT PARAMAKUDI

Paramakudi was the first stopping-place after leaving Ramnad, and there was a demonstration on a large scale, including the presentation of the following address:

SREEMAT VIVEKANANDA SWAMI

We, the citizens of Paramakudi, respectfully beg to accord to your Holiness a most hearty welcome to this place after your successful spiritual campaign of nearly four years in the Western world.

We share with our countrymen the feelings of joy and pride at the philanthropy which prompted you to attend the Parliament of Religions held at Chicago, and lay before the representatives of the religious world the sacred but hidden treasures of our ancient land. You have by your wide exposition of the sacred truths contained in the Vedic literature disabused the enlightened minds of the West of the prejudices entertained by them against our ancient faith, and convinced them of its universality and adaptability for intellects of all shades and in all ages.

The presence amongst us of your Western disciples is proof positive that your religious teachings have not only been understood in theory, but have also borne practical fruits. The magnetic influence of your august person reminds us of our ancient holy Rishis whose realisation of the Self by asceticism and self-control made them the true guides and preceptors of the human race.

In conclusion, we most earnestly pray to the All-Merciful that your Holiness may long be spared to continue to bless and spiritualise the whole of mankind.

With best regards.

We beg to subscribe ourselves,

Your Holiness' most obedient and devoted DISCIPLES

and SERVANTS.

In the course of his reply the Swami said:

It is almost impossible to express my thanks for the kindness and cordiality with which you have received me. But if I may be permitted to say so, I will add that my love for my country, and especially for my countrymen, will be the same whether they receive me with the utmost cordiality or spurn me from the country. For in the Gitâ Shri Krishna says—men should work for work's sake only, and love for love's sake. The work that has been done by me in the Western world has been very little; there is no one present here who could not have done a hundred times more work in the West than has been done by me. And I am anxiously waiting for the day when mighty minds will arise, gigantic spiritual minds, who will be ready to go forth from India to the ends of the world to teach spirituality and renunciation—those ideas which have come from the forests of India and belong to Indian soil alone.

There come periods in the history of the human race when, as it were, whole nations are seized with a sort of world-weariness, when they find that all their plans are slipping between their fingers, that old institutions and systems are crumbling into dust, that their hopes are all blighted and everything seems to be out of joint. Two attempts have been made in the world to found social life: the one was upon religion, and the other was upon social necessity. The one was founded upon spirituality, the other upon materialism; the one upon transcendentalism, the other upon realism. The one looks beyond the horizon of this little material world and is bold enough to begin life there, even apart from the other. The other, the second, is content to take its stand on the things of the world and expects to find a firm footing there. Curiously enough, it seems that at times the spiritual side prevails, and then the materialistic side—in wave-like motions following each other. In the same country there will be different tides. At one time the full flood of materialistic ideas prevails, and everything in this life—prosperity, the education which procures more pleasures, more food—will become glorious at first and then that will degrade and degenerate. Along with the prosperity will rise to white heat all the inborn jealousies and hatreds of the human race. Competition and merciless cruelty will be the watchword of the day. To quote a very commonplace and not very elegant English proverb, "Everyone for himself, and the devil take the hindmost", becomes the motto of the day. Then people think that the whole scheme of life is a failure. And the world would be destroyed had not spirituality come to the rescue and lent a helping hand to the sinking world. Then the world gets new hope and finds a new basis for a new building, and another wave of spirituality comes, which in time again declines. As a rule, spirituality brings a class of men who lay exclusive claim to the special powers of the world. The immediate effect of this is a reaction towards materialism, which opens the door to scores of exclusive claims, until the time comes when not only all the spiritual powers of the race, but all its material powers and privileges are centred in the hands of a very few; and these few, standing on the necks of the masses of the people, want to rule them. Then society has to help itself, and materialism comes to the rescue.

If you look at India, our motherland, you will see that the same thing is going on now. That you are here today to welcome one who went to Europe to preach Vedanta would have been impossible had not the materialism of Europe opened the way for it. Materialism has come to the rescue of India in a certain sense by throwing open the doors of life to everyone, by destroying the exclusive privileges of caste, by opening up to discussion the inestimable treasures which were hidden away in the hands of a very few who have even lost the use of them.

Half has been stolen and lost; and the other half which remains is in the hands of men who, like dogs in the manger, do not eat themselves and will not allow others to do so. On the other hand, the political systems that we are struggling for in India have been in Europe for ages, have been tried for centuries, and have been found wanting One after another, the institutions, systems, and everything connected with political government have been condemned as useless; and Europe is restless, does not know where to turn. The material tyranny is tremendous. The wealth and power of a country are in the hands of a few men who do not work but manipulate the work of millions of human beings. By this power they can deluge the whole earth with blood. Religion and all things are under their feet; they rule and stand supreme. The Western world is governed by a handful of Shylocks. All those things that you hear about—constitutional government, freedom, liberty, and parliaments—are but jokes.

The West is groaning under the tyranny of the Shylocks, and the East is groaning under the tyranny of the priests; each must keep the other in check. Do not think that one alone is to help the world. In this creation of the impartial Lord, He has made equal every particle in the universe. The worst, most demoniacal man has some virtues which the greatest saint has not; and the lowest worm may have certain things which the highest man has not. The poor labourer, who you think has so little enjoyment in life, has not your intellect, cannot understand the Vedanta Philosophy and so forth; but compare your body with his, and you will see, his body is not so sensitive to pain as yours. If he gets severe cuts on his body, they heal up more quickly than yours would. His life is in the senses, and he enjoys there. His life also is one of equilibrium and balance. Whether on the ground of materialism, or of intellect, or of spirituality,

the compensation that is given by the Lord to every one
impartially is exactly the same. Therefore we must not
think that we are the saviours of the world. We can teach
the world, a good many things, and we can learn a good
many things from it too. We can teach the world only
what it is waiting for. The whole of Western civilisation
will crumble to pieces in the next fifty years if there is
no spiritual foundation. It is hopeless and perfectly useless to attempt to govern mankind with the sword. You
will find that the very centres from which such ideas as
government by force sprang up are the very first centres
to degrade and degenerate and crumble to pieces.
Europe, the centre of the manifestation of material
energy, will crumble into dust within fifty years if she
is not mindful to change her position, to shift her ground
and make spirituality the basis of her life. And what will
save Europe is the religion of the Upanishads.

Apart from the different sects, philosophies, and
scriptures, there is one underlying doctrine—the belief in
the soul of man, the Âtman—common to all our sects ;
and that can change the whole tendency of the world.
With Hindus, Jains, and Buddhists, in fact everywhere
in India, there is the idea of a spiritual soul which is the
receptacle of all power. And you know full well that
there is not one system of philosophy in India which
teaches you that you can get power or purity or perfection from outside; but they all tell you that these are
your birthright, your nature. Impurity is a mere super-
imposition under which your real nature has become
hidden. But the real *you* is already perfect, already
strong. You do not require any assistance to govern
yourself ; you are already self-restrained. The only
difference is in knowing it or not knowing it. Therefore
the one difficulty has been summed up in the word,
Avidyâ. What makes the difference between God and
man, between the saint and the sinner? Only ignorance.

What is the difference between the highest man and the lowest worm that crawls under your feet? Ignorance. That makes all the difference. For inside that little crawling worm is lodged infinite power, and knowledge, and purity—the infinite divinity of God Himself. It is unmanifested ; it will have to be manifested.

This is the one great truth India has to teach to the world, because it is nowhere else. This is spirituality, the science of the soul. What makes a man stand up and work? Strength. Strength is goodness, weakness is sin. If there is one word that you find coming out like a bomb from the Upanishads, bursting like a bomb-shell upon masses of ignorance, it is the word fearlessness. And the only religion that ought to be taught is the religion of *fearlessness*. Either in this world or in the world of religion, it is true that fear is the sure cause of degradation and sin. It is fear that brings misery, fear that brings death, fear that breeds evil. And what causes fear? Ignorance of our own nature. Each of us is heir-apparent to the Emperor of emperors; we are of the substance of God Himself. Nay, according to the Advaita, we are God Himself though we have forgotten our own nature in thinking of ourselves as little men. We have fallen from that nature and thus made differences—I am a little better than you, or you than I, and so on. This idea of oneness is the great lesson India has to give, and mark you, when this is understood, it changes the whole aspect of things, because you look at the world through other eyes than you have been doing before. And this world is no more a battlefield where each soul is born to struggle with every other soul and the strongest gets the victory and the weakest goes to death. It becomes a playground where the Lord is playing like a child, and we are His playmates, His fellow-workers. This is only a play, however terrible, hideous, and dangerous it may appear. We have mistaken its aspect. When we have known the nature of the soul, hope comes to the weakest, to the most degraded, to the most miserable sinner. Only, declares your Shâstra, despair not. For you are the same whatever you do, and you cannot change your nature. Nature itself cannot destroy nature. Your nature is pure. It may be hidden for millions of aeons, but at last it will conquer and come out. Therefore the Advaita brings hope to every one and not despair. Its teaching is not through fear ; it teaches, not of devils who are always on the watch to snatch you if you miss your footing— it has nothing to do with devils—but says that you have taken your fate in your own hands. Your own Karma has manufactured for you this body, and nobody did it for you. The Omnipresent Lord has been hidden through ignorance, and the responsibility is on yourself. You have not to think that you were brought into the world without your choice and left in this most horrible place, but to know that you have yourself manufactured your body bit by bit just as you are doing it this very moment. You yourself eat ; nobody eats for you. You assimilate what you eat ; no one does it for you. You make blood, and muscles, and body out of the food ; nobody does it for you. So you have done all the time. One link in a chain explains the infinite chain. If it is true for one moment that you manufacture your body, it is true for every moment that has been or will come. And all the responsibility of good and evil is on you. This is the great hope. What I have done, that I can undo. And at the same time our religion does not take away from mankind the mercy of the Lord. That is always there. On the other hand, He stands beside this tremendous current of good and evil. He the bondless, the ever-merciful, is always ready to help us to the other shore, for His mercy is great, and it always comes to the pure in heart.

Your spirituality, in a certain sense, will have to form the basis of the new order of society. If I had more time,

I could show you how the West has yet more to learn
from some of the conclusions of the Advaita, for in these
days of materialistic science the ideal of the Personal
God does not count for much. But yet, even if a man
has a very crude form of religion and wants temples
and forms, he can have as many as he likes; if he wants
a Personal God to love, he can find here the noblest
ideas of a Personal God such as were never attained
anywhere else in the world. If a man wants to be a
rationalist and satisfy his reason, it is also here that he
can find the most rational ideas of the Impersonal.

REPLY TO THE ADDRESS OF WELCOME AT SHIVAGANGA AND MANAMADURA

At Manamadura, the following address of welcome from the Zemindars and citizens of Shivaganga and Manamadura was presented to the Swami:

TO SRI SWAMI VIVEKANANDA

MOST REVERED SIR,

We, the Zemindars and citizens of Shivaganga and Manamadura, beg to offer you a most hearty welcome. In the most sanguine moments of our life, in our widest dreams, we never contemplated that you, who were so near our hearts, would be in such close proximity to our homes. The first wire intimating your inability to come to Shivaganga cast a deep gloom on our hearts, and but for the subsequent silver lining to the cloud our disappointment would have been extreme. When we first heard that you had consented to honour our town with your presence, we thought we had realised our highest ambition. The mountain promised to come to Mohammed, and our joy knew no bounds. But when the mountain was obliged to withdraw its consent, and our worst fears were roused that we might not be able even to go to the mountain, you were graciously pleased to give way to our importunities.

Despite the almost insurmountable difficulties of the voyage, the noble self-sacrificing spirit with which you have conveyed the grandest message of the East to the West, the masterly way in which the mission has been executed, and the marvellous and unparalleled success which has crowned your philanthropic efforts have earned for you an undying glory. At a time when Western bread-winning materialism was making the strongest inroads on Indian religious convictions, when the sayings

and writings of our sages were beginning to be numbered,
the advent of a new master like you has already marked
an era in the annals of religious advancement, and we
hope that in the fullness of time you will succeed in dis-
intergrating the dross that is temporarily covering the
genuine gold of Indian philosophy, and, casting it in the
powerful mint of your intellect, will make it current coin
throughout the whole globe. The catholicity with which
you were able triumphantly to bear the flag of Indian
philosophic thought among the heterogeneous religionists
assembled in the Parliament of Religions enables us to
hope that at no distant date you, just like your contemporary in the political sphere, will rule an empire over
which the sun never sets, only with this difference that
hers is an empire over matter, and yours will be over
mind. As she has beaten all records in political history
by the length and beneficience of her reign, so we earnestly
pray to the Almighty that you will be spared long enough
to consummate the labour of love that you have so dis-
interestedly undertaken and thus to outshine all your
predecessors in spiritual history.

We are,

Most Revered Sir,

Your most dutiful and devoted
Servants.

The Swami's reply was to the following effect:

I cannot express the deep debt of gratitude which
you have laid upon me by the kind and warm welcome
which has just been accorded to me by you. Unfortunately I am not just now in a condition to make a very
big speech, however much I may wish it. In spite of the
beautiful adjectives which our Sanskrit friend has been
so kind to apply to me, I have a body after all, foolish
though it may be ; and the body always follows the
promptings, conditions, and laws of matter. As such,

there is such a thing as fatigue and weariness as regards
the material body.

It is a great thing to see the wonderful amount of
joy and appreciation expressed in every part of the
country for the little work that has been done by me in
the West. I look at it only in this way: I want to apply
it to those great souls who are coming in the future. If
the little bit of work that has been done by me receives
such approbation from the nation, what must be the
approbation that the spiritual giants, the world-movers
coming after us, will get from this nation? India is the
land of religion ; the Hindu understands religion and
religion alone. Centuries of education have always been
in that line ; and the result is that it is the one concern
in life ; and you all know well that it is so. It is not
necessary that every one should be a shopkeeper; it is
not necessary even that every one should be a school-
master ; it is not necessary that every one should be a
fighter ; but in this world there will be different nations
producing the harmony of result.

Well, perhaps we are fated by Divine Providence
to play the spiritual note in this harmony of nations, and
it rejoices me to see that we have not yet lost the grand
traditions which have been handed down to us by the
most glorious forefathers of whom any nation can be
proud. It gives me hope, it gives me adamatine faith
in the destiny of the race. It cheers me, not for the
personal attention paid to me, but to know that the heart
of the nation is there, and is still sound. India is still
living ; who says she is dead ? But the West wants to see
us active. If they want to see us active on the field of
battle, they will be disappointed—that is not our field—
just as we would be disappointed if we hoped to see
a military nation active on the field of spirituality. But
let them come here and see that we are equally active,
and how the nation is living and is as alive as ever. We

should dispel the idea that we have degenerated at all. So far so good.

But now I have to say a few harsh words, which I hope you will not take unkindly. For the complaint has just been made that European materialism has wellnigh swamped us. It is not all the fault of the Europeans, but a good deal our own. We, as Vedantists, must always look at things from an introspective viewpoint, from its subjective relations. We, as Vedantists, know for certain that there is no power in the universe to injure us unless we first injure ourselves. One-fifth of the population of India have become Mohammedans. Just as before that, going further back, two-thirds of the population in ancient times had become Buddhists, one-fifth are now Mohammedans, Christians are already more than a million.

Whose fault is it ? One of our historians says in ever-memorable language: Why should these poor wretches starve and die of thirst when the perennial fountain of life is flowing by ? The question is: What did we do for these people who forsook their own religion? Why should they have become Mohammedans ? I heard of an honest girl in England who was going to become a streetwalker. When a lady asked her not to do so, her reply was, "That is the only way I can get sympathy. I can find none to help me now ; but let me be a fallen, down-trodden woman, and then perhaps merciful ladies will come and take me to a home and do everything they can for me." We are weeping for these renegades now, but what did we do for them before ? Let every one of us ask ourselves, what have we learnt ; have we taken hold of the torch of truth, and if so, how far did we carry it ? We did not help them then. This is the question we should ask ourselves. That we did not do so was our own fault, our own Karma. Let us blame none, let us blame our own Karma.

Materialism, or Mohammedanism, or Christianity, or any other *ism* in the world could never have succeeded but that you allowed them. No bacilli can attack the human frame until it is degraded and degenerated by vice, bad food, privation, and exposure ; the healthy man passes scatheless through masses of poisonous bacilli. But yet there is time to change our ways. Give up all those old discussions, old fights about things which are meaningless, which are nonsensical in their very nature. Think of the last six hundred or seven hundred years of degradation when grown-up men by hundreds have been discussing for years whether we should drink a glass of water with the right hand or the left, whether the hand should be washed three times or four times, whether we should gargle five or six times. What can you expect from men who pass their lives in discussing such momentous questions as these and writing most learned philosophies on them! There is a danger of our religion getting into the kitchen. We are neither Vedantists, most of us now, nor Paurânics, nor Tântrics. We are just "Don't-touchists". Our religion is in the kitchen. Our God is the cooking-pot, and our religion is, "Don't touch me, I am holy". If this goes on for another century, every one of us will be in a lunatic asylum. It is a sure sign of softening of the brain when the mind cannot grasp the higher problems of life ; all originality is lost, the mind has lost all its strength, its activity, and its power of thought, and just tries to go round and round the smallest curve it can find. This state of things has first to be thrown overboard, and then we must stand up, be active and strong; and then we shall recognise our heritage to that infinite treasure, the treasure our fore-fathers have left for us, a treasure that the whole world requires today. The world will die if this treasure is not distributed. Bring it out, distribute it broadcast. Says Vyâsa: Giving alone is the one work in this Kali Yuga;

and of all the gifts, giving spiritual life is the highest
gift possible ; the next gift is secular knowledge ; the next,
saving the life of man ; and the last, giving food to the
needy. Of food we have given enough ; no nation is more
charitable than we. So long as there is a piece of bread in
the home of the beggar, he will give half of it. Such a
phenomenon can be observed only in India. We have
enough of that, let us go for the other two, the gifts of
spiritual and secular knowledge. And if we were all brave
and had stout hearts, and with absolute sincerity put our
shoulders to the wheel, in twenty-five years the whole
problem would be solved, and there would be nothing left
here to fight about ; the whole Indian world would be once
more Aryan.

This is all I have to tell you now. I am not given
much to talking about plans ; I rather prefer to do and
show, and then talk about my plans. I have my plans,
and mean to work them out if the Lord wills it, if life is
given to me. I do not know whether I shall succeed or
not, but it is a great thing to take up a grand ideal in life
and then give up one's whole life to it. For what otherwise is the value of life, this vegetating, little, low life of
man ? Subordinating it to one high ideal is the only value
that life has. This is the great work to be done in India.
I welcome the present religious revival ; and I should be
foolish if I lost the opportunity of striking the iron while
it is hot.

REPLY TO THE ADDRESS OF WELCOME
AT MADURA[1]

The Swami was presented with an address of welcome by the Hindus of Madura, which read as follows:

MOST REVERED SWAMI,

We, the Hindu Public of Madura, beg to offer you our most heartfelt and respectful welcome to our ancient and holy city. We realise in you a living example of the Hindu Sannyâsin, who, renouncing all worldly ties and attachments calculated to lead to the gratification of the self, is worthily engaged in the noble duty of living for others and endeavouring to raise the spiritual condition of mankind. You have demonstrated in your own person that the true essence of the Hindu religion is not necessarily bound up with rules and rituals, but that it is a sublime philosophy capable of giving peace and solace to the distressed and afflicted.

You have taught America and England to admire that philosophy and that religion which seeks to elevate every man in the best manner suited to his capacities and environments. Although your teachings have for the last three years been delivered in foreign lands, they have not been the less eagerly devoured in this country, and they have not a little tended to counteract the growing materialism imported from a foreign soil.

India lives to this day, for it has a mission to fulfil in the spiritual ordering of the universe. The appearance of a soul like you at the close of this cycle of the Kali Yuga is to us a sure sign of the incarnation in the near future of great souls through whom that mission will be fulfilled.

[1] Spelt now as Madurai.

Madura, the seat of ancient learning, Madura the favoured city of the God Sundareshwara, the holy Dwadashântakshetram of Yogis, lags behind no other Indian city in its warm admiration of your exposition of Indian Philosophy and in its grateful acknowledgments of your priceless services for humanity.

We pray that you may be blessed with a long life of vigour and strength and usefulness.

The Swami replied in the following terms:

I wish I could live in your midst for several days and fulfil the conditions that have just been pointed out by your most worthy Chairman of relating to you my experiences in the West and the result of all my labours there for the last four years. But, unfortunately, even Swamis have bodies ; and the continuous travelling and speaking that I have had to undergo for the last three weeks make it impossible for me to deliver a very long speech this evening. I will, therefore, satisfy myself with thanking you very cordially for the kindness that has been shown to me, and reserve other things for some day in the future when under better conditions of health we shall have time to talk over more various subjects than we can do in so short a time this evening. Being in Madura, as the guest of one of your well-known citizens and noblemen, the Raja of Ramnad, one fact comes prominently to my mind. Perhaps most of you are aware that it was the Raja who first put the idea into my mind of going to Chicago, and it was he who all the time supported it with all his heart and influence. A good deal, therefore, of the praise that has been bestowed upon me in this address, ought to go to this noble man of Southern India. I only wish that instead of becoming a Raja he had become a Sannyâsin, for that is what he is really fit for.

Wherever there is a thing really needed in one part of

the world, the complement will find its way there and
supply it with new life. This is true in the physical world
as well as in the spiritual. If there is a want of spirituality
in one part of the world, and at the same time that
spirituality exists elsewhere, whether we consciously
struggle for it or not, that spirituality will find its way
to the part where it is needed and balance the inequality.
In the history of the human race, not once or twice, but
again and again, it has been the destiny of India in the
past to supply spirituality to the world. We find that
whenever either by mighty conquest or by commercial
supremacy different parts of the world have been kneaded
into one whole race and bequests have been made from
one corner to the other, each nation, as it were, poured
forth its own quota, either political, social, or spiritual.
India's contribution to the sum total of human knowledge
has been spirituality, philosophy. These she contributed
even long before the rising of the Persian Empire ; the
second time was during the Persian Empire ; for the third
time during the ascendancy of the Greeks ; and now for
the fourth time during the ascendancy of the English, she
is going to fulfil the same destiny once more. As Western
ideas of organisation and external civilisation are penetrating and pouring into our country, whether we will have
them or not, so Indian spirituality and philosophy are
deluging the lands of the West. None can resist it, and
no more can we resist some sort of material civilisation
from the West. A little of it, perhaps, is good for us, and
a little spiritualisation is good for the West ; thus the
balance will be preserved. It is not that we ought to learn
everything from the West, or that they have to learn
everything from us, but each will have to supply and hand
down to future generations what it has for the future
accomplishment of that dream of ages—the harmony of
nations, an ideal world. Whether that ideal world will
ever come I do not know, whether that social perfection

will ever be reached I have my own doubts ; but whether
it comes or not, each one of us will have to work for the
idea as if it will come tomorrow, and as if it only depends
on his work, and his alone. Each one of us will have to
believe that every one else in the world has done his work,
and the only work remaining to be done to make the world
perfect has to be done by himself. This is the responsibility
we have to take upon ourselves.

In the meanwhile, in India there is a tremendous
revival of religion. There is danger ahead as well as
glory; for revival sometimes breeds fanaticism, sometimes
goes to the extreme, so that often it is not even in the
power of those who start the revival to control it when
it has gone beyond a certain length. It is better, therefore,
to be forewarned. We have to find our way between the
Scylla of old superstitious orthodoxy and the Charybdis
of materialism—of Europeanism, of soullessness, of the
so-called reform—which has penetrated to the foundation
of Western progress. These two have to be taken care of.
In the first place, we cannot become Western ; therefore
imitating the Westerns is useless. Suppose you can
imitate the Westerns, that moment you will die, you will
have no more life in you. In the second place, it is
impossible. A stream is taking its rise, away beyond
where time began, flowing through millions of ages of
human history; do you mean to get hold of that stream
and push it back to its source, to a Himalayan glacier ?
Even if that were practicable, it would not be possible
for you to be Europeanised. If you find it is impossible
for the European to throw off the few centuries of culture
which there is in the West, do you think it is possible
for you to throw off the culture of shining scores of
centuries? It cannot be. We must also remember that
in every little village-god and every little superstitious
custom is that which we are accustomed to call our religious faith. But local customs are infinite and contra-

dictory. Which are we to obey, and which not to obey?
The Brâhmin of Southern India, for instance, would
shrink in horror at the sight of another Brahmin eating
meat; a Brahmin in the North thinks it a most glorious
and holy thing to do—he kills goats by the hundred in
sacrifice. If you put forward your custom, they are equally
ready with theirs. Various are the customs all over India,
but they are local. The greatest mistake made is that
ignorant people always think that this local custom is the
essence of our religion.

But beyond this there is a still greater difficulty.
There are two sorts of truth we find in our Shâstras, one
that is based upon the eternal nature of man—the one
that deals with the eternal relation of God, soul, and
nature; the other, with local circumstances, environments
of the time, social institutions of the period, and so forth.
The first class of truths is chiefly embodied in our Vedas,
our scriptures; the second in the Smritis, the Purânas.
etc. We must remember that for all periods the Vedas
are the final goal and authority, and if the Puranas differ
in any respect from the Vedas, that part of the Puranas is
to be rejected without mercy. We find, then, that in all
these Smritis the teachings are different. One Smriti says,
this is the custom, and this should be the practice of this
age. Another one says, this is the practice of this age,
and so forth. This is the Âchâra which should be the
custom of the Satya Yuga, and this is the Achara which
should be the custom of the Kali Yuga, and so forth.
Now this is one of the most glorious doctrines that you
have, that eternal truths, being based upon the nature of
man, will never change so long as man lives ; they are
for all times, omnipresent, universal virtues. But the
Smritis speak generally of local circumstances, of duties
arising from different environments, and they change in
the course of time. This you have always to remember
that because a little social custom is going to be changed

you are not going to lose your religion, not at all.
Remember these customs have already been changed.
There was a time in this very India when, without eating
beef, no Brahmin could remain a Brahmin; you read in
the Vedas how, when a Sannyasin, a king, or a great
man came into a house, the best bullock was killed; how
in time it was found that as we were an agricultural race,
killing the best bulls meant annihilation of the race.
Therefore the practice was stopped, and a voice was
raised against the killing of cows. Sometimes we find
existing then what we now consider the most horrible
customs. In course of time other laws had to be made.
These in turn will have to go, and other Smritis will come.
This is one fact we have to learn that the Vedas being
eternal will be one and the same throughout all ages,
but the Smritis will have an end. As time rolls on, more
and more of the Smritis will go, sages will come, and
they will change and direct society into better channels,
into duties and into paths which accord with the necessity
of the age, and without which it is impossible that society
can live. Thus we have to guide our course, avoiding
these two dangers; and I hope that every one of us here
will have breadth enough, and at the same time faith
enough, to understand what that means, which I suppose.
is the inclusion of everything, and not the exclusion. I
want the intensity of the fanatic plus the extensity of the
materialist. Deep as the ocean, broad as the infinite skies,
that is the sort of heart we want. Let us be as progressive
as any nation that ever existed, and at the same time as
faithful and conservative towards our traditions as Hindus
alone know how to be.

In plain words, we have first to learn the distinction
between the essentials and the non-essentials in everything. The essentials are eternal, the non-essentials have
value only for a certain time; and if after a time they
are not replaced by something essential, they are posi-

tively dangerous. I do not mean that you should stand up and revile all your old customs and institutions. Certainly not; you must not revile even the most evil one of them. Revile none. Even those customs that are now appearing to be positive evils, have been positively life-giving in times past; and if we have to remove these, we must not do so with curses, but with blessings and gratitude for the glorious work these customs have done for the preservation of our race. And we must also remember that the leaders of our societies have never been either generals or kings, but Rishis. And who are the Rishis? The Rishi as he is called in the Upanishads is not an ordinary man, but a Mantra-drashtâ. He is a man who sees religion, to whom religion is not merely book-learning, not argumentation, nor speculation, nor much talking, but actual realisation, a coming face to face with truths which transcend the senses. This is Rishihood, and that Rishihood does not belong to any age, or time, or even to sects or caste. Vâtsyâyana says, truth must be realised; and we have to remember that you, and I, and every one of us will be called upon to become Rishis; and we must have faith in ourselves; we must become world-movers, for everything is in us. We must see Religion face to face, experience it, and thus solve our doubts about it; and then standing up in the glorious light of Rishihood each one of us will be a giant; and every word falling from our lips will carry behind it that infinite sanction of security; and before us evil will vanish by itself without the necessity of cursing any one, without the necessity of abusing any one, without the necessity of fighting any one in the world. May the Lord help us, each one of us here, to realise the Rishihood for our own salvation and for that of others!

THE MISSION OF THE VEDANTA

On the occasion of his visit to Kumbakonam, the Swamiji was presented with the following address by the local Hindu community:

REVERED SWAMIN,

On behalf of the Hindu inhabitants of this ancient and religiously important town of Kumbakonam, we request permission to offer you a most hearty welcome on your return from the Western World to our own holy land of great temples and famous saints and sages. We are highly thankful to God for the remarkable success of your religious mission in America and in Europe, and for His having enabled you to impress upon the choicest representatives of the world's great religions assembled at Chicago that both the Hindu philosophy and religion are so broad and so rationally catholic as to have in them the power to exalt and to harmonise all ideas of God and of human spirituality.

The conviction that the cause of Truth is always safe in the hands of Him who is the life and soul of the universe has been for thousands of years part of our living faith ; and if today we rejoice at the results of your holy work in Christian lands, it is because the eyes of men in and outside of India are thereby being opened to the inestimable value of the *spiritual* heritage of the *pre-eminently religious* Hindu nation. The success of your work has naturally added great lustre to the already renowned name of your great Guru ; it has also raised us in the estimation of the civilised world ; more than all, it has made us feel that we too, as a people, have reason to be proud of the achievements of our past, and that the absence of telling aggressiveness in our civilisation is in no way a sign of its exhausted or decaying condition. With clear-sighted, devoted, and altogether unselfish workers like you in our midst, the future of the Hindu nation cannot but be bright and hopeful. May the God of the universe who is also the great God of all nations bestow on you health and long life, and make you increasingly strong and wise in the discharge of your high and noble function as a worthy teacher of Hindu religion and philosophy.

A second address was also presented by the Hindu students of the town.

The Swami then delivered the following address on the Mission of the Vedanta:

A very small amount of religious work performed brings a large amount of result. If this statement of the Gîtâ wanted an illustration, I am finding every day the truth of that great saying in my humble life. My work has been very insignificant indeed, but the kindness and the cordiality of welcome that have met me at every step of my journey from Colombo to this city are simply beyond all expectation. Yet, at the same time, it is worthy of our traditions as Hindus, it is worthy of our race; for here we are, the Hindu race, whose vitality, whose life-principle, whose very soul, as it were, is in religion. I have seen a little of the world, travelling among the races of the East and the West; and everywhere I find among nations one great ideal which forms the backbone, so to speak, of that race. With some it is politics, with others it is social culture; others again may have intellectual culture and so on for their national background. But this, our motherland, has religion and religion alone for its basis, for its backbone, for the bed-rock upon which the whole building of its life has been based. Some of you may remember that in my reply to the kind address which the people of Madras sent over to me in America, I pointed out the fact that a peasant in India has, in many respects, a better religious education than many a gentleman in the West, and today, beyond all doubt, I myself am verifying my own words. There was a time when I did feel rather discontented at the want of information among the masses of India and the lack of thirst among them for information, but now I understand it. Where their interest lies, there they are more eager for information than the masses of any other race that I have seen or have travelled among. Ask our peasants about the momentous political changes in Europe, the upheavals that are going on in European society—they do not know anything of them, nor do they care to know ; but the peasants, even in Ceylon, detached from India in many ways, cut off from a living interest in India—I found the very peasants working in the fields there were already acquainted with the fact that there had been a Parliament of Religions in America, that an Indian Sannyâsin had gone over there, and that he had had some success.

Where, therefore, their interest is, there they are as eager for information as any other race ; and religion is the one and sole interest of the people of India. I am not just now discussing whether it is good to have the vitality of the race in religious ideals or in political ideals, but so far it is clear to us that, for good or for evil, our vitality is concentrated in our religion. You cannot change it. You cannot destroy it and put in its place another. You cannot transplant a large growing tree from one soil to another and make it immediately take root there. For good or for evil, the religious ideal has been flowing into India for thousands of years; for good or for evil, the Indian atmosphere has been filled with ideals of religion for shining scores of centuries; for good or for evil, we have been born and brought up in the very midst of these ideas of religion, till it has entered into our very blood and tingled with every drop in our veins, and has become one with our constitution, become the very vitality of our lives. Can you give such religion up without the rousing of the same energy in reaction, without filling the channel which that mighty river has cut out for itself in the course of thousands of years? Do you want that the Gangâ should go back to its icy bed and begin a new course? Even if that were possible, it would be impossible for this country to give up her charateristic course of religious life and take up for herself a new career of politics or something else. You can work only under the law of least resistance, and this religious line is the line of least resistance in India. This is the line of life, this is the line of growth, and this is the line of well-being in India—to follow the track of religion.

Ay, in other countries religion is only one of the many necessities in life. To use a common illustration which I am in the habit of using, my lady has many things in her parlour, and it is the fashion nowadays to have a Japanese vase, and she must procure it; it does not look well to be without it. So my lady, or my gentleman, has many other occupations in life, and also a little bit of religion must come in to complete it. Consequently he or she has a little religion. Politics, social improvement, in one word, this world, is the goal of mankind in the West, and God and religion come in quietly as helpers to attain that goal. Their God is, so to speak, the Being who helps to cleanse and to furnish this world for them; that is apparently all the value of God for them. Do you not know how for the last hundred or two hundred years you have been hearing again and again out of the lips of men who ought to have known better, from the mouths of those who pretend at least to know better, that all the arguments they produce against the Indian religion is this—that our religion does not conduce to well-being in this world, that it does not bring gold to us, that it does not make us robbers of nations, that it does not make the strong stand upon the bodies of the

weak and feed themselves with the life-blood of the weak.
Certainly our religion does not do that. It cannot send
cohorts, under whose feet the earth trembles, for the purpose of destruction and pillage and the ruination of races.
Therefore they say—what is there in this religion ? It does
not bring any grist to the grinding mill, any strength to
the muscles ; what is there in such a religion ?

They little dream that that is the very argument with
which we prove our religion, because it does not make for
this world. Ours is the only true religion because, according to it, this little sense-world of three days' duration is
not to be made the end and aim of all, is not to be our
great goal. This little earthly horizon of a few feet is
not that which bounds the view of our religion. Ours is
away beyond, and still beyond ; beyond the senses,
beyond space, and beyond time, away, away beyond, till
nothing of this world is left and the universe itself becomes like a drop in the transcendent ocean of the glory
of the soul. Ours is the true religion because it teaches
that God alone is true, that this world is false and fleeting, that all your gold is but as dust, that all your power
is finite, and that life itself is oftentimes an evil ; therefore it is, that ours is the true religion. Ours is the true
religion because, above all, it teaches renunciation and
stands up with the wisdom of ages to tell and to declare
to the nations who are mere children of yesterday in
comparison with us Hindus—who own the hoary antiquity of the wisdom, discovered by our ancestors here in
India—to tell them in plain words: "Children, you are
slaves of the senses ; there is only finiteness in the senses,
there is only ruination in the senses ; the three short days
of luxury here bring only ruin at last. Give it all up,
renounce the love of the senses and of the world ; that
is the way of religion." Through renunciation is the way
to the goal and not through enjoyment. Therefore ours is
the only true religion.

Ay, it is a curious fact that while nations after nations have come upon the stage of the world, played their parts vigorously for a few moments, and died almost without leaving a mark or a ripple on the ocean of time, here we are living, as it were, an eternal life. They talk a great deal of the new theories about the survival of the fittest, and they think that it is the strength of the muscles which is the fittest to survive. If that were true, any one of the aggressively known old world nations would have lived in glory today, and we, the weak Hindus, who never conquered even one other race or nation, ought to have died out; yet we live here three hundred million strong! (A young English lady once told me: What have the Hindus done? They never even conquered a single race!) And it is not at all true that all its energies are spent, that atrophy has overtaken its body: that is not true. There is vitality enough, and it comes out in torrents and deluges the world when the time is ripe and requires it.

We have, as it were, thrown a challenge to the whole world from the most ancient times. In the West, they are trying to solve the problem how much a man can possess, and we are trying here to solve the problem on how little a man can live. This struggle and this difference will still go on for some centuries. But if history has any truth in it and if prognostications ever prove true, it must be that those who train themselves to live on the least and control themselves well will in the end gain the battle, and that those who run after enjoyment and luxury, however vigorous they may seem for the moment, will have to die and become annihilated. There are times in the history of a man's life, nay, in the history of the lives of nations, when a sort of world-weariness becomes painfully predominant. It seems that such a tide of world-weariness has come upon the Western world. There, too, they have their thinkers, great men; and they

are already finding out that this race after gold and power
is all vanity of vanities; many, nay, most of the cultured
men and women there, are already weary of this competition, this struggle, this brutality of their commercial
civilisation, and they are looking forward towards something better. There is a class which still clings on to
political and social changes as the only panacea for the
evils in Europe, but among the great thinkers there, other
ideals are growing. They have found out that no amount
of political or social manipulation of human conditions
can cure the evils of life. It is a change of the soul itself
for the better that alone will cure the evils of life. No
amount of force, or government, or legislative cruelty will
change the conditions of a race, but it is spiritual culture
and ethical culture alone that can change wrong racial
tendencies for the better. Thus these races of the West
are eager for some new thought, for some new philosophy ; the religion they have had, Christianity, altough
good and glorious in many respects, has been imperfectly
understood, and is, as understood hitherto, found to be
insufficient. The thoughtful men of the West find in our
ancient philosophy, especially in the Vedanta, the new
impulse of thought they are seeking, the very spiritual food
and drink for which they are hungering and thirsting. And
it is no wonder that this is so.

    I have become used to hear all sorts of wonderful
claims put forward in favour of every religion under the
sun. You have also heard, quite within recent times, the
claims put forward by Dr. Barrows, a great friend of mine,
that Christianity is the only universal religion. Let me
consider this question awhile and lay before you my
reasons why I think that it is Vedanta, and Vedanta
alone that can become the universal religion of man,
and that no other is fitted for the role. Excepting our
own almost all the other great religions in the world
are inevitably connected with the life or lives of one or

more of their founders. All their theories, their teachings, their doctrines, and their ethics are built round the life of a personal founder, from whom they get their sanction, their authority, and their power ; and strangely enough, upon the historicity of the founder's life is built, as it were, all the fabric of such religions. If there is one blow dealt to the historicity of that life, as has been the case in modern times with the lives of almost all the so-called founders of religion—we know that half of the details of such lives is not now seriously believed in, and that the other half is seriously doubted—if this becomes the case, if that rock of historicity, as they pretend to call it, is shaken and shattered, the whole building tumbles down, broken absolutely, never to regain its lost status.

Every one of the great religions in the world excepting our own, is built upon such historical characters ; but ours rests upon principles. There is no man or woman who can claim to have created the Vedas. They are the embodiment of eternal principles ; sages discovered them ; and now and then the names of these sages are mentioned —just their names; we do not even know who or what they were. In many cases we do not know who their fathers were, and almost in every case we do not know when and where they were born. But what cared they, these sages, for their names? They were the preachers of principles, and they themselves, so far as they went, tried to become illustrations of the principles they preached. At the same time, just as our God is an Impersonal and yet a Personal God, so is our religion a most intensely impersonal one—a religion based upon principles—and yet with an infinite scope for the play of persons ; for what religion gives you more Incarnations, more prophets and seers, and still waits for infinitely more? The *Bhâgavata* says that Incarnations are infinite, leaving ample scope for as many as you like to come. Therefore if any one or more of these persons in India's

religious history, any one or more of these Incarnations, and
any one or more of our prophets are proved not to have
been historical, it does not injure our religion at all; even
then it remains firm as ever, because it is based upon principles, and not upon persons. It is in vain we try to gather
all the peoples of the world around a single personality.
It is difficult to make them gather together even round
eternal and universal principles. If it ever becomes possible to bring the largest portion of humanity to one way of
thinking in regard to religion, mark you, it must be always
through principles and not through persons. Yet as I have
said, our religion has ample scope for the authority and
influence of persons. There is that most wonderful theory
of Ishta which gives you the fullest and the freest choice
possible among these great religious personalities. You
may take up any one of the prophets or teachers as your
guide and the object of your special adoration ; you are
even allowed to think that he whom you have chosen
is the greatest of the prophets, greatest of all the Avatâras;
there is no harm in that, but you must keep to a firm
background of eternally true principles. The strange fact
here is that the power of our Incarnations has been holding good with us only so far as they are illustrations of
the principles in the Vedas. The glory of Shri Krishna
is that he has been the best preacher of our eternal religion of principles and the best commentator on the
Vedanta that ever lived in India.

The second claim of the Vedanta upon the attention of the world is that, of all the scriptures in the world,
it is the one scripture the teaching of which is in entire
harmony with the results that have been attained by the
modern scientific investigations of external nature. Two
minds in the dim past of history, cognate to each other
in form and kinship and sympathy, started, being placed
in different routes. The one was the ancient Hindu
mind, and the other the ancient Greek mind. The former

started by analysing the internal world. The latter started in search of that goal beyond by analysing the external world. And even through the various vicissitudes of their history, it is easy to make out these two vibrations of thought as tending to produce similar echoes of the goal beyond. It seems clear that the conclusions of modern materialistic science can be acceptable, harmoniously with their religion, only to the Vedantins or Hindus as they are called. It seems clear that modern materialism can hold its own and at the same time approach spirituality by taking up the conclusions of the Vedanta. It seems to us, and to all who care to know, that the conclusions of modern science are the very conclusions the Vedanta reached ages ago ; only, in modern science they are written in the language of matter. This then is another claim of the Vedanta upon modern Western minds, its rationality, the wonderful rationalism of the Vedanta. I have myself been told by some of the best Western scientific minds of the day, how wonderfully rational the conclusions of the Vedanta are. I know one of them personally who scarcely has time to eat his meal or go out of his laboratory, but who yet would stand by the hour to attend my lectures on the Vedanta ; for, as he expresses it, they are so scientific, they so exactly harmonise with the aspirations of the age and with the conclusions to which modern science is coming at the present time.

Two such scientific conclusions drawn from comparative religion, I would specially like to draw your attention to: the one bears upon the idea of the universality of religions, and the other on the idea of the oneness of things. We observe in the histories of Babylon and among the Jews an interesting religious phenomenon happening. We find that each of these Babylonian and Jewish peoples was divided into so many tribes, each tribe having a god of its own, and that these little tribal gods

had often a generic name. The gods among the
Babylonians were all called Baals, and among them Baal
Merodach was the chief. In course of time one of these
many tribes would conquer and assimilate the other
racially allied tribes, and the natural result would be that
the god of the conquering tribe would be placed at the
head of all the gods of the other tribes. Thus the so-
called boasted monotheism of the Semites was created.
Among the Jews the gods went by the name of Molochs.
Of these there was one Moloch who belonged to the tribe
called Israel, and he was called the Moloch-Yahveh or
Moloch-Yava. In time, this tribe of Israel slowly conquered
some of the other tribes of the same race, destroyed their
Molochs, and declared its own Moloch to be the Supreme
Moloch of all the Molochs. And I am sure, most of you
know the amount of bloodshed, of tyranny, and of brutal
savagery that this religious conquest entailed. Later on,
the Babylonians tried to destroy this supremacy of
Moloch-Yahveh, but could not succeed in doing so.

It seems to me, that such an attempt at tribal self-
assertion in religious matters might have taken place on
the frontiers and India also. Here, too, all the various tribes
of the Aryans might have come into conflict with one
another for declaring the supremacy of their several tribal
gods; but India's history was to be otherwise, was to be
different from that of the Jews. India alone was to be, of
all lands, the land of toleration and of spirituality; and
therefore the fight between tribes and their gods did not
long take place here. For one of the greatest sages that was
ever born found out here in India even at that distant
time, which history cannot reach, and into whose gloom
even tradition itself dares not peep—in that distant time
the sage arose and declared, एकं सद् विप्रा बहुधा वदन्ति—"He
who exists is one ; the sages call Him variously." This is
one of the most memorable sentences that was ever uttered,
one of the grandest truths that was ever discovered. And

for us Hindus this truth has been the very backbone of
our national existence. For throughout the vistas of the
centuries of our national life, this one idea—एकं सद् विप्रा
बहुधा वदन्ति—comes down, gaining in volume and in fullness till it has permeated the whole of our national
existence, till it has mingled in our blood, and has become
one with us. We live that grand truth in every vein, and
our country has become the glorious land of religious toleration. It is here and here alone that they build temples
and churches for the religions which have come with the
object of condemning our own religion. This is one very
great principle that the world is waiting to learn from us.
Ay, you little know how much of intolerance is yet abroad.
It struck me more than once that I should have to leave
my bones on foreign shores owing to the prevalence of
religious intolerance. Killing a man is nothing for religion's sake; tomorrow they may do it in the very heart of
the boasted civilisation of the West, if today they are not
really doing so. Outcasting in its most horrible forms
would often come down upon the head of a man in the
West if he dared to say a word against his country's
accepted religion. They talk glibly and smoothly here in
criticism of our caste laws. If you go to the West and live
there as I have done, you will know that even some of the
biggest professors you hear of are arrant cowards and dare
not say, for fear of public opinion, a hundredth part of
what they hold to be really true in religious matters.

Therefore the world is waiting for this grand idea of
universal toleration. It will be a great acquisition to civilisation. Nay, no civilisation can long exist unless this idea
enters into it. No civilisation can grow unless fanaticism,
bloodshed, and brutality stop. No civilisation can begin
to lift up its head until we look charitably upon one
another ; and the first step towards that much-needed
charity is to look charitably and kindly upon the religious
convictions of others. Nay more, to understand that not

only should we be charitable, but positively helpful to
each other, however different our religious ideas and convictions may be. And that is exactly what we do in India
as I have just related to you. It is here in India that
Hindus have built and are still building churches for
Christians and mosques for Mohammedans. That is the
thing to do. In spite of their hatred, in spite of their
brutality, in spite of their cruelty, in spite of their tyranny,
and in spite of the vile language they are given to utter-
ing, we will and must go on building churches for the
Christians and mosques for the Mohammedans until we
conquer through love, until we have demonstrated to the
world that love alone is the fittest thing to survive and
not hatred, that it is gentleness that has the strength
to live on and to fructify, and not mere brutality and
physical force.

The other great idea that the world wants from us
today, the thinking part of Europe, nay, the whole world
—more, perhaps, the lower classes than the higher, more
the masses than the cultured, more the ignorant than the
educated, more the weak than the strong—is that eternal
grand idea of the spiritual oneness of the whole universe.
I need not tell you today, men from Madras University,
how the modern researches of the West have demonstrated
through physical means the oneness and the solidarity of
the whole universe ; how, physically speaking, you and I,
the sun, moon, and stars are but little waves or wavelets
in the midst of an infinite ocean of matter ; how Indian
psychology demonstrated ages ago that, similarly, both
body and mind are but mere names or little wavelets in
the ocean of matter, the Samashti ; and how, going one
step further, it is also shown in the Vedanta that behind
that idea of the unity of the whole show, the real Soul is
one. There is but one Soul throughout the universe, all is
but One Existence. This great idea of the real and basic
solidarity of the whole universe has frightened many,

even in this country. It even now finds sometimes more opponents than adherents. I tell you, nevertheless, that it is the one great life-giving idea which the world wants from us today, and which the mute masses of India want for their uplifting, for none can regenerate this land of ours without the practical application and effective operation of this ideal of the oneness of things.

The rational West is earnestly bent upon seeking out the rationality, the *raison d' être* of all its philosophy and its ethics ; and you all know well that ethics cannot be derived from the mere sanction of any personage, however great and divine he may have been. Such an explanation of the authority of ethics appeals no more to the highest of the world's thinkers ; they want something more than human sanction for ethical and moral codes to be binding, they want some eternal principle of truth as the sanction of ethics. And where is that eternal sanction to be found except in the only Infinite Reality that exists in you and in me and in all, in the Self, in the Soul? The infinite oneness of the Soul is the eternal sanction of all morality, that you and I are not only brothers—every literature voicing man's struggle towards freedom has preached that for you—but that you and I are really one. This is the dictate of Indian philosophy. This oneness is the rationale of all ethics and all spirituality. Europe wants it today just as much as our downtrodden masses do, and this great principle is even now unconsciously forming the basis of all the latest political and social aspirations that are coming up in England, in Germany, in France, and in America. And mark it, my friends, that in and through all the literature voicing man's struggle towards freedom, towards universal freedom, again and again you find the Indian Vedantic ideals coming out prominently. In some cases the writers do not know the source of their inspiration, in some cases they try to appear very original, and a few there are, bold and grateful enough to mention the source and acknowledge their indebtedness to it.

When I was in America, I heard once the complaint made that I was preaching too much of Advaita, and too little of dualism. Ay, I know what grandeur, what oceans of love, what infinite, ecstatic blessings and joy there are in the dualistic love-theories of worship and religion. I know it all. But this is not the time with us to weep even in joy ; we have had weeping enough ; no more is this the time for us to become soft. This softness has been with us till we have become like masses of cotton and are dead. What our country now wants are muscles of iron and nerves of steel, gigantic wills which nothing can resist, which can penetrate into the mysteries and the secrets of the universe, and will accomplish their purpose in any fashion even if it meant going down to the bottom of the ocean and meeting death face to face. That is what we want, and that can only be created, established, and strengthened by understanding and realising the ideal of the Advaita, that ideal of the one-ness of all. Faith, faith, faith in ourselves, faith, faith in God—this is the secret of greatness. If you have faith in all the three hundred and thirty millions of your mytho-logical gods, and in all the gods which foreigners have now and again introduced into your midst, and still have no faith in yourselves, there is no salvation for you. Have faith in yourselves, and stand up on that faith and be strong ; that is what we need. Why is it that we three hundred and thirty millions of people have been ruled for the last one thousand years by any and every handful of foreigners who chose to walk over our prostrate bodies? Because they had faith in themselves and we had not. What did I learn in the West, and what did I see behind those frothy sayings of the Christian sects repeating that man was a fallen and hopelessly fallen sinner? There I saw that inside the national hearts of both Europe and

America reside the tremendous power of the men's faith in themselves. An English boy will tell you, "I am an Englishman, and I can do anything." The American boy will tell you the same thing, and so will any European boy. Can our boys say the same thing here? No, nor even the boy's fathers. We have lost faith in ourselves. Therefore to preach the Advaita aspect of the Vedanta is necessary to rouse up the hearts of men, to show them the glory of their souls. It is, therefore, that I preach this Advaita ; and I do so not as a sectarian, but upon universal and widely acceptable grounds.

It is easy to find out the way of reconciliation that will not hurt the dualist or the qualified monist. There is not one system in India which does not hold the doctrine that God is within, that Divinity resides within all things. Every one of our Vedantic systems admits that all purity and perfection and strength are in the soul already. According to some, this perfection sometimes becomes, as it were, contracted, and at other times it becomes expanded again. Yet it is there. According to the Advaita, it neither contracts nor expands, but becomes hidden and uncovered now and again. Pretty much the same thing in effect. The one may be a more logical statement than the other, but as to the result, the practical conclusions, both are about the same ; and this is the one central idea which the world stands in need of, and nowhere is the want more felt than in this, our own motherland.

Ay, my friends, I must tell you a few harsh truths. I read in the newspaper how, when one of our fellows is murdered or ill-treated by an Englishman, howls go up all over the country; I read and I weep, and the next moment comes to my mind the question: Who is responsible for it all? As a Vedantist I cannot but put that question to myself. The Hindu is a man of introspection ; he wants to see things in and through himself, through the subjective vision. I, therefore, ask myself: Who is responsible? And the answer comes every time: Not the English; no, they are not responsible ; it is we who are responsible for all our misery and all our degradation, and we alone are responsible. Our aristocratic ancestors went on treading the common masses of our country underfoot, till they became helpless, till under this torment the poor, poor people nearly forgot that they were human beings. They have been compelled to be merely hewers of wood and drawers of water for centuries, so much so, that they are made to believe that they are born as slaves, born as hewers of wood and drawers of water. With all our boasted education of modern times, if anybody says a kind word for them, I often find our men shrink at once from the duty of lifting them up, these poor downtrodden people. Not only so, but I also find that all sorts of most demoniacal and brutal arguments, culled from the crude ideas of hereditary transmission and other such gibberish from the Western world, are brought forward in order to brutalise and tyrannise over the poor all the more. At the Parliament of Religions in America, there came among others a young man, a born Negro, a real African Negro, and he made a beautiful speech. I became interested in the young man and now and then talked to him, but could learn nothing about him. But one day in England, I met some Americans ; and this is what they told me. This boy was the son of a Negro chief who lived in the heart of Africa, and that one day another chief became angry with the father of this boy and murdered him and murdered the mother also, and they were cooked and eaten ; he ordered the child to be killed also and cooked and eaten ; but the boy fled, and after passing through great hardships and having travelled a distance of several hundreds of miles, he reached the seashore, and there he was taken into an American vessel and brought over to America. And this boy made that speech! After that, what was I to think of your doctrine of heredity!

Ay, Brâhmins, if the Brahmin has more aptitude for learning on the ground of heredity than the Pariah, spend no more money on the Brahmin's education, but spend all on the Pariah. Give to the weak, for there all the gift is needed. If the Brahmin is born clever, he can educate himself without help. If the others are not born clever, let them have all the teaching and the teachers they want. This is justice and reason as I understand it. Our poor people, these downtrodden masses of India, therefore, require to hear and to know what they really are. Ay, let every man and woman and child, without respect of caste or birth, weakness or strength, hear and learn that behind the strong and the weak, behind the high and the low, behind every one, there is that Infinite Soul, assuring the infinite possibility and the infinite capacity of all to become great and good. Let us proclaim to every soul: उत्तिष्ठत जाग्रत प्राप्य वरान्निबोधत—Arise, awake, and stop not till the goal is reached. Arise, awake! Awake from this hypnotism of weakness. *None* is really weak; the soul is infinite, omnipotent, and omniscient. Stand up, assert yourself, proclaim the God within you, do not deny Him! Too much of inactivity, too much of weakness, too much of hypnotism has been and is upon our race. O ye modern Hindus, de-hypnotise yourselves. The way to do that is found in your own sacred books. Teach yourselves, teach every one his real nature, call upon the sleeping soul and see how it awakes. Power will come, glory will come, goodness will come, purity will come, and everything that is excellent will come when this sleeping soul is roused to self-conscious activity. Ay, if there is anything in the Gita that I like, it is these two verses, coming out strong as the very gist, the very essence, of Krishna's teaching—"He who sees the Supreme Lord dwelling alike in all beings, the Imperishable in things that perish, he sees indeed. For seeing the Lord as the same, everywhere present, he does not destroy the Self by the Self, and thus he goes to the highest goal."

Thus there is a great opening for the Vedanta to do beneficent work both here and elsewhere. This wonderful idea of the sameness and omnipresence of the Supreme Soul has to be preached for the amelioration and elevation of the human race here as elsewhere. Wherever there is evil and wherever there is ignorance and want of knowledge, I have found out by experience that all evil comes, as our scriptures say, relying upon differences, and that all good comes from faith in equality, in the underlying sameness and oneness of things. This is the great Vedantic ideal. To have the ideal is one thing, and to apply it practically to the details of daily life is quite another thing. It is very good to point out an ideal, but where is the practical way to reach it?

Here naturally comes the difficult and the vexed question of caste and of social reformation, which has been uppermost for centuries in the minds of our people. I must frankly tell you that I am neither a caste-breaker nor a mere social reformer. I have nothing to do directly with your castes or with your social reformation. Live in any caste you like, but that is no reason why you should hate another man or another caste. It is love and love alone that I preach, and I base my teaching on the great Vedantic truth of the sameness and omnipresence of the Soul of the Universe. For nearly the past one hundred years, our country has been flooded with social reformers and various social reform proposals. Personally, I have no fault to find with these reformers. Most of them are good, well-meaning men, and their aims too are very laudable on certain points ; but it is quite a patent fact that this one hundred years of social reform has produced no permanent and valuable result appreciable throughout the country. Platform speeches have been made by the thousand, denunciations in volumes after volumes have been hurled upon the devoted head of the Hindu race and its civilisation, and yet no good practical result has been achieved; and where is the reason for that? The reason is not hard to find. It is in the denunciation itself. As I told you before, in the first place, we must try to keep our historically acquired character as a people. I grant that we have to take a great many things from other nations, that we have to learn many lessons from outside; but I am sorry to say that most of our modern reform movements have been inconsiderate imitations of Western means and methods of work; and that surely will not do for India; therefore, it is that all our recent reform movements have had no result.

In the second place, denunciation is not at all the way to do good. That there are evils in our society even a child can see; and in what society are there no evils? And let me take this opportunity, my countrymen, of telling you that in comparing the different races and nations of the world I have been among, I have come to the conclusion that our people are on the whole the most moral and the most godly, and our institutions are, in their plan and purpose, best suited to make mankind happy. I do not, therefore, want any reformation. My ideal is growth, expansion, development on national lines. As I look back upon the history of my country, I do not find in the whole world another country which has done quite so much for the improvement of the human mind. Therefore I have no words of condemnation for my nation. I tell them, "You have done well; only try to do better." Great things have been done in the past in this land, and there is both time and room for greater things to be done yet. I am sure you know that we cannot stand still. If we stand still, we die. We have either to go forward or to go backward. We have either to progress or to degenerate. Our ancestors did great things in the past, but we have to grow into a fuller life and march beyond even their great achievements. How can we now go back and degenerate ourselves? That cannot be; that must not be; going back will lead to national decay and death. Therefore let us go forward and do yet greater things; that is what I have to tell you.

I am no preacher of any momentary social reform. I am not trying to remedy evils, I only ask you to go forward and to complete the practical realisation of the scheme of human progress that has been laid out in the most perfect order by our ancestors. I only ask you to work to realise more and more the Vedantic ideal of the solidarity of man and his inborn divine nature. Had I the time, I would gladly show you how everything we have now to do was laid out years ago by our ancient law-givers, and how they actually anticipated all the different changes that have taken place and are still to take place in our national institutions. They also were breakers of caste, but they were not like our modern men. They did not mean by the breaking of caste that all the people in a city should sit down together to a dinner of beef-steak and champagne, nor that all fools and lunatics in the country should marry when, where, and whom they chose and reduce the country to a lunatic asylum, nor did they believe that the prosperity of a nation is to be gauged by the number of husbands its widows get. I have yet to see such a prosperous nation.

The ideal man of our ancestors was the Brahmin. In all our books stands out prominently this ideal of the Brahmin. In Europe there is my Lord the Cardinal, who is struggling hard and spending thousands of pounds to prove the nobility of his ancestors, and he will not be satisfied until he has traced his ancestry to some dreadful tyrant who lived on a hill and watched the people passing by, and whenever he had the opportunity, sprang out on them and robbed them. That was the business of these nobility-bestowing ancestors, and my Lord Cardinal is not satisfied until he can trace his ancestry to one of these. In India, on the other hand, the greatest princes seek to trace their descent to some ancient sage who dressed in a bit of loin-cloth, lived in a forest, eating roots and studying the Vedas. It is there that the Indian prince goes to trace his ancestry. You are of the high caste when you can trace your ancestry to a Rishi, and not otherwise.

Our ideal of high birth, therefore, is different from that of others. Our ideal is the Brahmin of spiritual culture and renunciation. By the Brahmin ideal what do I mean? I mean the ideal Brahmin-ness in which worldliness is altogether absent and true wisdom is abundantly present. That is the ideal of the Hindu race. Have you not heard how it is declared that he, the Brahmin, is not amenable to law, that he has no law, that he is not governed by kings, and that his body cannot be hurt? That is perfectly true. Do not understand it in the light thrown upon it by interested and ignorant fools, but understand it in the light of the true and original Vedantic conception. If the Brahmin is he who has killed all selfishness and who lives and works to acquire and propagate wisdom and the power of love—if a country is altogether inhabited by such Brahmins, by men and women who are spiritual and moral and good, is it strange to think of that country as being above and beyond all law? What police, what military are necessary to govern them? Why should any one govern them at all? Why should they live under a government? They are good and noble, and they are the men of God; these are our ideal Brahmins, and we read that in the Satya Yuga there was only one caste, and that was the Brahmin. We read in the Mahâbhârata that the whole world was in the beginning peopled with Brahmins, and that as they began to degenerate, they became divided into different castes, and that when the cycle turns round, they will all go back

to that Brahminical origin. This cycle is turning round
now, and I draw your attention to this fact. Therefore our
solution of the caste question is not degrading those who
are already high up, is not running amuck through food
and drink, is not jumping out of our own limits in order
to have more enjoyment, but it comes by every one of us,
fulfilling the dictates of our Vedantic religion, by our
attaining spirituality, and by our becoming the ideal
Brahmin. There is a law laid on each one of you in this
land by your ancestors, whether you are Aryans or non-
Aryans, Rishis or Brahmins, or the very lowest outcasts.
The command is the same to you all, that you must make
progress without stopping, and that from the highest man
to the lowest Pariah, every one in this country has to try
and become the ideal Brahmin. This Vedantic idea is
applicable not only here but over the whole world. Such
is our ideal of caste as meant for raising all humanity slowly
and gently towards the realisation of that great ideal of
the spiritual man who is non-resisting, calm, steady, wor-
shipful, pure, and meditative. In that ideal there is God.

How are these things to be brought about? I must
again draw your attention to the fact that cursing and
vilifying and abusing do not and cannot produce anything
good. They have been tried for years and years, and no
valuable result has been obtained. Good results can be
produced only through love, through sympathy. It is a
great subject, and it requires several lectures to elucidate
all the plans that I have in view, and all the ideas that are,
in this connection, coming to my mind day after day. I
must, therefore, conclude, only reminding you of this fact
that this ship of our nation, O Hindus, has been usefully
plying here for ages. Today, perhaps, it has sprung a
leak ; today, perhaps, it has become a little worn out.
And if such is the case, it behoves you and me to try our
best to stop the leak and holes. Let us tell our countrymen
of the danger, let them awake and help us. I will cry at

the top of my voice from one part of this country to the other, to awaken the people to the situation and their duty. Suppose they do not hear me, still I shall not have one word of abuse for them, not one word of cursing. Great has been our nation's work in the past; and if we cannot do greater things in the future, let us have this consolation that we can sink and die together in peace. Be patriots, love the race which has done such great things for us in the past. Ay, the more I compare notes, the more I love you, my fellow-countrymen ; you are good and pure and gentle. You have been always tyrannised over, and such is the irony of this material world of Mâyâ. Never mind that; the Spirit will triumph in the long run. In the meanwhile let us work and let us not abuse our country, let us not curse and abuse the weather-beaten and work-worn institutions of our thrice-holy motherland. Have no word of condemnation even for the most superstitious and the most irrational of its institutions, for they also must have served some good in the past. Remember always that there is not in the world any other country whose institutions are really better in their aims and objects than the institutions of this land. I have seen castes in almost every country in the world, but nowhere is their plan and purpose so glorious as here. If caste is thus unavoidable, I would rather have a caste of purity and culture and self-sacrifice, than a caste of dollars. Therefore utter no words of condemnation. Close your lips and let your hearts open. Work out the salvation of this land and of the whole world, each of you thinking that the entire burden is on your shoulders. Carry the light and the life of the Vedanta to every door, and rouse up the divinity that is hidden within every soul. Then, whatever may be the measure of your success, you will have this satisfaction that you have lived, worked, and died for a great cause. In the success of this cause, howsoever brought about, is centred the salvation of humanity here and hereafter.

REPLY TO THE ADDRESS OF WELCOME
AT MADRAS

When the Swami Vivekananda arrived at Madras an address of welcome was presented to him by the Madras Reception Committee. It read as follows:

REVERED SWAMIN,

On behalf of your Hindu co-religionists in Madras, we offer you a most hearty welcome on the occasion of your return from your Religious Mission in the West. Our object in approaching you with this address is not the performance of any merely formal or ceremonial function; we come to offer you the love of our hearts and to give expression to our feeling of thankfulness for the services which you, by the grace of God, have been able to render to the great cause of Truth by proclaiming India's lofty religious ideals.

When the Parliament of Religions was organised at Chicago, some of our countrymen felt naturally anxious that our noble and ancient religion should be worthily represented therein and properly expounded to the American nation, and through them to the Western world at large. It was then our privilege to meet you and to realise once again, what has so often proved true in the history of nations, that with the hour rises the man who is to help forward the cause of Truth. When you undertook to represent Hinduism at the Parliament of Religions, most of us felt, from what we had known of your great gifts, that the cause of Hinduism would be ably upheld by its representative in that memorable religious assembly. Your representation of the doctrines of Hinduism at once clear, correct, and authoritative, not only produced a remarkable impression at the Parliament of Religions itself, but has also led a number of men and women even in foreign lands to realise that out of the fountain of Indian spirituality refreshing draughts of immortal life and love may be taken so as to bring about a larger, fuller, and holier evolution of humanity than has yet been witnessed on this globe of ours. We are particularly thankful to you for having called the attention of the representatives of the World's Great Religions to the characteristic Hindu doctrine of the Harmony and Brotherhood of Religions. No longer is it possible for really enlightened and earnest men to insist that Truth and Holiness are the exclusive possessions of any particular locality or body of men or system of doctrine and discipline, or to hold that any faith or philosophy will survive to the exclusion and destruction of all others. In your own happy language which brings out fully the sweet harmony in the heart of the Bhagavad-Gitâ, "The whole world of religions is only a travelling, a coming up of different men and women through various conditions and circumstances to the same goal."

Had you contented yourself with simply discharging this high and holy duty entrusted to your care, even then, your Hindu co-religionists would have been glad to recognise with joy and thankfulness the inestimable value of your work. But in making your way into Western countries you have also been the bearer of a message of light and peace to the whole of mankind, based on the old teachings of India's "Religion Eternal". In thanking you for all that you have done in the way of upholding the profound rationality of the religion of the Vedanta, it gives us great pleasure to allude to the great task you have in view, of establishing an active mission with permanent centres for the propagation of our religion and philosophy. The undertaking to which you propose to devote your energies is worthy of the holy traditions you represent and worthy, too, of the spirit of the great Guru who has inspired your life and its aims. We hope and trust that it may be given to us also to associate ourselves with you

in this noble work. We fervently pray to Him who is
the all-knowing and all-merciful Lord of the Universe to
bestow on you long life and full strength and to bless your
labours with that crown of glory and success which ever deserves to shine on the brow of immortal Truth.

Next was read the following address from the Maharaja of Khetri:

YOUR HOLINESS,

I wish to take this early opportunity of your arrival
and reception at Madras to express my feelings of joy
and pleasure on your safe return to India and to offer my
heartfelt congratulation on the great success which has
attended your unselfish efforts in Western lands, where
it is the boast of the highest intellects that, "Not an inch
of ground once conquered by science has ever been recon-
quered by religion"—although indeed science has hardly
ever claimed to oppose true religion. This holy land of
Âryâvarta has been singularly fortunate in having been
able to secure so worthy a representative of her sages at
the Parliament of Religions held at Chicago, and it is
entirely due to your wisdom, enterprise, and enthusiasm
that the Western world has come to understand what an
inexhaustible store of spirituality India has even today.
Your labours have now proved beyond the possibility of
doubt that the contradictions of the world's numerous
creeds are all reconciled in the universal light of the
Vedanta, and that all the peoples of the world have need
to understand and practically realise the great truth that
"Unity in variety" is nature's plan in the evolution of
the universe, and that only by harmony and brotherhood
among religions and by mutual toleration and help can
the mission and destiny of humanity be accomplished.
Under your high and holy auspices and the inspiring influence of your lofty teachings, we of the present genera
tion have the privilege of witnessing the inauguration of

a new era in the world's history, in which bigotry, hatred, and conflict may, I hope, cease, and peace, sympathy, and love reign among men.   And I in common with my people pray that the blessings of God may rest on you and your labours.

When the addresses had been read, the Swami left the hall and mounted to the box seat of a carriage in waiting.   Owing to the intense enthusiasm of the large crowd assembled to welcome him, the Swami was only able to make the following short reply, postponing his reply proper to a future occasion:

Man proposes and God disposes. It was proposed that the addresses and the replies should be carried in the English fashion.   But here God disposes—I am speaking to a scattered audience from a chariot in the Gîtâ fashion. Thankful we are, therefore, that it should have happened so.   It gives a zest to the speech, and strength to what I am going to tell you. I do not know whether my voice will reach all of you, but I will try my best. I never before had an opportunity of addressing a large open-air meeting.

The wonderful kindness, the fervent and enthusiastic joy with which I have been received from Colombo to Madras, and seem likely to be received all over India, have passed even my most sanguine expectations; but that only makes me glad, for it proves the assertion which I have made again and again in the past that as each nation has one ideal as its vitality, as each nation has one particular groove which is to become its own, so religion is the peculiarity of the growth of the Indian mind.   In other parts of the world, religion is one of the many considerations, in fact it is a minor occupation. In England, for instance, religion is part of the national policy. The English Church belongs to the ruling class, and as such, whether they believe in it or not, they all support it, thinking that it is their Church. Every gentleman and every lady is expected to belong to that Church. It is a sign of gentility. So with other countries, there is a great national power; either it is represented by politics or it is represented by some intellectual pursuits; either it is represented by militarism or by commercialism. There the heart of the nation beats, and religion is one of the many secondary ornamental things which that nation possesses.

Here in India, it is religion that forms the very core of the national heart. It is the backbone, the bed-rock, the foundation upon which the national edifice has been built. Politics, power, and even intellect form a secondary consideration here. Religion, therefore, is the one consideration in India. I have been told a hundred times of the want of information there is among the masses of the Indian people; and that is true. Landing in Colombo I found not one of them had heard of the political upheavals going on in Europe—the changes, the downfall of ministries, and so forth. Not one of them had heard of what is meant by socialism, and anarchism, and of this and that change in the political atmosphere of Europe. But that there was a Sannyâsin from India sent over to the Parliament of Religions, and that he had achieved some sort of success had become known to every man, woman, and child in Ceylon. It proves that there is no lack of information, nor lack of desire for information where it is of the character that suits them, when it falls in line with the necessities of their life. Politics and all these things never formed a necessity of Indian life, but religion and spirituality have been the one condition upon which it lived and thrived and has got to live in the future.

Two great problems are being decided by the nations of the world. India has taken up one side, and the rest of the world has taken the other side. And the problem is this: who is to survive? What makes one nation survive and the others die? Should love survive or hatred, should enjoyment survive or renunciation, should matter survive or the spirit, in the struggle of life? We think as our ancestors did, away back in pre-historic ages. Where even tradition cannot pierce the gloom of that past, there our glorious ancestors have taken up their side of the problem and have thrown the challenge to the world. Our solution is renunciation, giving up, fearlessness, and love; these are the fittest to survive. Giving up the senses makes a nation survive. As a proof of this, here is history today telling us of mushroom nations rising and falling almost every century—starting up from nothingness, making vicious play for a few days, and then melting. This big, gigantic race which had to grapple with some of the greatest problems of misfortunes, dangers, and vicissitudes such as never fell upon the head of any other nation of the world, survives because it has taken the side of renunciation; for without renunciation how can there be religion? Europe is trying to solve the other side of the problem as to how much a man can have, how much more power a man can possess by hook or by crook, by some means or other. Competition—cruel, cold, and heartless—is the law of Europe. Our law is caste—the breaking of competition, checking its forces, mitigating its cruelties, smoothing the passage of the human soul through this mystery of life.

At this stage the crowd became so unmanageable that the Swami could not make himself heard to advantage. He, therefore ended his address with these words:

Friends, I am very much pleased with your enthusiasm. It is marvellous. Do not think that I am displeased with you at all; I am, on the other hand, intensely pleased at the show of enthusiasm. That is what is required—tremendous enthusiasm. Only make it permanent; keep it up. Let not the fire die out. We want to work out great things in India. For that I require your help; such enthusiasm is necessary. It is impossible to hold this meeting any longer. I thank you very much

for your kindness and enthusiastic welcome. In calm
moments we shall have better thoughts and ideas to
exchange; now for the time, my friends, good-bye.
It is impossible to address you on all sides, therefore
you must content yourselves this evening with merely
seeing me. I will reserve my speech for some other
occasion. I thank you very much for your enthusiastic
welcome.

MY PLAN OF CAMPAIGN

(Delivered at the Victoria Hall, Madras)

As the other day we could not proceed, owing to the crowd, I shall take this opportunity of thanking the people of Madras for the uniform kindness that I have received at their hands. I do not know how better to express my gratitude for the beautiful words that have been expressed in the addresses than by praying to the Lord to make me worthy of the kind and generous expressions and by working all my life for the cause of our religion and to serve our motherland; and may the Lord make me worthy of them.

With all my faults, I think I have a little bit of boldness. I had a message from India to the West, and boldly I gave it to the American and the English peoples. I want, before going into the subject of the day, to speak a few bold words to you all. There have been certain circumstances growing around me, tending to thwart me, oppose my progress, and crush me out of existence if they could. Thank God they have failed, as such attempts will always fail. But there has been, for the last three years, a certain amount of misunderstanding, and so long as I was in foreign lands, I held my peace and did not even speak one word ; but now, standing upon the soil of my motherland, I want to give a few words of explanation. Not that I care what the result will be of these words—not that I care what feeling I shall evoke from you by these words. I care very little, for I am the same Sannyâsin that entered your city about four years ago with this staff and Kamandalu ; the same broad world is before me. Without further preface let me begin.

First of all, I have to say a few words about the

Theosophical Society. It goes without saying that a certain amount of good work has been done to India by the Society ; as such every Hindu is grateful to it, and especially to Mrs. Besant; for though I know very little of her, yet what little I know has impressed me with the idea that she is a sincere well-wisher of this motherland of ours, and that she is doing the best in her power to raise our country. For that, the eternal gratitude of every true-born Indian is hers, and all blessings be on her and hers for ever. But that is one thing—and joining the Society of the Theosophists is another. Regard and estimation and love are one thing, and swallowing everything any one has to say, without reasoning, without criticising, without analysing, is quite another. There is a report going round that the Theosophists helped the little achievements of mine in America and England. I have to tell you plainly that every word of it is wrong, every word of it is untrue. We hear so much tall talk in this world, of liberal ideas and sympathy with differences of opinion. That is very good, but as a fact, we find that one sympathises with another only so long as the other believes in everything he has to say, but as soon as he dares to differ, that sympathy is gone, that love vanishes. There are others, again, who have their own axes to grind, and if anything arises in a country which prevents the grinding of them, their hearts burn, any amount of hatred comes out, and they do not know what to do. What harm does it do to the Christian missionary that the Hindus are trying to cleanse their own houses? What injury will it do to the Brâhmo Samâj and other reform bodies that the Hindus are trying their best to reform themselves? Why should they stand in opposition? Why should they be the greatest enemies of these movements? Why?—I ask. It seems to me that their hatred and jealousy are so bitter that no why or how can be asked there.

Four years ago, when I, a poor, unknown, friendless

Sannyasin was going to America, going beyond the waters to America without any introductions or friends there, I called on the leader of the Theosophical Society. Naturally I thought he, being an American and a lover of India, perhaps would give me a letter of introduction to somebody there. He asked me, "Will you join my Society?" "No," I replied, "how can I? For I do not believe in most of your doctrines." "Then, I am sorry, I cannot do anything for you," he answered. That was not paving the way for me. I reached America, as you know, through the help of a few friends of Madras. Most of them are present here. Only one is absent, Mr. Justice Subramania Iyer, to whom my deepest gratitude is due. He has the insight of a genius and is one of the staunchest friends I have in this life, a true friend indeed, a true child of India. I arrived in America several months before the Parliament of Religions began. The money I had with me was little, and it was soon spent. Winter approached, and I had only thin summer clothes. I did not know what to do in that cold, dreary climate, for if I went to beg in the streets, the result would have been that I would have been sent to jail. There I was with the last few dollars in my pocket. I sent a wire to my friends in Madras. This came to be known to the Theosophists, and one of them wrote, "Now the devil is going to die; God bless us all." Was that paving the way for me? I would not have mentioned this now; but, as my countrymen wanted to know, it must come out. For three years I have not opened my lips about these things; silence has been my motto; but today the thing has come out. That was not all. I saw some Theosophists in the Parliament of Religions, and I wanted to talk and mix with them. I remember the looks of scorn which were on their faces, as much as to say, "What business has the worm to be here in the midst of the gods?" After I had got name and fame at the Parliament of Religions, then came tremendous work for me; but at every turn the Theosophists tried to cry me down. Theosophists were advised not to come and hear my lectures, for thereby they would lose all sympathy of the Society, because the laws of the esoteric section declare that any man who joins that esoteric section should receive instruction from Kuthumi and Moria, of course through their visible representatives—Mr. Judge and Mrs. Besant—so that, to join the esoteric section means to surrender one's independence. Certainly I could not do any such thing, nor could I call any man a Hindu who did any such thing. I had a great respect for Mr. Judge. He was a worthy man, open, fair, simple, and he was the best representative the Theosophists ever had. I have no right to criticise the dispute between him and Mrs. Besant when each claims that his or her Mahâtmâ is right. And the strange part of it is that the same Mahatma is claimed by both. Lord knows the truth: He is the Judge, and no one has the right to pass judgement when the balance is equal. Thus they prepared the way for me all over America!

They joined the other opposition—the Christian missionaries. There is not one black lie imaginable that these latter did not invent against me. They blackened my character from city to city, poor and friendless though I was in a foreign country. They tried to oust me from every house and to make every man who became my friend my enemy. They tried to starve me out; and I am sorry to say that one of my own countrymen took part against me in this. He is the leader of a reform party in India. This gentleman is declaring every day, "Christ has come to India." Is this the way Christ is to come to India? Is this the way to reform India? And this gentleman I knew from my childhood; he was one of my best friends; when I saw him—I had not met for a long time one of my countrymen —I was so glad, and this was the treatment I received from him. The day the Parliament cheered me, the day I became popular in Chicago, from that day his tone changed; and in an underhand way, he tried to do everything he could to

injure me. Is that the way that Christ will come to India?
Is that the lesson that he had learnt after sitting twenty
years at the feet of Christ? Our great reformers declare
that Christianity and Christian power are going to uplift
the Indian people. Is that the way to do it? Surely, if that
gentleman is an illustration, it does not look very hopeful.

One word more: I read in the organ of the social
reformers that I am called a Shudra and am challenged as
to what right a Shudra has to become a Sannyasin. To
which I reply: I trace my descent to one at whose feet
every Brahmin lays flowers when he utters the words—
यमाय धर्मराजाय चित्रगुप्ताय वै नमः —and whose descendants
are the purest of Kshatriyas. If you believe in your
mythology or your Paurânika scriptures, let these so-
called reformers know that my caste, apart from other
services in the past, ruled half of India for centuries. If my
caste is left out of consideration, what will there be left
of the present-day civilisation of India? In Bengal alone,
my blood has furnished them with their greatest philosopher, the greatest poet, the greatest historian, the greatest
archaeologist, the greatest religious preacher; my blood
has furnished India with the greatest of her modern scien-
tists. These detractors ought to have known a little of our
own history, and to have studied our three castes, and
learnt that the Brahmin, the Kshatriya, and the Vaishya
have equal right to be Sannyasins: the Traivarnikas have
equal right to the Vedas. This is only by the way. I
just refer to this, but I am not at all hurt if they call me
a Shudra. It will be a little reparation for the tyranny of
my ancestors over the poor. If I am a Pariah, I will be all
the more glad, for I am the disciple of a man, who—the
Brahmin of Brahmins—wanted to cleanse the house of a
Pariah. Of course the Pariah would not allow him; how
could he let this Brahmin Sannyasin come and cleanse
his house! And this man woke up in the dead of night,
entered surreptitiously the house of this Pariah, cleansed

his latrine, and with his long hair wiped the place, and that
he did day after day in order that he might make himself
the servant of all. I bear the feet of that man on my head;
he is my hero; that hero's life I will try to imitate. By
being the servant of all, a Hindu seeks to uplift himself.
That is how the Hindus should uplift the masses, and
not by looking for any foreign influence. Twenty years of
occidental civilisation brings to my mind the illustration
of the man who wants to starve his own friend in a foreign
land, simply because this friend is popular, simply because
he thinks that this man stands in the way of his making
money. And the other is the illustration of what genuine,
orthodox Hinduism itself will do at home. Let any one of
our reformers bring out that life, ready to serve even a
Pariah, and then I will sit at his feet and learn, and not
before that. One ounce of practice is worth twenty
thousand tons of big talk.

Now I come to the reform societies in Madras. They
have been very kind to me. They have given me very kind
words, and they have pointed out, and I heartily agree with
them, that there is a difference between the reformers of
Bengal and those of Madras. Many of you will remember
what I have very often told you, that Madras is in a very
beautiful state just now. It has not got into the play of
action and reaction as Bengal has done. Here there is
steady and slow progress all through; here is growth, and
not reaction. In many cases, and to a certain extent, there
is a revival in Bengal; but in Madras it is not a revival, it is
a growth, a natural growth. As such, I entirely agree with
what the reformers point out as the difference between the
two peoples; but there is one difference which they do not
understand. Some of these societies, I am afraid, try to in-
timidate me to join them. That is a strange thing for them
to attempt. A man who has met starvation face to face
for fourteen years of his life, who has not known where
he will get a meal the next day and where to sleep, cannot

be intimidated so easily. A man, almost without clothes, who dared to live where the thermometer registered thirty degrees below zero, without knowing where the next meal was to come from, cannot be so easily intimidated in India. This is the first thing I will tell them—I have a little will of my own. I have my little experience too; and I have a message for the world which I will deliver without fear and without care for the future. To the reformers I will point out that I am a greater reformer than any one of them. They want to reform only little bits. I want root-and-branch reform. Where we differ is in the method. Theirs is the method of destruction, mine is that of construction. I do not believe in reform; I believe in growth. I do not dare to put myself in the position of God and dictate to our society, "This way thou shouldst move and not that." I simply want to be like the squirrel in the building of Râma's bridge, who was quite content to put on the bridge his little quota of sand-dust. That is my position. This wonderful national machine has worked through ages, this wonderful river of national life is flowing before us. Who knows, and who dares to say, whether it is good and how it shall move? Thousands of circumstances are crowding round it, giving it a special impulse, making it dull at one time and quicker at another. Who dares command its motion? Ours is only to work, as the Gita says, without looking for results. Feed the national life with the fuel it wants, but the growth is its own ; none can dictate its growth to it. Evils are plentiful in our society, but so are there evils in every other society. Here the earth is soaked sometimes with widows' tears ; there in the West, the air is rent with the sighs of the unmarried. Here poverty is the great bane of life; there the life-weariness of luxury is the great bane that is upon the race. Here men want to commit suicide because they have nothing to eat; there they commit suicide because they have so much

to eat. Evil is everywhere; it is like chronic rheumatism.
Drive it from the foot, it goes to the head; drive it from
there, it goes somewhere else. It is a question of chasing
it from place to place; that is all. Ay, children, to try to
remedy evil is not the true way. Our philosophy teaches
that evil and good are eternally conjoined, the obverse
and the reverse of the same coin. If you have one, you
must have the other; a wave in the ocean must be at the
cost of a hollow elsewhere. Nay, all life is evil. No breath
can be breathed without killing some one else; not a
morsel of food can be eaten without depriving some one of
it. This is the law; this is philosophy. Therefore the only
thing we can do is to understand that all this work against
evil is more subjective than objective. The work against
evil is more educational than actual, however big we may
talk. This, first of all, is the idea of work against evil; and
it ought to make us calmer, it ought to take fanaticism
out of our blood. The history of the world teaches us that
wherever there have been fanatical reforms, the only result
has been that they have defeated their own ends. No
greater upheaval for the establishment of right and liberty
can be imagined than the war for the abolition of slavery
in America. You all know about it. And what has been
its results? The slaves are a hundred times worse off
today than they were before the abolition. Before the
abolition, these poor negroes were the property of somebody, and, as properties, they had to be looked after, so
that they might not deteriorate. Today they are the property of nobody. Their lives are of no value; they are
burnt alive on mere pretences. They are shot down without any law for their murderers; for they are niggers, they
are not human beings, they are not even animals; and that
is the effect of such violent taking away of evil by law
or by fanaticism. Such is the testimony of history against
every fanatical movement, even for doing good. I have
seen that. My own experience has taught me that.

Therefore I cannot join any one of these condemning societies. Why condemn? There are evils in every society; everybody knows it. Every child of today knows it; he can stand upon a platform and give us a harangue on the awful evils in Hindu society. Every uneducated foreigner who comes here globe-trotting takes a vanishing railway view of India and lectures most learnedly on the awful evils in India. We admit that there are evils. Everybody can show what evil is, but he is the friend of mankind who finds a way out of the difficulty. Like the drowning boy and the philosopher—when the philosopher was lecturing him, the boy cried, "Take me out of the water first"—so our people cry: "We have had lectures enough, societies enough, papers enough; where is the man who will lend us a hand to drag us out? Where is the man who really loves us? Where is the man who has sympathy for us?" Ay, that man is wanted. That is where I differ entirely from these reform movements. For a hundred years they have been here. What good has been done except the creation of a most vituperative, a most condemnatory literature? Would to God it was not here! They have criticised, condemned, abused the orthodox, until the orthodox have caught their tone and paid them back in their own coin; and the result is the creation of a literature in every vernacular which is the shame of the race, the shame of the country. Is this reform? Is this leading the nation to glory? Whose fault is this?

There is, then, another great consideration. Here in India, we have always been governed by kings; kings have made all our laws. Now the kings are gone, and there is no one left to make a move. The government dare not; it has to fashion its ways according to the growth of public opinion. It takes time, quite a long time, to make a healthy, strong, public opinion which will solve its own problems; and in the interim we shall have to wait. The whole problem of social reform, therefore, resolves itself into this: where are those who want reform? Make them first. Where are the people? The tyranny of a minority is the worst tyranny that the world ever sees. A few men who think that certain things are evil will not make a nation move. Why does not the nation move? First educate the nation, create your legislative body, and then the law will be forthcoming. First create the power, the sanction from which the law will spring. The kings are gone ; where is the new sanction, the new power of the people? Bring it up. Therefore, even for social reform, the first duty is to educate the people, and you will have to wait till that time comes. Most of the reforms that have been agitated for during the past century have been ornamental. Every one of these reforms only touches the first two castes, and no other. The question of widow marriage would not touch seventy per cent of the Indian women, and all such questions only reach the higher castes of Indian people who are educated, mark you, at the expense of the masses. Every effort has been spent in cleaning their own houses. But that is no reformation. You must go down to the basis of the thing, to the very root of the matter. That is what I call radical reform. Put the fire there and let it burn upwards and make an Indian nation. And the solution of the problem is not so easy, as it is a big and a vast one. Be not in a hurry, this problem has been known several hundred years.

Today it is the fashion to talk of Buddhism and Buddhistic agnosticism, especially in the South. Little do they dream that this degradation which is with us today has been left by Buddhism. This is the legacy which Buddhism has left to us. You read in books written by men who had never studied the rise and fall of Buddhism that the spread of Buddhism was owing to the wonderful ethics and the wonderful personality of Gautama Buddha.

I have every respect and veneration for Lord Buddha, but
mark my words, the spread of Buddhism was less owing
to the doctrines and the personality of the great preacher,
than to the temples that were built, the idols that were
erected, and the gorgeous ceremonials that were put
before the nation. Thus Buddhism progressed. The little
fire-places in the houses in which the people poured their
libations were not strong enough to hold their own against
these gorgeous temples and ceremonies ; but later on the
whole thing degenerated. It became a mass of corruption
of which I cannot speak before this audience ; but those
who want to know about it may see a little of it in those
big temples, full of sculptures, in Southern India; and
this is all the inheritance we have from the Buddhists.

Then arose the great reformer Shankarâchârya and
his followers, and during these hundreds of years, since
his time to the present day, there has been the slow bringing back of the Indian masses to the pristine purity of
the Vedantic religion. These reformers knew full well
the evils which existed, yet they did not condemn. They
did not say, "All that you have is wrong, and you must
throw it away." It can never be so. Today I read that
my friend Dr. Barrows says that in three hundred years
Christianity overthrew the Roman and Greek religious
influences. That is not the word of a man who has seen
Europe, and Greece, and Rome. The influence of Roman
and Greek religion is all there, even in Protestant
countries, only with changed names—old gods rechristened
in a new fashion. They change their names; the goddesses
become Marys and the gods become saints, and the ceremonials become new; even the old title of Pontifex
Maximus is there. So, sudden changes cannot be and
Shankaracharya knew it. So did Râmânuja. The only
way left to them was slowly to bring up to the highest
ideal the existing religion. If they had sought to apply
the other method, they would have been hypocrites, for

the very fundamental doctrine of their religion is evolution, the soul going towards the highest goal, through all these various stages and phases, which are, therefore, necessary and helpful. And who dares condemn them?

It has become a trite saying that idolatry is wrong, and every man swallows it at the present time without questioning. I once thought so, and to pay the penalty of that I had to learn my lesson sitting at the feet of a man who realised everything through idols; I allude to Ramakrishna Paramahamsa. If such Ramakrishna Paramahamsas are produced by idol-worship, what will you have—the reformer's creed or any number of idols? I want an answer. Take a thousand idols more if you can produce Ramakrishna Paramahamsas through idol-worship, and may God speed you! Produce such noble natures by any means you can. Yet idolatry is condemned! Why? Nobody knows. Because some hundreds of years ago some man of Jewish blood happened to condemn it? That is, he happened to condemn everybody else's idols except his own. If God is represented in any beautiful form or any symbolic form, said the Jew, it is awfully bad; it is sin. But if He is represented in the form of a chest, with two angels sitting on each side, and a cloud hanging over it, it is the holy of holies. If God comes in the form of a dove, it is holy. But if He comes in the form of a cow, it is heathen superstition; condemn it! That is how the world goes. That is why the poet says, "What fools we mortals be!" How difficult it is to look through each other's eyes, and that is the bane of humanity. That is the basis of hatred and jealousy, of quarrel and of fight. Boys, moustached babies, who never went out of Madras, standing up and wanting to dictate laws to three hundred millions of people with thousands of traditions at their back! Are you not ashamed? Stand back from such blasphemy and learn first your lessons! Irreverent boys, simply because you

can scrawl a few lines upon paper and get some fool to
publish them for you, you think you are the educators
of the world, you think you are the public opinion of
India! Is it so? This I have to tell to the social reformers
of Madras that I have the greatest respect and love for
them. I love them for their great hearts and their love
for their country, for the poor, for the oppressed. But
what I would tell them with a brother's love is that their
method is not right; It has been tried a hundred years
and failed. Let us try some new method.

Did India ever stand in want of reformers? Do you
read the history of India? Who was Ramanuja? Who
was Shankara? Who was Nânak? Who was Chaitanya?
Who was Kabir? Who was Dâdu? Who were all these
great preachers, one following the other, a galaxy of stars
of the first magnitude? Did not Ramanuja feel for the
lower classes? Did he not try all his life to admit even
the Pariah to his community? Did he not try to admit
even Mohammedans to his own fold? Did not Nanak
confer with Hindus and Mohammedans, and try to bring
about a new state of things? They all tried, and their
work is still going on. The difference is this. They had
not the fanfaronade of the reformers of today; they had
no curses on their lips as modern reformers have; their
lips pronounced only blessings. They never condemned.
They said to the people that the race must always grow.
They looked back and they said, "O Hindus, what you
have done is good, but, my brothers, let us do better."
They did not say, "You have been wicked, now let us be
good." They said, "You have been good, but let us now
be better." That makes a whole world of difference. We
must grow according to our nature. Vain is it to
attempt the lines of action that foreign societies have
engrafted upon us ; it is impossible. Glory unto God,
that it is impossible, that we cannot be twisted and
tortured into the shape of other nations. I do not

condemn the institutions of other races; they are good for them, but not for us. What is meat for them may be poison for us. This is the first lesson to learn. With other sciences, other institutions, and other traditions behind them, they have got their present system. We, with our traditions, with thousands of years of Karma behind us, naturally can only follow our own bent, run in our own grooves ; and that we shall have to do.

What is my plan then? My plan is to follow the ideas of the great ancient Masters. I have studied their work, and it has been given unto me to discover the line of action they took. They were the great originators of society. They were the great givers of strength, and of purity, and of life. They did most marvellous work. We have to do most marvellous work also. Circumstances have become a little different, and in consequence the lines of action have to be changed a little, and that is all. I see that each nation, like each individual, has one theme in this life, which is its centre, the principal note round which every other note comes to form the harmony. In one nation political power is its vitality, as in England, artistic life in another, and so on. In India, religious life forms the centre, the keynote of the whole music of national life; and if any nation attempts to throw off its national vitality—the direction which has become its own through the transmission of centuries—that nation dies if it succeeds in the attempt. And, therefore, if you succeed in the attempt to throw off your religion and take up either politics, or society, or any other things as your centre, as the vitality of your national life, the result will be that you will become extinct. To prevent this you must make all and everything work through that vitality of your religion. Let all your nerves vibrate through the backbone of your religion. I have seen that I cannot preach even religion to Americans without showing them its practical effect on social life. I could not preach

religion in England without showing the wonderful
political changes the Vedanta would bring. So, in India,
social reform has to be preached by showing how much
more spiritual a life the new system will bring; and
politics has to be preached by showing how much it will
improve the one thing that the nation wants—its spirituality. Every man has to make his own choice; so has
every nation. We made our choice ages ago, and we
must abide by it. And, after all, it is not such a bad
choice. Is it such a bad choice in this world to think not
of matter but of spirit, not of man but of God? That intense faith in another world, that intense hatred for this
world, that intense power of renunciation, that intense faith
in God, that intense faith in the immortal soul, is in you.
I challenge anyone to give it up. You cannot. You may try
to impose upon me by becoming materialists, by talking
materialism for a few months, but I know what you are;
if I take you by the hand, back you come as good theists
as ever were born. How can you change your nature?

So every improvement in India requires first of all an
upheaval in religion. Before flooding India with socialistic or political ideas, first deluge the land with spiritual
ideas. The first work that demands our attention is that
the most wonderful truths confined in our Upanishads, in
our scriptures, in our Purânas must be brought out from
the books, brought out from the monasteries, brought out
from the forests, brought out from the possession of
selected bodies of people, and scattered broadcast all
over the land, so that these truths may run like fire all
over the country from north to south and east to west,
from the Himalayas to Comorin, from Sindh to the
Brahmaputra. Everyone must know of them, because it
is said, "This has first to be heard, then thought upon,
and then meditated upon." Let the people hear first,
and whoever helps in making the people hear about the
great truths in their own scriptures cannot make for him-

self a better Karma today. Says our Vyâsa, "In the Kali Yuga there is one Karma left. Sacrifices and itremendous Tapasyâs are of no avail now. Of Karma one remains, and that is the Karma of giving." And of these gifts, the gift of spirituality and spiritual knowledge is the highest; the next gift is the gift of secular knowledge; the next is the gift of life; and the fourth is the gift of food. Look at this wonderfully charitable race; look at the amount of gifts that are made in this poor, poor country; look at the hospitality where a man can travel from the north to the south, having the best in the land, being treated always by everyone as if he were a friend, and where no beggar starves so long as there is a piece of bread anywhere!

In this land of charity, let us take up the energy of the first charity, the diffusion of spiritual knowledge. And that diffusion should not be confined within the bounds of India; it must go out all over the world. This has been the custom. Those that tell you that Indian thought never went outside of India, those that tell you that I am the first Sannyasin who went to foreign lands to preach, do not know the history of their own race. Again and again this phenomenon has happened. Whenever the world has required it, this perennial flood of spirituality has overflowed and deluged the world. Gifts of political knowledge can be made with the blast of trumpets and the march of cohorts. Gifts of secular knowledge and social knowledge can be made with fire and sword. But spiritual knowledge can only be given in silence like the dew that falls unseen and unheard, yet bringing into bloom masses of roses. This has been the gift of India to the world again and again Whenever there has been a great conquering race, bringing the nations of the world together, making roads and transit possible, immediately India arose and gave her quota of spiritual power to the sum total of the progress of the world. This happened ages before Buddha was born, and remnants

of it are still left in China, in Asia Minor, and in the
heart of the Malayan Archipelago. This was the case
when the great Greek conqueror united the four corners
of the then known world; then rushed out Indian
spirituality, and the boasted civilisation of the West is
but the remnant of that deluge. Now the same opportunity has again come; the power of England has linked
the nations of the world together as was never done before.
English roads and channels of communication rush from
one end of the world to the other. Owing to English
genius, the world today has been linked in such a fashion
as has never before been done. Today trade centres have
been formed such as have never been before in the history
of mankind. And immediately, consciously or unconsciously, India rises up and pours forth her gifts of
spirituality; and they will rush through these roads till
they have reached the very ends of the world. That I
went to America was not my doing or your doing; but
the God of India who is guiding her destiny sent me,
and will send hundreds of such to all the nations of the
world. No power on earth can resist it. This also has to
be done. You must go out to preach your religion, preach
it to every nation under the sun, preach it to every people.
This is the first thing to do. And after preaching spiritual
knowledge, along with it will come that secular knowledge and every other knowledge that you want; but
if you attempt to get the secular knowledge without
religion, I tell you plainly, vain is your attempt in India,
it will never have a hold on the people. Even the great
Buddhistic movement was a failure, partially on account
of that.

Therefore, my friends, my plan is to start institutions
in India, to train our young men as preachers of the truths
of our scriptures in India and outside India. Men, men,
these are wanted: everything else will be ready, but
strong, vigorous, believing young men, sincere to the

backbone, are wanted. A hundred such and the world becomes revolutionised. The will is stronger than anything else. Everything must go down before the will, for that comes from God and God Himself; a pure and a strong will is omnipotent. Do you not believe in it? Preach, preach unto the world the great truths of your religion; the world waits for them. For centuries people have been taught theories of degradation. They have been told that they are nothing. The masses have been told all over the world that they are not human beings. They have been so frightened for centuries, till they have nearly become animals. Never were they allowed to hear of the Âtman. Let them hear of the Atman—that even the lowest of the low have the Atman within, which never dies and never is born—of Him whom the sword cannot pierce, nor the fire burn, nor the air dry—immortal, without beginning or end, the all-pure, omnipotent, and omnipresent Atman! Let them have faith in themselves, for what makes the difference between the Englishman and you? Let them talk their religion and duty and so forth. I have found the difference. The difference is here, that the Englishman believes in himself and you do not. He believes in his being an Englishman, and he can do anything. That brings out the God within him, and he can do anything he likes. You have been told and taught that you can do nothing, and nonentities you are becoming every day. What we want is strength, so believe in yourselves. We have become weak, and that is why occultism and mysticism come to us—these creepy things; there may be great truths in them, but they have nearly destroyed us. Make your nerves strong. What we want is muscles of iron and nerves of steel. We have wept long enough. No more weeping, but stand on your feet and be men. It is a man-making religion that we want. It is man-making theories that we want. It is man-making education all round that we want. And here is the test of truth—anything that makes you weak physically, intellectually, and spiritually, reject as poison; there is no life in it, it cannot be true. Truth is strengthening. Truth is purity, truth is all-knowledge; truth must be strengthening, must be enlightening, must be invigorating. These mysticisms, in spite of some grains of truth in them, are generally weakening. Believe me, I have a lifelong experience of it, and the one conclusion that I draw is that it is weakening. I have travelled all over India, searched almost every cave here, and lived in the Himalayas. I know people who lived there all their lives. I love my nation, I cannot see you degraded, weakened any more than you are now. Therefore I am bound for your sake and for truth's sake to cry, "Hold!" and to raise my voice against this degradation of my race. Give up these weakening mysticisms and be strong. Go back to your Upanishads—the shining, the strengthening, the bright philosophy—and part from all these mysterious things, all these weakening things. Take up this philosophy; the greatest truths are the simplest things in the world, simple as your own existence. The truths of the Upanishads are before you. Take them up, live up to them, and the salvation of India will be at hand.

One word more and I have finished. They talk of patriotism. I believe in patriotism, and I also have my own ideal of patriotism. Three things are necessary for great achievements. First, feel from the heart. What is in the intellect or reason? It goes a few steps and there it stops. But through the heart comes inspiration. Love opens the most impossible gates; love is the gate to all the secrets of the universe. Feel, therefore, my would-be reformers, my would-be patriots! Do you feel? Do you feel that millions and millions of the descendants of gods and of sages have become next-door neighbours to brutes? Do you feel that millions are starving today, and millions have been starving for ages? Do you feel that ignorance has come over the land as a dark cloud? Does it make you restless? Does it make you sleepless? Has it gone into your blood, coursing through your veins, becoming consonant with your heartbeats? Has it made you almost mad? Are you seized with that one idea of the misery of ruin, and have you forgotten all about your name, your fame, your wives, your children, your property, even your own bodies? Have you done that? That is the first step to become a patriot, the very first step. I did not go to America, as most of you know, for the Parliament of Religions, but this demon of a feeling was in me and within my soul. I travelled twelve years all over India, finding no way to work for my countrymen, and that is why I went to America. Most of you know that, who knew me then. Who cared about this Parliament of Religions? Here was my own flesh and blood sinking every day, and who cared for them? This was my first step.

You may feel, then; but instead of spending your energies in frothy talk, have you found any way out, any practical solution, some help instead of condemnation, some sweet words to soothe their miseries, to bring them out of this living death ?

Yet that is not all. Have you got the will to surmount mountain-high obstructions? If the whole world stands against you sword in hand, would you still dare to do what you think is right? If your wives and children are against you, if all your money goes, your name dies, your wealth vanishes, would you still stick to it? Would you still pursue it and go on steadily towards your own goal? As the great King Bhartrihari says, "Let the sages blame or let them praise; let the goddess of fortune come or let her go wherever she likes; let death come today, or let it come in hundreds of years; he indeed is the steady man who does not move one inch from the way of truth." Have you got that steadfastness? If you have these three things, each one of you will work miracles. You need not write in the newspapers, you need not go about lecturing; your very face will shine. If you live in a cave, your thoughts will permeate even through the rock walls, will go vibrating all over the world for hundreds of years, maybe, until they will fasten on to some brain and work out there. Such is the power of thought, of sincerity, and of purity of purpose.

I am afraid I am delaying you, but one word more. This national ship, my countrymen, my friends, my children—this national ship has been ferrying millions and millions of souls across the waters of life. For scores of shining centuries it has been plying across this water, and through its agency, millions of souls have been taken to the other shore, to blessedness. But today, perhaps through your own fault, this boat has become a little damaged, has sprung a leak; and would you therefore curse it? Is it fit that you stand up and pronounce malediction upon it, one that has done more work than any other thing in the world? If there are holes in this national ship, this society of ours, we are its children. Let us go and stop the holes. Let us gladly do it with our hearts' blood; and if we cannot, then let us die. We will make a plug of our brains and put them into the ship, but condemn it never. Say not one harsh word against this society. I love it for its past greatness. I love you all because you are the children of gods, and because you are the children of the glorious forefathers. How then can I curse you! Never. All blessings be upon you! I have come to you, my children, to tell you all my plans. If you hear them I am ready to work with you. But if you will not listen to them, and even kick me out of India, I will come back and tell you that we are all sinking! I am come now to sit in your midst, and if we are to sink, let us all sink together, but never let curses rise to our lips.

VEDANTA IN ITS APPLICATION TO
INDIAN LIFE

There is a word which has become very common as
an appellation of our race and our religion. The word
"Hindu" requires a little explanation in connection with
what I mean by Vedantism. This word "Hindu" was the
name that the ancient Persians used to apply to the river
Sindhu. Whenever in Sanskrit there is an "s", in ancient
Persian it changes into "h", so that "Sindhu" became
"Hindu"; and you are all aware how the Greeks found it
hard to pronounce "h" and dropped it altogether, so that
we became known as Indians. Now this word "Hindu"
as applied to the inhabitants of the other side of the Indus,
whatever might have been its meaning in ancient times,
has lost all its force in modern times; for all the people
that live on this side of the Indus no longer belong to one
religion. There are the Hindus proper, the Mohammedans,
the Parsees, the Christians, the Buddhists, and Jains. The
word "Hindu" in its literal sense ought to include all
these; but as signifying the religion, it would not be proper
to call all these Hindus. It is very hard, therefore, to find
any common name for our religion, seeing that this religion
is a collection, so to speak, of various religions, of various
ideas, of various ceremonials and forms, all gathered
together almost without a name, and without a church,
and without an organisation. The only point where, perhaps, all our sects agree is that we all believe in the scriptures—the Vedas. This perhaps is certain that no man can
have a right to be called a Hindu who does not admit the
supreme authority of the Vedas. All these Vedas, as you
are aware, are divided into two portions—the Karma
Kânda and the Jnâna Kânda. The Karma Kanda includes

various sacrifices and ceremonials, of which the larger part
has fallen into disuse in the present age. The Jnana
Kanda, as embodying the spiritual teachings of the Vedas
known as the Upanishads and the Vedanta, has always
been cited as the highest authority by all our teachers,
philosophers, and writers, whether dualist, or qualified
monist, or monist. Whatever be his philosophy or sect,
every one in India has to find his authority in the Upanishads. If he cannot, his sect would be heterodox. Therefore, perhaps the one name in modern times which would
designate every Hindu throughout the land would be "Vedantist" or "Vaidika", as you may put it; and in that sense
I always use the words "Vedantism" and "Vedanta".
I want to make it a little clearer, for of late it has become
the custom of most people to identify the word Vedanta
with the Advaitic system of the Vedanta philosophy. We
all know that Advaitism is only one branch of the various
philosophic systems that have been founded on the
Upanishads. The followers of the Vishishtâdvaitic system
have as much reverence for the Upanishads as the
followers of the Advaita, and the Vishishtadvaitists claim
as much authority for the Vedanta as the Advaitist. So do
the dualists ; so does every other sect in India. But the
word Vedantist has become somewhat identified in the
popular mind with the word Advaitist, and perhaps with
some reason, because, although we have the Vedas for
our scriptures, we have Smritis and Purânas—subsequent
writings—to illustrate the doctrines of the Vedas; these of
course have not the same weight as the Vedas. And the
law is that wherever these Puranas and Smritis differ from
any part of the Shruti, the Shruti must be followed and
the Smriti rejected. Now in the expositions of the great
Advaitic philosopher Shankara, and the school founded by
him, we find most of the authorities cited are from the
Upanishads, very rarely is an authority cited from the
Smritis, except, perhaps, to elucidate a point which could

hardly be found in the Shrutis. On the other hand, other schools take refuge more and more in the Smritis and less and less in the Shrutis; and as we go to the more and more dualistic sects, we find a proportionate quantity of the Smritis quoted, which is out of all proportion to what we should expect from a Vedantist. It is, perhaps, because these gave such predominance to the Paurânika authorities that the Advaitist came to be considered as the Vedantist *par excellence,* if I may say so.

However it might have been, the word Vedanta must cover the whole ground of Indian religious life, and being part of the Vedas, by all acceptance it is the most ancient literature that we have; for whatever might be the idea of modern scholars, the Hindus are not ready to admit that parts of the Vedas were written at one time and parts were written at another time. They of course still hold on to their belief that the Vedas as a whole were produced at the same time, rather if I may say so, that they were never produced, but that they always existed in the mind of the Lord. This is what I mean by the word Vedanta, that it covers the ground of dualism, of qualified monism, and Advaitism in India. Perhaps we may even take in parts of Buddhism, and of Jainism too, if they would come in—for our hearts are sufficiently large. But it is they that will not come in, we are ready for upon severe analysis you will always find that the essence of Buddhism was all borrowed from the same Upanishads; even the ethics, the so-called great and wonderful ethics of Buddhism, were there word for word, in some one or other of the Upanishads; and so all the good doctrines of the Jains were there, minus their vagaries. In the Upanishads, also, we find the germs of all the subsequent development of Indian religious thought. Sometimes it has been urged without any ground whatsoever that there is no ideal of Bhakti in the Upanishads. Those that have been students of the Upanishads know that that is not true at all. There is enough of Bhakti in every Upanishad if you will only seek for it; but many of these ideas which are found so fully developed in later times in the Puranas and other Smritis are only in the germ in the Upanishads. The sketch, the skeleton, was there as it were. It was filled in in some of the Puranas. But there is not one full-grown Indian ideal that cannot be traced back to the same source—the Upanishads. Certain ludicrous attempts have been made by persons without much Upanishadic scholarship to trace Bhakti to some foreign source; but as you know, these have all been proved to be failures, and all that you want of Bhakti is there, even in the Samhitâs, not to speak of the Upanishads—it is there, worship and love and all the rest of it; only the ideals of Bhakti are becoming higher and higher. In the Samhita portions, now and then, you find traces of a religion of fear and tribulation; in the Samhitas now and then you find a worshipper quaking before a Varuna, or some other god. Now and then you will find they are very much tortured by the idea of sin, but the Upanishads have no place for the delineation of these things. There is no religion of fear in the Upanishads; it is one of Love and one of Knowledge.

These Upanishads are our scriptures. They have been differently explained, and, as I have told you already, whenever there is a difference between subsequent Pauranika literature and the Vedas, the Puranas must give way. But it is at the same time true that, as a practical result, we find ourselves ninety per cent Pauranika and ten per cent Vaidika—even if so much as that. And we all find the most contradictory usages prevailing in our midst and also religious opinions prevailing in our society which scarcely have any authority in the scriptures of the Hindus; and in many cases we read in books, and see with astonishment, customs of the country that neither have their authority in the Vedas nor in the Smritis or

Puranas, but are simply local. And yet each ignorant villager thinks that if that little local custom dies out, he will no more remain a Hindu. In his mind Vedantism and these little local customs have been indissolubly identified. In reading the scriptures it is hard for him to understand that what he is doing has not the sanction of the scriptures, and that the giving up of them will not hurt him at all, but on the other hand will make him a better man. Secondly, there is the other difficulty. These scriptures of ours have been very vast. We read in the *Mahâbhâshya* of Patanjali, that great philological work, that the Sâma-Veda had one thousand branches. Where are they all? Nobody knows. So with each of the Vedas; the major portion of these books have disappeared, and it is only the minor portion that remains to us. They were all taken charge of by particular families; and either these families died out, or were killed under foreign persecution, or somehow became extinct; and with them, that branch of the learning of the Vedas they took charge of became extinct also. This fact we ought to remember, as it always forms the sheet-anchor in the hands of those who want to preach anything new or to defend anything even against the Vedas. Wherever in India there is a discussion between local custom and the Shrutis, and whenever it is pointed out that the local custom is against the scriptures, the argument that is forwarded is that it is not, that the customs existed in the branch of the Shrutis which has become extinct and so has been a recognised one. In the midst of all these varying methods of reading and commenting on our scriptures, it is very difficult indeed to find the thread that runs through all of them; for we become convinced at once that there must be some common ground underlying all these varying divisions and subdivisions. There must be harmony, a common plan, upon which all these little bits of buildings have been constructed, some basis common to this apparently hopeless mass of confusion which we call our religion. Otherwise it could not have stood so long, it could not have endured so long.

Coming to our commentators again, we find another difficulty. The Advaitic commentator, whenever an Advaitic text comes, preserves it just as it is; but the same commentator, as soon as a dualistic text presents itself, tortures it if he can, and brings the most queer meaning out of it. Sometimes the "Unborn" becomes a "goat", such are the wonderful changes effected. To suit the commentator, "Aja" the Unborn is explained as "Ajâ" a she-goat. In the same way, if not in a still worse fashion, the texts are handled by the dualistic commentator. Every dualistic text is preserved, and every text that speaks of non-dualistic philosophy is tortured in any fashion he likes. This Sanskrit language is so intricate, the Sanskrit of the Vedas is so ancient, and the Sanskrit philology so perfect, that any amount of discussion can be carried on for ages in regard to the meaning of one word. If a Pandit takes it into his head, he can render anybody's prattle into correct Sanskrit by force of argument and quotation of texts and rules. These are the difficulties in our way of understanding the Upanishads. It was given to me to live with a man who was as ardent a dualist, as ardent an Advaitist, as ardent a Bhakta, as a Jnani. And living with this man first put it into my head to understand the Upanishads and the texts of the scriptures from an independent and better basis than by blindly following the commentators ; and in my opinion and in my researches, I came to the conclusion that these texts are not at all contradictory. So we need have no fear of text-torturing at all! The texts are beautiful, ay, they are most wonderful; and they are not contradictory, but wonderfully harmonious, one idea leading up to the other. But the one fact I found is that in all the Upanishads, they begin with dualistic ideas, with worship and all that, and end with a grand flourish of Advaitic ideas.

Therefore I now find in the light of this man's life that the dualist and the Advaitist need not fight each other. Each has a place, and a great place in the national life. The dualist must remain, for he is as much part and parcel of the national religious life as the Advaitist. One cannot exist without the other; one is the fulfilment of the other; one is the building, the other is the top; the one the root, the other the fruit, and so on. Therefore any attempt to torture the texts of the Upanishads appears to me very ridiculous. I begin to find out that the language is wonderful. Apart from all its merits as the greatest philosophy, apart from its wonderful merit as theology, as showing the path of salvation to mankind, the Upanishadic literature is the most wonderful painting of sublimity that the world has. Here comes out in full force that individuality of the human mind, that introspective, intuitive Hindu mind. We have paintings of sublimity elsewhere in all nations, but almost without exception you will find that their ideal is to grasp the sublime in the muscles. Take for instance, Milton, Dante, Homer, or any of the Western poets. There are wonderfully sublime passages in them; but there it is always a grasping at infinity through the senses, the muscles, getting the ideal of infinite expansion, the infinite of space. We find the same attempts made in the Samhita portion. You know some of those wonderful Riks where creation is described; the very heights of expression of the sublime in expansion and the infinite in space are attained. But they found out very soon that the Infinite cannot be reached in that way, that even infinite space, and expansion, and infinite external nature could not express the ideas that were struggling to find expression in their minds, and so they fell back upon other explanations. The language became new in the Upanishads; it is almost negative, it is some-

times, chaotic, sometimes taking you beyond the senses,
pointing out to you something which you cannot grasp,
which you cannot sense, and at the same time you feel
certain that it is there. What passage in the world can
compare with this?—न तत्र सूर्यो भाति न चन्द्रतारकं नेमा विद्युतो
भान्ति कुतोऽयमग्निः ।—"There the sun cannot illumine, nor the
moon nor the stars, the flash of lightning cannot illumine
the place, what to speak of this mortal fire." Again, where
can you find a more perfect expression of the whole
philosophy of the world, the gist of what the Hindus ever
thought, the whole dream of human salvation, painted in
language more wonderful, in figure more marvellous than
this?

द्वा सुपर्णा सयुजा सखाया समानं वृक्षं परिषस्वजाते ।
तयोरन्यः पिप्पलं स्वाद्वत्त्यनश्नन्नन्यो अभिचाकशीति ॥
समाने वृक्षे पुरुषो निमग्नोऽनीशया शोचति मुह्यमानः ।
जुष्टं यदा पश्यत्यन्यमीशमस्य महिमानमिति वीतशोकः ॥

Upon the same tree there are two birds of beautiful
plumage, most friendly to each other, one eating the fruits,
the other sitting there calm and silent without eating—the
one on the lower branch eating sweet and bitter fruits in
turn and becoming happy and unhappy, but the other one
on the top, calm and majestic; he eats neither sweet nor
bitter fruits, cares neither for happiness nor misery, immersed in his own glory. This is the picture of the human
soul. Man is eating the sweet and bitter fruits of this life,
pursuing gold, pursuing his senses, pursuing the vanities of
life—hopelessly, madly careering he goes. In other places
the Upanishads have compared the human soul to the
charioteer, and the senses to the mad horses unrestrained.
Such is the career of men pursuing the vanities of life,
children dreaming golden dreams only to find that they are
but vain, and old men chewing the cud of their past deeds,
and yet not knowing how to get out of this network. This
is the world. Yet in the life of every one there come
golden moments; in the midst of the deepest sorrows,

nay, of the deepest joys, there come moments when a part
of the cloud that hides the sunlight moves away as it
were, and we catch a glimpse, in spite of ourselves of
something beyond—away, away beyond the life of the
senses; away, away beyond its vanities, its joys, and its
sorrows; away, away beyond nature, or our imaginations
of happiness here or hereafter; away beyond all thirst
for gold, or for fame, or for name, or for posterity. Man
stops for a moment at this glimpse and sees the other
bird calm and majestic, eating neither sweet nor bitter
fruits, but immersed in his own glory, Self-content, Self-
satisfied. As the Gita says, यस्त्वात्मरतिरेव स्यादात्मतृप्तश्च मानवः
आत्मन्येव च संतुष्टस्य कार्यं न विद्यते ॥—"He whose devotion
is to the Atman, he who does not want anything beyond
Atman, he who has become satisfied in the Atman, what
work is there for him to do?" Why should he drudge?
Man catches a glimpse, then again he forgets and goes
on eating the sweet and bitter fruits of life; perhaps
after a time he catches another glimpse, and the lower
bird goes nearer and nearer to the higher bird as blows
after blows are received. If he be fortunate to receive
hard knocks, then he comes nearer and nearer to his
companion, the other bird, his life, his friend; and as he
approaches him, he finds that the light from the higher
bird is playing round his own plumage; and as he comes
nearer and nearer, lo! the transformation is going on.
The nearer and nearer he comes, he finds himself melting
away, as it were, until he has entirely disappeared. He
did not really exist; it was but the reflection of the other
bird who was there calm and majestic amidst the moving
leaves. It was all his glory, that upper bird's. He then
becomes fearless, perfectly satisfied, calmly serene. In this
figure, the Upanishads take you from the dualistic to the
utmost Advaitic conception.

Endless examples can be cited, but we have no time
in this lecture to do that or to show the marvellous poetry

of the Upanishads, the painting of the sublime, the grand conceptions. But one other idea I must note, that the language and the thought and everything come direct, they fall upon you like a sword-blade, strong as the blows of a hammer they come. There is no mistaking their meanings. Every tone of that music is firm and produces its full effect; no gyrations, no mad words, no intricacies in which the brain is lost. No signs of degradation are there—no attempts at too much allegorising, too much piling of adjectives after adjectives, making it more and more intricate, till the whole of the sense is lost, and the brain becomes giddy, and man does not know his way out from the maze of that literature. There was none of that yet. If it be human literature, it must be the production of a race which had not yet lost any of its national vigour.

Strength, strength is what the Upanishads speak to me from every page. This is the one great thing to remember, it has been the one great lesson I have been taught in my life; strength, it says, strength, O man, be not weak. Are there no human weaknesses?—says man. There are, say the Upanishads, but will more weakness heal them, would you try to wash dirt with dirt? Will sin cure sin, weakness cure weakness? Strength, O man, strength, say the Upanishads, stand up and be strong. Ay, it is the only literature in the world where you find the word "Abhih", "fearless", used again and again; in no other scripture in the world is this adjective applied either to God or to man. Abhih, fearless! And in my mind rises from the past the vision of the great Emperor of the West, Alexander the Great, and I see, as it were in a picture, the great monarch standing on the bank of the Indus, talking to one of our Sannyâsins in the forest; the old man he was talking to, perhaps naked, stark naked, sitting upon a block of stone, and the Emperor, astonished at his wisdom, tempting him with gold and honour to come over to Greece. And this man smiles at his gold, and smiles at his temptations, and refuses; and then the Emperor standing on his authority as an Emperor, says, "I will kill you if you do not come", and the man bursts into a laugh and says, "You never told such a falsehood in your life, as you tell just now. Who can kill me? Me you kill, Emperor of the material world! Never! For I am Spirit unborn and undecaying: never was I born and never do I die; I am the Infinite, the Omnipresent, the Omniscient; and you kill me, child that you are!" That is strength, that is strength! And the more I read the Upanishads, my friends, my countrymen, the more I weep for you, for therein is the great practical application. Strength, strength for us. What we need is strength, who will give us strength? There are thousands to weaken us, and of stories we have had enough. Every one of our Puranas, if you press it, gives out stories enough to fill three-fourths of the libraries of the world. Everything that can weaken us as a race we have had for the last thousand years. It seems as if during that period the national life had this one end in view, viz how to make us weaker and weaker till we have become real earthworms, crawling at the feet of every one who dares to put his foot on us. Therefore, my friends, as one of your blood, as one that lives and dies with you, let me tell you that we want strength, strength, and every time strength. And the Upanishads are the great mine of strength. Therein lies strength enough to invigorate the whole world; the whole world can be vivified, made strong, energised through them. They will call with trumpet voice upon the weak, the miserable, and the downtrodden of all races, all creeds, and all sects to stand on their feet and be free. Freedom, physical freedom, mental freedom, and spiritual freedom are the watchwords of the Upanishads.

Ay, this is the one scripture in the world, of all others, that does not talk of salvation, but of freedom. Be free from the bonds of nature, be free from weakness! And it shows to you that you have this freedom already in you. That is another peculiarity of its teachings. You are a Dvaitist; never mind, you have got to admit that by its very nature the soul is perfect; only by certain actions of the soul has it become contracted. Indeed, Râmânuja's theory of contraction and expansion is exactly what the modern evolutionists call evolution and atavism. The soul goes back, becomes contracted as it were, its powers become potential; and by good deeds and good thoughts it expands again and reveals its natural perfection. With the Advaitist the one difference is that he admits evolution in nature and not in the soul. Suppose there is a screen, and there is a small hole in the screen. I am a man standing behind the screen and looking at this grand assembly. I can see only very few faces here. Suppose the hole increases ; as it increases, more and more of this assembly is revealed 'to me, and in full when the hole has become identified with the screen—there is nothing between you and me in this case. Neither you changed nor I changed; all the change was in the screen. You were the same from first to last; only the screen changed. This is the Advaitist's position with regard to evolution—evolution of nature and manifestation of the Self within. Not that the Self can by any means be made to contract. It is unchangeable, the Infinite One. It was covered, as it were, with a veil, the veil of Mâyâ, and as this Maya veil becomes thinner and thinner, the inborn, natural glory of the soul comes out and becomes more manifest. This is the one great doctrine which the world is waiting to learn from India. Whatever they may talk, however they may try to boast, they will find out day after day that no society can stand without admitting this. Do you not find how everything is being revolutionised? Do you not see how it was the custom to take for granted that everything was wicked until it proved itself good? In education, in punishing criminals, in treating lunatics, in the treatment of common diseases even, that was the old law. What is the modern law? The modern law says, the body itself is healthy; it cures diseases of its own nature. Medicine can at the best but help the storing up of the best in the body. What says it of criminals? It takes for granted that however low a criminal may be, there is still the divinity within, which does not change, and we must treat criminals accordingly. All these things are now changing, and reformatories and penitentiaries are established. So with everything. Consciously or unconsciously that Indian idea of the divinity within every one is expressing itself even in other countries. And in your books is the explanation which other nations have to accept. The treatment of one man to another will be entirely revolutionised, and these old, old ideas of pointing to the weakness of mankind will have to go. They will have received their death-blow within this century. Now people may stand up and criticise us. I have been criticised, from one end of the world to the other, as one who preaches the diabolical idea that there is no sin! Very good. The descendants of these very men will bless me as the preacher of virtue, and not of sin. I am the teacher of virtue, not of sin. I glory in being the preacher of light, and not of darkness.

The second great idea which the world is waiting to receive from our Upanishads is the solidarity of this universe. The old lines of demarcation and differentiation are vanishing rapidly. Electricity and steam-power are placing the different parts of the world in intercommunication with each other, and, as a result, we Hindus no longer say that every country beyond our own land is peopled with demons and hobgoblins, nor do the people of Christain countries say that India is only peopled by cannibals and savages. When we go out of our country, we find the same brother-man, with the same strong hand to help, with the same lips to say godspeed; and sometimes they are better than in the country in which we are born. When they come here, they find the same brotherhood, the same cheer, the same godspeed. Our Upanishads say that the cause of all misery is ignorance; and that is perfectly true when applied to every state of life, either social or spiritual. It is ignorance that makes us hate each other, it is through ignorance that we do not know and do not love each other. As soon as we come to know each other, love comes, must come, for are we not one? Thus we find solidarity coming in spite of itself. Even in politics and sociology, problems that were only national twenty years ago can no more be solved on national grounds only. They are assuming huge proportions, gigantic shapes. They can only be solved when looked at in the broader light of international grounds. International organisations, international combinations, international laws are the cry of the day. That shows the solidarity. In science, every day they are coming to a similar broad view of matter. You speak of matter, the whole universe as one mass, one ocean of matter, in which you and I, the sun and the moon, and everything else are but the names of different little whirlpools and nothing more. Mentally speaking, it is one universal ocean of thought in which you and I are similar little whirlpools; and as spirit it moveth not, it changeth not. It is the One Unchangeable, Unbroken, Homogeneous Atman. The cry for morality is coming also, and that is to be found in our books. The explanation of morality, the fountain of ethics, that also the world wants; and that it will get here.

What do we want in India? If foreigners want these things, we want them twenty times more. Because, in spite of the greatness of the Upanishads, in spite of our boasted ancestry of sages, compared to many other races, I must tell you that we are weak, very weak. First of all is our physical weakness. That physical weakness is the cause of at least one-third of our miseries. We are lazy, we cannot work; we cannot combine, we do not love each other; we are intensely selfish, not three of us

can come together without hating each other, without being jealous of each other. That is the state in which we
are—hopelessly disorganised mobs, immensely selfish,
fighting each other for centuries as to whether a certain
mark is to be put on our forehead this way or that way,
writing volumes and volumes upon such momentous
questions as to whether the look of a man spoils my food
or not! This we have been doing for the past few centuries. We cannot expect anything high from a race
whose whole brain energy has been occupied in such
wonderfully beautiful problems and researches! And are
we not ashamed of ourselves? Ay, sometimes we are;
but though we think these things frivolous, we cannot
give them up. We speak of many things parrot-like, but
never do them; speaking and not doing has become a
habit with us. What is the cause of that? Physical weakness. This sort of weak brain is not able to do anything;
we must strengthen it. First of all, our young men must
be strong. Religion will come afterwards. Be strong,
my young friends; that is my advice to you. You will be
nearer to Heaven through football than through the
study of the Gita. These are bold words; but I have to
say them, for I love you. I know where the shoe pinches.
I have gained a little experience. You will understand
the Gita better with your biceps, your muscles, a little
stronger. You will understand the mighty genius and the
mighty strength of Krishna better with a little of strong
blood in you. You will understand the Upanishads better
and the glory of the Atman when your body stands firm
upon your feet, and you feel yourselves as men. Thus we
have to apply these to our needs.

People get disgusted many times at my preaching
Advaitism. I do not mean to preach Advaitism, or Dvaitism, or any *ism* in the world. The only *ism* that we require
now is this wonderful idea of the soul—its eternal might,
its eternal strength, its eternal purity, and its eternal per-

fection. If I had a child I would from its very birth begin to tell it, "Thou art the Pure One". You have read in one of the Puranas that beautiful story of queen Madâlasâ, how as soon as she has a child she puts her baby with her own hands in the cradle, and how as the cradle rocks to and fro, she begins to sing, "Thou art the Pure One, the Stainless, the Sinless, the Mighty One, the Great One." Ay, there is much in that. Feel that you are great and you become great. What did I get as my experience all over the world, is the question. They may talk about sinners—and if all Englishmen really believed that they were sinners, Englishmen would be no better than the negroes in Central Africa. God bless them that they do not believe it! On the other hand, the Englishman believes he is born the lord of the world. He believes he is great and can do anything in the world; if he wants to go to the sun or the moon, he believes he can ; and that makes him great. If he had believed his priests that he was a poor miserable sinner, going to be barbecued through all eternity, he would not be the same Englishman that he is today. So I find in every nation that, in spite of priests and superstition, the divine within lives and asserts itself. We have lost faith. Would you believe me, we have less faith than the Englishman and woman—a thousand times less faith! These are plain words; but I say these, I cannot help it. Don't you see how Englishmen and women, when they catch our ideals, become mad as it were ; and although they are the ruling class, they come to India to preach our own religion notwithstanding the jeers and ridicule of their own countrymen? How many of you could do that? And why cannot you do that? Do you not know it? You know more than they do; you are more wise than is good for you, that is your difficulty! Simply because your blood is only like water, your brain is sloughing, your body is weak! You must change the body. Physical weakness is the cause and nothing else. You have talked of reforms, of ideals, and all these things for the past hundred years ; but when it comes to practice, you are not to be found anywhere—till you have disgusted the whole world, and the very name of reform is a thing of ridicule! And what is the cause? Do you not know? You know too well. The only cause is that you are weak, weak, weak; your body is weak, your mind is weak, you have no faith in yourselves! Centuries and centuries, a thousand years of crushing tyranny of castes and kings and foreigners and your own people have taken out all your strength, my brethren. Your backbone is broken, you are like downtrodden worms. Who will give you strength? Let me tell you, strength, strength is what we want. And the first step in getting strength is to uphold the Upanishads, and believe—"I am the Soul", "Me the sword cannot cut; nor weapons pierce; me the fire cannot burn; me the air cannot dry; I am the Omnipotent, I am the Omniscient." So repeat these blessed, saving words. Do not say we are weak; we can do anything and everything. What can we not do? Everything can be done by us; we all have the same glorious soul, let us believe in it. Have faith, as Nachiketâ. At the time of his father's sacrifice, faith came unto Nachiketa; ay, I wish that faith would come to each of you; and every one of you would stand up a giant, a world-mover with a gigantic intellect —an infinite God in every respect. That is what I want you to become. This is the strength that you get from the Upanishads, this is the faith that you get from there.

Ay, but it was only for the Sannyâsin! Rahasya (esoteric)! The Upanishads were in the hands of the Sannyasin; he went into the forest! Shankara was a little kind and said even Grihasthas (householders) may study the Upanishads, it will do them good; it will not hurt them. But still the idea is that the Upanishads talked only of the forest life of the recluse. As I told you the other day, the only commentary, the authoritative com-

mentary on the Vedas, has been made once and for all
by Him who inspired the Vedas—by Krishna in the
Gita. It is there for every one in every occupation
of life. These conceptions of the Vedanta must come
out, must remain not only in the forest, not only in
the cave, but they must come out to work at the bar and
the bench, in the pulpit, and in the cottage of the poor
man, with the fishermen that are catching fish, and with
the students that are studying. They call to every man,
woman, and child whatever be their occupation, wherever
they may be. And what is there to fear! How can
the fishermen and all these carry out the ideals of the
Upanishads? The way has been shown. It is infinite;
religion is infinite, none can go beyond it; and whatever
you do sincerely is good for you. Even the least thing
well done brings marvellous results; therefore let every
one do what little he can. If the fisherman thinks that he
is the Spirit, he will be a better fisherman; if the student
thinks he is the Spirit, he will be a better student. If the
lawyer thinks that he is the Spirit, he will be a better
lawyer, and so on, and the result will be that the castes
will remain for ever. It is in the nature of society to form
itself into groups; and what will go will be these privileges.
Caste is a natural order; I can perform one duty in social
life, and you another; you can govern a country, and I
can mend a pair of old shoes, but that is no reason why
you are greater than I, for can you mend my shoes? Can
I govern the country? I am clever in mending shoes, you
are clever in reading Vedas, but that is no reason why you
should trample on my head. Why if one commits murder
should he be praised, and if another steals an apple why
should he be hanged? This will have to go. Caste is good.
That is the only natural way of solving life. Men must
form themselves into groups, and you cannot get rid of
that. Wherever you go, there will be caste. But that
does not mean that there should be these privileges.

They should be knocked on the head. If you teach
Vedanta to the fisherman, he will say, I am as good a man
as you; I am a fisherman, you are a philosopher, but I
have the same God in me as you have in you. And that
is what we want, no privilege for any one, equal chances
for all; let every one be taught that the divine is within,
and every one will work out his own salvation.

Liberty is the first condition of growth. It is wrong, a
thousand times wrong, if any of you dares to say, "I will
work out the salvation of this woman or child." I am asked
again and again, what I think of the widow problem and
what I think of the woman question. Let me answer once
for all—am I a widow that you ask me that nonsense?
Am I a woman that you ask me that question again and
again? Who are you to solve women's problems? Are
you the Lord God that you should rule over every widow
and every woman? Hands off! They will solve their
own problems. O tyrants, attempting to think that you
can do anything for any one! Hands off! The Divine
will look after all. Who are you to assume that you know
everything? How dare you think, O blasphemers, that
you have the right over God? For don't you know that
every soul is the Soul of God? Mind your own Karma;
a load of Karma is there in you to work out. Your nation
may put you upon a pedestal, your society may cheer
you up to the skies, and fools may praise you: but He
sleeps not, and retribution will be sure to follow, here
or hereafter.

Look upon every man, woman, and every one as God.
You cannot help anyone, you can only serve: serve the
children of the Lord, serve the Lord Himself, if you have
the privilege. If the Lord grants that you can help any
one of His children, blessed you are; do not think too
much of yourselves. Blessed you are that that privilege
was given to you when others had it not. Do it only as a
worship. I should see God in the poor, and it is for my

salvation that I go and worship them. The poor and the miserable are for our salvation, so that we may serve the Lord, coming in the shape of the diseased, coming in the shape of the lunatic, the leper, and the sinner! Bold are my words; and let me repeat that it is the greatest privilege in our life that we are allowed to serve the Lord in all these shapes. Give up the idea that by ruling over others you can do any good to them. But you can do just as much as you can in the case of the plant; you can supply the growing seed with the materials for the making up of its body, bringing to it the earth, the water, the air, that it wants. It will take all that it wants by its own nature, it will assimilate and grow by its own nature.

Bring all light into the world. Light, bring light! Let light come unto every one; the task will not be finished till every one has reached the Lord. Bring light to the poor; and bring more light to the rich, for they require it more than the poor. Bring light to the ignorant, and more light to the educated, for the vanities of the education of our time are tremendous! Thus bring light to all and leave the rest unto the Lord, for in the words of the same Lord, "To work you have the right and not to the fruits thereof." "Let not your work produce results for *you*, and at the same time may you never be without work."

May He who taught such grand ideas to our fore-fathers ages ago help us to get strength to carry into practice His commands!

THE SAGES OF INDIA

In speaking of the sages of India, my mind goes back to those periods of which history has no record, and tradition tries in vain to bring the secrets out of the gloom of the past. The sages of India have been almost innumerable, for what has the Hindu nation been doing for thousands of years except producing sages? I will take, therefore, the lives of a few of the most brilliant ones, the epoch-makers, and present them before you, that is to say, my study of them.

In the first place, we have to understand a little about our scriptures. Two ideals of truth are in our scriptures; the one is, what we call the eternal, and the other is not so authoritative, yet binding under particular circumstances, times, and places. The eternal relations which deal with the nature of the soul, and of God, and the relations between souls and God are embodied in what we call the Shrutis, the Vedas. The next set of truths is what we call the Smritis, as embodied in the words of Manu, Yâjnavalkya, and other writers and also in the Purânas, down to the Tantras. The second class of books and teachings is subordinate to the Shrutis, inasmuch as whenever any one of these contradicts anything in the Shrutis, the Shrutis must prevail. This is the law. The idea is that the framework of the destiny and goal of man has been all delineated in the Vedas, the details have been left to be worked out in the Smritis and Puranas. As for general directions, the Shrutis are enough ; for spiritual life, nothing more can be said, nothing more can be known. All that is necessary has been known, all the advice that is necessary to lead the soul to perfection has been completed in the Shrutis ; the details alone were left out, and these the Smritis have supplied from time to time.

Another peculiarity is that these Shrutis have many sages as the recorders of the truths in them, mostly men, even some women. Very little is known of their personalities, the dates of their birth, and so forth, but their best thoughts, their best discoveries, I should say, are preserved there, embodied in the sacred literature of our country, the Vedas. In the Smritis, on the other hand, personalities are more in evidence. Startling, gigantic, impressive, world-moving persons stand before us, as it were, for the first time, sometimes of more magnitude even than their teachings.

This is a peculiarity which we have to understand— that our religion preaches an Impersonal Personal God. It preaches any amount of impersonal laws *plus* any amount of personality, but the very fountain-head of our religion is in the Shrutis, the Vedas, which are perfectly impersonal; the persons all come in the Smritis and Puranas—the great Avatâras, Incarnations of God, Prophets, and so forth. And this ought also to be observed that except our religion, every other religion in the world depends upon the life or lives of some personal founder or founders. Christianity is built upon the life of Jesus Christ, Mohammedanism upon Mohammed, Buddhism upon Buddha, Jainism upon the Jinas, and so on. It naturally follows that there must be in all these religions a good deal of fight about what they call the historical evidences of these great personalities. If at any time the historical evidences about the existence of these personages in ancient times become weak, the whole building of the religion tumbles down and is broken to pieces. We escaped this fate because our religion is not based upon persons but on principles. That you obey your religion is not because it came through the authority of a sage, no, not even of an Incarnation. Krishna is not the authority of the Vedas, but the Vedas are the authority of Krishna himself. His glory is that he is the greatest preacher of the Vedas that ever existed. So with the other Incarnations; so with all our sages. Our first principle is that all that is necessary for the perfection of man and for attaining unto freedom is there in the Vedas. You cannot find anything new. You cannot go beyond a perfect unity, which is the goal of all knowledge; this has been already reached there, and it is impossible to go beyond the unity. Religious knowledge became complete when Tat Twam Asi (Thou art That) was discovered, and that was in the Vedas. What remained was the guidance of people from time to time according to different times and places, according to different circumstances and environments; people had to be guided along the old, old path, and for this these great teachers came, these great sages. Nothing can bear out more clearly this position than the celebrated saying of Shri Krishna in the Gîtâ: "Whenever virtue subsides and irreligion prevails, I create Myself for the protection of the good; for the destruction of all immorality I am coming from time to time." This is the idea in India.

What follows? That on the one hand, there are these eternal principles which stand upon their own foundations without depending on any reasoning even, much less on the authority of sages however great, of Incarnations however brilliant they may have been. We may remark that as this is the unique position in India, our claim is that the Vedanta only can be the universal religion, that it is already the existing universal religion in the world, because it teaches principles and not persons. No religion built upon a person can be taken up as a type by all the races of mankind. In our own country we find that there have been so many grand characters; in even a small city many persons are taken up as types by the different minds in that one city. How is it possible that one person as Mohammed or Buddha or Christ, can be taken up as the one type for the whole world, nay, that the whole of morality, ethics, spirituality, and religion can be true only from the sanction of that one person, and one person alone? Now, the Vedantic religion does not require any such personal authority. Its sanction is the eternal nature of man, its ethics are based upon the eternal spiritual solidarity of man, already existing, already attained and not to be attained. On the other hand, from the very earliest times, our sages have been feeling conscious of this fact that the vast majority of mankind require a personality. They must have a Personal God in some form or other. The very Buddha who declared against the existence of a Personal God had not died fifty years before his disciples manufactured a Personal God out of him. The Personal God is necessary, and at the same time we know that instead of and better than vain imaginations of a Personal God, which in ninety-nine cases out of a hundred are unworthy of human worship, we have in this world, living and walking in our midst, living Gods, now and then. These are more worthy of worship than any imaginary God, any creation of our imagination, that is to say, any idea of God which we can form. Shri Krishna is much greater than any idea of God you or I can have. Buddha is a much higher idea, a more living and idolised idea, than the ideal you or I can conceive of in our minds; and therefore it is that they always command the worship of mankind even to the exclusion of all imaginary deities.

This our sages knew, and, therefore, left it open to all Indian people to worship such great personages, such Incarnations. Nay, the greatest of these Incarnations goes further: "Wherever an extraordinary spiritual power is manifested by external man, know that I am there; it is from Me that that manifestation comes." That leaves the door open for the Hindu to worship the Incarnations of all the countries in the world. The Hindu can worship any sage and any saint from any country whatsoever, and as a fact we know that we go and worship many times in the churches of the Christians, and many, many times in the Mohammedan mosques, and that is good. Why not? Ours, as I have said, is the universal religion.

It is inclusive enough, it is broad enough to include all the ideals. All the ideals of religion that already exist in the world can be immediately included, and we can patiently wait for all the ideals that are to come in the future to be taken in the same fashion, embraced in the infinite arms of the religion of the Vedanta.

This, more or less, is our position with regard to the great sages, the Incarnations of God. There are also secondary characters. We find the word Rishi again and again mentioned in the Vedas, and it has become a common word at the present time. The Rishi is the great authority. We have to understand that idea. The definition is that the Rishi is the Mantra-drashtâ, the seer of thought. What is the proof of religion?—this was asked in very ancient times. There is no proof in the senses was the declaration. यतो वाचो निवर्तन्ते अप्राप्य मनसा सह —"From whence words reflect back with thought without reaching the goal." न तत्र चक्षुर्गच्छति न वागगच्छति नो मनः । —"There the eyes cannot reach, neither can speech, nor the mind"— that has been the declaration for ages and ages. Nature outside cannot give us any answer as to the existence of the soul, the existence of God, the eternal life, the goal of man, and all that. This mind is continually changing, always in a state of flux; it is finite, it is broken into pieces. How can nature tell of the Infinite, the Unchangeable, the Unbroken, the Indivisible, the Eternal? It never can. And whenever mankind has striven to get an answer from dull dead matter, history shows how disastrous the results have been. How comes, then, the knowledge which the Vedas declare? It comes through being a Rishi. This knowledge is not in the senses; but are the senses the be-all and the end-all of the human being? Who dare say that the senses are the all-in-all of man? Even in our lives, in the life of every one of us here, there come moments of calmness, perhaps, when we see before us the death of one we loved, when some shock comes to us, or when extreme

blessedness comes to us. Many other occasions there are
when the mind, as it were, becomes calm, feels for the
moment its real nature; and a glimpse of the Infinite
beyond, where words cannot reach nor the mind go, is
revealed to us. This happens in ordinary life, but it has
to be heightened, practised, perfected. Men found out ages
ago that the soul is not bound or limited by the senses, no,
not even by consciousness. We have to understand that
this consciousness is only the name of one link in the infinite chain. Being is not identical with consciousness, but
consciousness is only one part of Being. Beyond consciousness is where the bold search lies Consciousness is bound by
the senses. Beyond that, beyond the senses, men must go
in order to arrive at truths of the spiritual world, and there
are even now persons who succeed in going beyond the
bounds of the senses. These are called Rishis, because they
come face to face with spiritual truths.

The proof, therefore, of the Vedas is just the same
as the proof of this table before me, Pratyaksha, direct
perception. This I see with the senses, and the truths of
spirituality we also see in a superconscious state of the
human soul. This Rishi-state is not limited by time or
place, by sex or race. Vâtsyâyana boldly declares that
this Rishihood is the common property of the descendants
of the sage, of the Aryan, of the non-Aryan, of even the
Mlechchha. This is the sageship of the Vedas, and constantly we ought to remember this ideal of religion in
India, which I wish other nations of the world would also
remember and learn, so that there may be less fight and
less quarrel. Religion is not in books, nor in theories,
nor in dogmas, nor in talking, not even in reasoning. It
is being and becoming. Ay, my friends, until each one
of you has become a Rishi and come face to face with
spiritual facts, religious life has not begun for you. Until
the superconscious opens for you, religion is mere talk,
it is nothing but preparation. You are talking second-

hand, third-hand, and here applies that beautiful saying of Buddha when he had a discussion with some Brâhmins. They came discussing about the nature of Brahman, and the great sage asked, "Have you seen Brahman?" "No", said the Brahmin ; "Or your father?" "No, neither has he" ; "Or your grandfather?" "I don't think even he saw Him." "My friend, how can you discuss about a person whom your father and grandfather never saw, and try to put each other down?" That is what the whole world is doing. Let us say in the language of the Vedanta, "This Âtman is not to be reached by too much talk, no, not even by the highest intellect, no, not even by the study of the Vedas themselves."

Let us speak to all the nations of the world in the language of the Vedas: Vain are your fights and your quarrels; have you seen God whom you want to preach? If you have not seen, vain is your preaching; you do not know what you say; and if you have seen God, you will not quarrel, your very face will shine. An ancient sage of the Upanishads sent his son out to learn about Brahman, and the child came back, and the father asked, "What have you learnt?" The child replied he had learnt so many sciences. But the father said, "That is nothing, go back." And the son went back, and when he returned again the father asked the same question, and the same answer came from the child. Once more he had to go back. And the next time he came, his whole face was shining ; and his father stood up and declared, "Ay, today, my child, your face shines like a knower of Brahman." When you have known God, your very face will be changed, your voice will be changed, your whole appearance will be changed. You will be a blessing to mankind ; none will be able to resist the Rishi. This is the Rishihood, the ideal in our religion. The rest, all these talks and reasonings and philosophies and dualisms and monisms, and even the Vedas themselves are but pre-

parations, secondary things. The other is primary. The
Vedas, grammar, astronomy, etc., all these are secondary;
that is supreme knowledge which makes us realise the
Unchangeable One. Those who realised are the sages
whom we find in the Vedas ; and we understand how this
Rishi is the name of a type, of a class, which every one
of us, as true Hindus, is expected to become at some
period of our life, and becoming which, to the Hindu,
means salvation. Not belief in doctrines, not going to
thousands of temples, nor bathing in all the rivers in the
world, but becoming the Rishi, the Mantra-drashta—that
is freedom, that is salvation.

Coming down to later times, there have been great
world-moving sages, great Incarnations of whom there
have been many ; and according to the *Bhâgavata*, they
also are infinite in number, and those that are worshipped
most in India are Râma and Krishna. Rama, the ancient
idol of the heroic ages, the embodiment of truth, of
morality, the ideal son, the ideal husband, the ideal father,
and above all, the ideal king, this Rama has been presented before us by the great sage Vâlmiki. No language
can be purer, none chaster, none more beautiful and at
the same time simpler than the language in which the
great poet has depicted the life of Rama. And what to
speak of Sitâ? You may exhaust the literature of the world
that is past, and I may assure you that you will have
to exhaust the literature of the world of the future, before
finding another Sita. Sita is unique; that character was
depicted once and for all. There may have been several
Ramas, perhaps, but never more than one Sita! She is
the very type of the true Indian woman, for all the Indian
ideals of a perfected woman have grown out of that one
life of Sita ; and here she stands these thousands of
years, commanding the worship of every man, woman,
and child throughout the length and breadth of the land
of Âryâvarta. There she will always be, this glorious

Sita, purer than purity itself, all patience, and all suffering. She who suffered that life of suffering without a murmur, she the ever-chaste and ever-pure wife, she the ideal of the people, the ideal of the gods, the great Sita, our national God she must always remain. And every one of us knows her too well to require much delineation. All our mythology may vanish, even our Vedas may depart, and our Sanskrit language may vanish for ever, but so long as there will be five Hindus living here, even if only speaking the most vulgar patois, there will be the story of Sita present. Mark my words: Sita has gone into the very vitals of our race. She is there in the blood of every Hindu man and woman; we are all children of Sita. Any attempt to modernise our women, if it tries to take our women away from that ideal of Sita, is immediately a failure, as we see every day. The women of India must grow and develop in the footprints of Sita, and that is the only way.

The next is He who is worshipped in various forms, the favourite ideal of men as well as of women, the ideal of children, as well as of grown-up men. I mean He whom the writer of the *Bhagavata* was not content to call an Incarnation but says, "The other Incarnations were but parts of the Lord. He, Krishna, was the Lord Himself." And it is not strange that such adjectives are applied to him when we marvel at the many-sidedness of his character. He was the most wonderful Sannyâsin, and the most wonderful householder in one; he had the most wonderful amount of Rajas, power, and was at the same time living in the midst of the most wonderful renunciation. Krishna can never be understood until you have studied the Gita, for he was the embodiment of his own teaching. Every one of these Incarnations came as a living illustration of what they came to preach. Krishna, the preacher of the Gita, was all his life the embodiment of that Song Celestial; he was the great illustration of non-attachment. He gives up his throne and never cares for it. He, the leader of India, at whose

word kings come down from their thrones, never wants to
be a king. He is the simple Krishna, ever the same
Krishna who played with the Gopis. Ah, that most marvellous passage of his life, the most difficult to understand,
and which none ought to attempt to understand until he
has become perfectly chaste and pure, that most marvellous expansion of love, allegorised and expressed in that
beautiful play at Vrindâban, which none can understand
but he who has become mad with love, drunk deep of the
cup of love! Who can understand the throes of the love of
the Gopis—the very ideal of love, love that wants nothing,
love that even does not care for heaven, love that does not
care for anything in this world or the world to come? And
here, my friends, through this love of the Gopis has been
found the only solution of the conflict between the Personal
and the Impersonal God. We know how the Personal God
is the highest point of human life; we know that it is
philosophical to believe in an Impersonal God immanent
in the universe, of whom everything is but a manifestation.
At the same time our souls hanker after something concrete, something which we want to grasp, at whose feet we
can pour out our soul, and so on. The Personal God is
therefore the highest conception of human nature. Yet
reason stands aghast at such an idea. It is the same old, old
question which you find discussed in the *Brahma-Sutras*,
which you find Draupadi discussing with Yudhishthira in
the forest: If there is a Personal God, all-merciful, all-
powerful, why is the hell of an earth here, why did He
create this?—He must be a partial God. There was no
solution, and the only solution that can be found is what
you read about the love of the Gopis. They hated every
adjective that was applied to Krishna; they did not care to
know that he was the Lord of creation, they did not care to
know that he was almighty, they did not care to know that
he was omnipotent, and so forth. The only thing they
understood was that he was infinite Love, that was all.

The Gopis understood Krishna only as the Krishna of Vrindaban. He, the leader of the hosts, the King of kings, to them was the shepherd, and the shepherd for ever. "I do not want wealth, nor many people, nor do I want learning; no, not even do I want to go to heaven. Let me be born again and again, but Lord, grant me this, that I may have love for Thee, and that for love's sake." A great landmark in the history of religion is here, the ideal of love for love's sake, work for work's sake, duty for duty's sake, and it for the first time fell from the lips of the greatest of Incarnations, Krishna, and for the first time in the history of humanity, upon the soil of India. The religions of fear and of temptations were gone for ever, and in spite of the fear of hell and temptation of enjoyment in heaven, came the grandest of ideals, love for love's sake, duty for duty's sake, work for work's sake.

And what a love! I have told you just now that it is very difficult to understand the love of the Gopis. There are not wanting fools, even in the midst of us, who cannot understand the marvellous significance of that most marvellous of all episodes. There are, let me repeat, impure fools, even born of our blood, who try to shrink from that as if from something impure. To them I have only to say, first make yourselves pure; and you must remember that he who tells the history of the love of the Gopis is none else but Shuka Deva. The historian who records this marvellous love of the Gopis is one who was born pure, the eternally pure Shuka, the son of Vyâsa. So long as there is selfishness in the heart, so long is love of God impossible; it is nothing but shopkeeping: "I give you something; O Lord, you give me something in return"; and says the Lord, "If you do not do this, I will take good care of you when you die. I will roast you all the rest of your lives, perhaps", and so on. So long as such ideas are in the brain, how can one understand the mad throes of the Gopis' love? "O for one, one kiss of those lips! One who has been kissed by Thee, his thirst for Thee increases for ever, all sorrows vanish, and he forgets love for everything else but for Thee and Thee alone." Ay, forget first the love for gold, and name and fame, and for this little trumpery world of ours. Then, only then, you will understand the love of the Gopis, too holy to be attempted without giving up everything, too sacred to be understood until the soul has become perfectly pure. People with ideas of sex, and of money, and of fame, bubbling up every minute in the heart, daring to criticise and understand the love of the Gopis! That is the very essence of the Krishna Incarnation. Even the Gita, the great philosophy itself, does not compare with that madness, for in the Gita the disciple is taught slowly how to walk towards the goal, but here is the madness of enjoyment, the drunkenness of love, where disciples and teachers and teachings and books and all these things have become one; even the ideas of fear, and God, and heaven—everything has been thrown away. What remains is the madness of love. It is forgetfulness of everything, and the lover sees nothing in the world except that Krishna and Krishna alone, when the face of every being becomes a Krishna, when his own face looks like Krishna, when his own soul has become tinged with the Krishna colour. That was the great Krishna!

Do not waste your time upon little details. Take up the framework, the essence of the life. There may be many historical discrepancies, there may be interpolations in the life of Krishna. All these things may be true; but, at the same time, there must have been a basis, a foundation for this new and tremendous departure. Taking the life of any other sage or prophet, we find that that prophet is only the evolution of what had gone before him, we find that that prophet is only preaching the ideas that had been scattered about his own country even in his own times. Great doubts may exist even as to whether that prophet existed or not. But here, I challenge any one to show

whether these things, these ideals—work for work's sake,
love for love's sake, duty for duty's sake, were not original
ideas with Krishna, and as such, there must have been
someone with whom these ideas originated. They could
not have been borrowed from anybody else. They were
not floating about in the atmosphere when Krishna was
born. But the Lord Krishna was the first preacher of this;
his disciple Vyasa took it up and preached it unto mankind. This is the highest idea to picture. The highest thing
we can get out of him is Gopijanavallabha, the Beloved of
the Gopis of Vrindaban. When that madness comes in
your brain, when you understand the blessed Gopis, then
you will understand what love is. When the whole world
will vanish, when all other considerations will have died
out, when you will become pure-hearted with no other
aim, not even the search after truth, then and then alone
will come to you the madness of that love, the strength
and the power of that infinite love which the Gopis had,
that love for love's sake. That is the goal. When you have
got that, you have got everything.

To come down to the lower stratum—Krishna, the
preacher of the Gita. Ay, there is an attempt in India
now which is like putting the cart before the horse. Many
of our people think that Krishna as the lover of the Gopis
is something rather uncanny, and the Europeans do not
like it much. Dr. So-and-so does not like it. Certainly
then, the Gopis have to go! Without the sanction of
Europeans how can Krishna live? He cannot! In the
Mahâbhârata there is no mention of the Gopis except in
one or two places, and those not very remarkable places.
In the prayer of Draupadi there is mention of a Vrindaban
life, and in the speech of Shishupâla there is again mention of this Vrindaban. All these are interpolations! What
the Europeans do not want must be thrown off. They are
interpolations, the mention of the Gopis and of Krishna
too! Well, with these men, steeped in commercialism,

where even the ideal of religion has become commercial,
they are all trying to go to heaven by doing something
here; the bania wants compound interest, wants to lay
by something here and enjoy it there. Certainly the Gopis
have no place in such a system of thought. From that
ideal lover we come down to the lower stratum of Krishna,
the preacher of the Gita. Than the Gita no better commentary on the Vedas has been written or can be written.
The essence of the Shrutis, or of the Upanishads, is hard to
be understood, seeing that there are so many commentators, each one trying to interpret in his own way. Then
the Lord Himself comes, He who is the inspirer of the
Shrutis, to show us the meaning of them, as the preacher of
the Gita, and today India wants nothing better, the world
wants nothing better than that method of interpretation.
It is a wonder that subsequent interpreters of the scriptures,
even commenting upon the Gita, many times could not
catch the meaning, many times could not catch the drift.
For what do you find in the Gita, and what in modern
commentators? One non-dualistic commentator takes up
an Upanishad ; there are so many dualistic passages, and
he twists and tortures them into some meaning, and
wants to bring them all into a meaning of his own. If
a dualistic commentator comes, there are so many non-
dualistic texts which he begins to torture, to bring them
all round to dualistic meaning. But you find in the Gita
there is no attempt at torturing any one of them. They
are all right, says the Lord ; for slowly and gradually the
human soul rises up and up, step after step, from the
gross to the fine, from the fine to the finer, until it reaches
the Absolute, the goal. That is what is in the Gita.
Even the Karma Kânda is taken up, and it is shown that
although it cannot give salvation direct, but only indirectly,
yet that is also valid ; images are valid indirectly ; ceremonies, forms, everything is valid only with one condition,
purity of the heart. For worship is valid and leads to

the goal if the heart is pure and the heart is sincere; and all these various modes of worship are necessary, else why should they be there? Religions and sects are not the work of hypocrites and wicked people who invented all these to get a little money, as some of our modern men want to think. However reasonable that explanation may seem, it is not true, and they were not invented that way at all. They are the outcome of the necessity of the human soul. They are all here to satisfy the hankering and thirst of different classes of human minds, and you need not preach against them. The day when that necessity will cease, they will vanish along with the cessation of that necessity; and so long as that necessity remains, they must be there in spite of your preaching, in spite of your criticism. You may bring the sword or the gun into play, you may deluge the world with human blood, but so long as there is a necessity for idols, they must remain. These forms, and all the various steps in religion will remain, and we understand from the Lord Shri Krishna why they should.

A rather sadder chapter of India's history comes now. In the Gita we already hear the distant sound of the conflicts of sects, and the Lord comes in the middle to harmonise them all; He, the great preacher of harmony, the greatest teacher of harmony, Lord Shri Krishna. He says, "In Me they are all strung like pearls upon a thread." We already hear the distant sounds, the murmurs of the conflict, and possibly there was a period of harmony and calmness, when it broke out anew, not only on religious grounds, but most possibly on caste grounds—the fight between the two powerful factors in our community, the kings and the priests. And from the topmost crest of the wave that deluged India for nearly a thousand years, we see another glorious figure, and that was our Gautama Shâkyamuni. You all know about his teachings and preachings. We worship him as God incarnate, the greatest, the boldest preacher of morality that the world ever saw, the greatest Karma-Yogi ; as disciple of himself, as it were, the same Krishna came to show how to make his theories practical. There came once again the same voice that in the Gita preached, "Even the least bit done of this religion saves from great fear". "Women, or Vaishyas, or even Shudras, all reach the highest goal." Breaking the bondages of all, the chains of all, declaring liberty to all to reach the highest goal, come the words of the Gita, rolls like thunder the mighty voice of Krishna: "Even in this life they have conquered relativity, whose minds are firmly fixed upon the sameness, for God is pure and the same to all, therefore such are said to be living in God." "Thus seeing the same Lord equally present everywhere, the sage does not injure the Self by the self, and thus reaches the highest goal." As it were to give a living example of this preaching, as it were to make at least one part of it practical, the preacher himself came in another form, and this was Shakyamuni, the preacher to the poor and the miserable, he who rejected even the language of the gods to speak in the language of the people, so that he might reach the hearts of the people, he who gave up a throne to live with beggars, and the poor, and the downcast, he who pressed the Pariah to his breast like a second Rama.

You all know about his great work, his grand character. But the work had one great defect, and for that we are suffering even today. No blame attaches to the Lord. He is pure and glorious, but unfortunately such high ideals could not be well assimilated by the different uncivilised and uncultured races of mankind who flocked within the fold of the Aryans. These races, with varieties of superstition and hideous worship, rushed within the fold of the Aryans and for a time appeared as if they had become civilised, but before a century had passed they brought out their snakes, their ghosts, and all the other things their ancestors used to worship, and thus the whole of India became one degraded mass of superstition. The earlier

Buddhists in their rage against the killing of animals had denounced the sacrifices of the Vedas; and these sacrifices used to be held in every house. There was a fire burning, and that was all the paraphernalia of worship. These sacrifices were obliterated, and in their place came gorgeous temples, gorgeous ceremonies, and gorgeous priests, and all that you see in India in modern times. I smile when I read books written by some modern people who ought to have known better, that the Buddha was the destroyer of Brahminical idolatry. Little do they know that Buddhism created Brahminism and idolatry in India.

There was a book written a year or two ago by a Russian gentleman, who claimed to have found out a very curious life of Jesus Christ, and in one part of the book he says that Christ went to the temple of Jagannâth to study with the Brahmins, but became disgusted with their exclusiveness and their idols, and so he went to the Lamas of Tibet instead, became perfect, and went home. To any man who knows anything about Indian history, that very statement proves that the whole thing was a fraud, because the temple of Jagannath is an old Buddhistic temple. We took this and others over and re-Hinduised them. We shall have to do many things like that yet. That is Jagannath, and there was not one Brahmin there then, and yet we are told that Jesus Christ came to study with the Brahmins there. So says our great Russian archaeologist.

Thus, in spite of the preaching of mercy to animals, in spite of the sublime ethical religion, in spite of the hair-splitting discussions about the existence or non-existence of a permanent soul, the whole building of Buddhism tumbled down piecemeal; and the ruin was simply hideous. I have neither the time nor the inclination to describe to you the hideousness that came in the wake of Buddhism. The most hideous ceremonies, the most horrible, the most obscene books that human hands ever wrote or the human brain ever conceived, the most bestial forms that ever passed under the name of religion, have all been the creation of degraded Buddhism.

But India has to live, and the spirit of the Lord descended again. He who declared, "I will come whenever virtue subsides", came again, and this time the manifestation was in the South, and up rose that young Brahmin of whom it has been declared that at the age of sixteen he had completed all his writings; the marvellous boy Shankarâchârya arose. The writings of this boy of sixteen are the wonders of the modern world, and so was the boy. He wanted to bring back the Indian world to its pristine purity, but think of the amount of the task before him. I have told you a few points about the state of things that existed in India. All these horrors that you are trying to reform are the outcome of that reign of degradation. The Tartars and the Baluchis and all the hideous races of mankind came to India and became Buddhists, and assimilated with us, and brought their national customs, and the whole of our national life became a huge page of the most horrible and the most bestial customs. That was the inheritance which that boy got from the Buddhists, and from that time to this, the whole work in India is a reconquest of this Buddhistic degradation by the Vedanta. It is still going on, it is not yet finished. Shankara came, a great philosopher, and showed that the real essence of Buddhism and that of the Vedanta are not very different, but that the disciples did not understand the Master and have degraded themselves, denied the existence of the soul and of God, and have become atheists. That was what Shankara showed, and all the Buddhists began to come back to the old religion. But then they had become accustomed to all these forms; what could be done?

Then came the brilliant Râmânuja. Shankara, with his great intellect, I am afraid, had not as great a heart. Ramanuja's heart was greater. He felt for the downtrodden, he sympathised with them. He took up the ceremonies, the accretions that had gathered, made them pure so far as they could be, and instituted new ceremonies, new methods of worship, for the people who absolutely required them. At the same time he opened the door to the highest spiritual worship from the Brahmin to the Pariah. That was Ramanuja's work. That work rolled on, invaded the North, was taken up by some great leaders there; but that was much later, during the Mohammedan rule; and the brightest of these prophets of comparatively modern times in the North was Chaitanya.

You may mark one characteristic since the time of Ramanuja—the opening of the door of spirituality to every one. That has been the watchword of all prophets succeeding Ramanuja, as it had been the watchword of all the prophets before Shankara. I do not know why Shankara should be represented as rather exclusive; I do not find anything in his writings which is exclusive. As in the case of the declarations of the Lord Buddha, this exclusiveness that has been attributed to Shankara's teachings is most possibly not due to his teachings, but to the incapacity of his disciples. This one great Northern sage, Chaitanya, represented the mad love of the Gopis. Himself a Brahmin, born of one of the most rationalistic families of the day, himself a professor of logic fighting and gaining a word-victory—for, this he had learnt from his childhood as the highest ideal of life and yet through the mercy of some sage the whole life of that man became changed; he gave up his fight, his quarrels, his professorship of logic and became one of the greatest teachers of Bhakti the world has ever known—mad Chaitanya. His Bhakti rolled over the whole land of Bengal, bringing solace to every one. His love knew no bounds. The saint or the sinner, the Hindu or the Mohammedan, the pure or the impure, the prostitute, the streetwalker—all had a share in his love, all had a share in his mercy; and even to the present day, although greatly degenerated, as

everything does become in time, his sect is the refuge of
the poor, of the downtrodden, of the outcast, of the
weak, of those who have been rejected by all society.
But at the same time I must remark for truth's sake that
we find this: In the philosophic sects we find wonderful
liberalism. There is not a man who follows Shankara who
will say that all the different sects of India are really
different. At the same time he was a tremendous up-
holder of exclusiveness as regards caste. But with every
Vaishnavite preacher we find a wonderful liberalism as to
the teaching of caste questions, but exclusiveness as regards
religious questions.

The one had a great head, the other a large heart,
and the time was ripe for one to be born, the embodiment
of both this head and heart; the time was ripe for one to
be born who in one body would have the brilliant intellect
of Shankara and the wonderfully expansive, infinite heart
of Chaitanya; one who would see in every sect the same
spirit working, the same God; one who would see God
in every being, one whose heart would weep for the poor,
for the weak, for the outcast, for the downtrodden, for
every one in this world, inside India or outside India ;
and at the same time whose grand brilliant intellect would
conceive of such noble thoughts as would harmonise all
conflicting sects, not only in India but outside of India,
and bring a marvellous harmony, the universal religion
of head and heart into existence. Such a man was born,
and I had the good fortune to sit at his feet for years.
The time was ripe, it was necessary that such a man
should be born, and he came; and the most wonderful
part of it was that his life's work was just near a city
which was full of Western thought, a city which had run
mad after these occidental ideas, a city which had
become more Europeanised than any other city in India.
There he lived, without any book-learning whatsoever;
this great intellect never learnt even to write his own

name,[1] but the most brilliant graduates of our university found in him an intellectual giant. He was a strange man, this Shri Ramakrishna Paramahamsa. It is a long, long story, and I have no time to tell anything about him tonight. Let me now only mention the great Shri Ramakrishna, the fulfilment of the Indian sages, the sage for the time, one whose .teaching is just now, in the present time, most beneficial. And mark the divine power working behind the man. The son of a poor priest, born in an out-of-the-way village, unknown and unthought of, today is worshipped literally by thousands in Europe and America, and tomorrow will be worshipped by thousands more. Who knows the plans of the Lord!

Now, my brothers, if you do not see the hand, the finger of Providence, it is because you are blind, born blind indeed. If time comes, and another opportunity, I will speak to you more fully about him. Only let me say now that if I have told you one word of truth, it was his and his alone, and if I have told you many things which were not true, which were not correct, which were not beneficial to the human race, they were all mine, and on me is the responsibility.

---

[1] Later research has shown that although Shri Ramakrishna was almost illiterate in the Western sense, he could read and write Bengali.

THE WORK BEFORE US

(Delivered at the Triplicane Literary Society, Madras)

The problem of life is becoming deeper and broader every day as the world moves on. The watchword and the essence have been preached in the days of yore when the Vedantic truth was first discovered, the solidarity of all life. One atom in this universe cannot move without dragging the whole world along with it. There cannot be any progress without the whole world following in the wake, and it is becoming every day clearer that the solution of any problem can never be attained on racial, or national, or narrow grounds. Every idea has to become broad till it covers the whole of this world, every aspiration must go on increasing till it has engulfed the whole of humanity, nay, the whole of life, within its scope. This will explain why our country for the last few centuries has not been what she was in the past. We find that one of the causes which led to this degeneration was the narrowing of our view, narrowing the scope of our actions.

Two curious nations there have been—sprung of the same race, but placed in different circumstances and environments, working out the problems of life each in its own particular way. I mean the ancient Hindu and the ancient Greek. The Indian Aryan—bounded on the north by the snow-caps of the Himalayas, with fresh-water rivers like rolling oceans surrounding him in the plains, with eternal forests which, to him, seemed to be the end of the world—turned his vision inward; and given the natural instinct, the superfine brain of the Aryan, with this sublime scenery surrounding him, the natural result was that he became introspective. The analysis of his own mind was the great theme of the Indo-Aryan. With the Greek, on the other hand, who arrived at a part of the earth which was more beautiful than sublime, the beautiful islands of the Grecian Archipelago, nature all around him generous yet simple— his mind naturally went outside. It wanted to analyse the external world. And as a result we find that from India have sprung all the analytical sciences, and from Greece all the sciences of generalisation. The Hindu mind went on in its own direction and produced the most marvellous results. Even at the present day, the logical capacity of the Hindus, and the tremendous power which the Indian brain still possesses, is beyond compare. We all know that our boys pitched against the boys of any other country triumph always. At the same time when the national vigour went, perhaps one or two centuries before the Mohammedan conquest of India, this national faculty became so much exaggerated that it degraded itself, and we find some of this degradation in everything in India, in art, in music, in sciences, in everything. In art, no more was there a broad conception, no more the symmetry of form and sublimity of conception, but the tremendous attempt at the ornate and florid style had arisen. The originality of the race seemed to have been lost. In music no more were there the soul-stirring ideas of the ancient Sanskrit music, no more did each note stand, as it were, on its own feet, and produce the marvellous harmony, but each note had lost its individuality. The whole of modern music is a jumble of notes, a confused mass of curves. That is a sign of degradation in music. So, if you analyse your idealistic conceptions, you will find the same attempt at ornate figures, and loss of originality. And even in religion, your special field, there came the most horrible degradations. What can you expect of a race which for hundreds of years has been busy in discussing such momentous problems as whether we should drink a glass of water with the right hand or the left? What more degradation can there

be than that the greatest minds of a country have been
discussing about the kitchen for several hundreds of years,
discussing whether I may touch you or you touch me, and
what is the penance for this touching! The themes of the
Vedanta, the sublimest and the most glorious conceptions
of God and soul ever preached on earth, were half-lost,
buried in the forests, preserved by a few Sannyâsins, while
the rest of the nation discussed the momentous questions
of touching each other, and dress, and food. The Mohammedan conquest gave us many good things, no doubt;
even the lowest man in the world can teach something to
the highest; at the same time it could not bring vigour
into the race. Then for good or evil, the English conquest
of India took place. Of course every conquest is bad, for
conquest is an evil, foreign government is an evil, no
doubt; but even through evil comes good sometimes, and
the great good of the English conquest is this: England,
nay the whole of Europe, has to thank Greece for its
civilisation. It is Greece that speaks through everything
in Europe. Every building, every piece of furniture has
the impress of Greece upon it; European science and art
are nothing but Grecian. Today the ancient Greek is
meeting ·the ancient Hindu on the soil of India. Thus
slowly and silently the leaven has come; the broadening,
the life-giving and the revivalist movement that we
see all around us has been worked out by these forces
together. A broader and more generous conception of life
is before us; and although at first we have been deluded
a little and wanted to narrow things down, we are finding
out today that these generous impulses which are at work,
these broader conceptions of life, are the logical interpretation of what is in our ancient books. They are the
carrying out, to the rigorously logical effect, of the primary
conceptions of our own ancestors. To become broad, to
go out, to amalgamate, to universalise, is the end of our
aims. And all the time we have been making ourselves

smaller and smaller, and dissociating ourselves, contrary to the plans laid down in our scriptures.

Several dangers are in the way, and one is that of the extreme conception that we are *the* people in the world. With all my love for India, and with all my patriotism and veneration for the ancients, I cannot but think that we have to learn many things from other nations. We must be always ready to sit at the feet of all, for, mark you, every one can teach us great lessons. Says our great law-giver, Manu: "Receive some good knowledge even from the low-born, and even from the man of lowest birth learn by service the road to heaven." We, therefore, as true children of Manu, must obey his commands and be ready to learn the lessons of this life or the life hereafter from any one who can teach us. At the same time we must not forget that we have also to teach a great lesson to the world. We cannot do without the world outside India ; it was our foolishness that we thought we could, and we have paid the penalty by about a thousand years of slavery. That we did not go out to compare things with other nations, did not mark the workings that have been all around us, has been the one great cause of this degradation of the Indian mind. We have paid the penalty ; let us do it no more. All such foolish ideas that Indians must not go out of India are childish. They must be knocked on the head ; the more you go out and travel among the nations of the world, the better for you and for your country. If you had done that for hundreds of years past, you would not be here today at the feet of every nation that wants to rule India. The first manifest effect of life is expansion. You must expand if you want to live. The moment you have ceased to expand, death is upon you, danger is ahead. I went to America and Europe, to which you so kindly allude; I have to, because that is the first sign of the revival of national life, expansion. This reviving national life, expanding inside, threw me off, and thousands will be thrown off in that way. Mark my words, it has got to come if this nation lives at all. This question, therefore, is the greatest of the signs of the revival of national life, and through this expansion our quota of offering to the general mass of human knowledge, our contribution to the general upheaval of the world, is going out to the external world.

Again, this is not a new thing. Those of you who think that the Hindus have been always confined within the four walls of their country through all ages, are entirely mistaken ; you have not studied the old books, you have not studied the history of the race aright if you think so. Each nation must give in order to live. When you give life, you will have life ; when you receive, you must pay for it by giving to all others; and that we have been living for so many thousands of years is a fact that stares us in the face, and the solution that remains is that we have been always giving to the outside world, whatever the ignorant may think. But the gift of India is the gift of religion and philosophy, and wisdom and spirituality. And religion does not want cohorts to march before its path and clear its way. Wisdom and philosophy do not want to be carried on floods of blood. Wisdom and philosophy do not march upon bleeding human bodies, do not march with violence but come on the wings of peace and love, and that has always been so. Therefore we had to give. I was asked by a young lady in London, "What have you Hindus done ? You have never even conquered a single nation." That is true from the point of view of the Englishman, the brave, the heroic, the Kshatriya—conquest is the greatest glory that one man can have over another. That is true from his point of view, but from ours it is quite the opposite. If I ask myself what has been the cause of India's greatness, I answer, because we have never conquered. That is our glory. You are hearing every day, and sometimes, I am sorry to say, from men who ought to know better, denunciations of our religion, because it is not at all a conquering religion. To my mind that is the argument why our religion is truer than any other religion, because it never conquered, because it never shed blood, because its mouth always shed on all, words of blessing, of peace, words of love and sympathy. It is here and here alone that the ideals of toleration were first preached. And it is here and here alone that toleration and sympathy have become practical ; it is theoretical in every other country ; it is here and here alone, that the Hindu builds mosques for the Mohammedans and churches for the Christians.

So, you see, our message has gone out to the world many a time, but slowly, silently, unperceived. It is on a par with everything in India. The one characteristic of Indian thought is its silence, its calmness. At the same time the tremendous power that is behind it is never expressed by violence. It is always the silent mesmerism of Indian thought. If a foreigner takes up our literature to study, at first it is disgusting to him ; there is not the same stir, perhaps, the same amount of go that rouses him instantly. Compare the tragedies of Europe with our tragedies. The one is full of action, that rouses you for the moment, but when it is over there comes the reaction, and everything is gone, washed off as it were from your brains. Indian tragedies are like the mesmerist's power, quiet, silent, but as you go on studying them they fascinate you ; you cannot move ; you are bound ; and whoever has dared to touch our literature has felt the bondage, and is there bound for ever. Like the gentle dew that falls unseen and unheard, and yet brings into blossom the fairest of roses, has been the contribution of India to the thought of the world. Silent, unperceived, yet omnipotent in its effect, it has revolutionised the thought of the world, yet nobody knows when it did so. It was once remarked to me,. "How difficult it is to ascertain the name of any writer in India", to which I replied, "That is the Indian idea." Indian writers are not like modern writers who steal ninety per cent of their ideas from other authors, while only ten per cent is their own, and they take care to write a preface in which they say, "For these ideas I am responsible". Those great master minds producing momentous results in the hearts of mankind were content to write their books without even putting their names, and to die quietly, leaving the books to posterity. Who knows the writers of our philosophy, who knows the writers of our Purânas ? They all pass under the generic name of Vyâsa, and Kapila, and so on. They have been true children of Shri Krishna. They have been true followers of the Gita; they practically carried out the great mandate, "To work you have the right, but not to the fruits thereof."

Thus India is working upon the world, but one condition is necessary. Thoughts like merchandise can only run through channels made by somebody. Roads have to be made before even thought can travel from one place to another, and whenever in the history of the world a great conquering nation has arisen, linking the different parts of the world together, then has poured through these channels the thought of India and thus entered into the veins of every race. Before even the Buddhists were born, there are evidences accumulating every day that Indian thought penetrated the world. Before Buddhism, Vedanta had penetrated into China, into Persia, and the Islands of the Eastern Archipelago. Again when the mighty mind of the Greek had linked the different parts of the Eastern world together there came Indian thought ; and Christianity with all its boasted civilisation is but a collection of little bits of Indian thought. Ours is the religion of which Buddhism with all its greatness is a rebel child, and of which Christianity is a very patchy imitation. One of these cycles has again arrived. There is the tremendous power of England which has linked the different parts of the world together. English roads no more are content like Roman roads to run over lands, but they have also ploughed the

deep in all directions. From ocean to ocean run the roads
of England. Every part of the world has been linked to
every other part, and electricity plays a most marvellous
part as the new messenger. Under all these circumstances
we find again India reviving and ready to give her own
quota to the progress and civilisation of the world. And
that I have been forced, as it were, by nature, to go over
and preach to America and England is the result. Every
one of us ought to have seen that the time had arrived.
Everything looks propitious, and Indian thought, philosophical and spiritual, must once more go over and
conquer the world. The problem before us, therefore, is
assuming larger proportions every day. It is not only that
we must revive our own country—that is a small matter ;
I am an imaginative man—and my idea is the conquest
of the whole world by the Hindu race.

There have been great conquering races in the world.
We also have been great conquerors. The story of our
conquest has been described by that noble Emperor of
India, Asoka, as the conquest of religion and of spirituality.
Once more the world must be conquered by India. This
is the dream of my life, and I wish that each one of you
who hear me today will have the same dream in your
minds, and stop not till you have realised the dream. They
will tell you every day that we had better look to our own
homes first and then go to work outside. But I will tell
you in plain language that you work best when you work
for others. The best work that you ever did for yourselves
was when you worked for others, trying to disseminate
your ideas in foreign languages beyond the seas, and this
very meeting is proof how the attempt to enlighten other
countries with your thoughts is helping your own country.
One-fourth of the effect that has been produced in this
country by my going to England and America would not
have been brought about, had I confined my ideas only to
India. This is the great ideal before us, and every one

must be ready for it—the conquest of the whole world by
India—nothing less than that, and we must all get ready
for it, strain every nerve for it. Let foreigners come and
flood the land with their armies, never mind. Up, India,
and conquer the world with your spirituality! Ay, as
has been declared on this soil first, love must conquer
hatred, hatred cannot conquer itself. Materialism and all
its miseries can never be conquered by materialism. Armies
when they attempt to conquer armies only multiply and
make brutes of humanity. Spirituality must conquer the
West. Slowly they are finding out that what they want is
spirituality to preserve them as nations. They are waiting
for it, they are eager for it. Where is the supply to come
from? Where are the men ready to go out to every
country in the world with the messages of the great sages
of India ? Where are the men who are ready to sacrifice
everything, so that this message shall reach every corner
of the world? Such heroic souls are wanted to help the
spread of truth. Such heroic workers are wanted to go
abroad and help to disseminate the great truths of the
Vedanta. The world wants it ; without it the world will
be destroyed. The whole of the Western world is on a
volcano which may burst tomorrow, go to pieces tomorrow. They have searched every corner of the world
and have found no respite. They have drunk deep of the
cup of pleasure and found it vanity. Now is the time to
work so that India's spiritual ideas· may penetrate deep
into the West. Therefore young men of Madras, I specially
ask you to remember this. We must go out, we must
conquer the world through our spirituality and philosophy.
There is no other alternative, we must do it or die. The
only condition of national life, of awakened and vigorous
national life, is the conquest of the world by Indian thought.

At the same time we must not forget that what I mean
by the conquest of the world by spiritual thought is the
sending out of the life-giving principles, not the hundreds

of superstitions that we have been hugging to our breasts
for centuries. These have to be weeded out even on this
soil, and thrown aside, so that they may die for ever. These
are the causes of the degradation of the race and will lead
to softening of the brain. That brain which cannot think
high and noble thoughts, which has lost all power of
originality, which has lost all vigour, that brain which is
always poisoning itself with all sorts of little superstitions
passing under the name of religion, we must beware of.
In our sight, here in India, there are several dangers. Of
these, the two, Scylla and Charybdis, rank materialism and
its opposite arrant superstition, must be avoided. There
is the man today who after drinking the cup of Western
wisdom, thinks that he knows everything. He laughs at
the ancient sages. All Hindu thought to him is arrant
trash—philosophy mere child's prattle, and religion the
superstition of fools. On the other hand, there is the man
educated, but a sort of monomaniac, who runs to the other
extreme and wants to explain the omen of this and that.
He has philosophical and metaphysical, and Lord knows
what other puerile explanations for every superstition that
belongs to his peculiar race, or his peculiar gods, or his
peculiar village. Every little village superstition is to him
a mandate of the Vedas, and upon the carrying out of it,
according to him, depends the national life. You must
beware of this. I would rather see every one of you rank
atheists than superstitious fools, for the atheist is alive and
you can make something out of him. But if superstition
enters, the brain is gone, the brain is softening, degradation has seized upon the life. Avoid these two. Brave, bold
men, these are what we want. What we want is vigour in
the blood, strength in the nerves, iron muscles and nerves
of steel, not softening namby-pamby ideas. Avoid all
these. Avoid all mystery. There is no mystery in religion.
Is there any mystery in the Vedanta, or in the Vedas, or in
the Samhitâs, or in the Puranas? What secret societies did

the sages of yore establish to preach their religion? What sleight-of-hand tricks are there recorded as used by them to bring their grand truths to humanity? Mystery mongering and superstition are always signs of weakness. These are always signs of degradation and of death. Therefore beware of them; be strong, and stand on your own feet. Great things are there, most marvellous things. We may call them supernatural things so far as our ideas of nature go, but not one of these things is a mystery. It was never preached on this soil that the truths of religion were mysteries or that they were the property of secret societies sitting on the snow-caps of the Himalayas. I have been in the Himalayas. You have not been there ; it is several hundreds of miles from your homes. I am a Sannyâsin, and I have been for the last fourteen years on my feet. These mysterious societies do not exist anywhere. Do not run after these superstitions. Better for you and for the race that you become rank atheists, because you would have strength, but these are degradation and death. Shame on humanity that strong men should spend their time on these superstitions, spend all their time in inventing allegories to explain the most rotten superstitions of the world. Be bold ; do not try to explain everything that way. The fact is that we have many superstitions, many bad spots and sores on our body—these have to be excised, cut off, and destroyed—but these do not destroy our religion, our national life, our spirituality. Every principle of religion is safe, and the sooner these black spots are purged away, the better the principles will shine, the more gloriously. Stick to them.

You hear claims made by every religion as being the universal religion of the world. Let me tell you in the first place that perhaps there never will be such a thing, but if there is a religion which can lay claim to be that, it is only our religion and no other, because every other religion depends on some person or persons. All the other religions

have been built round the life of what they think a historical man; and what they think the strength of religion is
really the weakness, for disprove the historicity of the man
and the whole fabric tumbles to the ground. Half the lives
of these great founders of religions have been broken into
pieces, and the other half doubted very seriously. As such,
every truth that had its sanction only in their words vanishes into air. But the truths of our religion, although we have
persons by the score, do not depend upon them. The
glory of Krishna is not that he was Krishna, but that he was
the great teacher of Vedanta. If he had not been so, his
name would have died out of India in the same way as the
name of Buddha has done. Thus our allegiance is to the
principles always, and not to the persons. Persons are but
the embodiments, the illustrations of the principles. If the
principles are there, the persons will come by the thousands
and millions. If the principle is safe, persons like Buddha
will be born by the hundreds and thousands. But if the
principle is lost and forgotten and the whole of national
life tries to cling round a so-called historical person, woe
unto that religion, danger unto that religion! Ours is the
only religion that does not depend on a person or persons;
it is based upon principles. At the same time there is room
for millions of persons. There is ample ground for introducing persons, but each one of them must be an illustration of the principles. We must not forget that. These
principles of our religion are all safe, and it should be the
life-work of every one of us to keep them safe, and to keep
them free from the accumulating dirt and dust of ages. It
is strange that in spite of the degradation that seized upon
the race again and again, these principles of the Vedanta
were never tarnished. No one, however wicked, ever
dared to throw dirt upon them. Our scriptures are the best
preserved scriptures in the world. Compared to other
books there have been no interpolations, no text-torturing,
no destroying of the essence of the thought in them. It is

there just as it was first, directing the human mind towards the ideal, the goal.

You find that these texts have been commented upon by different commentators, preached by great teachers, and sects founded upon them; and you find that in these books of the Vedas there are various apparently contradictory ideas. There are certain texts which are entirely dualistic, others are entirely monistic. The dualistic commentator, knowing no better, wishes to knock the monistic texts on the head. Preachers and priests want to explain them in the dualistic meaning. The monistic commentator serves the dualistic texts in a similar fashion. Now this is not the fault of the Vedas. It is foolish to attempt to prove that the whole of the Vedas is dualistic. It is equally foolish to attempt to prove that the whole of the Vedas is non-dualistic. They are dualistic and non-dualistic both. We understand them better today in the light of newer ideas. These are but different conceptions leading to the final conclusion that both dualistic and monistic conceptions are necessary for the evolution of the mind, and therefore the Vedas preach them. In mercy to the human race the Vedas show the various steps to the higher goal. Not that they are contradictory, vain words used by the Vedas to delude children; they are necessary not only for children, but for many a grown-up man. So long as we have a body and so long as we are deluded by the idea of our identity with the body, so long as we have five senses and see the external world, we must have a Personal God. For if we have all these ideas, we must take as the great Râmânuja has proved, all the ideas about God and nature and the individualised soul; when you take the one you have to take the whole triangle—we cannot avoid it. Therefore as long as you see the external world, to avoid a Personal God and a personal soul is arrant lunacy. But there may be times in the lives of sages when the human mind transcends as it were its own limitations, when man goes even beyond nature, to the realm of which the Shruti declares, "whence words fall back with the mind without reaching it"; "There the eyes cannot reach nor speech nor mind"; "We cannot say that we know it, we cannot say that we do not know it" There the human soul transcends all limitations, and then and then alone flashes into the human soul the conception of monism: I and the whole universe are one; I and Brahman are one. And this conclusion you will find has not only been reached through knowledge and philosophy, but parts of it through the power of love. You read in the *Bhâgavata*, when Krishna disappeared and the Gopis bewailed his disappearance, that at last the thought of Krishna became so prominent in their minds that each one forgot her own body and thought she was Krishna, and began to decorate herself and to play as he did. We understand, therefore, that this identity comes even through love. There was an ancient Persian Sufi poet, and one of his poems says, "I came to the Beloved and beheld the door was closed; I knocked at the door and from inside a voice came, 'Who is there?' I replied, 'I am'. The door did not open. A second time I came and knocked at the door and the same voice asked, 'Who is there?' 'I am so-and-so.' The door did not open. A third time I came and the same voice asked, 'Who is there?' 'I am Thyself, my Love', and the door opened."

There are, therefore, many stages, and we need not quarrel about them even if there have been quarrels among the ancient commentators, whom all of us ought to revere; for there is no limitation to knowledge, there is no omniscience exclusively the property of any one in ancient or modern times. If there have been sages and Rishis in the past, be sure that there will be many now. If there have been Vyâsas and Vâlmikis and Shankarâchâryas in ancient times, why may not each one of you become a Shankaracharya? This is another point of our religion that you must always remember, that in all other scriptures inspiration is quoted as their authority, but this inspiration is limited to a very few persons, and through them the truth came to the masses, and we have all to obey them. Truth came to Jesus of Nazareth, and we must all obey him. But the truth came to the Rishis of India —the Mantra-drashtâs, the seers of thought—and will come to all Rishis in the future, not to talkers, not to book-swallowers, not to scholars, not to philologists, but to seers of thought. The Self is not to be reached by too much talking, not even by the highest intellects, not even by the study of the scriptures. The scriptures themselves say so. Do you find in any other scripture such a bold assertion as that—not even by the study of the Vedas will you reach the Âtman? You must open your heart. Religion is not going to church, or putting marks on the forehead, or dressing in a peculiar fashion; you may paint yourselves in all the colours of the rainbow, but if the heart has not been opened, if you have not realised God, it is all vain. If one has the colour of the heart, he does not want any external colour. That is the true religious realisation. We must not forget that colours and all these things are good so far as they help; so far they are all welcome. But they are apt to degenerate and instead of helping they retard, and a man identifies religion with externalities. Going to the temple becomes tantamount to spiritual life. Giving something to a priest becomes tantamount to religious life. These are dangerous and pernicious, and should be at once checked. Our scriptures declare again and again that even the knowledge of the external senses is not religion. That is religion which makes us realise the Unchangeable One, and that is the religion for every one. He who realises transcendental truth, he who realises the Atman in his own nature, he who comes face to face with God, sees God alone in everything, has become a Rishi. And there is no religious life for you until you have become a Rishi. Then alone religion begins for you, now is only the preparation. Then religion dawns upon you, now you are only undergoing intellectual gymnastics and physical tortures.

We must, therefore, remember that our religion lays down distinctly and clearly that every one who wants salvation must pass through the stage of Rishihood—must become a Mantra-drashta, must see God. That is salvation; that is the law laid down by our scriptures. Then it becomes easy to look into the scripture with our own eyes, understand the meaning for ourselves, to analyse just what we want, and to understand the truth for ourselves. This is what has to be done. At the same time we must pay all reverence to the ancient sages for their work. They were great, these ancients, but we want to be greater. They did great work in the past, but we must do greater work than they. They had hundreds of Rishis in ancient India. We will have millions—we are going to have, and the sooner every one of you believes in this, the better for India and the better for the world. Whatever you believe, that you will be. If you believe yourselves to be sages, sages you will be tomorrow. There is nothing to obstruct you. For if there is one common doctrine that runs through all our apparently fighting and contradictory sects, it is that all glory, power, and purity are within the soul already; only according to Ramanuja, the soul contracts and expands at times, and according to Shankara, it comes under a delusion. Never mind these differences. All admit the truth that the power is there—potential or manifest it is there—and the sooner you believe that, the better for you. All power is within you; you can do anything and everything. Believe in that, do not believe that you are weak; do not believe that you are half-crazy lunatics, as most of us do nowadays. You can do anything and everything without even the guidance of any one. All power is there. Stand up and express the divinity within you.

THE FUTURE OF INDIA

This is the ancient land where wisdom made its home before it went into any other country, the same India whose influx of spirituality is represented, as it were, on the material plane, by rolling rivers like oceans, where the eternal Himalayas, rising tier above tier with their snow-caps, look as it were into the very mysteries of heaven. Here is the same India whose soil has been trodden by the feet of the greatest sages that ever lived. Here first sprang up inquiries into the nature of man and into the internal world. Here first arose the doctrines of the immortality of the soul, the existence of a supervising God, an immanent God in nature and in man, and here the highest ideals of religion and philosophy have attained their culminating points. This is the land from whence, like the tidal waves, spirituality and philosophy have again and again rushed out and deluged the world, and this is the land from whence once more such tides must proceed in order to bring life and vigour into the decaying races of mankind. It is the same India which has withstood the shocks of centuries, of hundreds of foreign invasions, of hundreds of upheavals of manners and customs. It is the same land which stands firmer than any rock in the world, with its undying vigour, indestructible life. Its life is of the same nature as the soul, without beginning and without end, immortal; and we are the children of such a country.

Children of India, I am here to speak to you today about some practical things, and my object in reminding you about the glories of the past is simply this. Many times have I been told that looking into the past only degenerates and leads to nothing, and that we should look to the future. That is true. But out of the past is built

the future. Look back, therefore, as far as you can, drink
deep of the eternal fountains that are behind, and after
that, look forward, march forward and make India brighter,
greater, much higher than she ever was. Our ancestors
were great. We must first recall that. We must learn the
elements of our being, the blood that courses in our veins;
we must have faith in that blood and what it did in the
past; and out of that faith and consciousness of past
greatness, we must build an India yet greater than what
she has been. There have been periods of decay and
degradation. I do not attach much importance to them;
we all know that. Such periods have been necessary. A
mighty tree produces a beautiful ripe fruit. That fruit falls
on the ground, it decays and rots, and out of that decay
springs the root and the future tree, perhaps mightier than
the first one. This period of decay through which we have
passed was all the more necessary. Out of this decay is
coming the India of the future ; it is sprouting, its first
leaves are already out; and a mighty, gigantic tree, the
Urdhvamula, is here, already beginning to appear; and it is
about that that I am going to speak to you.

The problems in India are more complicated, more
momentous, than the problems in any other country.
Race, religion, language, government—all these together
make a nation. The elements which compose the nations
of the world are indeed very few, taking race after race,
compared to this country. Here have been the Aryan, the
Dravidian, the Tartar, the Turk, the Mogul, the European
—all the nations of the world, as it were, pouring their
blood into this land. Of languages the most wonderful
conglomeration is here ; of manners and customs there is
more difference between two Indian races than between
the European and the Eastern races.

The one common ground that we have is our sacred
tradition, our religion. That is the only common ground,
and upon that we shall have to build. In Europe, political

THE FUTURE OF INDIA

ideas form the national unity. In Asia, religious ideals form the national unity. The unity in religion, therefore, is absolutely necessary as the first condition of the future of India. There must be the recognition of one religion throughout the length and breadth of this land. What do I mean by one religion? Not in the sense of one religion as held among the Christians, or the Mohammedans, or the Buddhists. We know that our religion has certain common grounds, common to all our sects, however varying their conclusions may be, however different their claims may be. So there are certain common grounds; and within their limitation this religion of ours admits of a marvellous variation, an infinite amount of liberty to think and live our own lives. We all know that, at least those of us who have thought; and what we want is to bring out these life-giving common principles of our religion, and let every man, woman, and child, throughout .the length and breadth of this country, understand them, know them, and try to bring them out in their lives. This is the first step; and, therefore, it has to be taken.

We see how in Asia, and especially in India, race difficulties, linguistic difficulties, social difficulties, national difficulties, all melt away before this unifying power of religion. We know that to the Indian mind there is nothing higher than religious ideals, that this is the key-note of Indian life, and we can only work in the line of least resistance. It is not only true that the ideal of religion is the highest ideal; in the case of India it is the only possible means of work; work in any other line, without first strengthening this, would be disastrous. Therefore the first plank in the making of a future India, the first step that is to be hewn out of that rock of ages, is this unification of religion. All of us have to be taught that we Hindus—dualists, qualified monists, or monists, Shaivas, Vaishnavas, or Pâshupatas—to whatever denomination we may belong, have certain common ideas

behind us, and that the time has come when for the well-
being of ourselves, for the well-being of our race, we must
give up all our little quarrels and differences. Be sure, these
quarrels are entirely wrong; they are condemned by our
scriptures, forbidden by our forefathers; and those great
men from whom we claim our descent, whose blood is
in our veins, look down with contempt on their children
quarrelling about minute differences.

With the giving up of quarrels all other improvements will come. When the life-blood is strong and pure,
no disease germ can live in that body. Our life-blood is
spirituality. If it flows clear, if it flows strong and pure
and vigorous, everything is right; political, social, any
other material defects, even the poverty of the land, will
all be cured if that blood is pure. For if the disease germ
be thrown out, nothing will be able to enter into the blood.
To take a simile from modern medicine, we know that
there must be two causes to produce a disease, some
poison germ outside, and the state of the body. Until the
body is in a state to admit the germs, until the body is
degraded to a lower vitality so that the germs may enter
and thrive and multiply, there is no power in any germ
in the world to produce a disease in the body. In fact,
millions of germs are continually passing through everyone's body; but so long as it is vigorous, it never is
conscious of them. It is only when the body is weak that
these germs take possession of it and produce disease.
Just so with the national life. It is when the national body
is weak that all sorts of disease germs, in the political
state of the race or in its social state, in its educational
or intellectual state, crowd into the system and produce
disease. To remedy it, therefore, we must go to the root
of this disease and cleanse the blood of all impurities.
The one tendency will be to strengthen the man, to make
the blood pure, the body vigorous, so that it will be able
to resist and throw off all external poisons.

We have seen that our vigour, our strength, nay, our national life is in our religion. I am not going to discuss now whether it is right or not, whether it is correct or not, whether it is beneficial or not in the long run, to have this vitality in religion, but for good or evil it is there; you cannot get out of it, you have it now and for ever, and you have to stand by it, even if you have not the same faith that I have in our religion. You are bound by it, and if you give it up, you are smashed to pieces. That is the life of our race and that must be strengthened. You have withstood the shocks of centuries simply because you took great care of it, you sacrificed everything else for it. Your forefathers underwent everything boldly, even death itself, but preserved their religion. Temple after temple was broken down by the foreign conqueror, but no sooner had the wave passed than the spire of the temple rose up again. Some of these old temples of Southern India and those like Somnâth of Gujarat will teach you volumes of wisdom, will give you a keener insight into the history of the race than any amount of books. Mark how these temples bear the marks of a hundred attacks and a hundred regenerations, continually destroyed and continually springing up out of the ruins, rejuvenated and strong as ever! That is the national mind, that is the national life-current. Follow it and it leads to glory. Give it up and you die; death will be the only result, annihilation the only effect, the moment you step beyond that life-current. I do not mean to say that other things are not necessary. I do not mean to say that political or social improvements are not necessary, but what I mean is this, and I want you to bear it in mind, that they are secondary here and that religion is primary. The Indian mind is first religious, then anything else. So this is to be strengthened, and how to do it? I will lay before you my ideas. They have been in my mind for a long time, even years before I left the shores of

Madras for America, and that I went to America and
England was simply for propagating those ideas. I did
not care at all for the Parliament of Religions or anything
else; it was simply an opportunity ; for it was really those
ideas of mine that took me all over the world.

My idea is first of all to bring out the gems of
spirituality that are stored up in our books and in the
possession of a few only, hidden, as it were, in monasteries
and in forests—to bring them out; to bring the knowledge
out of them, not only from the hands where it is hidden,
but from the still more inaccessible chest, the language
in which it is preserved, the incrustation of centuries
of Sanskrit words. In one word, I want to make them
popular. I want to bring out these ideas and let them be
the common property of all, of every man in India, whether
he knows the Sanskrit language or not. The great difficulty
in the way is the Sanskrit language—the glorious language
of ours; and this difficulty cannot be removed until—if
it is possible—the whole of our nation are good Sanskrit
scholars. You will understand the difficulty when I tell
you that I have been studying this language all my life,
and yet every new book is new to me. How much more
difficult would it then be for people who never had time to
study the language thoroughly! Therefore the ideas must
be taught in the language of the people ; at the same time,
Sanskrit education must go on along with it, because the
very sound of Sanskrit words gives a prestige and a power
and a strength to the race. The attempts of the great
Râmânuja and of Chaitanya and of Kabir to raise the lower
classes of India show that marvellous results were attained
during the lifetime of those great prophets; yet the later
failures have to be explained, and cause shown why the
effect of their teachings stopped almost within a century
of the passing away of these great Masters. The secret is
here. They raised the lower classes ; they had all the
wish that these should come up, but they did not apply

their energies to the spreading of the Sanskrit language among the masses. Even the great Buddha made one false step when he stopped the Sanskrit language from being studied by the masses. He wanted rapid and immediate results, and translated and preached in the language of the day, Pâli. That was grand ; he spoke in the language of the people, and the people understood him. That was great ; it spread the ideas quickly and made them reach far and wide. But along with that, Sanskrit ought to have spread. Knowledge came, but the prestige was not there, culture was not there. It is culture that withstands shocks, not a simple mass of knowledge. You can put a mass of knowledge into the world, but that will not do it much good. There must come culture into the blood. We all know in modern times of nations which have masses of knowledge, but what of them? They are like tigers, they are like savages, because culture is not there. Knowledge is only skin-deep, as civilisation is, and a little scratch brings out the old savage. Such things happen; this is the danger. Teach the masses in the vernaculars, give them ideas; they will get information, but something more is necessary; give them culture. Until you give them that, there can be no permanence in the raised condition of the masses. There will be another caste created, having the advantage of the Sanskrit language, which will quickly get above the rest and rule them all the same. The only safety, I tell you men who belong to the lower castes, the only way to raise your condition is to study Sanskrit, and this fighting and writing and frothing against the higher castes is in vain, it does no good, and it creates fight and quarrel, and this race, unfortunately already divided, is going to be divided more and more. The only way to bring about the levelling of caste is to appropriate the culture, the education which is the strength of the higher castes. That done, you have what you want.

In connection with this I want to discuss one question

which has a particular bearing with regard to Madras. There is a theory that there was a race of mankind in Southern India called Dravidians, entirely differing from another race in Northern India called the Aryans, and that the Southern India Brâhmins are the only Aryans that came from the North, the other men of Southern India belong to an entirely different caste and race to those of Southern India Brahmins. Now I beg your pardon, Mr. Philologist, this is entirely unfounded. The only proof of it is that there is a difference of language between the North and the South. I do not see any other difference. We are so many Northern men here, and I ask my European friends to pick out the Northern and Southern men from this assembly. Where is the difference? A little difference of language. But the Brahmins are a race that came here speaking the Sanskrit language! Well then, they took up the Dravidian language and forgot their Sanskrit. Why should not the other castes have done the same? Why should not all the other castes have come one after the other from Northern India, taken up the Dravidian language, and so forgotten their own? That is an argument working both ways. Do not believe in such silly things. There may have been a Dravidian people who vanished from here, and the few who remained lived in forests and other places. It is quite possible that the language may have been taken up, but all these are Aryans who came from the North. The whole of India is Aryan, nothing else.

Then there is the other idea that the Shudra caste are surely the aborigines. What are they? They are slaves. They say history repeats itself. The Americans, English, Dutch, and the Portuguese got hold of the poor Africans and made them work hard while they lived, and their children of mixed birth were born in slavery and kept in that condition for a long period. From that wonderful example, the mind jumps back several thousand years

THE FUTURE OF INDIA

and fancies that the same thing happened here, and our archaeologist dreams of India being full of dark-eyed aborigines, and the bright Aryan came from—the Lord knows where. According to some, they came from Central Tibet, others will have it that they came from Central Asia. There are patriotic Englishmen who think that the Aryans were all red-haired. Others, according to their idea, think that they were all black-haired. If the writer happens to be a black-haired man, the Aryans were all black-haired. Of late, there was an attempt made to prove that the Aryans lived on the Swiss lakes. I should not be sorry if they had been all drowned there, theory and all. Some say now that they lived at the North Pole. Lord bless the Aryans and their habitations! As for the truth of these theories, there is not one word in our scriptures, not one, to prove that the Aryan ever came from anywhere outside of India, and in ancient India was included Afghanistan. There it ends. And the theory that the Shudra caste were all non-Aryans and they were a multitude, is equally illogical and equally irrational. It could not have been possible in those days that a few Aryans settled and lived there with a hundred thousand slaves at their command. These slaves would have eaten them up, made "chutney" of them in five minutes. The only explanation is to be found in the Mahâbhârata, which says that in the beginning of the Satya Yuga there was one caste, the Brahmins, and then by difference of occupations they went on dividing themselves into different castes, and that is the only true and rational explanation that has been given. And in the coming Satya Yuga all the other castes will have to go back to the same condition.

The solution of the caste problem in India, therefore, assumes this form, not to degrade the higher castes, not to crush out the Brahmin. The Brahminhood is the ideal of humanity in India, as wonderfully put forward by Shankarâchârya at the beginning of his commentary on the Gitâ, where he speaks about the reason for Krishna's coming as a preacher for the preservation of Brahminhood, of Brahminness. That was the great end. This Brahmin, the man of God, he who has known Brahman, the ideal man, the perfect man, must remain; he must not go. And with all the defects of the caste now, we know that we must all be ready to give to the Brahmins this credit, that from them have come more men with real Brahminness in them than from all the other castes. That is true. That is the credit due to them from all the other castes. We must be bold enough, must be brave enough to speak of their defects, but at the same time we must give the credit that is due to them. Remember the old English proverb, "Give every man his due". Therefore, my friends, it is no use fighting among the castes. What good will it do? It will divide us all the more, weaken us all the more, degrade us all the more. The days of exclusive privileges and exclusive claims are gone, gone for ever from the soil of India, and it is one of the great blessings of the British Rule in India. Even to the Mohammedan Rule we owe that great blessing, the destruction of exclusive privilege. That Rule was, after all, not all bad; nothing is all bad, and nothing is all good. The Mohammedan conquest of India came as a salvation to the downtrodden, to the poor. That is why one-fifth of our people have become Mohammedans. It was not the sword that did it all. It would be the height of madness to think it was all the work of sword and fire. And one-fifth—one-half—of your Madras people will become Christians if you do not take care. Was there ever a sillier thing before in the world than what I saw in Malabar country? The poor Pariah is not allowed to pass through the same street as the high-caste man, but if he changes his name to a hodge-podge English name, it is all right; or to a Mohammedan name, it is all right. What inference would you draw except that these Malabaris are all lunatics, their

Ramakrishna Vedanta Centre
Blind Lane
Bourne End
Buckinghamshire
SL8 5LF

Ramakrishna Vedanta Centre
Telephone: 01628 526464

Vedanta Books: Sri Ramakrishna, Sri Sarada
Devi, Swami Vivekananda, Upanishads,
Bhagavad Gita, Shankaracharya, Philosophy
of India, Meditation, and Spiritual Life

Please send me your book list and information
on Vedanta.
Name:
Address:

homes so many lunatic asylums, and that they are to be treated with derision by every race in India until they mend their manners and know better. Shame upon them that such wicked and diabolical customs are allowed ; their own children are allowed to die of starvation, but as soon as they take up some other religion they are well fed. There ought to be no more fight between the castes.

The solution is not by bringing down the higher, but by raising the lower up to the level of the higher. And that is the line of work that is found in all our books, in spite of what you may hear from some people whose knowledge of their own scriptures and whose capacity to understand the mighty plans of the ancients are only zero. They do not understand, but those do that have brains, that have the intellect to grasp the whole scope of the work. They stand aside and follow the wonderful procession of national life through the ages. They can trace it step by step through all the books, ancient and modern. What is the plan? The ideal at one end is the Brahmin and the ideal at the other end is the Chandâla, and the whole work is to raise the Chandala up to the Brahmin. Slowly and slowly you find more and more privileges granted to them. There are books where you read such fierce words as these: "If the Shudra hears the Vedas, fill his ears with molten lead, and if he remembers a line, cut his tongue out. If he says to the Brahmin, 'You Brahmin', cut his tongue out". This is diabolical old barbarism no doubt ; that goes without saying; but do not blame the law-givers, who simply record the customs of some section of the community. Such devils sometimes arose among the ancients. There have been devils everywhere more or less in all ages. Accordingly, you will find that later on, this tone is modified a little, as for instance, "Do not disturb the Shudras, but do not teach them higher things". Then gradually we find in other Smritis, especially in those that have full power now, that if the Shudras imitate the manners and customs of the Brahmins they do well, they ought to be encouraged. Thus it is going on. I have no time to place before you all these workings, nor how they can be traced in detail ; but coming to plain facts, we find that all the castes are to rise slowly and slowly. There are thousands of castes, and some are even getting admission into Brahminhood, for what prevents any caste from declaring they are Brahmins? Thus caste, with all its rigour, has been created in that manner. Let us suppose that there are castes here with ten thousand people in each. If these put their heads together and say, we will call ourselves Brahmins, nothing can stop them ; I have seen it in my own life. Some castes become strong, and as soon as they all agree, who is to say nay? Because whatever it was, each caste was exclusive of the other. It did not meddle with others' affairs ; even the several divisions of one caste did not meddle with the other divisions, and those powerful epoch-makers, Shankaracharya and others, were the great caste-makers. I cannot tell you all the wonderful things they fabricated, and some of you may resent what I have to say. But in my travels and experiences I have traced them out, and have arrived at most wonderful results. They would sometimes get hordes of Baluchis and at once make them Kshatriyas, also get hold of hordes of fishermen and make them Brahmins forthwith. They were all Rishis and sages, and we have to bow down to their memory. So, be you all Rishis and sages ; that is the secret. More or less we shall all be Rishis. What is meant by a Rishi? The pure one. Be pure first, and you will have power. Simply saying, "I am a Rishi", will not do ; but when you are a Rishi you will find that others obey you instinctively. Something mysterious emanates from you, which makes them follow you, makes them hear you, makes them unconsciously, even against their will, carry out your plans. That is Rishihood.

Now as to the details, they of course have to be worked out through generations. But this is merely a suggestion in order to show you that these quarrels should cease. Especially do I regret that in modern times there should be so much dissension between the castes. This must stop. It is useless on both sides, especially on the side of the higher caste, the Brahmin, because the day for these privileges and exclusive claims is gone. The duty of every aristocracy is to dig its own grave, and the sooner it does so, the better. The more it delays, the more it will fester and the worse death it will die. It is the duty of the Brahmin, therefore, to work for the salvation of the rest of mankind in India. If he does that, and so long as he does that, he is a Brahmin, but he is no Brahmin when he goes about making money. You on the other hand should give help only to the real Brahmin who deserves it; that leads to heaven. But sometimes a gift to another person who does not deserve it leads to the other place, says our scripture. You must be on your guard about that. He only is the Brahmin who has no secular employment. Secular employment is not for the Brahmin but for the other castes. To the Brahmins I appeal, that they must work hard to raise the Indian people by teaching them what they know, by giving out the culture that they have accumulated for centuries. It is clearly the duty of the Brahmins of India to remember what real Brahminhood is. As Manu says, all these privileges and honours are given to the Brahmin, because "with him is the treasury of virtue". He must open that treasury and distribute its valuables to the world. It is true that he was the earliest preacher to the Indian races, he was the first to renounce everything in order to attain to the higher realisation of life before others could reach to the idea. It was not his fault that he marched ahead of the other castes. Why did not the other castes so understand and do as he did? Why did they sit down and be lazy, and let the Brahmins win the race?

But it is one thing to gain an advantage, and another thing to preserve it for evil use. Whenever power is used for evil, it becomes diabolical; it must be used for good only. So this accumulated culture of ages of which the Brahmin has been the trustee, he must now give to the people at large, and it was because he did not give it to the people that the Mohammedan invasion was possible. It was because he did not open this treasury to the people from the beginning, that for a thousand years we have been trodden under the heels of every one who chose to come to India. It was through that we have become degraded, and the first task must be to break open the cells that hide the wonderful treasures which our common ancestors accumulated; bring them out and give them to everybody and the Brahmin must be the first to do it. There is an old superstition in Bengal that if the cobra that bites, sucks out his own poison from the patient, the man must survive. Well then, the Brahmin must suck out his own poison. To the non-Brahmin castes I say, wait, be not in a hurry. Do not seize every opportunity of fighting the Brahmin, because, as I have shown, you are suffering from your own fault. Who told you to neglect spirituality and Sanskrit learning? What have you been doing all this time? Why have you been indifferent? Why do you now fret and fume because somebody else had more brains, more energy, more pluck and go, than you? Instead of wasting your energies in vain discussions and quarrels in the newspapers, instead of fighting and quar- relling in your own homes—which is sinful—use all your energies in acquiring the culture which the Brahmin has, and the thing is done. Why do you not become Sanskrit scholars? Why do you not spend millions to bring Sanskrit education to all the castes of India? That is the question. The moment you do these things, you are equal to the Brahmin. That is the secret of power in India.

Sanskrit and prestige go together in India. As soon as you have that, none dares say anything against you. That is the one secret ; take that up. The whole universe, to use the ancient Advaitist's simile, is in a state of self-hypnotism. It is will that is the power. It is the man of strong will that throws, as it were, a halo round him and brings all other people to the same state of vibration as he has in his own mind. Such gigantic men do appear. And what is the idea? When a powerful individual appears, his personality infuses his thoughts into us, and many of us come to have the same thoughts, and thus we become powerful. Why is it that organisations are so powerful? Do not say organisation is material. Why is it, to take a case in point, that forty millions of Englishmen rule three hundred millions of people here? What is the psychological explanation? These forty millions put their wills together and that means infinite power, and you three hundred millions have a will each separate from the other. Therefore to make a great future India, the whole secret lies in organisation, accumulation of power, co-ordination of wills.

Already before my mind rises one of the marvellous verses of the Rig-Veda Samhitâ which says, "Be thou all of one mind, be thou all of one thought, for in the days of yore, the gods being of one mind were enabled to receive oblations." That the gods can be worshipped by men is because they are of one mind. Being of one mind is the secret of society. And the more you go on fighting and quarrelling about all trivialities such as "Dravidian" and "Aryan", and the question of Brahmins and non-Brahmins and all that, the further you are off from that accumulation of energy and power which is going to make the future India. For mark you, the future India depends entirely upon that. That is the secret—accumulation of will-power, co-ordination, bringing them all, as it were, into one focus. Each Chinaman thinks in his own way, and a handful of Japanese all think in the same way, and you know the result. That is how it goes throughout the history of the world. You find in every case, compact little nations always governing and ruling huge unwieldy nations, and this is natural, because it is easier for the little compact nations to bring their ideas into the same focus, and thus they become developed. And the bigger the nation, the more unwieldy it is. Born, as it were, a disorganised mob, they cannot combine. All these dissensions must stop.

There is yet another defect in us. Ladies, excuse me, but through centuries of slavery, we have become like a nation of women. You scarcely can get three women together for five minutes in this country or any other country, but they quarrel. Women make big societies in European countries, and make tremendous declarations of women's power and so on; then they quarrel, and some man comes and rules them all. All over the world they still require some man to rule them. We are like them. Women we are. If a woman comes to lead women, they all begin immediately to criticise her, tear her to pieces, and make her sit down. If a man comes and gives them a little harsh treatment, scolds them now and then, it is all right, they have been used to that sort of mesmerism. The whole world is full of such mesmerists and hypnotists. In the same way, if one of our countrymen stands up and tries to become great, we all try to hold him down, but if a foreigner comes and tries to kick us, it is all right. We have been used to it, have we not? And slaves must become great masters! So give up being a slave. For the next fifty years this alone shall be our keynote—this, our great Mother India. Let all other vain gods disappear for the time from our minds. This is the only god that is awake, our own race—"everywhere his hands, everywhere his feet, everywhere his ears, he covers everything." All other gods are sleeping. What vain gods shall we go after and yet cannot worship the god that we see all round us, the Virât? When we have worshipped this, we shall be able to worship all other gods. Before we can crawl half a mile, we want to cross the ocean like Hanumân! It cannot be. Everyone going to be a Yogi, everyone going to meditate! It cannot be. The whole day mixing with the world with Karma Kânda, and in the evening sitting down and blowing through your nose! Is it so easy? Should Rishis come flying through the air, because you have blown three times through the nose? Is it a joke? It is all nonsense. What is needed is Chittashuddhi, purification of the heart. And how does that come? The first of all worship is the worship of the Virat—of those all around us. Worship It. Worship is the exact equivalent of the Sanskrit word, and no other English word will do. These are all our gods—men and animals; and the first gods we have to worship are our countrymen. These we have to worship, instead of being jealous of each other and fighting each other. It is the most terrible Karma for which we are suffering, and yet it does not open our eyes!

Well, the subject is so great that I do not know where to stop, and I must bring my lecture to a close by placing before you in a few words the plans I want to carry out in Madras. We must have a hold on the spiritual and secular education of the nation. Do you understand that? You must dream it, you must talk it, you must think it, and you must work it out. Till then there is no salvation for the race. The education that you are getting now has some good points, but it has a tremendous disadvantage which is so great that the good things are all weighed down. In the first place it is not a man-making education, it is merely and entirely a negative education. A negative education or any training that is based on negation, is worse than death. The child is taken to school, and the first thing he learns is that his father is a fool, the second thing that his grandfather is a lunatic, the third thing that all his teachers are hypocrites, the fourth that all the sacred books are lies! By the time he is sixteen he is a mass of negation, lifeless and boneless. And the result is that fifty years of such education has not produced one original man in the three Presidencies. Every man of originality that has been produced has been educated elsewhere, and not in this country, or they have gone to the old universities once more to cleanse themselves of superstitions. Education is not the amount of information that is put into your brain and runs riot there, undigested, all your life. We must have life-building, man-making, character-making assimilation of ideas. If you have assimilated five ideas and made them your life and character, you have more education than any man who has got by heart a whole library यथा खरश्चन्दनभारवाही भारस्य वेत्ता न तु चन्दनस्य ।— "The ass carrying its load of sandalwood knows only the weight and not the value of the sandalwood." If education is identical with information, the libraries are the greatest sages in the world, and encyclopaedias are the Rishis. The ideal, therefore, is that we must have the whole education of our country, spiritual and secular, in our own hands, and it must be on national lines, through national methods as far as practical.

Of course this is a very big scheme, a very big plan. I do not know whether it will ever work out. But we must begin the work. But how? Take Madras, for instance. We must have a temple, for with Hindus religion must come first. Then, you may say, all sects will quarrel about it. But we will make it a non-sectarian temple, having only "Om" as the symbol, the greatest symbol of any sect. If there is any sect here which believes that "Om" ought not to be the symbol, it has no right to call itself Hindu. All will have the right to interpret Hinduism, each one according to his own sect ideas,

but we must have a common temple. You can have your
own images and symbols in other places, but do not
quarrel here with those who differ from you. Here should
be taught the common grounds of our different sects, and
at the same time the different sects should have perfect
liberty to come and teach their doctrines, with only one
restriction, that is, not to quarrel with other sects. Say
what you have to say, the world wants it; but the world
has no time to hear what you think about other people;
you can keep that to yourselves.

Secondly, in connection with this temple there should
be an institution to train teachers who must go about
preaching religion and giving secular education to our
people; they must carry both. As we have been already
carrying religion from door to door, let us along with it
carry secular education also. That can be easily done.
Then the work will extend through these bands of
teachers and preachers, and gradually we shall have
similar temples in other places, until we have covered the
whole of India. That is my plan. It may appear gigantic,
but it is much needed. You may ask, where is the money.
Money is not needed. Money is nothing. For the last
twelve years of my life, I did not know where the next
meal would come from; but money and everything else
I want must come, because they are my slaves, and not
I theirs; money and everything else must come. Must—
that is the word. Where are the men? That is the
question. Young men of Madras, my hope is in you.
Will you respond to the call of your nation? Each one of
you has a glorious future if you dare believe me. Have a
tremendous faith in yourselves, like the faith I had when
I was a child, and which I am working out now. Have
that faith, each one of you, in yourself—that eternal power
is lodged in every soul—and you will revive the whole of
India. Ay, we will then go to every country under the
sun, and our ideas will before long be a component of the

many forces that are working to make up every nation in the world. We must enter into the life of every race in India and abroad; we shall have to *work* to bring this about. Now for that, I want young men. "It is the young, the strong, and healthy, of sharp intellect that will reach the Lord", say the Vedas. This is the time to decide your future—while you possess the energy of youth, not when you are worn out and jaded, but in the freshness and vigour of youth. Work—this is the time; for the freshest, the untouched, and unsmelled flowers alone are to be laid at the feet of the Lord, and such He receives. Rouse yourselves, therefore, or life is short. There are greater works to be done than aspiring to become lawyers and picking quarrels and such things. A far greater work is this sacrifice of yourselves for the benefit of your race, for the welfare of humanity. What is in this life? You are Hindus, and there is the instinctive belief in you that life is eternal. Sometimes I have young men come and talk to me about atheism; I do not believe a Hindu can become an atheist. He may read European books, and persuade himself he is a materialist, but it is only for a time. It is not in your blood. You cannot believe what is not in your constitution; it would be a hopeless task for you. Do not attempt that sort of thing. I once attempted it when I was a boy, but it could not be. Life is short, but the soul is immortal and eternal, and one thing being certain, death, let us therefore take up a great ideal and give up our whole life to it. Let this be our determination, and may He, the Lord, who "comes again and again for the salvation of His own people", to quote from our scriptures—may the great Kṛiṣhṇa bless us and lead us all to the fulfilment of our aims!

ON CHARITY

During his stay in Madras the Swami presided at the annual meeting of the Chennapuri Annadâna Samâjam, an institution of a charitable nature, and in the course of a brief address referred to a remark by a previous speaker deprecating special alms-giving to the Brâhmin over and above the other castes. Swamiji pointed out that this had its good as well as its bad side. All the culture, practically, which the nation possessed, was among the Brahmins, and they also had been the thinkers of the nation. Take away the means of living which enabled them to be thinkers, and the nation as a whole would suffer. Speaking of the indiscriminate charity of India as compared with the legal charity of other nations, he said, the outcome of their system of relief was that the vagabond of India was contented to receive readily what he was given readily and lived a peaceful and contented life: while the vagabond in the West, unwilling to go to the poor-house—for man loves liberty more than food—turned a robber, the enemy of society, and necessitated the organisation of a system of magistracy, police, jails, and other establishments. Poverty there must be, so long as the disease known as civilisation existed: and hence the need for relief. So that they had to choose between the indiscriminate charity of India, which, in the case of Sannyâsins at any rate, even if they were not sincere men, at least forced them to learn some little of their scriptures before they were able to obtain food ; and the discriminate charity of Western nations which necessitated a costly system of poor-law relief, and in the end succeeded only in changing mendicants into criminals.

ADDRESS OF WELCOME PRESENTED AT CALCUTTA AND REPLY

On his arrival in Calcutta, the Swami Vivekananda was greeted with intense enthusiasm, and the whole of his progress through the decorated streets of the city was thronged with an immense crowd waiting to have a sight of him. The official reception was held a week later, at the residence of the late Raja Radha Kanta Deb Bahadur at Sobha Bazar, when Raja Benoy Krishna Deb Bahadur took the chair. After a few brief introductory remarks from the Chairman, the following address was read and presented to him, enclosed in a silver casket:

TO SRIMAT VIVEKANANDA SWAMI

DEAR BROTHER,

We, the Hindu inhabitants of Calcutta and of several other places in Bengal, offer you on your return to the land of your birth a hearty welcome. We do so with a sense of pride as well as of gratitude, for by your noble work and example in various parts of the world you have done honour not only to our religion but also to our country and to our province in particular.

At the great Parliament of Religions which constituted a Section of the World's Fair held in Chicago in 1893, you presented the principles of the Aryan religion. The substance of your exposition was to most of your audience a revelation, and its manner overpowering alike by its grace and its strength. Some may have received it in a questioning spirit, a few may have criticised it, but its general effect was a revolution in the religious ideas of a large section of cultivated Americans. A new light had dawned on their mind, and with their accustomed earnestness and love of truth they determined to take full advantage of it. Your opportunities widened; your work grew. You had to meet call after call from many cities in many States, answer many queries, satisfy many doubts, solve many difficulties. You did all this work with energy, ability, and sincerity ; and it has led to lasting results. Your teaching has deeply influenced many an enlightened circle· in the American Commonwealth, has stimulated thought and research, and has in many instances definitely altered religious conceptions in the direction of an increased appreciation of Hindu ideals. The rapid growth of clubs and societies for the comparative study of religions and the investigation of spiritual truth is witness to your labour in the far West. You may be regarded as the founder of a College in London for the teaching of the Vedanta philosophy. Your lectures have been regularly delivered, punctually attended, and widely appreciated. Their influence has extended beyond the walls of the lecture-rooms. The love and esteem which have been evoked by your teaching are evidenced by the warm acknowledgements, in the address presented to you on the eve of your departure from London, by the students of the Vedanta philosophy in that town.

Your success as a teacher has been due not only to your deep and intimate acquaintance with the truths of the Aryan religion and your skill in exposition by speech and writing, but also, and largely, to your personality. Your lectures, your essays, and your books have high merits, spiritual and literary, and they could not but produce their effect. But it has been heightened in a manner that defies expression by the example of your simple, sincere, self-denying life, your modesty, devotion, and earnestness.

While acknowledging your services as a teacher of the sublime truths of our religion, we feel that we must render a tribute to the memory of your revered preceptor, Shri

Ramakrishna Paramahamsa. To him we largely owe even you. With his rare magical insight he early discovered the heavenly spark in you and predicted for you a career which happily is now in course of realisation. He it was that unsealed the vision and the faculty divine with which God had blessed you, gave to your thoughts and aspirations the bent that was awaiting the holy touch, and aided your pursuits in the region of the unseen. His most precious legacy to posterity was yourself.

Go on, noble soul, working steadily and valiantly in the path you have chosen. You have a world to conquer. You have to interpret and vindicate the religion of the Hindus to the ignorant, the sceptical, the wilfully blind. You have begun the work in a spirit which commands our admiration, and have already achieved a success to which many lands bear witness. But a great deal yet remains to be done ; and our own country, or rather we should say your own country, waits on you. The truths of the Hindu religion have to be expounded to large numbers of Hindus themselves. Brace yourself then for the grand exertion. We have confidence in you and in the righteousness of our cause. Our national religion seeks to win no material triumphs. Its purposes are spiritual; its weapon is a truth which is hidden away from material eyes and yields only to the reflective reason. Call on the world, and where necessary, on Hindus themselves, to open the inner eye, to transcend the senses, to read rightly the sacred books, to face the supreme reality, and realise their position and destiny as men. No one is better fitted than yourself to give the awakening or make the call, and we can only assure you of our hearty sympathy and loyal co-operation in that work which is apparently your mission ordained by Heaven.

We remain, dear brother,
Your loving FRIENDS AND ADMIRERS.

The Swami's reply was as follows:

One wants to lose the individual in the universal, one renounces, flies off, and tries to cut himself off from all associations of the body of the past, one works hard to forget even that he is a man; yet, in the heart of his heart, there is a soft sound, one string vibrating, one whisper, which tells him, East or West, home is best. Citizens of the capital of this Empire, before you I stand, not as a Sannyâsin, no, not even as a preacher, but I come before you the same Calcutta boy to talk to you as I used to do. Ay, I would like to sit in the dust of the streets of this city, and, with the freedom of childhood, open my mind to you, my brothers. Accept, therefore, my heartfelt thanks for this unique word that you have used, "Brother". Yes, I am your brother, and you are my brothers. I was asked by an English friend on the eve of my departure, "Swami, how do you like now your motherland after four years' experience of the luxurious, glorious, powerful West?" I could only answer, "India I loved before I came away. Now the very dust of India has become holy to me, the very air is now to me holy; it is now the holy land, the place of pilgrimage, the Tirtha." Citizens of Calcutta— my brothers—I cannot express my gratitude to you for the kindness you have shown, or rather I should not thank you at all, for you are my brothers, you have done only a brother's duty, ay, only a Hindu brother's duty ; for such family ties, such relationships, such love exist nowhere beyond the bounds of this motherland of ours.

The Parliament of Religions was a great affair, no doubt. From various cities of this land, we have thanked the gentlemen who organised the meeting, and they deserved all our thanks for the kindness that has been shown to us; but yet allow me to construe for you the history of the Parliament of Religions. They wanted a horse, and they wanted to ride it. There were people there who wanted to make it a heathen show, but it was ordained otherwise; it could not help being so. Most of them were kind, but we have thanked them enough.

On the other hand, my mission in America was not to the Parliament of Religions. That was only something by the way, it was only an opening, an opportunity, and for that we are very thankful to the members of the Parliament; but really, our thanks are due to the great people of the United States, the American nation, the warm-hearted, hospitable, great nation of America, where more than anywhere else the feeling of brotherhood has been developed. An American meets you for five minutes on board a train, and you are his friend, and the next moment he invites you as a guest to his home and opens the secret of his whole living there. That is the character of the American race, and we highly appreciate it. Their kindness to me is past all narration, it would take me years yet to tell you how I have been treated by them most kindly and most wonderfully. So are our thanks due to the other nation on the other side of the Atlantic. No one ever landed on English soil with more hatred in his heart for a race than I did for the English, and on this platform are present English friends who can bear witness to the fact; but the more I lived among them and saw how the machine was working—the English national life—and mixed with them, I found where the heartbeat of the nation was, and the more I loved them. There is none among you here present, my brothers, who loves the English people more than I do now. You have to see what is going on there, and you have to mix with them. As the philosophy, our national philosophy of the Vedanta, has summarised all misfortune, all misery, as coming from that one cause, ignorance, herein also we must understand that the difficulties that arise between us and the English people are mostly due to that ignorance; we do not know them, they do not know us.

Unfortunately, to the Western mind, spirituality, nay,

even morality, is eternally connected with worldly prosperity; and as soon as an Englishman or any other Western man lands on our soil and finds a land of poverty and of misery, he forthwith concludes that there cannot be any religion here, there cannot be any morality even. His own experience is true. In Europe, owing to the inclemency of the climate and many other circumstances, poverty and sin go together, but not so in India. In India, on the other hand, my experience is that the poorer the man the better he is in point of morality. Now this takes time to understand, and how many foreign people are there who will stop to understand this, the very secret of national existence in India? Few are there who will have the patience to study the nation and understand. Here, and here alone, is the only race where poverty does not mean crime, poverty does not mean sin; and here is the only race where not only poverty does not mean crime, but poverty has been deified, and the beggar's garb is the garb of the highest in the land. On the other hand, we have also similarly, patiently to study the social institutions of the West and not rush into mad judgments about them Their intermingling of the sexes, their different customs, their manners, have all their meaning, have all their grand sides, if you have the patience to study them. Not that I mean that we are going to borrow their manners and customs, not that they are going to borrow ours, for the manners and customs of each race are the outcome of centuries of patient growth in that race, and each one has a deep meaning behind it; and, therefore, neither are they to ridicule our manners and customs, nor we theirs.

Again, I want to make another statement before this assembly. My work in England has been more satisfactory to me than my work in America. The bold, brave, and steady Englishman, if I may use the expression, with his skull a little thicker than those of other people—if he has once an idea put into his brain, it never comes out;

and the immense practicality and energy of the race
makes it sprout up and immediately bear fruit. It is not
so in any other country. That immense practicality, that
immense vitality of the race, you do not see anywhere
else. There is less of imagination, but more of work, and
who knows the well-spring, the mainspring of the English
heart? How much of imagination and of feeling is there!
They are a nation of heroes, they are the true Kshatriyas;
their education is to hide their feelings and never to show
them. From their childhood they have been educated up
to that. Seldom will you find an Englishman manifesting
feeling, nay, even an Englishwoman. I have seen English-
women go to work and do deeds which would stagger
the bravest of Bengalis to follow. But with all this
heroic superstructure, behind this covering of the fighter,
there is a deep spring of feeling in the English heart.
If you once know how to reach it, if you get there, if
you have personal contact and mix with him, he will
open his heart, he is your friend for ever, he is your
servant. Therefore in my opinion, my work in England
has been more satisfactory than anywhere else. I firmly
believe that if I should die tomorrow the work in
England would not die, but would go on expanding all
the time.

Brothers, you have touched another chord in my
heart, the deepest of all, and that is the mention of my
teacher, my master, my hero, my ideal, my God in life—
Shri Ramakrishna Paramahamsa. If there has been anything achieved by me, by thoughts, or words, or deeds,
if from my lips has ever fallen one word that has helped
any one in the world, I lay no claim to it, it was his. But
if there have been curses falling from my lips, if there has
been hatred coming out of me, it is all mine and not his.
All that has been weak has been mine, and all that has
been life-giving, strengthening, pure, and holy, has been
his inspiration, his words, and he himself. Yes, my

friends, the world has yet to know that man. We read in
the history of the world about prophets and their lives,
and these come down to us through centuries of writings
and workings by their disciples. Through thousands of
years of chiselling and modelling, the lives of the great
prophets of yore come down to us ; and yet, in 'my
opinion, not one stands so high in brilliance as that life
which I saw with my own eyes, under whose shadow I
have lived, at whose feet I have learnt everything—the
life of Ramakrishna Paramahamsa. Ay, friends, you all
know the celebrated saying of the Gitâ:

यदा यदा हि धर्मस्य ग्लानिर्भवति भारत ।
अभ्युत्थानमधर्मस्य तदात्मानं सृजाम्यहम् ॥
परित्राणाय साधूनां विनाशाय च दुष्कृताम् ।
धर्मसंस्थापनार्थाय संभवामि युगे युगे ॥

"Whenever, O descendant of Bharata, there is decline
of Dharma, and rise of Adharma, then I body Myself
forth. For the protection of the good, for the destruction
of the wicked, and for the establishment of Dharma I
come into being in every age."

Along with it you have to understand one thing more.
Such a thing is before us today. Before one of these
tidal waves of spirituality comes, there are whirlpools of
lesser manifestation all over society. One of these comes
up, at first unknown, unperceived, and unthought of,
assuming proportion, swallowing, as it were, and assimi-
lating all the other little whirlpools, becoming immense,
becoming a tidal wave, and falling upon society with a
power which none can resist. Such is happening before
us. If you have eyes, you will see it. If your heart is
open, you will receive it. If you are truth-seekers, you
will find it. Blind, blind indeed is the man who does not
see the signs of the day! Ay, this boy born of poor
Brâhmin parents in an out-of-the-way village of which
very few of you have even heard, is literally being

worshipped in lands which have been fulminating against heathen worship for centuries. Whose power is it? Is it mine or yours? It is none else than the power which was manifested here as Ramakrishna Paramahamsa. For, you and I, and sages and prophets, nay, even Incarnations, the whole universe, are but manifestations of power more or less individualised, more or less concentrated. Here has been a manifestation of an immense power, just the very beginning of whose workings we are seeing, and before this generation passes away, you will see more wonderful workings of that power. It has come just in time for the regeneration of India, for we forget from time to time the vital power that must always work in India.

Each nation has its own peculiar method of work. Some work through politics, some through social reforms, some through other lines. With us, religion is the only ground along which we can move. The Englishman can understand even religion through politics. Perhaps the American can understand even religion through social reforms. But the Hindu can understand even politics when it is given through religion; sociology must come through religion, everything must come through religion. For that is the theme, the rest are the variations in the national life-music. And that was in danger. It seemed that we were going to change this theme in our national life, that we were going to exchange the backbone of our existence, as it were, that we were trying to replace a spiritual by a political backbone. And if we could have succeeded, the result would have been annihilation. But it was not to be. So this power became manifest. I do not care in what light you understand this great sage, it matters not how much respect you pay to him, but I challenge you face to face with the fact that here is a manifestation of the most marvellous power that has been for several centuries in India, and it is your duty, as Hindus, to study this power, to find what has been done for the regeneration, for the good of India, and for the good of the whole human race through it. Ay, long before ideas of universal religion and brotherly feeling between different sects were mooted and discussed in any country in the world, here, in sight of this city, had been living a man whose whole life was a Parliament of Religions as it should be.

The highest ideal in our scriptures is the impersonal, and would to God everyone of us here were high enough to realise that impersonal ideal; but, as that cannot be, it is absolutely necessary for the vast majority of human beings to have a personal ideal; and no nation can rise, can become great, can work at all, without enthusiastically coming under the banner of one of these great ideals in life. Political ideals, personages representing political ideals, even social ideals, commercial ideals, would have no power in India. We want spiritual ideals before us, we want enthusiastically to gather round grand spiritual names. Our heroes must be spiritual. Such a hero has been given to us in the person of Ramakrishna Parama-hamsa. If this nation wants to rise, take my word for it, it will have to rally enthusiastically round this name. It does not matter who preaches Ramakrishna Parama-hamsa, whether I, or you, or anybody else. But him I place before you, and it is for you to judge, and for the good of our race, for the good of our nation, to judge now, what you shall do with this great ideal of life. One thing we are to remember that it was the purest of all lives that you have ever seen, or let me tell you distinctly, that you have ever read of And before you is the fact that it is the most marvellous manifestation of soul-power that you can read of, much less expect to see. Within ten years of his passing away, this power has encircled the globe ; that fact is before you. In duty bound, therefore, for the good of our race, for the good of our religion, I place this great spiritual ideal before you. Judge him not through me. I am only a weak instrument. Let not his character be judged by seeing me. It was so great that if I or any other of his disciples spent hundreds of lives, we could not do justice to a millionth part of what he really was. Judge for yourselves; in the heart of your hearts is the Eternal Witness, and may He, the same Ramakrishna Paramahamsa, for the good of our nation, for the welfare of our country, and for the good of humanity, open your hearts, make you true and steady to work for the immense change which must come, whether we exert ourselves or not. For the work of the Lord does not wait for the like of you or me. He can raise His workers from the dust by hundreds and by thousands. It is a glory and a privilege that we are allowed to work at all under Him.

From this the idea expands. As you have pointed out to me, we have to conquer the world. That we have to! India must conquer the world, and nothing less than that is my ideal. It may be very big, it may astonish many of you, but it is so. We must conquer the world or die. There is no other alternative. The sign of life is expansion ; we must go out, expand, show life, or degrade, fester, and die. There is no other alternative. Take either of these, either live or die. Now, we all know about the petty jealousies and quarrels that we have in our country. Take my word, it is the same everywhere. The other nations with their political lives have foreign policies. When they find too much quarrelling at home, they look for somebody abroad to quarrel with, and the quarrel at home stops. We have these quarrels without any foreign policy to stop them. This must be our eternal foreign policy, preaching the truths of our Shâstras to the nations of the world. I ask you who are politically minded, do you require any other proof that this will unite us as a race? This very assembly is a sufficient witness.

Secondly, apart from these selfish considerations, there are the unselfish, the noble, the living examples behind us. One of the great causes of India's misery and downfall has been that she narrowed herself, went into her shell as the oyster does, and refused to give her jewels and her treasures to the other races of mankind, refused to give the life-giving truths to thirsting nations outside the Aryan fold. That has been the one great cause; that we did not go out, that we did not compare notes with other nations—that has been the one great cause of our downfall, and every one of you knows that that little stir, the little life that you see in India, begins from the day when Raja Rammohan Roy broke through the walls of that exclusiveness. Since that day, history in India has taken another turn, and now it is growing with accelerated motion. If we have had little rivulets in the past, deluges are coming, and none can resist them. Therefore we must go out, and the secret of life is to give and take. Are we to take always, to sit at the feet of the Westerners to learn everything, even religion? We can learn mechanism from them. We can learn many other things. But we have to teach them something, and that is our religion, that is our spirituality. For a complete civilisation the world is waiting, waiting for the treasures to come out of India, waiting for the marvellous spiritual inheritance of the race, which, through decades of degradation and misery, the nation has still clutched to her breast. The world is waiting for that treasure; little do you know how much of hunger and of thirst there is outside of India for these wonderful treasures of our forefathers. We talk here, we quarrel with each other, we laugh at and we ridicule everything sacred, till it has become almost a national vice to ridicule everything holy. Little do we understand the heart-pangs of millions waiting outside the walls, stretching forth their hands for a little sip of that nectar which our forefathers have preserved in this land of India. Therefore we must go out, exchange our spirituality for anything they have to give us; for the

marvels of the region of spirit we will exchange the
marvels of the region of matter. We will not be students
always, but teachers also. There cannot be friendship
without equality, and there cannot be equality when one
party is always the teacher and the other party sits always
at his feet. If you want to become equal with the Englishman or the American, you will have to teach as well as
to learn, and you have plenty yet to teach to the world
for centuries to come. This has to be done. Fire and
enthusiasm must be in our blood. We Bengalis have
been credited with imagination, and I believe we have
it. We have been ridiculed as an imaginative race, as
men with a good deal of feeling. Let me tell you, my
friends, intellect is great indeed, but it stops within certain
bounds. It is through the heart, and the heart alone, that
inspiration comes. It is through the feelings that the
highest secrets are reached; and therefore it is the Bengali,
the man of feeling, that has to do this work.

उत्तिष्ठत जाग्रत प्राप्य वरान्निबोधत ।—Arise, awake and
stop not till the desired end is reached. Young men of
Calcutta, arise, awake, for the time is propitious. Already
everything is opening out before us. Be bold and fear not.
It is only in our scriptures that this adjective is given
unto the Lord—Abhih, Abhih. We have to become Abhih,
fearless, and our task will be done. Arise, awake, for
your country needs this tremendous sacrifice. It is the
young men that will do it. "The young, the energetic,
the strong, the well-built, the intellectual"—for them is
the task. And we have hundreds and thousands of such
young men in Calcutta. If, as you say, I have done
something, remember that I was that good-for-nothing boy
playing in the streets of Calcutta. If I have done so much,
how much more will you do! Arise and awake, the world
is calling upon you. In other parts of India, there is
intellect, there is money, but enthusiasm is only in my
motherland. That must come out; therefore arise, young

men of Calcutta, with enthusiasm in your blood. Think
not that you are poor, that you have no friends. Ay,
who ever saw money make the man? It is man that
always makes money. The whole world has been made
by the energy of man, by the power of enthusiasm, by the
power of faith.

Those of you who have studied that most beautiful of
all the Upanishads, the Katha, will remember how the king
was going to make a great sacrifice, and, instead of giving
away things that were of any worth, he was giving away
cows and horses that were not of any use, and the book
says that at that time Shraddhâ entered into the heart
of his son Nachiketâ. I would not translate this word
Shraddha to you, it would be a mistake; it is a wonderful
word to understand, and much depends on it ; we will see
how it works, for immediately we find Nachiketa telling
himself, "I am superior to many, I am inferior to few, but
nowhere am I the last, I can also do something." And
this boldness increased, and the boy wanted to solve the
problem which was in his mind, the problem of death.
The solution could only be got by going to the house of
Death, and the boy went. There he was, brave Nachiketa,
waiting at the house of Death for three days, and you
know how he obtained what he desired. What we want
is this Shraddha. Unfortunately, it has nearly vanished
from India, and this is why we are in our present state.
What makes the difference between man and man is the
difference in this Shraddha and nothing else. What makes
one man great and another weak and low is this Shraddha.
My Master used to say, he who thinks himself weak will
become weak, and that is true. This Shraddha must
enter into you. Whatever of material power you see
manifested by the Western races is the outcome of this
Shraddha, because they believe in their muscles and if
you believe in your spirit, how much more will it work!
Believe in that infinite soul, the infinite power, which,

with consensus of opinion, your books and sages preach. That Âtman which nothing can destroy, in It is infinite power only waiting to be called out. For here is the great difference between all other philosophies and the Indian philosophy. Whether dualistic, qualified monistic, or monistic, they all firmly believe that everything is in the soul itself; it has only to come out and manifest itself. Therefore, this Shraddha is what I want, and what all of us here want, this faith in ourselves, and before you is the great task to get that faith. Give up the awful disease that is creeping into our national blood, that idea of ridiculing everything, that loss of seriousness. Give that up. Be strong and have this Shraddha, and everything else is bound to follow.

I have done nothing as yet; you have to do the task. If I die tomorrow the work will not die. I sincerely believe that there will be thousands coming up from the ranks to take up the work and carry it further and further, beyond all my most hopeful imagination ever painted. I have faith in my country, and especially in the youth of my country. The youth of Bengal have the greatest of all tasks that has ever been placed on the shoulders of young men. I have travelled for the last ten years or so over the whole of India, and my conviction is that from the youth of Bengal will come the power which will raise India once more to her proper spiritual place. Ay, from the youth of Bengal, with this immense amount of feeling and enthusiasm in the blood, will come those heroes who will march from one corner of the earth to the other, preaching and teaching the eternal spiritual truths of our forefathers. And this is the great work before you. Therefore, let me conclude by reminding you once more, "Arise, awake and stop not till the desired end is reached." Be not afraid, for all great power, throughout the history of humanity, has been with the people. From out of their ranks have come all the greatest geniuses of the world, and history

can only repeat itself. Be not afraid of anything. You
will do marvellous work. The moment you fear, you are
nobody. It is fear that is the great cause of misery in
the world. It is fear that is the greatest of all superstitions. It is fear that is the cause of our woes, and it is
fearlessness that brings heaven even in a moment.
Therefore, "Arise, awake, and stop not till the goal is
reached."

Gentlemen, allow me to thank you once more for all
the kindness that I have received at your hands. It is my
wish—my intense, sincere wish—to be even of the least
service to the world, and above all to my own country
and countrymen.

THE VEDANTA IN ALL ITS PHASES

(Delivered in Calcutta)

Away back, where no recorded history, nay, not even the dim light of tradition, can penetrate, has been steadily shining the light, sometimes dimmed by external circumstances, at others effulgent, but undying and steady, shedding its lustre not only over India, but permeating the whole thought-world with its power, silent, unperceived, gentle, yet omnipotent, like the dew that falls in the morning, unseen and unnoticed, yet bringing into bloom the fairest of roses: this has been the thought of the Upanishads, the philosophy of the Vedanta. Nobody knows when it first came to flourish on the soil of India. Guesswork has been vain. The guesses, especially of Western writers, have been so conflicting that no certain date can be ascribed to them. But we Hindus, from the spiritual standpoint, do not admit that they had any origin. This Vedanta, the philosophy of the Upanishads, I would make bold to state, has been the first as well as the final thought on the spiritual plane that has ever been vouchsafed to man.

From this ocean of the Vedanta, waves of light from time to time have been going Westward and Eastward. In the days of yore it travelled Westward and gave its impetus to the mind of the Greeks, either in Athens, or in Alexandria, or in Antioch. The Sânkhya system must clearly have made its mark on the minds of the ancient Greeks; and the Sankhya and all other systems in India had that one authority, the Upanishads, the Vedanta. In India, too, in spite of all these jarring sects that we see today and all those that have been in the past, the one authority, the basis of all these systems, has yet been the

Upanishads, the Vedanta. Whether you are a dualist, or a qualified monist, an Advaitist, or a Vishishtâdvaitist, a Shuddhâdvaitist, or any other Advaitist, or Dvaitist, or whatever you may call yourself, there stand behind you as authority, your Shâstras, your scriptures, the Upanishads. Whatever system in India does not obey the Upanishads cannot be called orthodox, and even the systems of the Jains and the Buddhists have been rejected from the soil of India only because they did not bear allegiance to the Upanishads. Thus the Vedanta, whether we know it or not, has penetrated all the sects in India, and what we call Hinduism, this mighty banyan with its immense, almost infinite ramifications, has been throughout interpenetrated by the influence of the Vedanta. Whether we are conscious of it or not, we think the Vedanta, we live in the Vedanta, we breathe the Vedanta, and we die in the Vedanta, and every Hindu does that. To preach Vedanta in the land of India, and before an Indian audience, seems, therefore, to be an anomaly. But it is the one thing that has to be preached, and it is the necessity of the age that it must be preached. For, as I have just told you, all the Indian sects must bear allegiance to the Upanishads; but among these sects there are many apparent contradictions. Many times the great sages of yore themselves could not understand the underlying harmony of the Upanishads. Many times, even sages quarrelled, so much so that it became a proverb that there are no sages who do not differ. But the time requires that a better interpretation should be given to this underlying harmony of the Upanishadic texts, whether they are dualistic, or non-dualistic, quasi-dualistic, or so forth. That has to be shown before the world at large, and this work is required as much in India as outside of India; and I, through the grace of God, had the great good fortune to sit at the feet of one whose whole life was such an interpretation, whose life, a thousandfold more than whose teaching, was a living commentary on the texts of the Upanishads, was in fact the spirit of the Upanishads living in a human form. Perhaps I have got a little of that harmony ; I do not know whether I shall be able to express it or not. But this is my attempt, my mission in life, to show that the Vedantic schools are not contradictory, that 'they all necessitate each other, all fulfil each other, and one, as it were, is the stepping-stone to the other, until the goal, the Advaita, the Tat Tvam Asi, is reached. There was a time in India when the Karma Kânda had its sway. There are many grand ideals, no doubt, in that portion of the Vedas. Some of our present daily worship is still according to the precepts of the Karma Kanda. But with all that, the Karma Kanda of the Vedas has almost disappeared from India. Very little of our life today is bound and regulated by the orders of the Karma Kanda of the Vedas. In our ordinary lives we are mostly Paurânikas or Tântrikas, and, even where some Vedic texts are used by the Brâhmins òf India, the adjustment of the texts is mostly not according to the Vedas, but according to the Tantras or the Puranas. As such, to call ourselves Vaidikas in the sense of following the Karma Kanda of the Vedas, I do not think, would be proper. But the other fact stands that we are all of us Vedantists. The people who call themselves Hindus had better be called Vedantists, and, as I have shown you, under that one name Vaidantika come in all our various sects, whether dualists or non-dualists.

The sects that are at the present time in India come to be divided in general into the two great classes of dualists and monists. The little differences which some of these sects insist upon, and upon the authority of which want to take new names as pure Advaitists, or qualified Advaitists, and so forth, do not matter much. As a classification, either they are dualists or monists, and of the sects existing at the present time, some of them are very new, and others seem to be reproductions of very ancient sects. The one class I would present by the life and philosophy of Râmânuja, and the other by Shankar-âchârya.

Ramanuja is the leading dualistic philosopher of later India, whom all the other dualistic sects have followed, directly or indirectly, both in the substance of their teaching and in the organisation of their sects even down to some of the most minute points of their organisation. You will be astonished if you compare Ramanuja and his work with the other dualistic Vaishnava sects in India, to see how much they resemble each other in organisation, teaching, and method. There is the great Southern preacher Madhva Muni, and following him, our great Chaitanya of Bengal who took up the philosophy of the Madhvas and preached it in Bengal. There are some other sects also in Southern India, as the qualified dualistic Shaivas. The Shaivas in most parts of India are Advaitists, except in some portions of Southern India and in Ceylon. But they also only substitute Shiva for Vishnu and are Ramanujists in every sense of the term except in the doctrine of the soul. The followers of Ramanuja hold that the soul is Anu, like a particle, very small, and the followers of Shankaracharya hold that it is Vibhu, omnipresent. There have been several non-dualistic sects. It seems that there have been sects in ancient times which Shankara's movement has entirely swallowed up and assimilated. You find sometimes a fling at Shankara himself in some of the commentaries, especially in that of Vijnâna Bhikshu who, although an Advaitist, attempts to upset the Mâyâvâda of Shankara. It seems there were schools who did not believe in this Mayavada, and they went so far as to call Shankara a crypto-Buddhist, Prachchhanna Bauddha, and they thought this Mayavada was taken from the Buddhists and brought within the Vedantic fold. However that may be, in modern times the Advaitists have all ranged themselves under Shankaracharya; and Shankaracharya and his disciples have been the great preachers of Advaita both in Southern and in Northern India. The influence of Shankaracharya did not penetrate much into our country of Bengal and in Kashmir and the Punjab, but in Southern India the Smârtas are all followers of Shankaracharya, and with Varanasi as the centre, his influence is simply immense even in many parts of Northern India.

Now both Shankara and Ramanuja laid aside all claim to originality. Ramanuja expressly tells us he is only following the great commentary of Bodhâyana. भगवद्बोधायन-कृतां विस्तीर्णां ब्रह्मसूत्रवृत्तिं पूर्वाचार्याः संचिक्षिपुः तन्मतानुसारेण सूत्राक्षराणि व्याख्यास्यन्ते । —"Ancient teachers abridged that extensive commentary on the *Brahma-sutras* which was composed by the Bhagavân Bodhayana; in accordance with their opinion, the words of the Sutra are explained." That is what Ramanuja says at the beginning of his commentary, the *Shri-Bhâshya*. He takes it up and makes of it a Samkshepa, and that is what we have today. I myself never had an opportunity of seeing this commentary of Bodhayana. The late Swami Dayânanda Saraswati wanted to reject every other commentary of the *Vyâsa-Sutras* except that of Bodhayana; and although he never lost an opportunity of having a fling at Ramanuja, he himself could never produce the Bodhayana. I have sought for it all over India, and never yet have been able to see it. But Ramanuja is very plain on the point, and he tells us that he is taking the ideas, and sometimes the very passages out of Bodhayana, and condensing them into the present Ramanuja Bhashya. It seems that Shankaracharya was also doing the same. There are a few places in his Bhashya which mention older commentaries, and when we know that his Guru and his Guru's Guru had been Vedantists of the same school as he, sometimes even more thorough-going, bolder even than

Shankara himself on certain points, it seems pretty plain that he also was not preaching anything very original, and that even in his Bhashya he himself had been doing the same work that Ramanuja did with Bodhayana, but from what Bhashya, it cannot be discovered at the present time.

All these Darshanas that you have ever seen or heard of are based upon Upanishadic authority. Whenever they want to quote a Shruti, they mean the Upanishads. They are always quoting the Upanishads. Following the Upanishads there come other philosophies of India, but every one of them failed in getting that hold on India which the philosophy of Vyasa got, although the philosophy of Vyasa is a development out of an older one, the Sankhya, and every philosophy and every system in India—I mean throughout the world—owes much to Kapila, perhaps the greatest name in the history of India in psychological and philosophical lines. The influence of Kapila is everywhere seen throughout the world. Wherever there is a recognised system of thought, there you can trace his influence; even if it be thousands of years back, yet he stands there, the shining, glorious, wonderful Kapila. His psychology and a good deal of his philosophy have been accepted by all the sects of India with but very little differences. In our own country, our Naiyâyika philosophers could not make much impression on the philosophical world of India. They were too busy with little things like species and genus, and so forth, and that most cumbersome terminology, which it is a life's work to study. As such, they were very busy with logic and left philosophy to the Vedantists, but every one of the Indian philosophic sects in modern times has adopted the logical terminology of the Naiyayikas of Bengal. Jagadisha, Gadâdhara, and Shiromani are as well known at Nadia as in some of the cities in Malabar. But the philosophy of Vyasa, the *Vyasa-Sutras*, is firm-seated and has attained the permanence of that which it intended to present to men, the Brahman of the Vedantic side of philosophy. Reason was entirely subordinated to the Shrutis, and as Shankaracharya declares, Vyasa did not care to reason at all. His idea in writing the Sutras was just to bring together, and with one thread to make a garland of the flowers of Vedantic texts. His Sutras are admitted so far as they are subordinate to the authority of the Upanishads, and no further.

And, as I have said, all the sects of India now hold these *Vyasa-Sutras* to be the great authority, and every new sect in India starts with a fresh commentary on the *Vyasa-Sutras* according to its light. The difference between some of these commentators is sometimes very great, sometimes the text-torturing is quite disgusting. The *Vyasa-Sutras* have got the place of authority, and no one can expect to found a sect in India until he can write a fresh commentary, on the *Vyasa-Sutras*.

Next in authority is the celebrated Gita. The great glory of Shankaracharya was his preaching of the Gita. It is one of the greatest works that this great man did among the many noble works of his noble life—the preaching of the Gita and writing the most beautiful commentary upon it. And he has been followed by all founders of the orthodox sects in India, each of whom has written a commentary on the Gita.

The Upanishads are many, and said to be one hundred and eight, but some declare them to be still larger in number. Some of them are evidently of a much later date, as for instance, the Allopanishad in which Allah is praised and Mohammed is called the Rajasullâ. I have been told that this was written during the reign of Akbar to bring the Hindus and Mohammedans together, and sometimes they got hold of some word, as Allah, or Illa in the Samhitâs, and made an Upanishad on it. So in this Allopanishad, Mohammed is the Rajasulla, whatever that may mean. There are other sectarian Upanishads of the same species, which you find to be entirely modern, and it has been so easy to write them, seeing that this language of the Samhitâ portion of the Vedas is so archaic that there is no grammar to it. Years ago I had an idea of studying the grammar of the Vedas, and I began with all earnestness to study Pânini and the *Mahâbhâshya*, but to my surprise I found that the best part of the Vedic grammar consists only of exceptions to rules. A rule is made, and after that comes a statement to the effect, "This rule will be an exception". So you see what an amount of liberty there is for anybody to write anything, the only safeguard being the dictionary of Yâska. Still, in this you will find, for the most part, but a large number of synonyms. Given all that, how easy it is to write any number of Upanishads you please. Just have a little knowledge of Sanskrit, enough to make words look like the old archaic words, and you have no fear of grammar. Then you bring in Rajasulla or any other Sulla you like. In that way many Upanishads have been manufactured, and I am told that that is being done even now. In some parts of India, I am perfectly certain, they are trying to manufacture such Upanishads among the different sects. But among the Upanishads are those, which, on the face of them, bear the evidence of genuineness, and these have been taken up by the great commentators and commented upon, especially by Shankara, followed by Ramanuja and all the rest.

There are one or two more ideas with regard to the Upanishads which I want to bring to your notice, for these are an ocean of knowledge, and to talk about the Upanishads, even for an incompetent person like myself, takes years and not one lecture only. I want, therefore, to bring to your notice one or two points in the study of the Upanishads. In the first place, they are the most wonderful poems in the world. If you read the Samhita portion of the Vedas, you now and then find passages of most marvellous beauty. For instance, the famous Shloka which describes Chaos—तम आसीत्तमसा गूढमग्रे etc.—"When darkness was hidden in darkness", so on it goes. One reads and feels the wonderful sublimity of the poetry. Do you mark this that outside of India, and inside also, there have been attempts at painting the sublime. But outside, it has always been the infinite in the muscles, the external world, the infinite of matter, or of space. When Milton or Dante, or any other great European poet, either ancient or modern, wants to paint a picture of the infinite, he tries to soar outside, to make you feel the infinite through the muscles. That attempt has been made here also. You find it in the Samhitas, the infinite of extension most marvellously painted and placed before the readers, such as has been done nowhere else. Mark that one sentence तम आसीत् तमसा गूढम्, and now mark the description of darkness by three poets. Take our own Kâlidâsa— "Darkness which can be penetrated with the point of a needle"; then Milton—"No light but rather darkness visible"; but come now to the Upanishad, "Darkness was covering darkness", "Darkness was hidden in darkness" We who live in the tropics can understand it, the sudden outburst of the monsoon, when in a moment, the horizon becomes darkened and clouds become covered with more rolling black clouds. So on, the poem goes; but yet, in the Samhita portion, all these attempts are external. As everywhere else, the attempts at finding the solution of the great problems of life have been through the external world. Just as the Greek mind or the modern European mind wants to find the solution of life and of all the sacred problems of Being by searching into the external world. so also did our forefathers, and just as the Europeans failed, they failed also. But the Western people never made a move more, they remained there, they failed in the search for the solution of the great problems of life and death in the external world, and there they remained, stranded; our forefathers also found it impossible, but

were bolder in declaring the utter helplessness of the senses
to find the solution. Nowhere else was the answer better
put than in the Upanishad: यतो वाचो निवर्तन्ते अप्राप्य मनसा सह ।
—"From whence words come back reflected, together
with the mind" ; न तत्रचक्षुर्गच्छति न वाग्गच्छति ।—"There the
eye cannot go, nor can speech reach". There are various
sentences which declare the utter helplessness of the
senses, but they did not stop there; they fell back upon
the internal nature of man, they went to get the answer
from their own soul, they became introspective; they
gave up external nature as a failure, as nothing could be
done there, as no hope, no answer could be found; they
discovered that dull, dead matter would not give them
truth, and they fell back upon the shining soul of man,
and there the answer was found.

तमेवैकं जानथ आत्मानम् अन्या वाचो विमुञ्चथ। —"Know
this Atman alone," they declared, "give up all other vain
words, and hear no other." In the Atman they found the
solution—the greatest of all Atmans, the God, the Lord of
this universe, His relation to the Atman of man, our duty
to Him, and through that our relation to each other. And
herein you find the most sublime poetry in the world.
No more is the attempt made to paint this Atman in the
language of matter. Nay, for it they have given up even all
positive language. No more is there any attempt to come
to the senses to give them the idea of the infinite, no
more is there an external, dull, dead, material, spacious,
sensuous infinite, but instead of that comes something
which is as fine as even that mentioned in the saying—

न तत्र सूर्यो भाति न चन्द्रतारकं नेमा विद्युतो भान्ति कुतोऽयमग्निः ।
तमेव भान्तमनुभाति सर्वं तस्य भासा सर्वमिदं विभाति ॥

What poetry in the world can be more sublime than
this! "There the sun cannot illumine, nor the moon, nor
the stars, there this flash of lightning cannot illumine ;
what to speak of this mortal fire!" Such poetry you find
nowhere else. Take that most marvellous Upanishad, the

Katha. What a wonderful finish, what a most marvellous
art displayed in that poem! How wonderfully it opens
with that little boy to whom Shraddhâ came, who wanted
to see Yama, and how that most marvellous of all
teachers, Death himself, teaches him the great lessons of
life and death! And what was his quest? To know the
secret of death.

The second point that I want you to remember is
the perfectly impersonal character of the Upanishads.
Although we find many names, and many speakers, and
many teachers in the Upanishads, not one of them stands
as an authority of the Upanishads, not one verse is based
upon the life of any one of them. These are simply
figures like shadows moving in the background, unfelt,
unseen, unrealised, but the real force is in the marvellous,
the brilliant, the effulgent texts of the Upanishads, perfectly impersonal. If twenty Yâjnavalkyas came and lived
and died, it does not matter; the texts are there. And
yet it is against no personality; it is broad and expansive
enough to embrace all the personalities that the world has
yet produced, and all that are yet to come. It has nothing
to say against the worship of persons, or Avatâras, or sages.
On the other hand, it is always upholding it. At the same
time, it is perfectly impersonal. It is a most marvellous
idea, like the God it preaches, the impersonal idea of the
Upanishads. For the sage, the thinker, the philosopher,
for the rationalist, it is as much impersonal as any modern
scientist can wish. And these are our scriptures. You
must remember that what the Bible is to the Christians,
what the Koran is to the Mohammedans, what the
Tripitaka is to the Buddhist, what the Zend Avesta is
to the Parsees, these Upanishads are to us. These and
nothing but these are our scriptures. The Purânas, the
Tantras, and all the other books, even the *Vyasa-Sutras*,
are of secondary, tertiary authority, but primary are the
Vedas. Manu, and the Puranas, and all the other books

are to be taken so far as they agree with the authority
of the Upanishads, and when they disagree they are to
be rejected without mercy. This we ought to remember
always, but unfortunately for India, at the present time
we have forgotten it. A petty village custom seems now
the real authority and not the teaching of the Upanishads.
A petty idea current in a wayside village in Bengal seems
to have the authority of the Vedas, and even something
better. And that word "orthodox", how wonderful its
influence! To the villager, the following of every little bit
of the Karma Kanda is the very height of "orthodoxy",
and one who does not do it is told, "Go away, you are
no more a Hindu." So there are, most unfortunately
in my motherland, persons who will take up one of
these Tantras and say, that the practice of this Tantra
is to be obeyed; he who does not do so is no more
orthodox in his views. Therefore it is better for us to
remember that in the Upanishads is the primary authority,
even the Grihya and Shrauta Sutras are subordinate to
the authority of the Vedas. They are the words of the
Rishis, our forefathers, and you have to believe them
if you want to become a Hindu. You may even believe
the most peculiar ideas about the Godhead, but if you
deny the authority of the Vedas, you are a Nâstika.
Therein lies the difference between the scriptures of the
Christians or the Buddhists and ours; theirs are all
Puranas, and not scriptures, because they describe the
history of the deluge, and the history of kings and reigning
families, and record the lives of great men, and so on.
This is the work of the Puranas, and so far as they agree
with the Vedas, they are good. So far as the Bible and the
scriptures of other nations agree with the Vedas, they are
perfectly good, but when they do not agree, they are no
more to be accepted. So with the Koran. There are
many moral teachings in these, and so far as they agree
with the Vedas they have the authority of the Puranas,

but no more. The idea is that the Vedas were never written; the idea is, they never came into existence. I was told once by a Christian missionary that their scriptures have a historical character, and therefore are true, to which I replied, "Mine have no historical character and *therefore* they are true; yours being historical, they were evidently made by some man the other day. Yours are man-made and mine are not; their non-historicity is in their favour." Such is the relation of the Vedas with all the other scriptures at the present day.

We now come to the teachings of the Upanishads. Various texts are there. Some are perfectly dualistic, while others are monistic. But there are certain doctrines which are agreed to by all the different sects of India. First, there is the doctrine of Samsâra or reincarnation of the soul. Secondly, they all agree in their psychology; first there is the body, behind that, what they call the Sukshma Sharira, the mind, and behind that even, is the Jiva. That is the great difference between Western and Indian psychology; in the Western psychology the mind is the soul, here it is not. The Antahkarana, the internal instrument, as the mind is called, is only an instrument in the hands of that Jiva, through which the Jiva works on the body or on the external world. Here they all agree, and they all also agree that this Jiva or Atman, Jivâtman as it is called by various sects, is eternal, without beginning; and that it is going from birth to birth, until it gets a final release. They all agree in this, and they also all agree in one other most vital point, which alone marks characteristically, most prominently, most vitally, the difference between the Indian and the Western mind, and it is this, that everything is in the soul. There is no inspiration, but properly speaking, expiration. All powers and all purity and all greatness—everything is in the soul. The Yogi would tell you that the Siddhis—Animâ, Laghimâ, and so on—that he wants to attain to are not

to be attained, in the proper sense of the word, but are
already there in the soul; the work is to make them
manifest. Patanjali, for instance, would tell you that
even in the lowest worm that crawls under your feet, all
the eightfold Yogi's powers are already existing. The
difference has been made by the body. As soon as it
gets a better body, the powers will become manifest, but
they are there. निमित्तमप्रयोजकं प्रकृतीनां वरणमेदस्तु ततः क्षेत्रिकवत् ।
—"Good and bad deeds are not the direct causes in the
transformations of nature, but they act as breakers of
obstacles to the evolutions of nature: as a farmer breaks
the obstacles to the course of water, which then runs
down by its own nature." Here Patanjali gives the celebrated example of the cultivator bringing water into his
field from a huge tank somewhere. The tank is already
filled and the water would flood his land in a moment,
only there is a mud-wall between the tank and his field.
As soon as the barrier is broken, in rushes the water out
of its own power and force. This mass of power and
purity and perfection is in the soul already. The only
difference is the Âvarana—this veil—that has been cast
over it. Once the veil is removed, the soul attains to
purity, and its powers become manifest. This, you ought
to remember, is the great difference between Eastern and
Western thought. Hence you find people teaching such
awful doctrines as that we are all born sinners, and
because we do not believe in such awful doctrines we are
all born wicked. They never stop to think that if we are
by our very nature wicked, we can never be good—for
how can nature change? If it changes, it contradicts
itself; it is not nature. We ought to remember this.
Here the dualist, and the Advaitist, and all others in
India agree.

The next point, which all the sects in India believe
in, is God. Of course their ideas of God will be different.
The dualists believe in a Personal God, and a personal

only. I want you to understand this word personal a
little more. This word personal does not mean that God
has a body, sits on a throne somewhere, and rules this
world, but means Saguna, with qualities. There are
many descriptions of the Personal God. This Personal
God as the Ruler, the Creator, the Preserver, and the
Destroyer of this universe is believed in by all the sects.
The Advaitists believe something more. They believe in a
still higher phase of this Personal God, which is personal-
impersonal. No adjective can illustrate where there is no
qualification, and the Advaitist would not give Him any
qualities except the three—Sat-Chit-Ananda, Existence,
Knowledge, and Bliss Absolute. This is what Shankara
did. But in the Upanishads themselves you find they
penetrate even further, and say, nothing can be predicated
of it except Neti, Neti, "Not this, Not this".

Here all the different sects of India agree. But taking
the dualistic side, as I have said, I will take Ramanuja as
the typical dualist of India, the great modern representative of the dualistic system. It is a pity that our people
in Bengal know so very little about the great religious
leaders in India, who have been born in other parts of
the country; and for the matter of that, during the whole
of the Mohammedan period, with the exception of our
Chaitanya, all the great religious leaders were born in
Southern India, and it is the intellect of Southern India
that is really governing India now; for even Chaitanya
belonged to one of these sects, a sect of the Mâdhvas.
According to Ramanuja, these three entities are eternal—
God, and soul, and nature. The souls are eternal, and
they will remain eternally existing, individualised through
eternity, and will retain their individuality all through.
Your soul will be different from my soul through all eternity, says Ramanuja, and so will this nature—which is an
existing fact, as much a fact as the existence of soul or
the existence of God—remain always different. And God

is interpenetrating, the essence of the soul, He is the Antaryâmin. In this sense Ramanuja sometimes thinks that God is one with the soul, the essence of the soul, and these souls—at the time of Pralaya, when the whole of nature becomes what he calls Sankuchita, contracted—become contracted and minute and remain so for a time. And at the beginning of the next cycle they all come out, according to their past Karma, and undergo the effect of that Karma. Every action that makes the natural inborn purity and perfection of the soul get contracted is a bad action, and every action that makes it come out and expand itself is a good action, says Ramanuja. Whatever helps to make the Vikâsha of the soul is good, and whatever makes it Sankuchita is bad. And thus the soul is going on, expanding or contracting in its actions, till through the grace of God comes salvation. And that grace comes to all souls, says Ramanuja, that are pure and struggle for that grace.

There is a celebrated verse in the Shrutis, आहारशुद्धौ सत्त्वशुद्धिः सत्त्वशुद्धौ ध्रुवा स्मृतिः "When the food is pure, then the Sattva becomes pure; when the Sattva is pure, then the Smriti"—the memory of the Lord, or the memory of our own perfection—if you are an Advaitist—"becomes truer, steadier, and absolute". Here is a great discussion. First of all, what is this Sattva? We know that according to the Sankhya—and it has been admitted by all our sects of philosophy—the body is composed of three sorts of materials—not qualities. It is the general idea that Sattva, Rajas, and Tamas are qualities. Not at all, not qualities but the materials of this universe, and with Âhâra-shuddhi, when the food is pure, the Sattva material becomes pure. The one theme of the Vedanta is to get this Sattva. As I have told you, the soul is already pure and perfect, and it is, according to the Vedanta, covered up by Rajas and Tamas particles. The Sattva particles are the most luminous, and the effulgence of the soul penetrates through them as easily as light through glass. So if the Rajas and Tamas particles go, and leave the Sattva particles, in this state the power and purity of the soul will appear, and leave the soul more manifest.

Therefore it is necessary to have this Sattva. And the text says, "When Ahara becomes pure". Ramanuja takes this word Ahara to mean food, and he has made it one of the turning points of his philosophy. Not only so, it has affected the whole of India, and all the different sects. Therefore it is necessary for us to understand what it means, for that, according to Ramanuja, is one of the principal factors in our life, Ahara-shuddhi. What makes food impure? asks Ramanuja. Three sorts of defects make food impure—first, Jâti-dosha, the defect in the very nature of the class to which the food belongs, as the smell in onions, garlic, and suchlike. The next is Âshraya-dosha, the defect in the person from whom the food comes; food coming from a wicked person will make you impure. I myself have seen many great sages in India following strictly that advice all their lives. Of course they had the power to know who brought the food, and even who had touched the food, and I have seen it in my own life, not once, but hundreds of times. Then Nimitta-dosha, the defect of impure things or influences coming in contact with food is another. We had better attend to that a little more now. It has become too prevalent in India to take food with dirt and dust and bits of hair in it. If food is taken from which these three defects have been removed, that makes Sattva-shuddhi, purifies the Sattva. Religion seems to be a very easy task then. Then every one can have religion if it comes by eating pure food only. There is none so weak or incompetent in this world, that I know, who cannot save himself from these defects. Then comes Shankaracharya, who says this word Ahara means thought collected in the mind; when that becomes pure, the Sattva becomes pure, and not before that. You may eat what

you like. If food alone would purify the Sattva, then feed
the monkey with milk and rice all its life; would it become
a great Yogi? Then the cows and the deer would be great
Yogis. As has been said, "If it is by bathing much that
heaven is reached, the fishes will get to heaven first. If
by eating vegetables a man gets to heaven, the cows and
the deer will get to heaven first."

But what is the solution? Both are necessary. Of
course the idea that Shankaracharya gives us of Ahara is
the primary idea. But pure food, no doubt, helps pure
thought; it has an intimate connection; both ought to be
there. But the defect is that in modern India we have
forgotten the advice of Shankaracharya and taken only the
"pure food" meaning. That is why people get mad with
me when I say, religion has got into the kitchen; and if
you had been in Madras with me, you would have agreed
with me. The Bengalis are better than that. In Madras
they throw away food if anybody looks at it. And with
all this, I do not see that the people are any the better
there. If only eating this and that sort of food and saving
it from the looks of this person and that person would
give them perfection, you would expect them all to be
perfect men, which they are not.

Thus, although these are to be combined and linked
together to make a perfect whole, do not put the cart
before the horse. There is a cry nowadays about this and
that food and about Varnâshrama, and the Bengalis are
the most vociferous in these cries. I would ask every
one of you, what do you know about this Varnashrama?
Where are the four castes today in this country? Answer
me; I do not see the four castes. Just as our Bengali
proverb has it, "A headache without a head", so you want
to make this Varnashrama here. There are not four castes
here. I see only the Brâhmin and the Shudra. If there are
the Kshatriyas and the Vaishyas, where are they and why
do not you Brahmins order them to take the Yajnopavita

and study the Vedas, as every Hindu ought to do? And
if the Vaishyas and the Kshatriyas do not exist, but only
the Brahmins and the Shudras, the Shâstras say that the
Brahmin must not live in a country where there are only
Shudras; so depart bag and baggage! Do you know what
the Shastras say about people who have been eating
Mlechchha food and living under a government of the
Mlechchhas, as you have for the past thousand years? Do
you know the penance for that? The penance would be
burning oneself with one's own hands. Do you want to
pass as teachers and walk like hypocrities? If you believe
in your Shastras, burn yourselves first like the one great
Brahmin did who went with Alexander the Great and
burnt himself because he thought he had eaten the food of
a Mlechchha. Do like that, and you will see that the
whole nation will be at your feet. You do not believe
in your own Shastras and yet want to make others believe
in them. If you think you are not able to do that in this
age, admit your weakness and excuse the weakness of
others, take the other castes up, give them a helping
hand, let them study the Vedas and become just as good
Âryans as any other Aryans in the world, and be you
likewise Aryans, you Brahmins of Bengal.

Give up this filthy Vâmâchâra that is killing your
country. You have not seen the other parts of India.
When I see how much the Vamachara has entered our
society, I find it a most disgraceful place with all its boast
of culture. These Vamachara sects are honeycombing
our society in Bengal. Those who come out in the day-
time and preach most loudly about Âchâra, it is they who
carry on the horrible debauchery at night and are backed
by the most dreadful books. They are ordered by the
books to do these things. You who are of Bengal know it.
The Bengali Shastras are the Vamachara Tantras. They
are published by the cart-load, and you poison the minds
of your children with them instead of teaching them your

Shrutis. Fathers of Calcutta, do you not feel ashamed
that such horrible stuff as these Vamachara Tantras, with
translations too, should be put into the hands of your
boys and girls, and their minds poisoned, and that they
should be brought up with the idea that these are the
Shastras of the Hindus? If you are ashamed, take them
away from your children, and let them read the true
Shastras, the Vedas, the Gita, the Upanishads.

According to the dualistic sects of India, the individual
souls remain as individuals throughout, and God creates
the universe out of pre-existing material only as the
efficient cause. According to the Advaitists, on the other
hand, God is both the material and the efficient cause of
the universe. He is not only the Creator of the universe,
but He creates it out of Himself. That is the Advaitist
position. There are crude dualistic sects who believe that
this world has been created by God out of Himself, and
at the same time God is eternally separate from the
universe, and everything is eternally subordinate to the
Ruler of the universe. There are sects too who also
believe that out of Himself God has evolved this universe,
and individuals in the long run attain to Nirvâna to give
up the finite and become the Infinite. But these sects have
disappeared. The one sect of Advaitists that you see in
modern India is composed of the followers of Shankara.
According to Shankara, God is both the material and the
efficient cause through Mâyâ, but not in reality. God has
not become this universe; but the universe is not, and
God is. This is one of the highest points to understand of
Advaita Vedanta, this idea of Maya. I am afraid I have
no time to discuss this one most difficult point in our
philosophy. Those of you who are acquainted with
Western philosophy will find something very similar in
Kant. But I must warn you, those of you who have
studied Professor Max Müller's writings on Kant, that
there is one idea most misleading. It was Shankara who

first found out the idea of the identity of time, space, and
causation with Maya, and I had the good fortune to find
one or two passages in Shankara's commentaries and send
them to my friend the Professor. So even that idea was
here in India. Now this is a peculiar theory—this Maya
theory of the Advaita Vedantists. The Brahman is all
that exists, but differentiation has been caused by this
Maya. Unity, the one Brahman, is the ultimate, the goal,
and herein is an eternal dissension again between Indian
and Western thought. India has thrown this challenge to
the world for thousands of years, and the challenge has
been taken up by different nations, and the result is that
they all succumbed and you live. This is the challenge
that this world is a delusion, that it is all Maya, that
whether you eat off the ground with your fingers or dine
off golden plates, whether you live in palaces and are one
of the mightest monarchs or are the poorest of beggars,
death is the one result; it is all the same, all Maya. That
is the old Indian theme, and again and again nations are
springing up trying to unsay it, to disprove it; becoming
great, with enjoyment as their watchword, power in their
hands, they use that power to the utmost, enjoy to the
utmost, and the next moment they die. We stand for ever
because we see that everything is Maya. The children of
Maya live for ever, but the children of enjoyment die.

Here again is another great difference. Just as you
find the attempts of Hegel and Schopenhauer in German
philosophy, so you will find the very same ideas brought
forward in ancient India. Fortunately for us, Hegelianism
was nipped in the bud and not allowed to sprout and cast
its baneful shoots over this motherland of ours. Hegel's
one idea is that the one, the absolute, is only chaos, and
that the individualised form is the greater. The world is
greater than the non-world, Samsâra is greater than
salvation. That is the one idea, and the more you plunge
into this Samsara the more your soul is covered with the

workings of life, the better you are. They say, do you
not see how we build houses, cleanse the streets, enjoy the
senses? Ay, behind that they may hide rancour, misery,
horror—behind every bit of that enjoyment.

On the other hand, our philosophers have from the
very first declared that every manifestation, what you call
evolution, is vain, a vain attempt of the unmanifested to
manifest itself. Ay, you the mighty cause of this
universe, trying to reflect yourself in little mud puddles!
But after making the attempt for a time you find out it
was all in vain and beat a retreat to the place from
whence you came. This is Vairâgya, or renunciation, and
the very beginning of religion. How can religion or morality begin without renunciation itself? The Alpha and
Omega is renunciation. "Give up," says the Veda, "give
up." That is the one way, "Give up". न प्रजया धनेन त्यागेनैके
ऽमृतत्वमानशुः —"Neither through wealth, nor through progeny, but by giving up alone that immortality is to be
reached." That is the dictate of the Indian books. Of course,
there have been great givers-up of the world, even sitting
on thrones. But even (King) Janaka himself had to renounce ; who was a greater renouncer than he? But in
modern times we all want to be called Janakas! They are
all Janakas (lit. fathers) of children—unclad, ill-fed, miserable children. The word Janaka can be applied to them in
that sense only; they have none of the shining, Godlike
thoughts as the old Janaka had. These are our modern
Janakas! A little less of this Janakism now, and come
straight to the mark! If you can give up, you will have
religion. If you cannot, you may read all the books that
are in the world, from East to West, swallow all the libraries, and become the greatest of Pandits, but if you have
Karma Kanda only, you are nothing; there is no spirituality. Through renunciation alone this immortality is to be
reached. It is the power, the great power, that cares not
even for the universe; then it is that   ब्रह्माण्डम्   गोष्पदायते ।

"The whole universe becomes like a hollow made by a cow's foot."

Renunciation, that is the flag, the banner of India, floating over the world, the one undying thought which India sends again and again as a warning to dying races, as a warning to all tyranny, as a warning to wickedness in the world. Ay, Hindus, let not your hold of that banner go. Hold it aloft. Even if you are weak and cannot renounce, do not lower the ideal. Say, "I am weak and cannot renounce the world", but do not try to be hypo-crites, torturing texts, and making specious arguments, and trying to throw dust in the eyes of people who are ignorant. Do not do that, but own you are weak. For the idea is great, that of renunciation. What matters it if millions fail in the attempt, if ten soldiers or even two return victorious! Blessed be the millions dead! Their blood has bought the victory. This renunciation is the one ideal throughout the different Vedic sects except one, and that is the Vallabhâchârya sect in Bombay Presidency, and most of you are aware what comes where renunciation does not exist. We want orthodoxy—even the hideous-ly orthodox, even those who smother themselves with ashes, even those who stand with their hands uplifted. Ay, we want them, unnatural though they be, for stand-ing for that idea of giving up, and acting as a warning to the race against succumbing to the effeminate luxuries that are creeping into India, eating into our very vitals, and tending to make the whole race a race of hypocrites. We want to have a little of asceticism. Renunciation conquered India in days of yore, it has still to conquer India. Still it stands as the greatest and highest of Indian ideals—this renunciation. The land of Buddha, the land of Ramanuja, of Ramakrishna Paramahamsa, the land of renunciation, the land where, from the days of yore, Karma Kanda was preached against, and even today there are hundreds who have given up everything, and become

Jivanmuktas—ay, will that land give up its ideals? Certainly not. There may be people whose brains have become turned by the Western luxurious ideals; there may be thousands and hundreds of thousands who have drunk deep of enjoyment, this curse of the West—the senses—the curse of the world; yet for all that, there will be other thousands in this motherland of mine to whom religion will ever be a reality, and who will be ever ready to give up without counting the cost, if need be.

Another ideal very common in all our sects, I want to place before you; it is also a vast subject. This unique idea that religion is to be realised is in India alone. नायमात्मा प्रवचनेन लभ्यो न मेधया न बहुना श्रुतेन—"This Atman is not to be reached by too much talking, nor is it to be reached by the power of intellect, nor by much study of the scriptures." Nay, ours is the only scripture in the world that declares, not even by the study of the scriptures can the Atman be realised—not talks, not lecturing, none of that, but It is to be realised. It comes from the teacher to the disciple. When this insight comes to the disciple, everything is cleared up and realisation follows.

One more idea. There is a peculiar custom in Bengal, which they call Kula-Guru, or hereditary Guruship. "My father was your Guru, now I shall be your Guru. My father was the Guru of your father, so shall I be yours." What is a Guru? Let us go back to the Shrutis—"He who knows the secret of the Vedas", not bookworms, not grammarians, not Pandits in general, but he who knows the meaning. यथा खरश्चन्दनभारवाही भारस्य वेत्ता न तु चन्दनस्य —"An ass laden with a load of sandalwood knows only the weight of the wood, but not its precious qualities"; so are these Pandits. We do not want such. What can they teach if they have no realisation? When I was a boy here, in this city of Calcutta, I used to go from place to place in search of religion, and everywhere I asked the lecturer after hearing very big lectures, "Have you seen God?"

The man was taken aback at the idea of seeing God; and
the only man who told me, "I have", was Ramakrishna
Paramahamsa, and not only so, but he said, "I will put
you in the way of seeing Him too". The Guru is not
a man who twists and tortures texts. वाग्वैखरी शब्दझरी शास्त्र-
व्याख्यानकौशलं वैदुष्यं विदुषां तद्वद्भुक्तये न तु मुक्तये ।—"Different ways
of throwing out words, different ways of explaining texts of
the scriptures, these are for the enjoyment of the learned,
not for freedom." Shrotriya, he who knows the secret of
the Shrutis, Avrijina, the sinless, and Akâmahata, unpierc-
ed by desire—he who does not want to make money by
teaching you—he is the Shânta, the Sâdhu, who comes as
the spring which brings the leaves and blossoms to various plants but does not ask anything from the plant, for
its very nature is to do good. It does good and there it is.
Such is the Guru, तीर्णाः स्वयं भीमभवार्णवं जनानहेतुनान्यानपि तारयन्तः
—"Who has himself crossed this terrible ocean of life, and
without any idea of gain to himself, helps others also to
cross the ocean." This is the Guru, and mark that none
else can be a Guru, for अविद्यायामन्तरे वर्तमानाः स्वयं धीराः पण्डि-
तम्मन्यमानाः । दन्द्रम्यमाणाः परियन्ति मूढाः अन्धेनैव नीयमाना यथान्धाः
—"Themselves steeped in darkness, but in the pride of
their hearts, thinking they know everything, the fools want
to help others, and they go round and round in many
crooked ways, staggering to and fro, and thus like the blind
leading the blind, both fall into the ditch." Thus say the
Vedas. Compare that and your present custom. You
are Vedantists, you are very orthodox, are you not? You
are great Hindus and very orthodox. Ay, what I want
to do is to make you more orthodox. The more orthodox
you are, the more sensible; and the more you think of
modern orthodoxy, the more foolish you are. Go back to
your old orthodoxy, for in those days every sound that
came from these books, every pulsation, was out of a
strong, steady, and sincere heart; every note was true.
After that came degradation in art, in science, in religion,

in everything, national degradation. We have no time to discuss the causes, but all the books written about that period breathe of the pestilence—the national decay; instead of vigour, only wails and cries. Go back, go back to the old days when there was strength and vitality. Be strong once more, drink deep of this fountain of yore, and that is the only condition of life in India.

According to the Advaitist, this individuality which we have today is a delusion. This has been a hard nut to crack all over the world. Forthwith you tell a man he is not an individual, he is so much afraid that his individuality, whatever that may be, will be lost! But the Advaitist says there never has been an individuality, you have been changing every moment of your life. You were a child and thought in one way, now you are a man and think another way, again you will be an old man and think differently. Everybody is changing. If so, where is your individuality? Certainly not in the body, or in the mind, or in thought. And beyond that is your Atman, and, says the Advaitist, this Atman is the Brahman Itself. There cannot be two infinites. There is only one individual and it is infinite. In plain words, we are rational beings, and we want to reason. And what is reason? More or less of classification, until you cannot go on any further. And the finite can only find its ultimate rest when it is classified into the infinite. Take up a finite thing and go on analysing it, but you will find rest nowhere until you reach the ultimate or infinite, and that infinite, says the Advaitist, is what alone exists. Everything else is Maya, nothing else has real existence; whatever is of existence in any material thing is this Brahman; we are this Brahman, and the shape and everything else is Maya. Take away the form and shape, and you and I are all one. But we have to guard against the word, "I". Generally people say, "If I am the Brahman, why cannot I do this and that?" But this is using the word in a different sense.

As soon as you think you are bound, no more you are
Brahman, the Self, who wants nothing, whose light is inside. All His pleasures and bliss are inside; perfectly satisfied with Himself, He wants nothing, expects nothing,
perfectly fearless, perfectly free. That is Brahman. In
That we are all one.

Now this seems, therefore, to be the great point of
difference between the dualist and the Advaitist. You
find even great commentators like Shankaracharya making
meanings of texts, which, to my mind, sometimes do not
seem to be justified. Sometimes you find Ramanuja dealing with texts in a way that is not very clear. The idea
has been even among our Pandits that only one of these
sects can be true and the rest must be false, although they
have the idea in the Shrutis, the most wonderful idea that
India has yet to give to the world: एकं सद्विप्रा बहुधा वदन्ति ।
—"That which exists is One ; sages call It by various
names." That has been the theme, and the working out of
the whole of this life-problem of the nation is the working
out of that theme—एकं सद्विप्रा बहुधा वदन्ति । Yea, except a very
few learned men, I mean, barring a very few spiritual
men, in India, we always forget this. We forget this great
idea, and you will find that there are persons among
Pandits—I should think ninety-eight per cent—who are
of opinion that either the Advaitist will be true, or the
Vishishtadvaitist will be true, or the Dvaitist will be true;
and if you go to Varanasi, and sit for five minutes in one
of the Ghâts there, you will have demonstration of what I
say. You will see a regular bull-fight going on about these
various sects and things.

Thus it remains. Then came one whose life was the
explanation, whose life was the working out of the harmony that is the background of all the different sects of
India, I mean Ramakrishna Paramahamsa. It is his life
that explains that both of these are necessary, that they
are like the geocentric and the heliocentric theories in

astronomy. When a child is taught astronomy, he is taught the geocentric first, and works out similar ideas of astronomy to the geocentric. But when he comes to finer points of astronomy, the heliocentric will be necessary, and he will understand it better. Dualism is the natural idea of the senses; as long as we are bound by the senses we are bound to see a God who is only Personal, and nothing but Personal, we are bound to see the world as it is. Says Ramanuja, "So long as you think you are a body, and you think you are a mind, and you think you are a Jiva, every act of perception will give you the three—Soul, and nature, and something as causing both." But yet, at the same time, even the idea of the body disappears where the mind itself becomes finer and finer, till it has almost disappeared, when all the different things that make us fear, make us weak, and bind us down to this body-life have disappeared. Then and then alone one finds out the truth of that grand old teaching. What is the teaching?

इहैव तैर्जितः सर्गो येषां साम्ये स्थितं मनः ।
निर्दोषं हि समं ब्रह्म तस्माद्ब्रह्मणि ते स्थिताः ॥

"Even in this life they have conquered the round of birth and death whose minds are firm-fixed on the sameness of everything, for God is pure and the same to all, and therefore such are said to be living in God."

समं पश्यन् हि सर्वत्र समवस्थितमीश्वरम् ।
न हिनस्त्यात्मनात्मानं ततो याति परां गतिम् ॥

"Thus seeing the Lord the same everywhere, he, the sage, does not hurt the Self by the self, and so goes to the highest goal."

ADDRESS OF WELCOME AT ALMORA
AND REPLY

On his arrival at Almora, Swamiji received an Address of Welcome in Hindi from the citizens of Almora, of which the following is a translation:

GREAT-SOULED ONE,

Since the time we heard that, after gaining spiritual conquest in the West, you had started from England for your motherland, India, we were naturally desirous of having the pleasure of seeing you. By the grace of the Almighty, that auspicious moment has at last come. The saying of the great poet and the prince of Bhaktas, Tulasidâsa, "A person who intensely loves another is sure to find him", has been fully realised today. We have assembled here to welcome you with sincere devotion. You have highly obliged us by your kindly taking so much trouble in paying a visit to this town again. We can hardly thank you enough for your kindness. Blessed are you! Blessed, blessed is the revered Gurudeva who initiated you into Yoga. Blessed is the land of Bhârata where, even in this fearful Kali Yuga, there exist leaders of Aryan races like yourself. Even at an early period of life, you have by your simplicity, sincerity, character, philanthropy, severe discipline, conduct, and the preaching of knowledge, acquired that immaculate fame throughout the world of which we feel so proud.

In truth, you have accomplished that difficult task which no one ever undertook in this country since the days of Shri Shankarâchârya. Which of us ever dreamt that a descendant of the old Indian Aryans, by dint of Tapas, would prove to the learned people of England and America the superiority of the ancient Indian religion over other creeds? Before the representatives of different religions, assembled in the world's Parliament of Religions held in Chicago, you so ably advocated the superiority of the ancient religion of India that their eyes were opened. In that great assembly, learned speakers defended their respective religions in their own way, but you surpassed them all. You completely established that no religion can compete with the religion of the Vedas. Not only this, but by preaching the ancient wisdom at various places in the continents aforesaid, you have attracted many learned men towards the ancient Aryan religion and philosophy. In England, too, you have planted the banner of the ancient religion, which it is impossible now to remove.

Up to this time, the modern civilised nations of Europe and America were entirely ignorant of the genuine nature of our religion, but you have with our spiritual teaching opened their eyes, by which they have come to know that the ancient religion, which owing to their ignorance they used to brand "as a religion of subtleties of conceited people or a mass of discourses meant for fools", is a mine of gems. Certainly, "It is better to have a virtuous and accomplished son than to have hundreds of foolish ones"; "It is the moon that singly with its light dispels all darkness and not all the stars put together." It is only the life of a good and virtuous son like yourself that is really useful to the world. Mother India is consoled in her decayed state by the presence of pious sons like you. Many have crossed the seas and aimlessly run to and fro, but it was only through the reward of your past good Karma that you have proved the greatness of our religion beyond the seas. You have made it the sole aim of your life by word, thought, and deed, to impart spiritual instruction to humanity. You are always ready to give religious instruction.

We have heard with great pleasure that you intend

establishing a Math (monastery) here, and we sincerely pray that your efforts in this direction may be crowned with success. The great Shankaracharya also, after his spiritual conquest, established a Math at Badarikâshrama in the Himalayas for the protection of the ancient religion. Similarly, if your desire is also fulfilled, India will be greatly benefited. By the establishment of the Math, we, Kumaonese, will derive special spiritual advantages, and we shall not see the ancient religion gradually disappearing from our midst.

From time immemorial, this part of the country has been the land of asceticism. The greatest of the Indian sages passed their time in piety and asceticism in this land; but that has become a thing of the past. We earnestly hope that by the establishment of the Math you will kindly make us realise it again. It was this sacred land which enjoyed the celebrity all over India of having true religion, Karma, discipline, and fair dealing, all of which seem to have been decaying by the efflux of time. And we hope that by your noble exertions this land will revert to its ancient religious state.

We cannot adequately express the joy we have felt at your arrivial here. May you live long, enjoying perfect health and leading a philanthropic life! May your spiritual powers be ever on the increase, so that through your endeavours the unhappy state of India may soon disappear!

Two other addresses were presented, to which the Swami made the following brief reply:

This is the land of dreams of our forefathers, in which was born Pârvati, the Mother of India. This is the holy land where every ardent soul in India wants to come at the end of its life, and to close the last chapter of its mortal career. On the tops of the mountains of this blessed land, in the depths of its caves, on the banks of its rushing torrents, have been thought out the most wonderful thoughts, a little bit of which has drawn so much admiration even from foreigners, and which have been pronounced by the most competent of judges to be incomparable. This is the land which, since my very childhood, I have been dreaming of passing my life in, and as all of you are aware, I have attempted again and again to live here; and although the time was not ripe, and I had work to do and was whirled outside of this holy place, yet it is the hope of my life to end my days somewhere in this Father of Mountains where Rishis lived, where philosophy was born. Perhaps, my friends, I shall not be able to do it, in the way that I had planned before—how I wish that silence, that unknownness would be given to me—yet I sincerely pray and hope, and almost believe, that my last days will be spent here, of all places on earth.

Inhabitants of this holy land, accept my gratitude for the kind praise that has fallen from you for my little work in the West. But at the same time, my mind does not want to speak of that, either in the East or in the West. As peak after peak of this Father of Mountains began to appear before my sight, all the propensities to work, that ferment that had been going on in my brain for years, seemed to quiet down, and instead of talking about what had been done and what was going to be done, the mind reverted to that one eternal theme which the Himalayas always teach us, that one theme which is reverberating in the very atmosphere of the place, the one theme the murmur of which I hear even now in the rushing whirlpools of its rivers—renunciation! सर्वं वस्तु भयान्वितं भुवि नृणां वैराग्यमेवाभयम्—"Everything in this life is fraught with fear. It is renunciation alone that makes one fearless." Yes, this is the land of renunciation.

The time will not permit me, and the circumstances are not fitting, to speak to you fully. I shall have to conclude, therefore, by pointing out to you that the

Himalayas stand for that renunciation, and the grand
lesson we shall ever teach to humanity will be renunciation. As our forefathers used to be attracted towards it
in the latter days of their lives, so strong souls from all
quarters of this earth, in time to come, will be attracted
to this Father of Mountains, when all this fight between
sects and all those differences in dogmas will not be
remembered any more, and quarrels between your religion
and my religion will have vanished altogether, when
mankind will understand that there is but one eternal religion, and that is the perception of the divine within, and
the rest is mere froth: such ardent souls will come here
knowing that the world is but vanity of vanities, knowing
that everything is useless except the worship of the Lord
and the Lord alone.

Friends, you have been very kind to allude to an idea
of mine, which is to start a centre in the Himalayas, and
perhaps I have sufficiently explained why it should be so,
why, above all others, this is the spot which I want to
select as one of the great centres to teach this universal
religion. These mountains are associated with the best
memories of our race; if these Himalayas are taken away
from the history of religious India, there will be very little
left behind. Here, therefore, must be one of those
centres, not merely of activity, but more of calmness, of
meditation, and of peace; and I hope some day to realise
it. I hope also to meet you at other times and have better
opportunities of talking to you. For the present, let me
thank you again for all the kindness that has been shown
to me, and let me take it as not only kindness shown to me
in person, but as to one who represents our religion. May
it never leave our hearts! May we always remain as pure
as we are at the present moment, and as enthusiastic for
spirituality as we are just now!

VEDIC TEACHING IN THEORY AND
PRACTICE

When the Swami's visit was drawing to a close, his
friends in Almora invited him to give a lecture in Hindi.
He consented to make the attempt for the first time. He
began slowly, and soon warmed to his theme, and found
himself building his phrases and almost his words as he
went along. Those best acquainted with the difficulties
and limitations of the Hindi language, still undeveloped
as a medium for oratory, expressed their opinion that a
personal triumph had been achieved by Swamiji and that
he had proved by his masterly use of Hindi that the
language had in it undreamt-of possibilities of development in the direction of oratory.

Another lecture was delivered at the English Club in
English, of which a brief summary follows.

The subject was "Vedic Teaching in Theory and
Practice". A short historical sketch of the rise of the worship of the tribal God and its spread through conquest of
other tribes was followed by an account of the Vedas.
Their nature, character, and teaching were briefly touched
upon. Then the Swami spoke about the soul, comparing
the Western method which seeks for the solution of vital
and religious mysteries in the outside world, with the
Eastern method which finding no answer in nature outside
turns its inquiry within. He justly claimed for his nation
the glory of being the discoverers of the introspective
method peculiar to themselves, and of having given to
humanity the priceless treasures of spirituality which are
the result of that method alone. Passing from this theme,
naturally so dear to the heart of a Hindu, the Swami
reached the climax of his power as a spiritual teacher

when he described the relation of the soul to God, its aspiration after and real unity with God. For some time it seemed as though the teacher, his words, his audience, and the spirit pervading them all were one. No longer was there any consciousness of "I" and "Thou", of "This" or "That". The different units collected there were for the time being lost and merged in the spiritual radiance which emanated so powerfully from the great teacher and held them all more than spellbound.

Those that have frequently heard him will recall similar experiences when he ceased to be Swami Vivekananda lecturing to critical and attentive hearers, when all details and personalities were lost, names and forms disappeared, only the Spirit remaining, uniting the speaker, hearer, and the spoken word.

BHAKTI

(Delivered at Sialkote, Punjab)

In response to invitations from the Punjab and Kashmir, the Swami Vivekananda travelled through those parts. He stayed in Kashmir for over a month and his work there was very much appreciated by the Maharaja and his brothers. He then spent a few days in visiting Murree, Rawalpindi, and Jammu, and at each of these places he delivered lectures. Subsequently he visited Sialkote and lectured twice, once in English and once in Hindi. The subject of the Swamiji's Hindi lecture was Bhakti, a summary of which, translated into English, is given below:

The various religions that exist in the world, although they differ in the form of worship they take, are really one. In some places the people build temples and worship in them, in some they worship fire, in others they prostrate themselves before idols, while there are many who do not believe at all in God. All are true, for, if you look to the real spirit, the real religion, and the truths in each of them, they are all alike. In some religions God is not worshipped, nay, His existence is not believed in, but good and worthy men are worshipped as if they were Gods. The example worthy of citation in this case is Buddhism. Bhakti is everywhere, whether directed to God or to noble persons. Upâsanâ in the form of Bhakti is everywhere supreme, and Bhakti is more easily attained than Jnâna. The latter requires favourable circumstances and strenuous practice. Yoga cannot be properly practised unless a man is physically very healthy and free from all worldly attachments. But Bhakti can be more easily practised by persons in every condition of life. Shândilya Rishi, who wrote about Bhakti, says that extreme love for God is Bhakti. Prahlâda speaks to the same effect. If a man does not get food one day, he is troubled; if his son dies, how agonising it is to him! The true Bhakta feels the same pangs in his heart when he yearns after God. The great quality of Bhakti is that it cleanses the mind, and the firmly established Bhakti for the Supreme Lord is alone sufficient to purify the mind. "O God, Thy names are innumerable, but in every name Thy power is manifest, and every name is pregnant with deep and mighty significance." We should think of God always and not consider time and place for doing so.

The different names under which God is worshipped are apparently different. One thinks that his method of worshipping God is the most efficacious, and another thinks that his is the more potent process of attaining salvation. But look at the true basis of all, and it is one. The Shaivas call Shiva the most powerful; the Vaishnavas hold to their all-powerful Vishnu; the worshippers of Devi will not yield to any in their idea that their Devi is the most omnipotent power in the universe. Leave inimical thoughts aside if you want to have permanent Bhakti. Hatred is a thing which greatly impedes the course of Bhakti, and the man who hates none reaches God. Even then the devotion for one's own ideal is necessary. Hanumân says, "Vishnu and Râma, I know, are one and the same, but after all, the lotus-eyed Rama is my best treasure." The peculiar tendencies with which a person is born must remain with him. That is the chief reason why the world cannot be of one religion—and God forbid that there should be one religion only—for the world would then be a chaos and not a cosmos. A man must follow the tendencies peculiar to himself; and if he gets a teacher to help him to advance along his own lines, he will progress. We should let a person go the way he intends to go, but if we try to force him into another path, he will lose what he has already attained and will become worthless. As the face of one person does not resemble that of another, so the nature of one differs from that of another, and why should he not be allowed to act accordingly? A river flows in a certain direction; and if you direct the course into a regular channel, the current becomes more rapid and the force is increased, but try to divert it from its proper course, and you will see the result; the volume as well as the force will be lessened. This life is very important, and it, therefore, ought to be guided in the way one's tendency prompts him. In India there was no enmity, and every religion was left unmolested; so religion has lived. It ought to be remembered that quarrels about religion arise from thinking that one alone has the truth and whoever does not believe as one does is a fool; while another thinks that the other is a hypocrite, for if he were not one, he would follow him.

If God wished that people should follow one religion, why have so many religions sprung up? Methods have been vainly tried to force one religion upon everyone. Even when the sword was lifted to make all people follow one religion, history tells us that ten religions sprang up in its place. One religion cannot suit all. Man is the product of two forces, action and reaction, which make him think. If such forces did not exercise a man's mind, he would be incapable of thinking. Man is a creature who thinks; Manushya (man) is a being with Manas (mind); and as soon as his thinking power goes, he becomes no better than an animal. Who would like such a man? God forbid that any such state should come upon the people of India. Variety in unity is necessary to keep man as man. Variety ought to be preserved in everything; for as long as there is variety the world will exist. Of course variety does not merely mean that one is small and the other is great; but if all play their parts equally well in their respective position in life, the variety is still preserved. In every religion there have been men good and able, thus making the religion to which they belonged worthy of respect; and as there are such people in every religion, there ought to be no hatred for any sect whatsoever.

Then the question may be asked, should we respect that religion which advocates vice? The answer will be certainly in the negative, and such a religion ought to be expelled at once, because it is productive of harm. All religion is to be based upon morality, and personal purity is to be counted superior to Dharma. In this connection it ought to be known that Âchâra means purity inside and outside. External purity can be attained by cleansing the body with water and other things which are recommended in the Shâstras. The internal man is to be purified by not speaking falsehood, by not drinking, by not doing immoral acts, and by doing good to others. If you do not commit any sin, if you do not tell lies, if you do not drink, gamble, or commit theft, it is good. But that is only your duty and you cannot be applauded for it. Some service to others is also to be done. As you do good to yourself, so you must do good to others.

Here I shall say something about food regulations. All the old customs have faded away, and nothing but a vague notion of not eating with this man and not eating with that man has been left among our countrymen. Purity by touch is the only relic left of the good rules laid down hundreds of years ago. Three kinds of food are forbidden in the Shastras. First, the food that is by its very nature defective, as garlic or onions. If a man eats too much of them it creates passion, and he may be led to commit immoralities, hateful both to God and man. Secondly, food contaminated by external impurities. We ought to select some place quite neat and clean in which to keep our food. Thirdly, we should avoid eating food touched by a wicked man, because contact with such produces bad ideas in us. Even if one be a son of a

Brâhmin, but is profligate and immoral in his habits, we should not eat food from his hands.

But the spirit of these observances is gone. What is left is this, that we cannot eat from the hands of any man who is not of the highest caste, even though he be the most wise and holy person. The disregard of those old rules is ever to be found in the confectioner's shop. If you look there, you will find flies hovering all over the confectionery, and the dust from the road blowing upon the sweetmeats, and the confectioner himself in a dress that is not very clean and neat. Purchasers should declare with one voice that they will not buy sweets unless they are kept in glass-cases in the Halwai's shop. That would have the salutary effect of preventing flies from conveying cholera and other plague germs to the sweets. We ought to improve, but instead of improving we have gone back. Manu says that we should not spit in water, but we throw all sorts of filth into the rivers. Considering all these things we find that the purification of one's outer self is very necessary. The Shâstrakâras knew that very well. But now the real spirit of this observance of purity about food is lost and the letter only remains. Thieves, drunkards, and criminals can be our caste-fellows, but if a good and noble man eats food with a person of a lower caste, who is quite as respectable as himself, he will be outcasted and lost for ever. This custom has been the bane of our country. It ought, therefore, to be distinctly understood that sin is incurred by coming in contact with sinners, and nobility in the company of good persons; and keeping aloof from the wicked is the external purification.

The internal purification is a task much more severe. It consists in speaking the truth, serving the poor, helping the needy, etc. Do we always speak the truth? What happens is often this. People go to the house of a rich person for some business of their own and flatter him by calling him benefactor of the poor and so forth, even though that man may cut the throat of a poor man coming to his house. What is this? Nothing but falsehood. And it is this that pollutes the mind. It is therefore, truly said that whatever a man says who has purified his inner self for twelve years without entertaining a single vicious idea during that period is sure to come true. This is the power of truth, and one who has cleansed both the inner and the outer self is alone capable of Bhakti. But the beauty is that Bhakti itself cleanses the mind to a great extent. Although the Jews, Mohammedans, and Christians do not set so much importance upon the excessive external purification of the body as the Hindus do, still they have it in some form or other; they find that to a certain extent it is always required. Among the Jews, idol-worship is condemned, but they had a temple in which was kept a chest which they called an ark, in which the Tables of the Law were preserved, and above the chest were two figures of angels with wings outstretched, between which the Divine Presence was supposed to manifest itself as a cloud. That temple has long since been destroyed, but the new temples are made exactly after the old fashion, and in the chest religious books are kept. The Roman Catholics and the Greek Christians have idol-worship in certain forms. The image of Jesus and that of his mother are worshipped. Among Protestants there is no idol-worship, yet they worship God in a personal form, which may be called idol-worship in another form. Among Parsees and Iranians fire-worship is carried on to a great extent. Among Mohammedans the prophets and great and noble persons are worshipped, and they turn their faces towards the Caaba when they pray. These things show that men at the first stage of religious development have to make use of something external, and when the inner self becomes purified they turn to more abstract conceptions. "When the Jiva is sought to be united with Brahman it is best, when meditation is practised it is mediocre, repetition of names is the lowest form, and external worship is the lowest of the low." But it should be distinctly understood that even in practising the last there is no sin. Everybody ought to do what he is able to do; and if he be dissuaded from that, he will do it in some other way in order to attain his end. So we should not speak ill of a man who worships idols. He is in that stage of growth, and, therefore, must have them; wise men should try to help forward such men and get them to do better. But there is no use in quarrelling about these various sorts of worship.

Some persons worship God for the sake of obtaining wealth, others because they want to have a son, and they think themselves Bhâgavatas (devotees). This is no Bhakti, and they are not true Bhagavatas. When a Sâdhu comes who professes that he can make gold, they run to him, and they still consider themselves Bhagavatas. It is not Bhakti if we worship God with the desire for a son; it is not Bhakti if we worship with the desire to be rich; it is not Bhakti even if we have a desire for heaven; it is not Bhakti if a man worships with the desire of being saved from the tortures of hell. Bhakti is not the outcome of fear or greediness. He is the true Bhagavata who says, "O God, I do not want a beautiful wife, I do not want knowledge or salvation. Let me be born and die hundreds of times. What I want is that I should be ever engaged in Thy service." It is at this stage—and when a man sees God in everything, and everything in God—that he attains perfect Bhakti. It is then that he sees Vishnu incarnated in everything from the microbe to Brahmâ, and it is then that he sees God manifesting Himself in everything, it is then that he feels that there is nothing without God, and it is then and then alone that thinking himself to be the most insignificant of all beings he worships God with the true spirit of a Bhakta. He then leaves Tirthas and external forms of worship far behind him, he sees every man to be the most perfect temple.

Bhakti is described in several ways in the Shastras. We say that God is our Father. In the same way we call Him Mother, and so on. These relationships are conceived in order to strengthen Bhakti in us, and they make us feel nearer and dearer to God. Hence these names are justifiable in one way, and that is that the words are simply words of endearment, the outcome of the fond love which a true Bhagavata feels for God. Take the story of Râdhâ and Krishna in Râsalîlâ. The story simply exemplifies the true spirit of a Bhakta, because no love in the world exceeds that existing between a man and a woman. When there is such intense love, there is no fear, no other attachment save that one which binds that pair in an inseparable and all-absorbing bond. But with regard to parents, love is accompanied with fear due to the reverence we have for them. Why should we care whether God created anything or not, what have we to do with the fact that He is our preserver? He is only our Beloved, and we should adore Him devoid of all thoughts of fear. A man loves God only when he has no other desire, when he thinks of nothing else and when he is mad after Him. That love which a man has for his beloved can illustrate the love we ought to have for God. Krishna is the God and Radha loves Him; read those books which describe that story, and then you can imagine the way you should love God. But how many understand this? How can people who are vicious to their very core and have no idea of what morality is understand all this? When people drive all sorts of worldly thoughts from their minds and live in a clear moral and spiritual atmosphere, it is then that they understand the abstrusest of thoughts even if they be un-educated. But how few are there of that nature! There is not a single religion which cannot be perverted by man. For example, he may think that the Âtman is quite separate from the body, and so, when committing sins with the body his Atman is unaffected. If religions were truly followed, there would not have been a single man, whether Hindu, Mohammedan, or Christian, who would not have been all purity. But men are guided by their own nature, whether good or bad ; there is no gainsaying that. But in the world, there are always some who get intoxicated when they hear of God, and shed tears of joy when they read of God. Such men are true Bhaktas.

At the initial stage of religious development a man thinks of God as his Master and himself as His servant. He feels indebted to Him for providing for his daily wants, and so forth. Put such thoughts aside. There is but one attractive power, and that is God; and it is in obedience to that attractive power that the sun and the moon and everything else move. Everything in this world, whether good or bad, belongs to God. Whatever occurs in our life, whether good or bad, is bringing us to Him. One man kills another because of some selfish purpose. But the motive behind is love, whether for himself or for any one else. Whether we do good or evil, the propeller is love. When a tiger kills a buffalo, it is because he or his cubs are hungry.

God is love personified. He is apparent in everything. Everybody is being drawn to Him whether he knows it or not. When a woman loves her husband, she does not understand that it is the divine in her husband that is the great attractive power. The God of Love is the one thing to be worshipped. So long as we think of Him only as the Creator and Preserver, we can offer Him external worship, but when we get beyond all that and think Him to be Love Incarnate, seeing Him in all things and all things in Him, it is then that supreme Bhakti is attained.

THE COMMON BASES OF HINDUISM

On his arrival at Lahore the Swamiji was accorded a grand reception by the leaders, both of the Ârya Samâj and of the Sanâtana Dharma Sabhâ. During his brief stay in Lahore, Swamiji delivered three lectures. The first of these was on "The Common Bases of Hinduism", the second on "Bhakti", and the third one was the famous lecture on "The Vedanta". On the first occasion he spoke as follows:

This is the land which is held to be the holiest even in holy Âryâvarta; this is the Brahmâvarta of which our great Manu speaks. This is the land from whence arose that mighty aspiration after the Spirit, ay, which in times to come, as history shows, is to deluge the world. This is the land where, like its mighty rivers, spiritual aspirations have arisen and joined their strength, till they travelled over the length and breadth of the world and declared themselves with a voice of thunder. This is the land which had first to bear the brunt of all inroads and invasions into India; this heroic land had first to bare its bosom to every onslaught of the outer barbarians into Aryavarta. This is the land which, after all its sufferings, has not yet entirely lost its glory and its strength. Here it was that in later times the gentle Nânak preached his marvellous love for the world. Here it was that his broad heart was opened and his arms outstretched to embrace the whole world, not only of Hindus, but of Mohammedans too. Here it was that one of the last and one of the most glorious heroes of our race, Guru Govinda Singh, after shedding his blood and that of his dearest and nearest for the cause of religion, even when deserted by those for whom this blood was shed, retired into the South to die like a wounded lion struck to the heart, without a word against his country, without a single word of murmur.

Here, in this ancient land of ours, children of the land of five rivers, I stand before you, not as a teacher, for I know very little to teach, but as one who has come from the east to exchange words of greeting with the brothers of the west, to compare notes. Here am I, not to find out differences that exist among us, but to find where we agree. Here am I trying to understand on what ground we may always remain brothers, upon what foundations the voice that has spoken from eternity may become stronger and stronger as it grows. Here am I trying to propose to you something of constructive work and not destructive. For criticism the days are past, and we are waiting for constructive work. The world needs, at times, criticisms even fierce ones; but that is only for a time, and the work for eternity is progress and construction, and not criticism and destruction. For the last hundred years or so, there has been a flood of criticism all over this land of ours, where the full play of Western science has been let loose upon all the dark spots, and as a result the corners and the holes have become much more prominent than anything else. Naturally enough there arose mighty intellects all over the land, great and glorious, with the love of truth and justice in their hearts, with the love of their country, and above all, an intense love for their religion and their God ; and because these mighty souls felt so deeply, because they loved so deeply, they criticised everything they thought was wrong. Glory unto these mighty spirits of the past!   They have done so much good; but the voice of the present day is coming to us, telling, "Enough!"   There has been enough of criticism, there has been enough of fault-finding, the time has come for the rebuilding, the reconstructing; the time has come for us to gather all our scattered forces, to concentrate them into one focus, and through that, to lead the nation on its onward march, which for centuries almost has been stopped. The house has been cleansed ; let it be inhabited anew. The road has been cleared. March ahead, children of the Aryans!

Gentlemen, this is the motive that brings me before you, and at the start I may declare to you that I belong to no party and no sect. They are all great and glorious to me, I love them all, and all my life I have been attempting to find what is good and true in them. Therefore, it is my proposal tonight to bring before you points where we are agreed, to find out, if we can, a ground of agreement; and if through the grace of the Lord such a state of things be possible, let us take it up, and from theory carry it out into practice. We are Hindus. I do not use the word Hindu in any bad sense at all, nor do I agree with those that think there is any bad meaning in it. In old times, it simply meant people who lived on the other side of the Indus; today a good many among those who hate us may have put a bad interpretation upon it, but names are nothing. Upon us depends whether the name Hindu will stand for everything that is glorious, everything that is spiritual, or whether it will remain a name of opprobrium, one designating the downtrodden, the worthless, the heathen. If at present the word Hindu means anything bad, never mind; by our action let us be ready to show that this is the highest word that any language can invent. It has been one of the principles of my life not to be ashamed of my own ancestors. I am one of the proudest men ever born, but let me tell you frankly, it is not for myself, but on account of my ancestry. The more I have studied the past, the more I have looked back, more and more has this pride come to me, and it has given me the strength and courage of conviction, raised me up from the dust of the earth, and set me working out that great plan laid out by those great ancestors of ours. Children of those ancient Aryans, through the grace of the Lord may you have the same pride, may that faith in your ancestors come into your blood, may it become a part and parcel

of your lives, may it work towards the salvation of
the world!

Before trying to find out the precise point where we
are all agreed, the common ground of our national life, one
thing we must remember. Just as there is an individuality
in every man, so there is a national individuality. As one
man differs from another in certain particulars, in certain
characteristics of his own, so one race differs from another
in certain peculiar characteristics; and just as it is the
mission of every man to fulfil a certain purpose in the
economy of nature, just as there is a particular line set out
for him by his own past Karma, so it is with nations—each
nation has a destiny to fulfil, each nation has a message to
deliver, each nation has a mission to accomplish. Therefore, from the very start, we must have to understand the
mission of our own race, the destiny it has to fulfil, the
place it has to occupy in the march of nations, the note
which it has to contribute to the harmony of races. In our
country, when children, we hear stories how some serpents
have jewels in their heads, and whatever one may do
with the serpent, so long as the jewel is there, the serpent
cannot be killed. We hear stories of giants and ogres
who had souls living in certain little birds, and so long as
the bird was safe, there was no power on earth to kill these
giants; you might hack them to pieces, or do what you
liked to them, the giants could not die. So with nations,
there is a certain point where the life of a nation centres,
where lies the nationality of the nation, and until that is
touched, the nation cannot die. In the light of this we
can understand the most marvellous phenomenon that the
history of the world has ever known. Wave after wave of
barbarian conquest has rolled ove_ this devoted land of
ours. "Allah Ho Akbar!" has rent the skies for hundreds
of years, and no Hindu knew what moment would be his
last. This is the most suffering and the most subjugated
of all the historic lands of the world. Yet we still stand

practically the same race, ready to face difficulties again and again if necessary; and not only so, of late there have been signs that we are not only strong, but ready to go out, for the sign of life is expansion.

We find today that our ideas and thoughts are no more cooped up within the bounds of India, but whether we will it or not, they are marching outside, filtering into the literature of nations, taking their place among nations, and in some, even getting a commanding dictatorial position. Behind this we find the explanation that the great contribution to the sum total of the world's progress from India is the greatest, the noblest, the sublimest theme that can occupy the mind of man—it is philosophy and spirituality. Our ancestors tried many other things; they, like other nations, first went to bring out the secrets of external nature as we all know, and with their gigantic brains that marvellous race could have done miracles in that line of which the world could have been proud for ever. But they gave it up for something higher; something better rings out from the pages of the Vedas: "That science is the greatest which makes us know Him who never changes!" The science of nature, changeful, evanescent, the world of death, of woe, of misery, may be great, great indeed; but the science of Him who changes not, the Blissful One, where alone is peace, where alone is life eternal, where alone is perfection, where alone all misery ceases— that, according to our ancestors, was the sublimest science of all. After all, sciences that can give us only bread and clothes and power over our fellowmen, sciences that can teach us only how to conquer our fellow-beings, to rule over them, which teach the strong to domineer over the weak— those they could have discovered if they willed. But praise be unto the Lord, they caught at once the other side, which was grander, infinitely higher, infinitely more blissful, till it has become the national characteristic, till it has come down to us, inherited from father to son for thousands of

years, till it has become a part and parcel of us, till it
tingles in every drop of blood that runs through our veins,
till it has become our second nature, till the name of religion and Hindu have become one. This is the national
characteristic, and this cannot be touched. Barbarians with
sword and fire, barbarians bringing barbarous religions, not
one of them could touch the core, not one could touch the
"jewel", not one had the power to kill the "bird" which the
soul of the race inhabited. This, therefore, is the vitality of
the race, and so long as that remains, there is no power
under the sun that can kill the race. All the tortures and
miseries of the world will pass over without hurting us, and
we shall come out of the flames like Prahlâda, so long as we
hold on to this grandest of all our inheritances, spirituality.
If a Hindu is not spiritual I do not call him a Hindu. In
other countries a man may be political first, and then he
may have a little religion, but here in India the first and the
foremost duty of our lives is to be spiritual first, and then,
if there is time, let other things come. Bearing this in mind
we shall be in a better position to understand why, for our
national welfare, we must first seek out at the present day
all the spiritual forces of the race, as was done in days of
yore and will be done in all times to come. National union
in India must be a gathering up of its scattered spiritual
forces. A nation in India must be a union of those whose
hearts beat to the same spiritual tune.

There have been sects enough in this country. There
are sects enough, and there will be enough in the future,
because this has been the peculiarity of our religion that
in abstract principles so much latitude has been given
that, although afterwards so much detail has been worked
out, all these details are the working out of principles,
broad as the skies above our heads, eternal as nature
herself. Sects, therefore, as a matter of course, must
exist here, but what need not exist is sectarian quarrel.
Sects must be, but sectarianism need not. The world

would not be the better for sectarianism, but the world cannot move on without having sects. One set of men cannot do everything. The almost infinite mass of energy in the world cannot be managed by a small number of people. Here, at once we see the necessity that forced this division of labour upon us—the division into sects. For the use of spiritual forces let there be sects; but is there any need that we should quarrel when our most ancient books declare that this differentiation is only apparent, that in spite of all these differences there is a thread of harmony, that beautiful unity, running through them all? Our most ancient books have declared: एकं सद्विप्रा बहुधा वदन्ति । —"That which exists is One; sages call Him by various names." Therefore, if there are these sectarian struggles, if there are these fights among the different sects, if there is jealousy and hatred between the different sects in India, the land where all sects have always been honoured, it is a shame on us who dare to call ourselves the descendants of those fathers.

There are certain great principles in which, I think, we—whether Vaishnavas, Shaivas, Shâktas, or Gânapatyas, whether belonging to the ancient Vedantists or the modern ones, whether belonging to the old rigid sects or the modern reformed ones—are all óne, and whoever calls himself a Hindu, believes in these principles. Of course there is a difference in the interpretation, in the explanation of these principles, and that difference should be there, and it should be allowed, for our standard is not to bind every man down to our position. It would be a sin to force every man to work out our own interpretation of things, and to live by our own methods. Perhaps all who are here will agree on the first point that we believe the Vedas to be the eternal teachings of the secrets of religion. We all believe that this holy literature is without beginning and without end, coeval with nature, which is without beginning and without end; and that all our

religious differences, all our religious struggles must end
when we stand in the presence of that holy book; we are
all agreed that this is the last court of appeal in all our
spiritual differences. We may take different points of view
as to what the Vedas are. There may be one sect which
regards one portion as more sacred than another, but that
matters little so long as we say that we are all brothers in
the Vedas, that out of these venerable, eternal, marvellous
books has come everything that we possess today, good,
holy, and pure. Well, therefore, if we believe in all this,
let this principle first of all be preached broadcast throughout the length and breadth of the land. If this be true,
let the Vedas have that prominence which they always
deserve, and which we all believe in. First, then, the
Vedas. The second point we all believe in is God, the
creating, the preserving power of the whole universe, and
unto whom it periodically returns to come out at other
periods and manifest this wonderful phenomenon, called
the universe. We may differ as to our conception of God.
One may believe in a God who is entirely personal,
another may believe in a God who is personal and yet not
human, and yet another may believe in a God who is
entirely impersonal, and all may get their support from the
Vedas. Still we are all believers in God; that is to say,
that man who does not believe in a most marvellous
Infinite Power from which everything has come, in which
everything lives, and to which everything must in the end
return, cannot be called a Hindu. If that be so, let us try
to preach that idea all over the land. Preach whatever conception you have to give, there is no difference, we are not
going to fight over it, but preach God; that is all we want.
One idea may be better than another, but, mind you, not
one of them is bad. One is good, another is better, and
again another may be the best, but the word bad does not
enter the category of our religion. Therefore, may the
Lord bless them all who preach the name of God in what-

ever form they like! The more He is preached, the
better for this race. Let our children be brought up in this
idea, let this idea enter the homes of the poorest and the
lowest, as well as of the richest and the highest—the idea
of the name of God.

The third idea that I will present before you is that,
unlike all other races of the world, we do not believe that
this world was created only so many thousand years ago,
and is going to be destroyed eternally on a certain day. Nor
do we believe that the human soul has been created along
with this universe just out of nothing. Here is another
point I think we are all able to agree upon. We believe
in nature being without beginning and without end; only
at psychological periods this gross material of the outer
universe goes back to its finer state, thus to remain for a
certain period, again to be projected outside to manifest
all this infinite panorama we call nature. This wavelike
motion was going on even before time began, through
eternity, and will remain for an infinite period of time.

Next, all Hindus believe that man is not only a gross
material body; not only that within this there is the finer
body, the mind, but there is something yet greater—for the
body changes and so does the mind—something beyond,
the Âtman—I cannot translate the word to you for any
translation will be wrong—that there is something beyond
even this fine body, which is the Atman of man, which has
neither beginning nor end, which knows not what death is.
And then this peculiar idea, different from that of all other
races of men, that this Atman inhabits body after body
until there is no more interest for it to continue to do so,
and it becomes free, not to be born again, I refer to the
theory of Samsâra and the theory of eternal souls taught
by our Shâstras. This is another point where we all agree,
whatever sect we may belong to. There may be differences
as to the relation between the soul and God. According
to one sect the soul may be eternally different from God,

according to another it may be a spark of that infinite fire, yet again according to others it may be one with that Infinite. It does not matter what our interpretation is, so long as we hold on to the one basic belief that the soul is infinite, that this soul was never created, and therefore will never die, that it had to pass and evolve into various bodies, till it attained perfection in the human one—in that we are all agreed. And then comes the most differentiating, the grandest, and the most wonderful discovery in the realms of spirituality that has ever been made. Some of you, perhaps, who have been studying Western thought, may have observed already that there is another radical difference severing at one stroke all that is Western from all that is Eastern. It is this that we hold, whether we are Shâktas, Sauras, or Vaishnavas, even whether we are Bauddhas or Jainas, we all hold in India that the soul is by its nature pure and perfect, infinite in power and blessed. Only, according to the dualist, this natural blissfulness of the soul has become contracted by past bad work, and through the grace of God it is again going to open out and show its perfection; while according to the monist, even this idea of contraction is a partial mistake, it is the veil of Mâyâ that causes us to think the soul has lost its powers, but the powers are there fully manifest. Whatever the difference may be, we come to the central core, and there is at once an irreconcilable difference between all that is Western and Eastern. The Eastern is looking inward for all that is great and good. When we worship, we close our eyes and try to find God within. The Western is looking up outside for his God. To the Western their religious books have been inspired, while with us our books have been expired; breath-like they came, the breath of God, out of the hearts of sages they sprang, the Mantra-drashtâs.

This is one great point to understand, and, my friends, my brethren,, let me tell you, this is the one point we shall have to insist upon in the future. For I am firmly

III—25

convinced, and I beg you to understand this one fact—no
good comes out of the man who day and night thinks he
is nobody. If a man, day and night, thinks he is miserable,
low, and nothing, nothing he becomes. If you say yea, yea,
"I am, I am", so shall you be; and if you say "I am not",
think that you are not, and day and night meditate upon
the fact that you are nothing, ay, nothing shall you be.
That is the great fact which you ought to remember. We
are the children of the Almighty, we are sparks of the infinite, divine fire. How can we be nothings? We are everything, ready to do everything, we can do everything, and
man must do everything. This faith in themselves was in
the hearts of our ancestors, this faith in themselves was the
motive power that pushed them forward and forward in
the march of civilisation; and if there has been degeneration, if there has been defect, mark my words, you will
find that degradation to have started on the day our people
lost this faith in themselves. Losing faith in one's self
means losing faith in God. Do you believe in that infinite,
good Providence working in and through you? If you
believe that this Omnipresent One, the Antaryâmin, is
present in every atom, is through and through, Ota-prota,
as the Sanskrit word goes, penetrating your body, mind
and soul, how can you lose heart? I may be a little bubble
of water, and you may be a mountain-high wave. Never
mind! The infinite ocean is the background of me as well
as of you. Mine also is that infinite ocean of life, of power,
of spirituality, as well as yours. I am already joined—from
my very birth, from the very fact of my life—I am in Yoga
with that infinite life and infinite goodness and infinite
power, as you are, mountain-high though you may be.
Therefore, my brethren, teach this life-saving, great, ennobling, grand doctrine to your children, even from their
very birth. You need not teach them Advaitism; teach
them Dvaitism, or any "ism" you please, but we have seen
that this is the common "ism" all through India; this

marvellous doctrine of the soul, the perfection of the soul, is commonly believed in by all sects. As says our great philosopher Kapila, if purity has not been the nature of the soul, it can never attain purity afterwards, for anything that was not perfect by nature, even if it attained to perfection, that perfection would go away again. If impurity is the nature of man, then man will have to remain impure, even though he may be pure for five minutes. The time will come when this purity will wash out, pass away, and the old natural impurity will have its sway once more. Therefore, say all our philosophers, good is our nature, perfection is our nature, not imperfection, not impurity—and we should remember that. Remember the beautiful example of the great sage who, when he was dying, asked his mind to remember all his mighty deeds and all his mighty thoughts. There you do not find that he was teaching his mind to remember all his weaknesses and all his follies. Follies there are, weakness there must be, but remember your real nature always—that is the only way to cure the weakness, that is the only way to cure the follies.

It seems that these few points are common among all the various religious sects in India, and perhaps in future upon this common platform, conservative and liberal religionists, old type and new type, may shake hands. Above all, there is another thing to remember, which I am sorry we forget from time to time, that religion, in India, means realisation and nothing short of that. "Believe in the doctrine, and you are safe", can never be taught to us, for we do not believe in that. You are what you make yourselves. You are, by the grace of God and your own exertions, what you are. Mere believing in certain theories and doctrines will not help you much. The mighty word that came out from the sky of spirituality in India was Anubhuti, realisation, and ours are the only books which declare again and again: "The Lord is to be *seen*". Bold, brave words indeed, but true to their very core; every sound, every vibration is true. Religion is to be realised, not only heard; it is not in learning some doctrine like a parrot. Neither is it mere intellectual assent—that is nothing; but it must come into us. Ay, and therefore the greatest proof that we have of the existence of a God is not because our reason says so, but because God has been seen by the ancients as well as by the moderns. We believe in the soul not only because there are good reasons to prove its existence, but, above all, because there have been in the past thousands in India, there are still many who have realised, and there will be thousands in the future who will realise and see their own souls. And there is no salvation for man until he sees God, realises his own soul. Therefore, above all, let us understand this, and the more we understand it the less we shall have of sectarianism in India, for it is only that man who has realised God and seen Him, who is religious. In him the knots have been cut asunder, in him alone the doubts have subsided; he alone has become free from the fruits of action who has seen Him who is nearest of the near and farthest of the far. Ay, we often mistake mere prattle for religious truth, mere intellectual perorations for great spiritual realisation, and then comes sectarianism, then comes fight. If we once understand that this realisation is the only religion, we shall look into our own hearts and find how far we are towards realising the truths of religion. Then we shall understand that we ourselves are groping in darkness, and are leading others to grope in the same darkness, then we shall cease from sectarianism, quarrel, and fight. Ask a man who wants to start a sectarian fight, "Have you seen God? Have you seen the Atman? If you have not, what right have you to preach His name—you walking in darkness trying to lead me into the same darkness—the blind leading the blind, and both falling into the ditch?"

Therefore, take more thought before you go and find

fault with others. Let them follow their own path to realisation so long as they struggle to see truth in their own hearts; and when the broad, naked truth will be seen, then they will find that wonderful blissfulness which marvellously enough has been testified to by every seer in India, by every one who has realised the truth. Then words of love alone will come out of that heart, for it has already been touched by Him who is the essence of Love Himself. Then and then alone, all sectarian quarrels will cease, and we shall be in a position to understand, to bring to our hearts, to embrace, to intensely love the very word Hindu and every one who bears that name. Mark me, then and then alone you are a Hindu when the very name sends through you a galvanic shock of strength. Then and then alone you are a Hindu when every man who bears the name, from any country, speaking our language or any other language, becomes at once the nearest and the dearest to you. Then and then alone you are a Hindu when the distress of anyone bearing that name comes to your heart and makes you feel as if your own son were in distress. Then and then alone you are a Hindu when you will be ready to bear everything for them, like the great example I have quoted at the beginning of this lecture, of your great Guru Govind Singh. Driven out from this country, fighting against its oppressors, after having shed his own blood for the defence of the Hindu religion, after having seen his children killed on the battlefield—ay, this example of the great Guru, left even by those for whose sake he was shedding his blood and the blood of his own nearest and dearest—he, the wounded lion, retired from the field calmly to die in the South, but not a word of curse escaped his lips against those who had ungratefully forsaken him! Mark me, every one of you will have to be a Govind Singh, if you want to do good to your country. You may see thousands of defects in your countrymen, but mark their Hindu blood. They are the first Gods you will have to worship even if they do everything to hurt you, even if everyone of them send out a curse to you, you send out to them words of love. If they drive you out, retire to die in silence like that mighty lion, Govind Singh. Such a man is worthy of the name of Hindu; such an ideal ought to be before us always. All our hatchets let us bury; send out this grand current of love all round.

Let them talk of India's regeneration as they like. Let me tell you as one who has been working—at least trying to work—all his life, that there is no regeneration for India until you be spiritual. Not only so, but upon it depends the welfare of the whole world. For I must tell you frankly that the very foundations of Western civilisation have been shaken to their base. The mightiest buildings, if built upon the loose sand foundations of materialism, must come to grief one day, must totter to their destruction some day. The history of the world is our witness. Nation after nation has arisen and based its greatness upon materialism, declaring man was all matter. Ay, in Western language, a man gives up the ghost, but in our language a man gives up his body. The Western man is a body first, and then he has a soul; with us a man is a soul and spirit, and he has a body. Therein lies a world of difference. All such civilisations, therefore, as have been based upon such sand foundations as material comfort and all that, have disappeared one after another, after short lives, from the face of the world ; but the civilisation of India and the other nations that have stood at India's feet to listen and learn, namely, Japan and China, live even to the present day, and there are signs even of revival among them. Their lives are like that of the Phoenix, a thousand times destroyed, but ready to spring up again more glorious. But a materialistic civilisation once dashed down, never can come up again ; that building once thrown down is broken into pieces once for all. Therefore have patience and wait, the future is in store for us.

Do not be in a hurry, do not go out to imitate anybody else. This is another great lesson we have to remember ; imitation is not civilisation. I may deck myself out in a Raja's dress, but will that make me a Raja? An ass in a lion's skin never makes a lion. Imitation, cowardly imitation, never makes for progress. It is verily the sign of awful degradation in a man. Ay, when a man has begun to hate himself, then the last blow has come. When a man has begun to be ashamed of his ancestors, the end has come. Here am I, one of the least of the Hindu race, yet proud of my race, proud of my ancestors. I am proud to call myself a Hindu, I am proud that I am one of your unworthy servants. I am proud that I am a countryman of yours, you the descendants of the sages, you the descendants of the most glorious Rishis the world ever saw. Therefore have faith in yourselves, be proud of your ancestors, instead of being ashamed of them. And do not imitate, do not imitate! Whenever you are under the thumb of others, you lose your own independence. If you are working, even in spiritual things, at the dictation of others, slowly you lose all faculty, even of thought. Bring out through your own exertions what you have, but do not imitate, yet take what is good from others. We have to learn from others. You put the seed in the ground, and give it plenty of earth, and air, and water to feed upon; when the seed grows into the plant and into a gigantic tree, does it become the earth, does it become the air, or does it become the water? It becomes the mighty plant, the mighty tree, after its own nature, having absorbed everything that was given to it. Let that be your position. We have indeed many things to learn from others, yea, that man who refuses to learn is already dead. Declares our Manu: आददीत परां विद्यां प्रयत्नादवरादपि । अन्त्यादपि परं धर्मं स्त्रीरत्नं दुष्कुलादपि ।—"Take the jewel of a woman for your wife, though she be of inferior descent. Learn supreme knowledge with service even from the man of

low birth; and even from the Chandâla, learn by serving
him the way to salvation." Learn everything that is
good from others, but bring it in, and in your own way
absorb it; do not become others. Do not be dragged
away out of this Indian life; do not for a moment think
that it would be better for India if all the Indians dressed,
ate, and behaved like another race. You know the difficulty of giving up a habit of a few years. The Lord
knows how many thousands of years are in your blood;
this national specialised life has been flowing in one way,
the Lord knows for how many thousands of years ; and
do you mean to say that that mighty stream, which has
nearly reached its ocean, can go back to the snows of its
Himalayas again? That is impossible! The struggle to
do so would only break it. Therefore, make way for the
life-current of the nation. Take away the blocks that bar
the way to the progress of this mighty river, cleanse its
path, clear the channel, and out it will rush by its own
natural impulse, and the nation will go on careering and
progressing.

These are the lines which I beg to suggest to you
for spiritual work in India. There are many other great
problems which, for want of time, I cannot bring before
you this night. For instance, there is the wonderful
question of caste. I have been studying this question, its
pros and cons, all my life; I have studied it in nearly
every province in India. I have mixed with people of all
castes in nearly every part of the country, and I am too
bewildered in my own mind to grasp even the very significance of it. The more I try to study it, the more I get
bewildered. Still at last I find that a little glimmer of light
is before me, I begin to feel its significance just now.
Then there is the other great problem about eating and
drinking. That is a great problem indeed. It is not so
useless a thing as we generally think. I have come to the
conclusion that the insistence which we make now about

eating and drinking is most curious and is just going against what the Shastras required, that is- to say, we come to grief by neglecting the proper purity of the food we eat and drink; we have lost the true spirit of it.

There are several other questions which I want to bring before you and show how these problems can be solved, how to work out the ideas; but unfortunately the meeting could not come to order until very late, and I do not wish to detain you any longer now. I will, therefore, keep my ideas about caste and other things for a future occasion.

Now, one word more and I will finish about these spiritual ideas. Religion for a long time has come to be static in India. What we want is to make it dynamic. I want it to be brought into the life of everybody. Religion, as it always has been in the past, must enter the palaces of kings as well as the homes of the poorest peasants in the land. Religion, the common inheritance, the universal birthright of the race, must be brought free to the door of everybody. Religion in India must be made as free and as easy of access as is God's air. And this is the kind of work we have to bring about in India, but not by getting up little sects and fighting on points of difference. Let us preach where we all agree and leave the differences to remedy themselves. As I have said to the Indian people again and again, if there is the darkness of centuries in a room and we go into the room and begin to cry, "Oh, it is dark, it is dark!", will the darkness go? Bring in the light and the darkness will vanish at once. This is the secret of reforming men. Suggest to them higher things; believe in man first. Why start with the belief that man is degraded and degenerated? I have never failed in my faith in man in any case, even taking him at his worst. Wherever I had faith in man, though at first the prospect was not always bright, yet it triumphed in the long run. Have faith in man, whether he appears to you to be a very learned one or a most ignorant one. Have faith in man, whether he appears to be an angel or the very devil himself. Have faith in man first, and then having faith in him, believe that if there are defects in him, if he makes mistakes, if he embraces the crudest and the vilest doctrines, believe that it is not from his real nature that they come, but from the want of higher ideals. If a man goes towards what is false, it is because he cannot get what is true. Therefore the only method of correcting what is false is by supplying him with what is true. Do this, and let him compare. You give him the truth, and there your work is done. Let him compare it in his own mind with what he has already in him; and, mark my words, if you have really given him the truth, the false must vanish, light must dispel darkness, and truth will bring the good out. This is the way if you want to reform the country spiritually; this is the way, and not fighting, not even telling people that what they are doing is bad. Put the good before them, see how eagerly they take it, see how the divine that never dies, that is always living in the human, comes up awakened and stretches out its hand for all that is good, and all that is glorious.

May He who is the Creator, the Preserver, and the Protector of our race, the God of our forefathers, whether called by the name of Vishnu, or Shiva, or Shakti, or Ganapati, whether He is worshipped as Saguna or as Nirguna, whether He is worshipped as personal or as impersonal, may He whom our forefathers knew and addressed by the words, एकं सद्विप्रा बहुधा वदन्ति ।—"That which exists is One; sages call Him by various names"— may He enter into us with His mighty love; may He shower His blessings on us, may He make us understand each other, may He make us work for each other with real love, with intense love for truth, and may not the least desire for our own personal fame, our own personal prestige, our own personal advantage, enter into this great work of the spiritual regeneration of India!

BHAKTI

(Delivered at Lahore on the 9th November, 1897)

There is a sound which comes to us like a distant echo in the midst of the roaring torrents of the Upanishads, at times rising in proportion and volume, and yet, throughout the literature of the Vedanta, its voice, though clear, is not very strong. The main duty of the Upanishads seems to be to present before us the spirit and the aspect of the sublime, and yet behind this wonderful sublimity there come to us here and there glimpses of poetry as we read; न तत्र सूर्यो भाति न चन्द्रतारकं नेमा विद्युतो भान्ति कुतोऽयमग्निः—"There the sun shines not, nor the moon, nor the stars, what to speak of this fire?" As we listen to the heart-stirring poetry of these marvellous lines, we are taken, as it were, off from the world of the senses, off even from the world of intellect, and brought to that world which can never be comprehended, and yet which is always with us. There is behind even this sublimity another ideal following as its shadow, one more acceptable to mankind, one more of daily use, one that has to enter into every part of human life, which assumes proportion and volume later on, and is stated in full and determined language in the Purânas, and that is the ideal of Bhakti. The germs of Bhakti are there already; the germs are even in the Samhitâ ; the germs a little more developed are in the Upanishads; but they are worked out in their details in the Puranas.

To understand Bhakti, therefore, we have got to understand these Puranas of ours. There have been great discussions of late as to their authenticity. Many a passage of uncertain meaning has been taken up and criticised. In many places it has been pointed out that the passages cannot stand the light of modern science and so forth. But, apart from all these discussions, apart from the scientific validity of the statements of the Puranas, apart from their valid or invalid geography, apart from their valid or invalid astronomy, and so forth, what we find for a certainty, traced out bit by bit almost in every one of these volumes, is this doctrine of Bhakti, illustrated, reillustrated, stated and restated, in the lives of saints and in the lives of kings. It seems to have been the duty of the Puranas to stand as illustrations for that great ideal of the beautiful, the ideal of Bhakti, and this, as I have stated, is so much nearer to the ordinary man. Very few indeed are there who can understand and appreciate, far less live and move, in the grandeur of the full blaze of the light of Vedanta, because the first step for the pure Vedantist is to be Abhih, fearless. Weakness has got to go before a man dares to become a Vedantist, and we know how difficult that is. Even those who have given up all connection with the world, and have very few bondages to make them cowards, feel in the heart of their hearts how weak they are at moments, at times how soft they become, how cowed down; much more so is it with men who have so many bondages, and have to remain as slaves to so many hundred and thousand things, inside of themselves and outside of themselves, men every moment of whose life is dragging-down slavery. To them the Puranas come with the most beautiful message of Bhakti.

For them the softness and the poetry are spread out, for them are told these wonderful and marvellous stories of a Dhruva and a Prahlâda, and of a thousand saints, and these illustrations are to make it practical. Whether you believe in the scientific accuracy of the Puranas or not, there is not one among you whose life has not been influenced by the story of Prahlada, or that of Dhruva, or of any one of these great Paurânika saints. We have not only to acknowledge the power of the Puranas in our own day, but we ought to be grateful to them as they gave

us in the past a more comprehensive and a better popular
religion than what the degraded later-day Buddhism was
leading us to. This easy and smooth idea of Bhakti has
been written and worked upon, and we have to embrace
it in our everyday practical life, for we shall see as we go
on how the idea has been worked out until Bhakti becomes
the essence of love. So long as there shall be such a
thing as personal and material love, one cannot go behind
the teachings of the Puranas. So long as there shall be
the human weakness of leaning upon somebody for
support, these Puranas, in some form or other, must
always exist. You can change their names; you can condemn those that are already existing, but immediately you
will be compelled to write another Purana. If there arises
amongst us a sage who will not want these old Puranas,
we shall find that his disciples, within twenty years of his
death, will make of his life another Purana. That will be
all the difference.

This is a necessity of the nature of man; for them
only are there no Puranas who have gone beyond all
human weakness and have become what is really
wanted of a Paramahamsa, brave and bold souls, who
have gone beyond the bondages of Mâyâ, the necessities
even of nature—the triumphant, the conquerors, the
gods of the world. The ordinary man cannot do without a personal God to worship; if he does not worship
a God in nature, he has to worship either a God in the
shape of a wife, or a child, or a father, or a friend, or a
teacher, or somebody else; and the necessity is still more
upon women than men. The vibration of light may be
everywhere; it may be in dark places, since cats and
other animals perceive it, but for us the vibration must
be in our plane to become visible. We may talk, therefore, of an Impersonal Being and so forth, but so long as
we are ordinary mortals, God can be seen in man alone.
Our conception of God and our worship of God are

naturally, therefore, human. "This body, indeed, is the
greatest temple of God." So we find that men have been
worshipped throughout the ages, and although we may
condemn or criticise some of the extravagances which
naturally follow, we find at once that the heart is sound,
that in spite of these extravagances, in spite of this going
into extremes, there is an essence, there is a true, firm
core, a backbone, to the doctrine that is preached. I am
not asking you to swallow without consideration any old
stories, or any unscientific jargon. I am not calling upon
you to believe in all sorts of Vâmâchâri explanations that,
unfortunately, have crept into some of the Puranas, but
what I mean is this, that there is an essence which ought
not to be lost, a reason for the existence of the Puranas,
and that is the teaching of Bhakti to make religion practical, to bring religion from its high philosophical flights
into the everyday lives of our common human beings.

[The lecturer defended the use of material helps in
Bhakti. Would to God man did not stand where he is,
but it is useless to fight against existing facts; man is a
material being now, however he may talk about spirituality
and all that. Therefore the material man has to be taken
in hand and slowly raised, until he becomes spiritual. In
these days it is hard for 99 per cent of us to understand
spirituality, much more so to talk about it. The motive
powers that are pushing us forward, and the efforts we are
seeking to attain, are all material. We can only work, in
the language of Herbert Spencer, in the line of least resistance, and the Puranas have the good and common sense
to work in the line of least resistance; and the successes
that have been attained by the Puranas have been marvellous and unique. The ideal of Bhakti is of course spiritual,
but the way lies through matter and we cannot help it.
Everything that is conducive to the attainment of this
spirituality in the material world, therefore, is to be taken
hold of and brought to the use of man to evolve the

spiritual being. Having pointed out that the Shâstras start by giving the right to study the Vedas to everybody, without distinction of sex, caste, or creed, he claimed that if making a material temple helps a man more to love God, welcome; if making an image of God helps a man in attaining to this ideal of love, Lord bless him and give him twenty such images if he pleases. If anything helps him to attain to that ideal of spirituality, welcome, so long as it is moral, because anything immoral will not help, but will only retard. He traced the opposition to the use of images in worship in India partly at least to Kabir, but on the other hand showed that India has had great philosophers and founders of religions who did not even believe in the existence of a Personal God and boldly preached that to the people, but yet did not condemn the use of images. At best they only said it was not a very high form of worship, and there was not one of the Puranas in which it was said that it was a very high form. Having referred historically to the use of image-worship by the Jews, in their belief that Jehovah resided in a chest, he condemned the practice of abusing idol-worship merely because others said it was bad. Though an image or any other material form could be used if it helped to make a man spiritual, yet there was no one book in our religion which did not very clearly state that it was the lowest form of worship, because it was worship through matter. The attempt that was made all over India to force this image-worship on everybody, he had no language to condemn; what business had anybody to direct and dictate to anyone what he should worship and through what? How could any other man know through what he would grow, whether his spiritual growth would be by worshipping an image, by worshipping fire, or by worshipping even a pillar? That was to be guided and directed by our own Gurus, and by the relation between the Guru and the Shishya. That explained the rule which Bhakti books laid

down for what was called the Ishta, that was to say, that
each man had to take up his own peculiar form of worship,
his own way of going towards God, and that chosen ideal
was his Ishta Devatâ. He was to regard other forms of
worship with sympathy, but at the same time to practise
his own form till he reached the goal and came to the
centre where no more material helps were necessary for
him. In this connection a word of warning was necessary
against a system prevalent in some parts of India, what
was called the Kula-Guru system, a sort of hereditary
Guruism. We read in the books that "He who knows the
essence of the Vedas, is sinless, and does not teach
another for love of gold or love of anything else, whose
mercy is without any cause, who gives as the spring which
does not ask anything from the plants and trees, for it is
its nature to do good, and brings them out once more into
life, and buds, flowers, and leaves come out, who wants
nothing, but whose whole life is only to do good"—such
a man could be a Guru and none else. There was another
danger, for a Guru was not a teacher alone; that was a
very small part of it. The Guru, as the Hindus believed,
transmitted spirituality to his disciples. To take a common
material example, therefore, if a man were not inoculated
with good virus, he ran the risk of being inoculated with
what was bad and vile, so that by being taught by a bad
Guru there was the risk of learning something evil. Therefore it was absolutely necessary that this idea of Kula-Guru
should vanish from India. Guruism must not be a trade;
that must stop, it was against the Shastras. No man ought
to call himself a Guru and at the same time help the
present state of things under the Kula-Guru system.

Speaking of the question of food, the Swami pointed
out that the present-day insistence upon the strict regulations as to eating was to a great extent superficial, and
missed the mark they were originally intended to cover.
He particularly instanced the idea that care should be

exercised as to who was allowed to touch food, and pointed out that there was a deep psychological significance in this, but that in the everyday life of ordinary men it was a care difficult or impossible to exercise. Here again the mistake was made of insisting upon a general observance of an idea which was only possible to one class, those who have entirely devoted their lives to spirituality, whereas the vast majority of men were still unsatiated with material pleasures, and until they were satiated to some extent it was useless to think of forcing spirituality on them.

The highest form of worship that had been laid down by the Bhakta was the worship of man. Really, if there were to be any sort of worship, he would suggest getting a poor man, or six, or twelve, as their circumstances would permit, every day to their homes, and serving them, thinking that they were Nârâyanas. He had seen charity in many countries and the reason it did not succeed was that it was not done with a good spirit. "Here, take this, and go away"—that was not charity, but the expression of the pride of the heart, to gain the applause of the world, that the world might know they were becoming charitable. Hindus must know that, according to the Smritis, the giver was lower than the receiver, for the receiver was for the time being God Himself. Therefore he would suggest such a form of worship as getting some of these poor Narayanas, or blind Narayanas, and hungry Narayanas into every house every day, and giving them the worship they would give to an image, feeding them and clothing them, and the next day doing the same to others. He did not condemn any form of worship, but what he went to say was that the highest form and the most necessary at present in India was this form of Narayana worship.

In conclusion, he likened Bhakti to a triangle. The first angle was that love knew no want, the second that love knew no fear. Love for reward or service of any kind was the beggar's religion, the shopkeeper's religion, with very little of real religion in it. Let them not become beggars, because, in the first place, beggary was the sign of atheism. "Foolish indeed is the man who living on the banks of the Gangâ digs a little well to drink water." So is the man who begs of God material objects. The Bhakta should be ready to stand up and say, "I do not want anything from you, Lord, but if you need anything from me I am ready to give." Love knew no fear. Had they not seen a weak, frail, little woman passing through a street, and if a dog barked, she flew off into the next house? The next day she was in the street, perhaps, with her child at her breast. And a lion attacked her. Where was she then? In the mouth of the lion to save her child. Lastly, love was unto love itself. The Bhakta at last comes to this, that love itself is God and nothing else. Where should man go to prove the existence of God? Love was the most visible of all visible things. It was the force that was moving the sun, the moon, and the stars, manifesting itself in men, women, and in animals, everywhere and in everything. It was expressed in material forces as gravitation and so on. It was everywhere, in every atom, manifesting everywhere. It was that infinite love, the only motive power of this universe, visible everywhere, and this was God Himself.[1]

---

[1] From the report published in *The Tribune*.

THE VEDANTA

(Delivered at Lahore on 12th November, 1897)

Two worlds there are in which we live, one the external, the other internal. Human progress has been made, from days of yore, almost in parallel lines along both these worlds. The search began in the external, and man at first wanted to get answers for all the deep problems from outside nature. Man wanted to satisfy his thirst for the beautiful and the sublime from all that surrounded him; he wanted to express himself and all that was within him in the language of the concrete ; and grand indeed were the answers he got, most marvellous ideas of God and worship, and most rapturous expressions of the beautiful. Sublime ideas came from the external world indeed. But the other, opening out for humanity later, laid out before him a universe yet sublimer, yet more beautiful, and infinitely more expansive. In the Karma Kânda portion of the Vedas, we find the most wonderful ideas of religion inculcated, we find the most wonderful ideas about an overruling Creator, Preserver, and Destroyer of the universe presented before us in language sometimes the most soul-stirring. Most of you perhaps remember that most wonderful Shloka in the Rig-Veda Samhitâ where you get the description of chaos, perhaps the sublimest that has ever been attempted yet. In spite of all this, we find it is only a painting of the sublime outside, we find that yet it is gross, that something of matter yet clings to it. Yet we find that it is only the expression of the Infinite in the language of matter, in the language of the finite, it is the infinite of the muscles and not of the mind; it is the infinite of space and not of thought. Therefore in the second portion of Jnâna Kânda, we find there is altogether a different procedure. The first was a search in external nature for the truths of the universe; it was an attempt to get the solution of the deep problems of life from the material world. यस्यैते हिमवन्तो महित्वा—"Whose glory these Himalayas declare". This is a grand idea, but yet it was not grand enough for India. The Indian mind had to fall back, and the research took a different direction altogether; from the external the search came to the internal, from matter to mind. There arose the cry, "When a man dies, what becomes of him?" अस्तीत्येके नायमस्तीति चैके—"Some say that he exists, others that he is gone; say, O king of Death, what is the truth?" An entirely different procedure we find here. The Indian mind got all that could be had from the external world, but it did not feel satisfied with that; it wanted to search further, to dive into its own soul, and the final answer came.

The Upanishads, or the Vedanta, or the Āranyakas, or Rahasya is the name of this portion of the Vedas. Here we find at once that religion has got rid of all external formalities. Here we find at once that spiritual things are told not in the language of matter, but in the language of the spirit; the superfine in the language of the superfine. No more any grossness attaches to it, no more is there any compromise with things of worldly concern. Bold, brave, beyond the conception of the present day, stand the giant minds of the sages of the Upanishads, declaring the noblest truths that have ever been preached to humanity, without any compromise, without any fear. This, my countrymen, I want to lay before you. Even the Jnana Kanda of the Vedas is a vast ocean; many lives are necessary to understand even a little of it. Truly has it been said of the Upanishads by Râmânuja that they form the head, the shoulders, the crest of the Vedas, and surely enough the Upanishads have become the Bible of modern India. The Hindus have the greatest respect for the Karma Kanda of the Vedas, but, for all practical purposes, we know that for ages by Shruti has been meant the Upanishads, and the Upanishads alone. We know that all our great philosophers, whether Vyâsa, Patanjali, or Gautama, and even the father of all philosophy, the great Kapila himself, whenever they wanted an authority for what they wrote, everyone of them found it in the Upanishads, and nowhere else, for therein are the truths that remain for ever.

There are truths that are true only in a certain line, in a certain direction, under certain circumstances, and for certain times—those that are founded on the institutions of the times. There are other truths which are based on the nature of man himself, and which must endure so long as man himself endures. These are the truths that alone can be universal, and in spite of all the changes that have come to India, as to our social surroundings, our methods of dress, our manner of eating, our modes of worship—these universal truths of the Shrutis, the marvellous Vedantic ideas, stand out in their own sublimity, immovable, unvanquishable, deathless, and immortal. Yet the germs of all the ideas that were developed in the Upanishads had been taught already in the Karma Kanda. The idea of the cosmos which all sects of Vedantists had to take for granted, the psychology which has formed the common basis of all the Indian schools of thought, had there been worked out already and presented before the world. A few words, therefore, about the Karma Kanda are necessary before we begin the spiritual portion, the Vedanta; and first of all I should like to explain the sense in which I use the word Vedanta.

Unfortunately there is the mistaken notion in modern India that the word Vedanta has reference only to the Advaita system; but you must always remember that in modern India the three Prasthânas are considered equally important in the study of all the systems of religion. First of all there are the Revelations, the Shrutis, by which I mean the Upanishads. Secondly, among our philosophies, the Sutras of Vyasa have the greatest prominence on account of their being the consummation of all the preceding systems of philosophy. These systems are not contradictory to one another, but one is based on another, and there is a gradual unfolding of the theme which culminates in the Sutras of Vyasa. Then, between the Upanishads and the Sutras, which are the systematising of the marvellous truths of the Vedanta, comes in the Gîtâ, the divine commentary of the Vedanta.

The Upanishads, the *Vyâsa-Sutras,* and the Gita, therefore, have been taken up by every sect in India that wants to claim authority for orthodoxy, whether dualist, or Vishishtâdvaitist, or Advaitist; the authorities of each of these are the three Prasthanas. We find that a Shankaracharya, or a Râmânuja, or a Madhvâchârya, or a Vallabhâchârya, or a Chaitanya—any one who wanted to propound a new sect—had to take up these three systems and write only a new commentary on them. Therefore it would be wrong to confine the word Vedanta only to one system which has arisen out of the Upanishads. All these are covered by the word Vedanta. The Vishishtadvaitist has as much right to be called a Vedantist as the Advaitist; in fact I will go a little further and say that what we really mean by the word Hindu is really the same as Vedantist. I want you to note that these three systems have been current in India almost from time immemorial; for you must not believe that Shankara was the inventor of the Advaita system. It existed ages before Shankara was born; he was one of its last representatives. So with the Vishishtadvaita system; it had existed ages before Ramanuja appeared, as we already know from the commentaries he has written; so with the dualistic systems that have existed side by side with the others. And with my little knowledge, I have come to the conclusion that they do not contradict each other.

Just as in the case of the six Darshanas, we find they

are a gradual unfolding of the grand principles whose music beginning far back in the soft low notes, ends in the triumphant blast of the Advaita, so also in these three systems we find the gradual working up of the human mind towards higher and higher ideals till everything is merged in that wonderful unity which is reached in the Advaita system. Therefore these three are not contradictory. On the other hand I am bound to tell you that this has been a mistake committed by not a few. We find that an Advaitist teacher keeps intact those texts which especially teach Advaitism, and tries to interpret the dualistic or qualified non-dualistic texts into his own meaning. Similarly we find dualistic teachers trying to read their dualistic meaning into Advaitic texts. Our Gurus were great men, yet there is a saying, "Even the faults of a Guru must be told". I am of opinion that in this only they were mistaken. We need not go into text-torturing, we need not go into any sort of religious dishonesty, we need not go into any sort of grammatical twaddle, we need not go about trying to put our own ideas into texts which were never meant for them, but the work is plain and becomes easier, once you understand the marvellous doctrine of Adhikârabheda.

It is true that the Upanishads have this one theme before them : कस्मिन्नु भगवो विज्ञाते सर्वमिदं विज्ञातं भवति ।—"What is that knowing which we know everything else?" In modern language, the theme of the Upanishads is to find an ultimate unity of things. Knowledge is nothing but finding unity in the midst of diversity. Every science is based upon this; all human knowledge is based upon the finding of unity in the midst of diversity; and if it is the task of small fragments of human knowledge, which we call our sciences, to find unity in the midst of a few 'different phenomena, the task becomes stupendous when the theme before us is to find unity in the midst of this marvellously diversified universe, where prevail unnumbered differences

in name and form, in matter and spirit—each thought
differing from every other thought, each form differing
from every other form. Yet, to harmonise these many
planes and unending Lokas, in the midst of this infinite
variety to find unity, is the theme of the Upanishads. On
the other hand, the old idea of Arundhati Nyâya applies.
To show a man the fine star Arundhati, one takes the big
and brilliant nearest to it, upon which he is asked to
fix his eyes first, and then it becomes quite easy to direct
his sight to Arundhati. This is the task before us, and to
prove my idea I have simply to show you the Upanishads,
and you will see it. Nearly every chapter begins with
dualistic teaching, Upâsanâ. God is first taught as some
one who is the Creator of this universe, its Preserver, and
unto whom everything goes at last. He is one to be worshipped, the Ruler, the Guide of nature, external and internal, yet appearing as if He were outside of nature and
external. One step further, and we find the same teacher
teaching that this God is not outside of nature, but immanent in nature. And at last both ideas are discarded, and
whatever is real is He; there is no difference. तत्त्वमसि श्वेतकेतो
—"Shvetaketu, That thou art." That Immanent One is at
last declared to be the same that is in the human soul.
Here is no compromise; here is no fear of others' opinions.
Truth, bold truth, has been taught in bold language, and
we need not fear to preach the truth in the same bold
language today, and, by the grace of God, I hope at least
to be one who dares to be that bold preacher.

To go back to our preliminaries. There are first two
things to be. understood—one, the psychological aspect
common to all the Vedantic schools, and the other, the
cosmological aspect. I will first take up the latter. Today
we find wonderful discoveries of modern science coming
upon us like bolts from the blue, opening our eyes to
marvels we never dreamt of. But many of these are only
re-discoveries of what had been found ages ago. It was

only the other day that modern science found that even in
the midst of the variety of forces there is unity. It has just
discovered that what it calls heat, magnetism, electricity,
and so forth, are all convertible into one unit force, and
as such, it expresses all these by one name, whatever you
may choose to call it. But this has been done even in the
Samhita ; old and ancient as it is, in it we meet with this
very idea of force I was referring to. All the forces,
whether you call them gravitation, or attraction, or repul-
sion, whether expressing themselves as heat, or electricity,
or magnetism, are nothing but the variations of that unit
energy. Whether they express themselves as thought,
reflected from Antahkarana, the inner organs of man, or
as action from an external organ, the unit from which they
spring is what is called Prâna. Again, what is Prana?
Prana is Spandana or vibration. When all this universe
shall have resolved back into its primal state, what becomes of this infinite force? Do they think that it becomes
extinct? Of course not. If it became extinct, what would
be the cause of the next wave, because the motion is going
in wave forms, rising, falling, rising again, falling again?
Here is the word Srishti, which expresses the universe.
Mark that the word does not mean creation. I am helpless
in talking English; I have to translate the Sanskrit words
as best as I can. It is Srishti, projection. At the end of
a cycle, everything becomes finer and finer and is resolved
back into the primal state from which it sprang, and there
it remains for a time quiescent, ready to spring forth
again. That is Srishti, projection. And what becomes of
all these forces, the Pranas? They are resolved back into
the primal Prana, and this Prana becomes almost motionless—not entirely motionless ; and that is what is described in the Vedic Sukta: "It vibrated without vibrations"—Ânidavâtam. There are many technical phrases
in the Upanishads difficult to understand. For instance,
take this word Vâta ; many times it means air and many

times motion, and often people confuse one with the
other. We must guard against that. And what becomes
of what you call matter? The forces permeate all matter ;
they all dissolve into Âkâsha, from which they again come
out; this Akasha is the primal matter. Whether you translate it as ether or anything else, the idea is that this Akasha
is the primal form of matter. This Akasha vibrates under
the action of Prana, and when the next Srishti is coming
up, as the vibration becomes quicker, the Akasha is lashed
into all these wave forms which we call suns, moons, and
systems.

        We read again: यदिदं किंच जगत् सर्वं प्राण एजति निःसृतम्
—"Everything in this universe has been projected, Prana
vibrating." You must mark the word Ejati, because it comes
from Eja—to vibrate. Nihsritam—projected. Yadidam
Kincha—whatever in this universe.

        This is a part of the cosmological side. There are
many details working into it. For instance, how the process takes place, how there is first ether, and how from
the ether come other things, how that ether begins to
vibrate, and from that Vâyu comes. But the one idea is
here that it is from the finer that the grosser has come.
Gross matter is the last to emerge and the most external,
and this gross matter had the finer matter before it. Yet
we see that the whole thing has been resolved into two,
but there is not yet a final unity. There is the unity of
force, Prana , there is the unity of matter, called Akasha.
Is there any unity to be found among them again? Can
they be melted into one? Our modern science is mute
here, it has not yet found its way out; and if it is doing
so, just as it has been slowly finding the same old Prana
and the same ancient Akasha, it will have to move along
the same lines.

        The next unity is the omnipresent impersonal Being
known by its old mythological name as Brahmâ, the four-
headed Brahma, and psychologically called Mahat. This

is where the two unite. What is called your mind is only
a bit of this Mahat caught in the trap of the brain, and the
sum total of all minds caught in the meshes of brains is
what you call Samashti, the aggregate, the universal.
Analysis had to go further; it was not yet complete. Here
we were each one of us, as it were, a microcosm, and the
world taken altogether is the macrocosm. But whatever is
in the Vyashti, the particular, we may safely conjecture that
a similar thing is happening also outside. If we had the
power to analyse our own minds, we might safely conjecture that the same thing is happening in the cosmic mind.
What is this mind is the question. In modern times, in
Western countries, as physical science is making rapid
progress, as physiology is step by step conquering stronghold after stronghold of old religions, the Western people
do not know where to stand, because to their great
despair, modern physiology at every step has identified
the mind with the brain. But we in India have known
that always. That is the first proposition the Hindu boy
learns that the mind is matter, only finer. The body is gross,
and behind the body is what we call the Sukshma Sharira,
the fine body, or mind. This is also material, only finer ;
and it is not the Âtman.

I will not translate this word to you in English, because
the idea does not exist in Europe; it is untranslatable.
The modern attempt of German philosophers is to translate the word Atman by the word "Self", and until that
word is universally accepted, it is impossible to use it. So,
call it as Self or anything, it is our Atman. This Atman
is the real man behind. It is the Atman that uses the
material mind as its instrument, its Antahkarana, as is the
psychological term for the mind. And the mind by
means of a series of internal organs works the visible
organs of the body. What is this mind? It was only the
other day that Western philosophers have come to know
that the eyes are not the real organs of vision, but that

behind these are other organs, the Indriyas, and if these
are destroyed, a man may have a thousand eyes, like
Indra, but there will be no sight for him. Ay, your
philosophy starts with this assumption that by vision is
not meant the external vision. The real vision belongs to
the internal organs, the brain-centres inside. You may call
them what you like, but it is not that the Indriyas are the
eyes, or the nose, or the ears. And the sum total of all
these Indriyas plus the Manas, Buddhi, Chitta, Ahamkâra,
etc., is what is called the mind, and if the modern physi-
ologist comes to tell you that the brain is what is called
the mind, and that the brain is formed of so many organs,
you need not be afraid at all; tell him that your philosophers knew it always; it is one of the very first principles
of your religion.

Well then, we have to understand now what is meant
by this Manas, Buddhi, Chitta, Ahamkara, etc. First of all,
let us take Chitta. It is the mind-stuff—a part of the Mahat
—it is the generic name for the mind itself, including all
its various states. Suppose on a summer evening, there is
a lake, smooth and calm, without a ripple on its surface.
And suppose some one throws a stone into this lake.
What happens? First there is the action, the blow given
to the water; next the water rises and sends a reaction
towards the stone, and that reaction takes the form of a
wave. First the water vibrates a little, and immediately
sends back a reaction in the form of a wave. The Chitta
let us compare to this lake, and the external objects are
like the stones thrown into it. As soon as it comes in contact with any external object by means of these Indriyas
—the Indriyas must be there to carry these external objects
inside—there is a vibration, what is called Manas,
indecisive. Next there is a reaction, the determinative
faculty, Buddhi, and along with this Buddhi flashes the
idea of Aham and the external object. Suppose there is a
mosquito sitting upon my hand. This sensation is carried

to my Chitta and it vibrates a little ; this is the psychological Manas. Then there is a reaction, and immediately comes the idea that I have a mosquito on my hand and that I shall have to drive it off. Thus these stones are thrown into the lake, but in the case of the lake every blow that comes to it is from the external world, while in the case of the lake of the mind, the blows may either come from the external world or the internal world. This whole series is what is called the Antahkarana.

Along with it, you ought to understand one thing more that will help us in understanding the Advaita system later on. It is this. All of you must have seen pearls and most of you know how pearls are formed. A grain of sand enters into the shell of a pearl oyster, and sets up an irritation there, and the oyster's body reacts towards the irritation and covers the little particle with its own juice. That crystallises and forms the pearl. So the whole universe is like that, it is the pearl which is being formed by us. What we get from the external world is simply the blow. Even to be conscious of that blow we have to react, and as soon as we react, we really project a portion of our own mind towards the blow, and when we come to know of it, it is really our own mind as it has been shaped by the blow. Therefore it is clear even to those who want to believe in a hard and fast realism of an external world, which they cannot but admit in these days of physiology —that supposing we represent the external world by "x", what we really know is "x" plus mind, and this mind-element is so great that it has covered the whole of that "x" which has remained unknown and unknowable throughout; and, therefore, if there is an external world, it is always unknown and unknowable. What we know of it is as it is moulded, formed, fashioned by our own mind. So with the internal world. The same applies to our own soul, the Atman. In order to know the Atman we shall have to know It through the mind; and, therefore, what little we know of this Atman is simply the Atman plus the mind. That is to say, the Atman covered over, fashioned. and moulded by the mind, and nothing more. We shall return to this a little later, but we will remember what has been told here.

The next thing to understand is this. The question arose that this body is the name of one continuous stream of matter—every moment we are adding material to it, and every moment material is being thrown off by it—like a river continually flowing, vast masses of water always changing places; yet all the same, we take up the whole thing in imagination, and call it the same river. What do we call the river? Every moment the water is changing, the shore is changing, every moment the environment is changing, what is the river then? It is the name of this series of changes. So with the mind. That is the great Kshanika Vijnâna Vâda doctrine, most difficult to understand, but most rigorously and logically worked out in the Buddhistic philosophy; and this arose in India in opposition to some part of the Vedanta. That had to be answered and we shall see later on how it could only be answered by Advaitism and by nothing else. We will see also how, in spite of people's curious notions about Advaitism, people's fright about Advaitism, it is the salvation of the world, because therein alone is to be found the reason of things. Dualism and other isms are very good as means of worship, very satisfying to the mind, and maybe, they have helped the mind onward; but if man wants to be rational and religious at the same time, Advaita is the one system in the world for him. Well, now, we shall regard the mind as a similar river, continually filling itself at one end and emptying itself at the other end. Where is that unity which we call the Atman? The idea is this, that in spite of this continuous change in the body, and in spite of this continuous change in the mind, there is in us something that is unchangeable, which makes our ideas of things appear unchangeable. When rays of light coming from different quarters fall upon a screen, or a wall, or upon something that is not changeable, then and then alone it is possible for them to form a unity, then and then alone it is possible for them to form one complete whole. Where is this unity in the human organs, falling upon which, as it were, the various ideas will come to unity and become one complete whole? This certainly cannot be the mind itself, seeing that it also changes. Therefore there must be something which is neither the body nor the mind, something which changes not, something permanent, upon which all our ideas, our sensations fall to form a unity and a complete whole; and this is the real soul, the Atman of man. And seeing that everything material, whether you call it fine matter, or mind, must be changeful, seeing that what you call gross matter, the external world, must also be changeful in comparison to that—this unchangeable something cannot be of material substance; therefore it is spiritual, that is to say, it is not matter—it is indestructible, unchangeable.

Next will come another question: Apart from those old arguments which only rise in the external world, the arguments in support of design—who created this external world, who created matter, etc.? The idea here is to know truth only from the inner nature of man, and the question arises just in the same way as it arose about the soul. Taking for granted that there is a soul, unchangeable, in each man, which is neither the mind nor the body, there is still a unity of idea among the souls, a unity of feeling, of sympathy. How is it possible that my soul can act upon your soul, where is the medium through which it can work, where is the medium through which it can act? How is it I can feel anything about your souls? What is it that is in touch both with your soul and with my soul? Therefore there is a metaphysical necessity of admitting another soul, for it must be a soul which acts in contact with all the

different souls, and in and through matter—one Soul which
covers and interpenetrates all the infinite number of souls
in the world, in and through which they live, in and
through which they sympathise, and love, and work for one
another. And this universal Soul is Paramâtman, the Lord
God of the universe. Again, it follows that because the
soul is not made of matter, since it is spiritual, it cannot
obey the laws of matter, it cannot be judged by the laws
of matter. It is, therefore, unconquerable, birthless,
deathless, and changeless.

नैनं छिन्दन्ति शस्त्राणि नैनं दहति पावकः ।
न चैनं क्लेदयन्त्यापो न शोषयति मारुतः ॥
नित्यः सर्वगतः स्थाणुरचलोऽयं सनातनः ॥

—"This Self, weapons cannot pierce, nor fire can burn,
water cannot wet, nor air can dry up. Changless, all-
pervading, unmoving, immovable, eternal is this Self of
man." We learn according to the Gita and the Vedanta
that this individual Self is also Vibhu, and according to
Kapila, is omnipresent. Of course there are sects in India
which hold that the Self is Anu, infinitely small; but what
they mean is Anu in manifestation; its real nature is Vibhu,
all-pervading.

There comes another idea, startling perhaps, yet a
characteristically Indian idea, and if there is any idea that
is common to all our sects, it is this. Therefore I beg you
to pay attention to this one idea and to remember it, for
this is the very foundation of everything that we have in
India. The idea is this. You have heard of the doctrine
of physical evolution preached in the Western world by
the German and the English savants. It tells us that the
bodies of the different animals are really one; the differences that we see are but different expressions of the same
series; that from the lowest worm to the highest and the
most saintly man it is but one—the one changing into the
other, and so on, going up and up, higher and higher, until
it attains perfection. We had that idea also. Declares our

Yogi Patanjali—जात्यन्तरपरिणामः प्रकृत्यापूरात् । One species—the Jâti is species—changes into another species—evolution; Parinâma means one thing changing into another, just as one species changes into another. Where do we differ from the Europeans? Patanjali says, Prakrityâpurât, "By the infilling of nature". The European says, it is competition, natural and sexual selection, etc. that forces one body to take the form of another. But here is another idea, a still better analysis, going deeper into the thing and saying, "By the infilling of nature". What is meant by this infilling of nature? We admit that the amoeba goes higher and higher until it becomes a Buddha; we admit that, but we are at the same time as much certain that you cannot get an amount of work out of a machine unless you have put it in in some shape or other. The sum total of the energy remains the same, whatever the forms it may take. If you want a mass of energy at one end, you have got to put it in at the other end; it may be in another form, but the amount of energy that should be produced out of it must be the same. Therefore, if a Buddha is the one end of the change, the very amoeba must have been the Buddha also. If the Buddha is the evolved amoeba, the amoeba was the involved Buddha also. If this universe is the manifestation of an almost infinite amount of energy, when this universe was in a state of Pralaya, it must have represented the same amount of involved energy. It cannot have been otherwise. As such, it follows that every soul is infinite. From the lowest worm that crawls under our feet to the noblest and greatest saints, all have this infinite power, infinite purity, and infinite everything. Only the difference is in the degree of manifestation. The worm is only manifesting just a little bit of that energy, you have manifested more, another god-man has manifested still more: that is all the difference. But that infinite power is there all the same. Says Patanjali: ततः क्षेत्रिकवत् । —"Like the peasant irrigating his field." Through a little corner of his field he brings water from a reservoir some-where, and perhaps he has got a little lock that prevents the water from rushing into his field. When he wants water, he has simply to open the lock, and in rushes the water of its own power. The power has not to be added, it is already there in the reservoir. So every one of us, every being, has as his own background such a reservoir of strength, infinite power, infinite purity, infinite bliss, and existence infinite—only these locks, these bodies, are hindering us from expressing what we really are to the fullest.

And as these bodies become more and more finely organised, as the Tamoguna becomes the Rajoguna, and as the Rajoguna becomes Sattvaguna, more and more of this power and purity becomes manifest, and therefore it is that our people have been so careful about eating and drinking, and the food question. It may be that the origi-nal ideas have been lost, just as with our marriage—which, though not belonging to the subject, I may take as an example. If I have another opportunity I will talk to you about these; but let me tell you now that the ideas behind our marriage system are the only ideas through which there can be a real civilisation. There cannot be anything else. If a man or a woman were allowed the freedom to take up any woman or man as wife or husband, if individual pleasure, satisfaction of animal instincts, were to be allowed to run loose in society, the result must be evil, evil children, wicked and demoniacal. Ay, man in every country is, on the one hand, producing these brutal children, and on the other hand multiplying the police force to keep these brutes down. The question is not how to destroy evil that way, but how to prevent the very birth of evil. And so long as you live in society your marriage certainly affects every member of it; and therefore society has the right to dictate whom you shall marry, and whom you shall not. And great ideas of this kind have been behind the system of marriage here, what they call the astrological Jâti of the bride and bridegroom. And in passing I may remark that according to Manu a child who is born of lust is not an Aryan. The child whose very conception and whose death is according to the rules of the Vedas, such is an Aryan. Yes, and less of these Aryan children are being produced in every country, and the result is the mass of evil which we call Kali Yuga. But we have lost all these ideals—it is true we cannot carry all these ideas to the fullest length now—it is perfectly true we have made almost a caricature of some of these great ideas. It is lamentably true that the fathers and mothers are not what they were in old times, neither is society so educated as it used to be, neither has society that love for individuals that it used to have. But, however faulty the working out may be, the principle is sound; and if its application has become defective, if one method has failed, take up the principle and work it out better; why kill the principle? The same applies to the food question. The work and details are bad, very bad indeed, but that does not hurt the principle. The principle is eternal and must be there. Work it out afresh and make a re-formed application.

This is the one great idea of the Atman which every one of our sects in India has to believe. Only, as we shall find, the dualists preach that this Atman by evil works becomes Sankuchita, i.e. all its powers and its nature become contracted, and by good works again that nature expands. And the Advaitist says that the Atman never expands nor contracts, but seems to do so. It appears to have become contracted. That is all the difference, but all have the one idea that our Atman has all the powers already, not that anything will come to It from outside, not that anything will drop into It from the skies. Mark you, your Vedas are not inspired, but expired, not that they came from anywhere outside, but they are the eternal laws living in every soul. The Vedas are in the soul of the ant,

in the soul of the god. The ant has only to evolve and get
the body of a sage or a Rishi, and the Vedas will come
out, eternal laws expressing themselves. This is the one
great idea to understand that our power is already ours,
our salvation is already within us. Say either that it has
become contracted, or say that it has been covered
with the veil of Mâyâ, it matters little; the idea is there
already; you must have to believe in that, believe in the
possibility of everybody—that even in the lowest man there
is the same possibility as in the Buddha. This is the
doctrine of the Atman.

But now comes a tremendous fight. Here are the
Buddhists, who equally analyse the body into a material
stream and as equally analyse the mind into another. And
as for this Atman, they state that It is unnecessary; so we
need not assume the Atman at all. What use of a substance,
and qualities adhering to the substance? We say,
Gunas, qualities, and qualities alone. It is illogical to
assume two causes where one will explain the whole thing.
And the fight went on, and all the theories which held the
doctrine of substance were thrown to the ground by the
Buddhists. There was a break-up all along the line of
those who held on to the doctrine of substance and qualities, that you have a soul, and I have a soul, and every one
has a soul separate from the mind and body, and that each
one is an individual.

So far we have seen that the idea of dualism is all
right ; for there is the body, there is then the fine body—
the mind—there is this Atman, and in and through all the
Atmans is that Paramâtman, God. The difficulty is here
that this Atman and Paramatman are both called substance, to which the mind and body and so-called substances adhere like so many qualities. Nobody has ever
seen a substance, none can ever conceive; what is the
use of thinking of this substance? Why not become a
Kshanikavâdin and say that whatever exists is this succes-

sion of mental currents and nothing more? They do not adhere to each other, they do not form a unit, one is chasing the other, like waves in the ocean, never complete, never forming one unit-whole. Man is a succession of waves, and when one goes away it generates another, and the cessation of these wave-forms is what is called Nirvâna. You see that dualism is mute before this; it is impossible that it can bring up any argument, and the dualistic God also cannot be retained here. The idea of a God that is omnipresent, and yet is a person who creates without hands, and moves without feet, and so on, and who has created the universe as a Kumbhakâra (potter) creates a Ghata (pot), the Buddhist declares, is childish, and that if this is God, he is going to fight this God and not worship it. This universe is full of misery ; if it is the work of a God, we are going to fight this God. And secondly, this God is illogical and impossible, as all of you are aware. We need not go into the defects of the "design theory", as all our Kshanikas have shown them full well ; and so this Personal God fell to pieces.

Truth, and nothing but truth, is the watchword of the Advaitist. सत्यमेव जयते नानृतं । सत्येन पन्था विततो देवयानः —"Truth alone triumphs, and not, untruth. Through truth alone the way to gods, Devayâna, lies." Everybody marches forward under that banner ; ay, but it is only to crush the weaker man's position by his own. You come with your dualistic idea of God to pick a quarrel with a poor man who is worshipping an image, and you think you are wonderfully rational, you can confound him ; but if he turns round and shatters your own Personal God and calls that an imaginary ideal, where are you? You fall back on faith and so on, or raise the cry of atheism, the old cry of a weak man—whosoever defeats him is an atheist. If you are to be rational, be rational all along the line, and if not, allow others the same privilege which you ask for yourselves. How can you prove the existence of this God? On the other hand, it can be almost disproved. There is not a shadow of a proof as to His existence, and there are very strong arguments to the contrary. How will you prove His existence, with your God, and His Gunas, and an infinite number of souls which are substance, and each soul an individual? In what are you an individual? You are not as a body, for you know today better than even the Buddhists of old knew that what may have been matter in the sun has just now become matter in you, and will go out and become matter in the plants; then where is your individuality, Mr. So-and-so? The same applies to the mind. Where is your individuality? You have one thought to-night and another tomorrow. You do not think the same way as you thought when you were a child ; and old men do not think the same way as they did when they were young. Where is your individuality then? Do not say it is in consciousness, this Ahamkara, because this only covers a small part of your existence. While I am talking to you, all my organs are working and I am not conscious of it. If consciousness is the proof of existence they do not exist then, because I am not conscious of them. Where are you then with your Personal God theories? How can you prove such a God?

Again, the Buddhists will stand up and declare—not only is it illogical, but immoral, for it teaches man to be a coward and to seek assistance outside, and nobody can give him such help. Here is the universe, man made it ; why then depend on an imaginary being outside whom nobody ever saw, or felt, or got help from? Why then do you make cowards of yourselves and teach your children that the highest state of man is to be like a dog, and go crawling before this imaginary being, saying that you are weak and impure, and that you are everything vile in this universe? On the other hand, the Buddhists may urge not only that you tell a lie, but that you bring a tremendous amount of evil upon your children; for, mark you, this world is one of hypnotisation. Whatever you tell yourself, that you become. Almost the first words the great Buddha uttered were: "What you think, that you are ; what you will think, that you will be." If this is true, do not teach yourself that you are nothing, ay, that you cannot do anything unless you are helped by somebody who does not live here, but sits above the clouds. The result will be that you will be more and more weakened every day. By constantly repeating, "we are very impure, Lord, make us pure", the result will be that you will hypnotise yourselves into all sorts of vices. Ay, the Buddhists say that ninety per cent of these vices that you see in every society are on account of this idea of a Personal God ; this is an awful idea of the human being that the end and aim of this expression of life, this wonderful expression of life, is to become like a dog. Says the Buddhist to the Vaishnava, if your ideal, your aim and goal is to go to the place called Vaikuntha where God lives, and there stand before Him with folded hands all through eternity, it is better to commit suicide than do that. The Buddhists may even urge that, that is why he is going to create annihilation, Nirvana, to escape this. I am putting these ideas before you as a Buddhist just for the time being, because nowadays all these Advaitic ideas are said to make you immoral, and I am trying to tell you how the other side looks. Let us face both sides boldly and bravely.

We have seen first of all that this cannot be proved, this idea of a Personal God creating the world; is there any child that can believe this today? Because a Kumbhakara creates a Ghata, therefore a God created the world! If this is so, then your Kumbhakara is God also; and if any one tells you that He acts without head and hands, you may take him to a lunatic asylum. Has ever your Personal God, the Creator of the world to whom you cry all your life, helped you—is the next challenge from modern science.

They will prove that any help you have had could have
been got by your own exertions, and better still, you need
not have spent your energy in that crying, you could have
done it better without that weeping and crying. And we
have seen that along with this idea of a Personal God
comes tyranny and priestcraft. Tyranny and priestcraft
have prevailed wherever this idea existed, and until the
lie is knocked on the head, say the Buddhists, tyranny will
not cease. So long as man thinks he has to cower before a
supernatural being, so long there will be priests to claim
rights and privileges and to make men cower before them,
while these poor men will continue to ask some priest to
act as interceder for them. You may do away with the
Brâhmin, but mark me, those who do so will put themselves in his place and will be worse, because the Brahmin
has a certain amount of generosity in him, but these up-
starts are always the worst of tyrannisers. If a beggar gets
wealth, he thinks the whole world is a bit of straw. So these
priests there must be, so long as this Personal God idea
persists, and it will be impossible to think of any great
morality in society. Priestcraft and tyranny go hand in
hand. Why was it invented? Because some strong men
in old times got people into their hands and said, you must
obey us or we will destroy you. That was the long and
short of it. महदुर्यं वज्रमुद्यतम् । —It is the idea of the thunder-
er who kills every one who does not obey him.

Next the Buddhist says, you have been perfectly
rational up to this point, that everything is the result of
the law of Karma. You believe in an infinity of souls, and
that souls are without birth or death, and this infinity of
souls and the belief in the law of Karma are perfectly logical no doubt. There cannot be a cause without an effect,
the present must have had its cause in the past and will
have its effect in the future. The Hindu says the Karma
is Jada (inert) and not Chaitanya (Spirit), therefore some
Chaitanya is necessary to bring this cause to fruition. Is

it so, that Chaitanya is necessary to bring the plant to fruition? If I plant the seed and add water, no Chaitanya is necessary. You may say there was some original Chaitanya there, but the souls themselves were the Chaitanya, nothing else is necessary. If human souls have it too, what necessity is there for a God, as say the Jains, who, unlike the Buddhists, believe in souls and do not believe in God. Where are you logical, where are you moral? And when you criticise Advaitism and fear that it will make for immorality, just read a little of what has been done in India by dualistic sects. If there have been twenty thousand Advaitist blackguards, there have also been twenty thousand Dvaitist blackguards. Generally speaking, there will be more Dvaitist blackguards, because it takes a better type of mind to understand Advaitism, and Advaitists can scarcely be frightened into anything. What remains for you Hindus, then? There is no help for you out of the clutches of the Buddhists. You may quote the Vedas, but he does not believe in them. He will say, "My Tripitakas say otherwise, and they are without beginning or end, not even written by Buddha, for Buddha says he is only reciting them; they are eternal." And he adds, "Yours are wrong, ours are the true Vedas, yours are manufactured by the Brahmin priests, therefore out with them." How do you escape?

Here is the way to get out. Take up the first objection, the metaphysical one, that substance and qualities are different. Says the Advaitist, they are not. There is no difference between substance and qualities. You know the old illustration, how the rope is taken for the snake, and when you see the snake you do not see the rope at all, the rope has vanished. Dividing the thing into substance and quality is a metaphysical something in the brains of philosophers, for never can they be in effect outside. You see qualities if you are an ordinary man, and substance if you are a great Yogi, but you never see both at the same time. So, Buddhists, your quarrel about substance and qualities has been but a miscalculation which does not stand on fact. But if substance is unqualified, there can only be one. If you take qualities off from the soul, and show that these qualities are in the mind really, superimposed on the soul, then there can never be two souls for it is qualification that makes the difference between one soul and another. How do you know that one soul is different from the other? Owing to certain differentiating marks, certain qualities. And where qualities do not exist, how can there be differentiation? Therefore there are not two souls, there is but One, and your Paramatman is unnecessary, it is this very soul. That One is called Paramatman, that very One is called Jivâtman, and so on; and you dualists, such as the Sânkhyas and others, who say that the soul is Vibhu, omnipresent, how can you make two infinites? There can be only one. What else? This One is the one Infinite Atman, everything else is its manifestation. There the Buddhist stops, but there it does not end.

The Advaitist position is not merely a weak one of criticism. The Advaitist criticises others when they come too near him, and just throws them away, that is all; but he propounds his own position. He is the only one that criticises, and does not stop with criticism and showing books. Here you are. You say the universe is a thing of continuous motion. In Vyashti (the finite) everything is moving ; you are moving, the table is moving, motion everywhere ; it is Samsâra, continuous motion ; it is Jagat. Therefore there cannot be an individuality in this Jagat, because individuality means that which does not change ; there cannot be any changeful individuality, it is a contradiction in terms. There is no such thing as individuality in this little world of ours, the Jagat. Thought and feeling, mind and body, men and animals and plants are in a continuous state of flux. But suppose you take the universe as a unit whole; can it change or move? Certainly not.

Motion is possible in comparison with something which is a little less in motion or entirely motionless. The universe as a whole, therefore, is motionless, unchangeable. You are therefore, an individual then and then alone when you are the whole of it, when the realisation of "I am the universe" comes. That is why the Vedantist says that so long as there are two, fear does not cease. It is only when one does not see another, does not feel another, when it is all one—then alone fear ceases, then alone death vanishes, then alone Samsara vanishes. Advaita teaches us, therefore, that man is individual in being universal, and not in being particular. You are immortal only when you are the whole. You are fearless and deathless only when you are the universe ; and then that which you call the universe is the same as that you call God, the same that you call existence, the same that you call the whole. It is the one undivided Existence which is taken to be the manifold world which we see, as also others who are in the same state of mind as we. People who have done a little better Karma and get a better state of mind, when they die, look upon it as Svarga and see Indras and so forth. People still higher will see it, the very same thing, as Brahma-Loka, and the perfect ones will neither see the earth nor the heavens, nor any Loka at all. The universe will have vanished, and Brahman will be in its stead.

Can we know this Brahman? I have told you of the painting of the Infinite in the Samhita. Here we shall find another side shown, the infinite internal. That was the infinite of the muscles. Here we shall have the Infinite of thought. There the Infinite was attempted to be painted in language positive ; here that language failed and the attempt has been to paint it in language negative. Here is this universe, and even admitting that it is Brahman, can we know it? No! No! You must understand this one thing again very clearly. Again and again this doubt will

come to you: If this is Brahman, how can we know it?
विज्ञातारमरे   केन   विजानीयात्   —"By what can the knower be
known?" How can the knower be known? The eyes
see everything; can they see themselves? They cannot.
The very fact of knowledge is a degradation. Children
of the Aryans, you must remember this, for herein lies a
big story. All the Western temptations that come to you,
have their metaphysical basis on that one thing—there is
nothing higher than sense-knowledge. In the East, we
say in our Vedas that this knowledge is lower than the
thing itself, because it is always a limitation. When you
want to know a thing, it immediately becomes limited by
your mind. They say, refer back to that instance of the
oyster making a pearl and see how knowledge is limitation, gathering a thing, bringing it into consciousness, and
not knowing it as a whole. This is true about all knowledge, and can it be less so about the Infinite? Can you
thus limit Him who is the substance of all knowledge,
Him who is the Sâkshi, the witness, without whom you
cannot have any knowledge, Him who has no qualities,
who is the Witness of the whole universe, the Witness
in our own souls? How can you know Him? By what
means can you bind Him up? Everything, the whole
universe, is such a false attempt. This infinite Atman is,
as it were, trying to see His own face, and all, from the
lowest animals to the highest of gods, are like so many
mirrors to reflect Himself in, and He is taking up still
others, finding them insufficient, until in the human body
He comes to know that it is the finite of the finite, all is
finite, there cannot be any expression of the Infinite in the
finite. Then comes the retrograde march, and this is what
is called renunciation, Vairâgya. Back from the senses,
back! Do not go to the senses is the watchword of
Vairagya. This is the watchword of all morality, this is
the watchword of all well-being; for you must remember
that with us the universe begins in Tapasyâ, in renuncia-

tion, and as you go back and back, all the forms are being manifested before you, and they are left aside one after the other until you remain what you really are. This is Moksha or liberation.

This idea we have to understand: विज्ञातारमरे केन विजानीयात् —"How to know the knower?" The knower cannot be known, because if it were known, it will not be the knower. If you look at your eyes in a mirror, the reflection is no more your eyes, but something else, only a reflection. Then if this Soul, this Universal, Infinite Being which you are, is only a witness, what good is it? It cannot live, and move about, and enjoy the world, as we do. People cannot understand how the witness can enjoy. "Oh," they say, "you Hindus have become quiescent, and good for nothing, through this doctrine that you are witnesses!" First of all, it is only the witness that can enjoy. If there is a wrestling match, who enjoys it, those who take part in it, or those who are looking on—the outsiders? The more and more you are the witness of anything in life, the more you enjoy it. And this is Ânanda ; and, therefore, infinite bliss can only be yours when you have become the witness of this universe; then alone you are a Mukta Purusha. It is the witness alone that can work without any desire, without any idea of going to heaven, without any idea of blame, without any idea of praise. The witness alone enjoys, and none else.

Coming to the moral aspect, there is one thing between the metaphysical and the moral aspect of Advaitism; it is the theory of Mâyâ. Everyone of these points in the Advaita system requires years to understand and months to explain. Therefore you will excuse me if I only just touch them en passant. This theory of Maya has been the most difficult thing to understand in all ages. Let me tell you in a few words that it is surely no theory, it is the combination of the three ideas Desha-Kâla-Nimitta—space, time, and causation—and this time

and space and cause have been further reduced into
Nâma-Rupa. Suppose there is a wave in the ocean.
The wave is distinct from the ocean only in its form and
name, and this form and this name cannot have any
separate existence from the wave ; they exist only with
the wave. The wave may subside, but the same amount
of water remains, even if the name and form that were
on the wave vanish for ever. So this Maya is what makes
the difference between me and you, between all animals
and man, between gods and men. In fact, it is this
Maya that causes the Atman to be caught, as it were, in
so many millions of beings, and these are distinguishable
only through name and form. If you leave it alone, let
name and form go, all this variety vanishes for ever, and
you are what you really are. This is Maya.

It is again no theory, but a statement of facts. When
the realist states that this table exists, what he means is,
that this table has an independent existence of its own,
that it does not depend on the existence of anything else
in the universe, and if this whole universe be destroyed and
annihilated, this table will remain just as it is now. A little
thought will show you that it cannot be so. Everything
here in the sense-world is dependent and interdependent,
relative and correlative, the existence of one depending
on the other. There are three steps, therefore, in our
knowledge of things; the first is that each thing is
individual and separate from every other ; and the next
step is to find that there is a relation and correlation
between all things; and the third is that there is only one
thing which we see as many. The first idea of God with
the ignorant is that this God is somewhere outside the
universe, that is to say, the conception of God is extremely
human; He does just what a man does, only on a bigger
and higher scale. And we have seen how that idea of
God is proved in a few words to be unreasonable and
insufficient. And the next idea is the idea of a power we

see manifested everywhere. This is the real Personal God we get in the *Chandi*, but, mark me, not a God that you make the reservoir of all good qualities only. You cannot have two Gods, God and Satan; you must have only one and dare to call Him good and bad. Have only one and take the logical consequences. We read in the *Chandi*: "We salute Thee, O Divine Mother, who lives in every being as peace. We salute Thee, O Divine Mother, who lives in all beings as purity." At the same time we must take the whole consequence of calling Him the All-formed. "All this is bliss, O Gârgi; wherever there is bliss there is a portion of the Divine." You may use it how you like. In this light before me, you may give a poor man a hundred rupees, and another man may forge your name, but the light will be the same for both. This is the second stage. And the third is that God is neither outside nature nor inside nature, but God and nature and soul and universe are all convertible terms. You never see two things; it is your metaphysical words that have deluded you. You assume that you are a body and have a soul, and that you are both together. How can that be? Try in your own mind. If there is a Yogi among you, he knows himself as Chaitanya, for him the body has vanished. An ordinary man thinks of himself as a body; the idea of spirit has vanished from him ; but because the metaphysical ideas exist that man has a body and a soul and all these things, you think they are all simultaneously there. One thing at a time. Do not talk of God when you see matter; you see the effect and the effect alone, and the cause you cannot see, and the moment you can see the cause, the effect will have vanished. Where is the world then, and who has taken it off?

"One that is present always as consciousness, the bliss absolute, beyond all bounds, beyond all compare, beyond all qualities, ever-free, limitless as the sky, without parts, the absolute, the perfect—such a Brahman, O sage, O

learned one, shines in the heart of the Jnâni in
Samâdhi. (*Vivekachudamani*, 408).

"Where all the changes of nature cease for ever, who
is thought beyond all thoughts, who is equal to all yet
having no equal, immeasurable, whom the Vedas declare,
who is the essence in what we call our existence, the
perfect—such a Brahman, O sage, O learned one, shines
in the heart of the Jnani in Samadhi. (Ibid., 409)

"Beyond all birth and death, the Infinite One, incomparable, like the whole universe deluged in water in
Mahâpralaya—water above, water beneath, water on all
sides, and on the face of that water not a wave, not a
ripple—silent and calm, all visions have died out, all fights
and quarrels and the war of fools and saints have ceased
for ever—such a Brahman, O sage, O learned one, shines
in the heart of the Jnani in Samadhi." (Ibid., 410)

That also comes, and when that comes the world has
vanished.

We have seen then that this Brahman, this Reality is
unknown and unknowable, not in the sense of the agnostic, but because to know Him would be a blasphemy,
because you are He already. We have also seen that this
Brahman is not this table and yet is this table. Take off
the name and form, and whatever is reality is He. He is
the reality in everything.

"Thou art the woman, thou the man, thou art the boy,
and the girl as well, thou the old man supporting thyself
on a stick, thou art all in all in the universe." That is the
theme of Advaitism. A few words more. Herein lies, we
find, the explanation of the essence of things. We have
seen how here alone we can take a firm stand against all
the onrush of logic and scientific knowledge. Here at last
reason has a firm foundation, and, at the same time, the
Indian Vedantist does not curse the preceding steps ; he
looks back and he blesses them, and he knows that they
were true, only wrongly perceived, and wrongly stated.

They were the same truth, only seen through the glass of Maya, distorted it may be—yet truth, and nothing but truth. The same God whom the ignorant man saw outside nature, the same whom the little-knowing man saw as interpenetrating the universe, and the same whom the sage realises as his own Self, as the whole universe itself—all are One and the same Being, the same entity seen from different standpoints, seen through different glasses of Maya, perceived by different minds, and all the difference was caused by that. Not only so, but one view must lead to the other. What is the difference between science and common knowledge? Go out into the streets in the dark, and if something unusual is happening there, ask one of the passers-by what is the cause of it. It is ten to one that he will tell you it is a ghost causing the phenomenon. He is always going after ghosts and spirits outside, because it is the nature of ignorance to seek for causes outside of effects. If a stone falls, it has been thrown by a devil or a ghost, says the ignorant man, but the scientific man says it is the law of nature, the law of gravitation.

What is the fight between science and religion everywhere? Religions are encumbered with such a mass of explanations which come from outside—one angel is in charge of the sun, another of the moon, and so on *ad infinitum*. Every change is caused by a spirit, the one common point of agreement being that they are all outside the thing. Science means that the cause of a thing is sought out by the nature of the thing itself. As step by step science is progressing, it has taken the explanation of natural phenomena out of the hands of spirits and angels. Because Advaitism has done likewise in spiritual matters, it is the most scientific religion. This universe has not been created by any extra-cosmic God, nor is it the work of any outside genius. It is self-creating, self-dissolving, self-manifesting, One Infinite Existence, the

Brahman. Tattvamasi Shvetaketo—"That thou art,
O Shvetaketu!"

Thus you see that this, and this alone, and none else,
can be the only scientific religion. And with all the prattle
about science that is going on daily at the present time in
modern half-educated India, with all the talk about
rationalism and reason that I hear every day, I expect that
whole sects of you will come over and dare to be
Advaitists, and dare to preach it to the world in the words
of Buddha, बहुजनहिताय बहुजनसुखाय—"For the good of many,
for the happiness of many." If you do not, I take you
for cowards. If you cannot get over your cowardice, if
your fear is your excuse, allow the same liberty to others,
do not try to break up the poor idol-worshipper, do not
call him a devil, do not go about preaching to every man
that does not agree entirely with you. Know first, that
you are cowards yourselves, and if society frightens you,
if your own superstitions of the past frighten you so much,
how much more will these superstitions frighten and bind
down those who are ignorant? That is the Advaita
position. Have mercy on others. Would to God that
the whole world were Advaitists tomorrow, not only in
theory, but in realisation. But if that cannot be, let us
do the next best thing; let us take the ignorant by the
hand, lead them always step by step just as they can go,
and know that every step in all religious growth in India
has been progressive. It is not from bad to good, but
from good to better.

Something more has to be told about the moral
relation. Our boys blithely talk nowadays; they learn
from somebody—the Lord knows from whom—that
Advaita makes people immoral, because if we are all one
and all God, what need of morality will there be at all!
In the first place, that is the argument of the brute, who
can only be kept down by the whip. If you are such
brutes, commit suicide rather than pass for human beings

who have to be kept down by the whip. If the whip is taken away, you will all be demons! You ought all to be killed if such is the case. There is no help for you ; you must always be living under this whip and rod, and there is no salvation, no escape for you.

In the second place, Advaita and Advaita alone explains morality. Every religion preaches that the essence of all morality is to do good to others. And why? Be unselfish. And why should I? Some God has said it? He is not for me. Some texts have declared it? Let them; that is nothing to me; let them all tell it. And if they do, what is it to me? Each one for himself, and somebody take the hindermost—that is all the morality in the world, at least with many. What is the reason that I should be moral? You cannot explain it except when you come to know the truth as given in the Gita: "He who sees everyone in himself, and himself in everyone, thus seeing the same God living in all, he, the sage, no more kills the Self by the self." Know through Advaita that whomsoever you hurt, you hurt yourself; they are all you. Whether you know it or not, through all hands you work, through all feet you move, you are the king enjoying in the palace, you are the beggar leading that miserable existence in the street; you are in the ignorant as well as in the learned, you are in the man who is weak, and you are in the strong; know this and be sympathetic. And that is why we must not hurt others. That is why I do not even care whether I have to starve, because there will be millions of mouths eating at the same time, and they are all mine. Therefore I should not care what becomes of me and mine, for the whole universe is mine, I am enjoying all the bliss at the same time; and who can kill me or the universe? Herein is morality. Here, in Advaita alone, is morality explained. The others teach it, but cannot give you its reason. Then, so far about explanation.

What is the gain? It is strength. Take off that veil of hypnotism which you have cast upon the world, send not out thoughts and words of weakness unto humanity. Know that all sins and all evils can be summed up in that one word, weakness. It is weakness that is the motive power in all evil doing; it is weakness that is the source of all selfishness; it is weakness that makes men injure others; it is weakness that makes them manifest what they are not in reality. Let them all know what they are; let them repeat day and night what they are. Soham. Let them suck it in with their mothers' milk, this idea of strength—I am He, I am He. This is to be heard first—श्रोतव्यो मन्तव्यो निदिध्यासितव्यः etc. And then let them think of it, and out of that thought, out of that heart will proceed works such as the world has never seen. What has to be done? Ay, this Advaita is said by some to be impracticable; that is to say, it is not yet manifesting itself on the material plane. To a certain extent that is true, for remember the saying of the Vedas:

ओमित्येकाक्षरं ब्रह्म ओमित्येकाक्षरं परम् ।
ओमित्येकाक्षरं ज्ञात्वा यो यदिच्छति तस्य तत् ॥

"Om, this is the Brahman; Om, this is the greatest reality; he who knows the secret of this Om, whatever he desires that he gets." Ay, therefore first know the secret of this Om, that you are the Om; know the secret of this Tattvamasi, and then and then alone whatever you want shall come to you. If you want to be great materially, believe that you are so. I may be a little bubble, and you may be a wave mountain-high, but know that for both of us the infinite ocean is the background, the infinite Brahman is our magazine of power and strength, and we can draw as much as we like, both of us, I the bubble and you the mountain-high wave. Believe, therefore, in yourselves. The secret of Advaita is: Believe in yourselves first, and then believe in anything else. In the history of the world, you will find that only those nations that have

believed in themselves have become great and strong. In
the history of each nation, you will always find that only
those individuals who have believed in themselves have
become great and strong. Here, to India, came an
Englishman who was only a clerk, and for want of funds
and other reasons he twice tried to blow his brains out;
and when he failed, he believed in himself, he believed
that he was born to do great things; and that man became
Lord Clive, the founder of the Empire. If he had believed
the Padres and gone crawling all his life—"O Lord, I am
weak, and I am low"—where would he have been? In
a lunatic asylum. You also are made lunatics by these
evil teachings. I have seen, all the world over, the bad
effects of these weak teachings of humility destroying the
human race. Our children are brought up in this way,
and is it a wonder that they become semi-lunatics?

This is teaching on the practical side. Believe, therefore, in yourselves, and if you want material wealth, work
it out; it will come to you. If you want to be intellectual,
work it out on the intellectual plane, and intellectual giants
you shall be. And if you want to attain to freedom, work
it out on the spiritual plane, and free you shall be and
shall enter into Nirvana, the Eternal Bliss. But one defect
which lay in the Advaita was its being worked out so
long on the spiritual plane only, and nowhere else; now
the time has come when you have to make it practical.
It shall no more be a Rahasya, a secret, it shall no more
live with monks in caves and forests, and in the
Himalayas; it must come down to the daily, everyday
life of the people; it shall be worked out in the palace
of the king, in the cave of the recluse; it shall be worked
out in the cottage of the poor, by the beggar in the street,
everywhere; anywhere it can be worked out. Therefore
do not fear whether you are a woman or a Shudra, for
this religion is so great, says Lord Krishna, that even a
little of it brings a great amount of good.

Therefore, children of the Aryans, do not sit idle; awake, arise, and stop not till the goal is reached. The time has come when this Advaita is to be worked out practically. Let us bring it down from heaven unto the earth; this is the present dispensation. Ay, the voices of our forefathers of old are telling us to bring it down from heaven to the earth. Let your teachings permeate the world, till they have entered into every pore of society, till they have become the common property of everybody, till they have become part and parcel of our lives, till they have entered into our veins and tingle with every drop of blood there.

Ay, you may be astonished to hear that as practical Vedantists the Americans are better than we are. I used to stand on the seashore at New York and look at the emigrants coming from different countries—crushed, down-trodden, hopeless, unable to look a man in the face, with a little bundle of clothes as all their possession, and these all in rags; if they saw a policeman they were afraid and tried to get to the other side of the foot-path. And, mark you, in six months those very men were walking erect, well clothed, looking everybody in the face; and what made this wonderful difference? Say, this man comes from Armenia or somewhere else where he was crushed down beyond all recognition, where everybody told him he was a born slave and born to remain in a low state all his life, and where at the least move on his part he was trodden upon. There everything told him, as it were, "Slave! you are a slave, remain so. Hopeless you were born, hopeless you must remain." Even the very air murmured round him, as it were, "There is no hope for you; hopeless and a slave you must remain", while the strong man crushed the life out of him. And when he landed in the streets of New York, he found a gentleman, well-dressed, shaking him by the hand; it made no difference that the one was in rags and the other well-clad. He went a step further and saw a restaurant, that there were gentlemen dining at a table, and he was asked to take a seat at the corner of the same table. He went about and found a new life, that there was a place where he was a man among men. Perhaps he went to Washington, shook hands with the President of the United States, and perhaps there he saw men coming from distant villages, peasants, and ill-clad, all shaking hands with the President. Then the veil of Maya slipped away from him. He is Brahman, he who has been hypnotised into slavery and weakness is once more awake, and he rises up and finds himself a man in a world of men. Ay, in this country of ours, the very birth-place of the Vedanta, our masses have been hypnotised for ages into that state. To touch them is pollution, to sit with them is pollution! Hopeless they were born, hopeless they must remain! And the result is that they have been sinking, sinking, sinking, and have come to the last stage to which a human being can come. For what country is there in the world where man has to sleep with the cattle? And for this, blame nobody else, do not commit the mistake of the ignorant. The effect is here and the cause is here too. We are to blame. Stand up, be bold, and take the blame on your own shoulders. Do not go about throwing mud at others; for all the faults you suffer from, you are the sole and only cause.

Young men of Lahore, understand this, therefore, this great sin, hereditary and national, is on our shoulders. There is no hope for us. You may make thousands of societies, twenty thousand political assemblages, fifty thousand institutions. These will be of no use until there is that sympathy, that love, that heart that thinks for all; until Buddha's heart comes once more into India, until the words of the Lord Krishna are brought to their practical use, there is no hope for us. You go on imitating the Europeans and their societies and their assemblages, but let me tell you a story, a fact that I saw with my own eyes.

A company of Burmans was taken over to London by some persons here, who turned out to be Eurasians. They exhibited these people in London, took all the money, and then took these Burmans over to the Continent, and left them there for good or evil. These poor people did not know a word of any European language, but the English Consul in Austria sent them over to London. They were helpless in London, without knowing anyone. But an English lady got to know of them, took these foreigners from Burma into her own house, gave them her own clothes, her bed, and everything, and then sent the news to the papers. And, mark you, the next day the whole nation was, as it were, roused. Money poured in, and these people were helped out and sent back to Burma. On this sort of sympathy are based all their political and other institutions; it is the rock-foundation of love, for themselves at least. They may not love the world; and the Burmans may be their enemies, but in England, it goes without saying, there is this great love for their own people, for truth and justice and charity to the stranger at the door. I should be the most ungrateful man if I did not tell you how wonderfully and how hospitably I was received in every country in the West. Where is the heart here to build upon? No sooner do we start a little joint-stock company than we try to cheat each other, and the whole thing comes down with a crash. You talk of imitating the English and building up as big a nation as they are. But where are the foundations? Ours are only sand, and, therefore, the building comes down with a crash in no time.

Therefore, young men of Lahore, raise once more that mighty banner of Advaita, for on no other ground can you have that wonderful love until you see that the same Lord is present everywhere. Unfurl that banner of love! "Arise, awake, and stop not till the goal is reached." Arise, arise once more, for nothing can be done without renunciation. If you want to help others, your little self must go. In the words of the Christians—you cannot serve God and Mammon at the same time. Have Vairagya. Your ancestors gave up the world for doing great things. At the present time there are men who give up the world to help their own salvation. Throw away everything, even your own salvation, and go and help others. Ay. you are always talking bold words, but here is practical Vedanta before you. Give up this little life of yours. What matters it if you die of starvation—you and I and thousands like us—so long as this nation lives? The nation is sinking, the curse of unnumbered millions is on our heads—those to whom we have been giving ditch-water to drink when they have been dying of thirst and while the perennial river of water was flowing past, the unnumbered millions whom we have allowed to starve in sight of plenty, the unnumbered millions to whom we have talked of Advaita and whom we have hated with all our strength, the unnumbered millions for whom we have invented the doctrine of Lokâchâra (usage), to whom we have talked theoretically that we are all the same and all are one with the same Lord, without even an ounce of practice. "Yet, my friends, it must be only in the mind and never in practice!" Wipe off this blot. "Arise and awake." What matters it if this little life goes? Everyone has to die, the saint or the sinner, the rich or the poor. The body never remains for anyone. Arise and awake and be perfectly sincere. Our insincerity in India is awful; what we want is character, that steadiness and character that make a man cling on to a thing like grim death.

"Let the sages blame or let them praise, let Lakshmi come today or let her go away, let death come just now or in a hundred years; he indeed is the sage who does not make one false step from the right path." Arise and awake, for the time is passing and all our energies will be frittered away in vain talking. Arise and awake, let minor

things, and quarrels over little details and fights over little
doctrines be thrown aside, for here is the greatest of all
works, here are the sinking millions. When the Mohammedans first came into India, what a great number of
Hindus were here; but mark, how today they have
dwindled down! Every day they will become less and less
till they wholly disappear. Let them disappear, but with
them will disappear the marvellous ideas, of which, with
all their defects and all their misrepresentations, they still
stand as representatives. And with them will disappear
this marvellous Advaita, the crest-jewel of all spiritual
thought. Therefore, arise, awake, with your hands
stretched out to protect the spirituality of the world. And
first of all, work it out for your own country. What we
want is not so much spirituality as a little of the bringing
down of the Advaita into the material world. First bread
and then religion. We stuff them too much with religion,
when the poor fellows have been starving. No dogmas
will satisfy the cravings of hunger. There are two curses
here: first our weakness, secondly, our hatred, our dried-
up hearts. You may talk doctrines by the millions, you
may have sects by the hundreds of millions; ay, but it
is nothing until you have the heart to feel. Feel for them
as your Veda teaches you, till you find they are parts of
your own bodies, till you realise that you and they, the
poor and the rich, the saint and the sinner, are all parts
of One Infinite Whole, which you call Brahman.

Gentlemen, I have tried to place before you a few
of the most brilliant points of the Advaita system, and now
the time has come when it should be carried into practice,
not only in this country but everywhere. Modern science
and its sledge-hammer blows are pulverising the porcelain
foundations of all dualistic religions everywhere. Not only
here are the dualists torturing texts till they will extend no
longer—for texts are not India-rubber—it is not only here
that they are trying to get into the nooks and corners to

protect themselves; it is still more so in Europe and America. And even there something of this idea will have to go from India. It has already got there. It will have to grow and increase and save their civilisations too. For in the West the old order of things is vanishing, giving way to a new order of things, which is the worship of gold, the worship of Mammon. Thus this old crude system of religion was better than the modern system, namely—competition and gold. No nation, however strong, can stand on such foundations, and the history of the world tells us that all that had such foundations are dead and gone. In the first place we have to stop the incoming of such a wave in India. Therefore preach the Advaita to every one, so that religion may withstand the shock of modern science. Not only so, you will have to help others; your thought will help out Europe and America. But above all, let me once more remind you that here is need of practical work, and the first part of that is that you should go to the sinking millions of India, and take them by the hand, remembering the words of the Lord Krishna:

इहैव तैर्जितः सर्गो येषां साम्ये स्थितं मनः ।
निर्दोषं हि समं ब्रह्म तस्मात् ब्रह्मणि ते स्थिताः ॥

"Even in this life they have conquered relative existence whose minds are firm-fixed on the sameness of everything, for God is pure and the same to all; therefore, such are said to be living in God."

VEDANTISM

At Khetri on 20th December 1897, Swami Vivekananda delivered a lecture on Vedantism in the hall of the Maharaja's bungalow in which he lodged with his disciples. The Swami was introduced by the Raja, who was the president of the meeting; and he spoke for more than an hour and a half. The Swami was at his best, and it was a matter of regret that no shorthand writer was present to report this interesting lecture at length. The following is a summary from notes taken down at the time:

Two nations of yore, namely the Greek and the Aryan, placed in different environments and circumstances—the former, surrounded by all that was beautiful, sweet, and tempting in nature, with an invigorating climate, and the latter, surrounded on every side by all that was sublime, and born and nurtured in a climate which did not allow of much physical exercise—developed two peculiar and different ideals of civilisation. The study of the Greeks was the outer infinite, while that of the Aryans was the inner infinite; one studied the macrocosm, and the other the microcosm. Each had its distinct part to play in the civilisation of the world. Not that one was required to borrow from the other, but if they compared notes both would be the gainers. The Aryans were by nature an analytical race. In the sciences of mathematics and grammar wonderful fruits were gained, and by the analysis of mind the full tree was developed. In Pythagoras, Socrates, Plato, and the Egyptian neo-Platonists, we can find traces of Indian thought.

The Swami then traced in detail the influence of Indian thought on Europe and showed how at different periods Spain, Germany, and other European countries were greatly influenced by it. The Indian prince, Dârâ-

Shuko, translated the Upanishads into Persian, and a Latin translation of the same was seen by Schopenhauer, whose philosophy was moulded by these. Next to him, the philosophy of Kant also shows traces of the teachings of the Upanishads. In Europe it is the interest in comparative philology that attracts scholars to the study of Sanskrit, though there are men like Deussen who take interest in philosophy for its own sake. The Swami hoped that in future much more interest would be taken in the study of Sanskrit. He then showed that the word "Hindu" in former times was full of meaning, as referring to the people living beyond the Sindhu or the Indus; it is now meaningless, representing neither the nation nor their religion, for on this side of the Indus, various races professing different religions live at the present day.

The Swami then dwelt at length on the Vedas and stated that they were not spoken by any person, but the ideas were evolving slowly and slowly until they were embodied in book form, and then that book became the authority. He said that various religions were embodied in books: the power of books seemed to be infinite. The Hindus have their Vedas, and will have to hold on to them for thousands of years more, but their ideas about them are to be changed and built anew on a solid foundation of rock. The Vedas, he said, were a huge literature. Ninety-nine per cent of them were missing; they were in the keeping of certain families, with whose extinction the books were lost. But still, those that are left now could not be contained even in a large hall like that. They were written in language archaic and simple; their grammar was very crude, so much so that it was said that some part of the Vedas had no meaning.

He then dilated on the two portions of the Vedas— the Karma Kânda and the Jnâna Kânda. The Karma Kanda, he said, were the Samhitâs and the Brâhmanas. The Brahmanas dealt with sacrifices. The Samhitas were songs composed in Chhandas known as Anushtup, Trishtup, Jagati, etc. Generally they praised deities such as Varuna or Indra; and the question arose who were these deities; and if any theories were raised about them, they were smashed up by other theories, and so on it went.

The Swami then proceeded to explain different ideas of worship. With the ancient Babylonians, the soul was only a double, having no individuality of its own and not able to break its connection with the body. This double was believed to suffer hunger and thirst, feelings and emotions like those of the old body. Another idea was that if the first body was injured the double would be injured also; when the first was annihilated, the double also perished; so the tendency grew to preserve the body, and thus mummies, tombs, and graves came into existence. The Egyptians, the Babylonians, and the Jews never got any farther than this idea of the double; they did not reach to the idea of the Âtman beyond.

Prof. Max Müller's opinion was that not the least trace of ancestral worship could be found in the Rig-Veda. There we do not meet with the horrid sight of mummies staring stark and blank at us. There the gods were friendly to man; communion between the worshipper and the worshipped was healthy. There was no moroseness, no want of simple joy, no lack of smiles or light in the eyes. The Swami said that dwelling on the Vedas he even seemed to hear the laughter of the gods. The Vedic Rishis might not have had finish in their expression, but they were men of culture and heart, and we are brutes in comparison to them. Swamiji then recited several Mantras in confirmation of what he had just said: "Carry him to the place where the Fathers live, where there is no grief or sorrow" etc. Thus the idea arose that the sooner the dead body was cremated the better. By degrees they came to know that there was a finer body that went to a place where there was all joy and no sorrow. In the Semitic type

of religion there was tribulation and fear; it was thought
that if a man saw God, he would die. But according to
the Rig-Veda, when a man saw God face to face then began
his real life.

Now the questions came to be asked: What were these
gods? Sometimes Indra came and helped man; sometimes
Indra drank too much Soma. Now and again, adjectives
such as all-powerful, all-pervading, were attributed to
him; the same was the case with Varuna. In this way it
went on, and some of these Mantras depicting the characteristics of these gods were marvellous, and the language
was exceedingly grand. The speaker here repeated the
famous *Nâsadiya Sukta* which describes the Pralaya
state and in which occurs the idea of "Darkness covering
darkness", and asked if the persons that described
these sublime ideas in such poetic thought were uncivilised
and uncultured, then what we should call ourselves. It was
not for him, Swamiji said, to criticise or pass any judgment
on those Rishis and their gods—Indra or Varuna. All this
was like a panorama, unfolding one scene after another,
and behind them all as a background stood out एकं सद्विप्रा
बहुधा वदन्ति —"That which exists is One; sages call It
variously." The whole thing was most mystical, marvellous, and exquisitely beautiful. It seemed even yet quite
unapproachable—the veil was so thin that it would rend,
as it were, at the least touch and vanish like a mirage.

Continuing, he said that one thing seemed to him
quite clear and possible that the Aryans too, like the
Greeks, went to outside nature for their solution, that
nature tempted them outside, led them step by step to the
outward world, beautiful and good. But here in India anything which was not sublime counted for nothing. It never
occurred to the Greeks to pry into the secrets after death.
But here from the beginning was asked again and again,
"What am I? What will become of me after death?"
There the Greek thought—the man died and went to

heaven. What was meant by going to heaven? It meant
going outside of everything; there was nothing inside,
everything was outside; his search was all directed outside, nay, he himself was, as it were, outside himself. And
when he went to a place which was very much like this
world minus all its sorrows, he thought he had got everything that was desirable and was satisfied; and there all
ideas of religion stopped. But this did not satisfy the Hindu
mind. In its analysis, these heavens were all included
within the material universe. "Whatever comes by combination", the Hindus said, "dies of annihilation". They
asked external nature, "Do you know what is soul?" and
nature answered, "No". "Is there any God?" Nature
answered, "I do not know". Then they turned away from
nature. They understood that external nature, however
great and grand, was limited in space and time. Then
there arose another voice; new sublime thoughts dawned
in their minds. That voice said—"Neti, Neti", "Not this,
not this". All the different gods were now reduced into
one; the suns, moons, and stars—nay, the whole universe
—were one, and upon this new ideal the spiritual basis of
religion was built.

न तत्र सूर्यो भाति न चन्द्रतारकं नेमा विद्युतो भान्ति कुतोऽयमग्निः ।
तमेव भान्तमनुभाति सर्वं तस्य भासा सर्वं मिदं विभाति ॥

—"There the sun doth not shine, neither the moon,
nor stars, nor lightning, what to speak of this fire. He
shining, everything doth shine. Through Him everything
shineth." No more is there that limited, crude, personal
idea; no more is there that little idea of God sitting in
judgment; no more is that search outside, but henceforth
it is directed inside. Thus the Upanishads became the
Bible of India. It was a vast literature, these Upanishads,
and all the schools holding different opinions in India came
to be established on the foundation of the Upanishads.

The Swami passed on to the dualistic, qualified
monistic, and Advaitic theories, and reconciled them by

saying that each one of these was like a step by which one passed before the other was reached; the final evolution to Advaitism was the natural outcome, and the last step was "Tattvamasi". He pointed out where even the great commentators Shankarâchârya, Râmânujâchârya, and Madhvâchârya had committed mistakes. Each one believed in the Upanishads as the sole authority, but thought that they preached one thing, one path only. Thus Shankaracharya committed the mistake in supposing that the whole of the Upanishads taught one thing, which was Advaitism, and nothing else; and wherever a passage bearing distinctly the Dvaita idea occurred, he twisted and tortured the meaning to make it support his own theory. So with Ramanuja and Madhvacharya when pure Advaitic texts occurred. It was perfectly true that the Upanishads had one thing to teach, but that was taught as a going up from one step to another. Swamiji regretted that in modern India the spirit of religion is gone; only the externals remain. The people are neither Hindus nor Vedantists. They are merely don't-touchists; the kitchen is their temple and Hândi Bartans (cooking pots) are their Devatâ (object of worship). This state of things must go. The sooner it is given up the better for our religion. Let the Upanishads shine in their glory, and at the same time let not quarrels exist amongst different sects.

As Swamiji was not keeping good health, he felt exhausted at this stage of his speech; so he took a little rest for half an hour, during which time the whole audience waited patiently to hear the rest of the lecture. He came out and spoke again for half an hour, and explained that knowledge was the finding of unity in diversity, and the highest point in every science was reached when it found the one unity underlying all variety. This was as true in physical science as in the spiritual.

THE INFLUENCE OF INDIAN SPIRITUAL THOUGHT IN ENGLAND

The Swami Vivekananda presided over a meeting at which the Sister Nivedita (Miss M. E. Noble) delivered a lecture on "The Influence of Indian Spiritual Thought in England" on 11th March, 1898, at the Star Theatre, Calcutta. Swami Vivekananda on rising to introduce Miss Noble spoke as follows:

LADIES AND GENTLEMEN,

When I was travelling through the Eastern parts of Asia, one thing especially struck me—that is the prevalence of Indian spiritual thought in Eastern Asiatic countries. You may imagine the surprise with which I noticed written on the walls of Chinese and Japanese temples some well-known Sanskrit Mantras, and possibly it will please you all the more to know that they were all in old Bengali characters, standing even in the present day as a monument of missionary energy and zeal displayed by our forefathers of Bengal.

Apart from these Asiatic countries, the work of India's spiritual thought is so widespread and unmistakable that even in Western countries, going deep below the surface, I found traces of the same influence still present. It has now become a historical fact that the spiritual ideas of the Indian people travelled towards both the East and the West in days gone by. Everybody knows now how much the world owes to India's spirituality, and what a potent factor in the present and the past of humanity have been the spiritual powers of India. These are things of the past. I find another most remarkable phenomenon, and that is that the most stupendous powers of civilisation, and progress towards humanity and social progress, have been effected by that wonderful race—I mean the Anglo-Saxon. I may go further and tell you that had it not been for the power of the Anglo-Saxons we should not have met here today to discuss, as we are doing, the influence of our Indian spiritual thought. And coming back to our own country, coming from the West to the East, I see the same Anglo-Saxon powers working here with all their defects, but retaining their peculiarly characteristic good features, and I believe that at last the grand result is achieved. The British idea of expansion and progress is forcing us up, and let us remember that the civilisation of the West has been drawn from the fountain of the Greeks, and that the great idea of Greek civilisation is that of *expression*. In India we *think*—but unfortunately sometimes we think so deeply that there is no power left for expression. Gradually, therefore, it came to pass that our force of expression did not manifest itself before the world, and what is the result of that? The result is this—we worked to hide everything we had. It began first with individuals as a faculty of hiding, and it ended by becoming a national habit of hiding—there is such a lack of power of expression with us that we are now considered a dead nation. Without expression, how can we live? The backbone of Western civilisation is—expansion and expression. This side of the work of the Anglo-Saxon race in India, to which I draw your attention, is calculated to rouse our nation once more to express itself, and it is inciting it to bring out its hidden treasures before the world by using the means of communication provided by the same mighty race. The Anglo-Saxons have created a future for India, and the space through which our ancestral ideas are now ranging is simply phenomenal. Ay, what great facilities had our forefathers when they delivered their message of truth and salvation? Ay, how did the great Buddha preach the noble doctrine of universal brotherhood? There were even then great facilities here, in our beloved India, for the attainment of real happiness, and we could easily send our ideas from one end of the world to the other. Now we have reached even the Anglo-Saxon race. This is the kind of interaction now going on, and we find that our message is heard, and not only heard but is being responded to. Already England has given us some of her great intellects to help us in our mission. Every one has heard and is perhaps familiar with my friend Miss Müller, who is now here on this platform. This lady, born of a very good family and well educated, has given her whole life to us out of love for India, and has made India her home and her family. Every one of you is familiar with the name of that noble and distinguished Englishwoman who has also given her whole life to work for the good of India and India's regeneration—I mean Mrs. Besant. Today, we meet on this platform two ladies from America who have the same mission in their hearts; and I can assure you that they also are willing to devote their lives to do the least good to our poor country. I take this opportunity of reminding you of the name of one of our countrymen—one who has seen England and America, one in whom I have great confidence, and whom I respect and love, and who would have been present here but for an engagement elsewhere—a man working steadily and silently for the good of our country, a man of great spirituality—I mean Mr. Mohini Mohan Chatterji. And now England has sent us another gift in Miss Margaret Noble, from whom we expect much. Without any more words of mine I introduce to you Miss Noble, who will now address you.

After Sister Nivedita had finished her interesting lecture, the Swami rose and said:

I have only a few words to say. We have an idea that we Indians can do something, and amongst the Indians we Bengalis may laugh at this idea; but I do not. My mission in life is to rouse a struggle in you. Whether you are an Advaitin, whether you are a qualified monist or dualist, it does not matter much. But let me draw your attention to one thing which unfortunately we always forget: that is—"O man, have faith in yourself." That is the way by which we can have faith in God. Whether you are an Advaitist or a dualist, whether you are a believer in the system of Yoga or a believer in Shankaráchárya, whether you are a follower of Vyása or Vishvámitra, it does not matter much. But the thing is that on this point Indian thought differs from that of all the rest of the world. Let us remember for a moment that, whereas in every other religion and in every other country, the power of the soul is entirely ignored—the soul is thought of as almost powerless, weak, and inert—we in India consider the soul to be eternal and hold that it will remain perfect through all eternity. We should always bear in mind the teachings of the Upanishads.

Remember your great mission in life. We Indians, and especially those of Bengal, have been invaded by a vast amount of foreign ideas that are eating into the very vitals of our national religion. Why are we so backward nowadays? Why are ninety-nine per cent of us made up of entirely foreign ideas and elements? This has to be thrown out if we want to rise in the scale of nations. If we want to rise, we must also remember that we have many things to learn from the West. We should learn from the West her arts and her sciences. From the West we have to learn the sciences of physical nature, while on the other hand the West has to come to us to learn and assimilate religion and spiritual knowledge. We Hindus must believe that we are the teachers of the world. We have been clamouring here for getting political rights and many other such things. Very well. Rights and privileges and other things can only come through friendship, and friendship can only be expected between two equals. When one of the parties is a beggar, what friendship can there be? It is all very well to speak so, but I say that without mutual co-operation we can never make ourselves strong men. So, I must call upon you to go out to England and America, not as beggars but as teachers of religion. The law of exchange must be applied to the best of our power. If we have to learn from them the ways and methods of making ourselves happy in this life, why, in return, should we not give them the methods and ways that would make them happy for all eternity? Above all, work for the good of humanity. Give up the so-called boast of your narrow orthodox life. Death is waiting for every one, and mark you this—the most marvellous historical fact—that all the nations of the world have to sit down patiently at the feet of India to learn the eternal truths embodied in her literature. India dies not. China dies not. Japan dies not. Therefore, we must always remember that our backbone is spirituality, and to do that we must have a guide who will show the path to us, that path about which I am talking just now. If any of you do not believe it, if there be a Hindu boy amongst us who is not ready to believe that his religion is pure spirituality, I do not call him a Hindu. I remember in one of the villages of Kashmir, while talking to an old Mohammedan lady I asked her in a mild voice, "What religion is yours?" She replied in her own language, "Praise the Lord! By the mercy of God, I am a Mussulman." And then I asked a Hindu, "What is your religion?" He plainly replied, "I am a Hindu." I remember that grand word of the Katha Upanishad—Shraddhâ or marvellous faith. An instance of Shraddha can be found in the life of Nachiketâ. To preach the doctrine of Shraddha or genuine faith is the mission of my life. Let me repeat to you that this faith is one of the potent factors of humanity and of all religions. First, have faith in yourselves. Know that though one may be a little bubble and another may be a mountain-high wave, yet behind both the bubble and the wave there is the infinite ocean. Therefore there is hope for every one. There is salvation for every one. Every one must sooner or later get rid of the bonds of Mâyâ. This is the first thing to do. Infinite hope begets infinite aspiration. If that faith comes to us, it will bring back our national life as it was in the days of Vyasa and Arjuna—the days when all our sublime doctrines of humanity were preached. Today we are far behindhand in spiritual insight and spiritual thoughts. India had plenty of spirituality, so much so that her spiritual greatness made India the greatest nation of the then existing races of the world; and if traditions and hopes are to be believed, those days will come back once more to us, and that depends upon you. You, young men of Bengal, do not look up to the rich and great men who have money. The poor did all the great and gigantic work of the world. You, poor men of Bengal, come up, you can do everything, and you must do everything. Many will follow your example, poor though you are. Be steady, and, above all, be pure and sincere to the backbone. Have faith in your destiny. You, young men of Bengal, are to work out the salvation of India. Mark that, whether you believe it or not, do not think that it will be done today or tomorrow. I believe in it as I believe in my own body and my own soul. Therefore my heart goes to you—young men of Bengal. It depends upon you who have no money; because you are poor, therefore you will work. Because you have nothing, therefore you will be sincere. Because you are sincere, you will be ready to renounce all. That is what I am just now telling you. Once more I repeat this to you. This is your mission in life, this is my mission in life. I do not care what philosophy you take up; only I am ready to prove here that throughout the whole of India, there runs a mutual and cordial string of eternal faith in the perfection of humanity, and I believe in it myself. And let that faith be spread over the whole land.

SANNYASA: ITS IDEAL AND PRACTICE

A parting Address was given to Swamiji by the junior Sannyâsins of the Math (Belur), on the eve of his leaving for the West for the second time. The following is the substance of Swamiji's reply as entered in the Math Diary on 19th June 1899:

This is not the time for a long lecture. But I shall speak to you in brief about a few things which I should like you to carry into practice. First, we have to understand the ideal, and then the methods by which we can make it practical. Those of you who are Sannyasins must try to do good to others, for Sannyasa means that. There is no time to deliver a long discourse on "Renunciation", but I shall very briefly characterise it as *the love of death*. Worldly people love life. The Sannyasin is to love death. Are we to commit suicide then? Far from it. For suicides are not lovers of death, as it is often seen that when a man trying to commit suicide fails, he never attempts it for a second time. What is the love of death then? We must die, that is certain ; let us die then for a good cause. Let all our actions—eating, drinking, and everything that we do—tend towards the sacrifice of our self. You nourish your body by eating. What good is there in doing that if you do not hold it as a sacrifice to the well-being of others? You nourish your minds by reading books. There is no good in doing that unless you hold it also as a sacrifice to the whole world. For the whole world is one; you are rated a very insignificant part of it, and therefore it is right for you that you should serve your millions of brothers rather than aggrandise this little self.

सर्वतः पाणिपादं तत् सर्वतोऽक्षिशिरोमुखम् ।
सर्वतः श्रुतिमल्लोके सर्वमावृत्य तिष्ठति ॥

"With hands and feet everywhere, with eyes, heads, and mouths everywhere, with ears everywhere in the universe, That exists pervading all." (Gita, XIII. 13)

Thus you must die a gradual death. In such a death is heaven, all good is stored therein—and in its opposite is all that is diabolical and evil.

Then as to the methods of carrying the ideals into practical life. First, we have to understand that we must not have any impossible ideal. An ideal which is too high makes a nation weak and degraded. This happened after the Buddhistic and the Jain reforms. On the other hand, too much practicality is also wrong. If you have not even a little imagination, if you have no ideal to guide you, you are simply a brute. So we must not lower our ideal, neither are we to lose sight of practicality. We must avoid the two extremes. In our country, the old idea is to sit in a cave and meditate and die. To go ahead of others in salvation is wrong. One must learn sooner or later that one cannot get salvation if one does not try to seek the salvation of his brothers. You must try to combine in your life immense idealism with immense practicality. You must be prepared to go into deep meditation now, and the next moment you must be ready to go and cultivate these fields (Swamiji said, pointing to the meadows of the Math). You must be prepared to explain the difficult intricacies of the Shâstras now, and the next moment to go and sell the produce of the fields in the market. You must be prepared for all menial services, not only here, but elsewhere also.

The next thing to remember is that the aim of this institution is to make men. You must not merely learn what the Rishis taught. Those Rishis are gone, and their opinions are also gone with them. You must be Rishis yourselves. You are also men as much as the greatest men that were ever born—even our Incarnations. What can mere book-learning do? What can meditation do even? What can the Mantras and Tantras do? You must stand on your own feet. You must have this new method —the method of man-making. The true *man* is he who is strong as strength itself and yet possesses a woman's heart. You must feel for the millions of beings around you, and yet you must be strong and inflexible and you must also possess obedience; though it may seem a little paradoxical —you must possess these apparently conflicting virtues. If your superior order you to throw yourself into a river and catch a crocodile, you must first obey and then reason with him. Even if the order be wrong, first obey and then contradict it. The bane of sects, especially in Bengal, is that if any one happens to have a different opinion, he immediately starts a new sect, he has no patience to wait. So you must have a deep regard for your Sangha. There is no place for disobedience here. Crush it out without mercy. No disobedient members here, you must turn them out. There must not be any traitors in the camp. You must be as free as the air, and as obedient as this plant and the dog.

WHAT HAVE I LEARNT ?

(Delivered at Dacca, 30th March, 1901)

At Dacca Swamiji delivered two lectures in English. The first was on "What have I learnt?" and the second one was "The Religion we are born in". The following is translated from a report in Bengali by a disciple, and it contains the substance of the first lecture:

First of all, I must express my pleasure at the opportunity afforded me of coming to Eastern Bengal to acquire an intimate knowledge of this part of the country, which I hitherto lacked in spite of my wanderings through many civilised countries of the West, as well as my gratification at the sight of majestic rivers, wide fertile plains, and picturesque villages in this, my own country of Bengal, which I had not the good fortune of seeing for myself before. I did not know that there was everywhere in my country of Bengal—on land and water—so much beauty and charm. But this much has been my gain that after seeing the various countries of the world I can now much more appreciate the beauties of my own land.

In the same way also, in search of religion, I had travelled among various sects—sects which had taken up the ideals of foreign nations as their own, and I had begged at the door of others, not knowing then that in the religion of my country, in our national religion, there was so much beauty and grandeur. It is now many years since I found Hinduism to be the most perfectly satisfying religion in the world. Hence I feel sad at heart when I see existing among my own countrymen, professing a peerless faith, such a widespread indifference to our religion—though I am very well aware of the unfavourable materialistic conditions in which they pass their lives—

owing to the diffusion of European modes of thought in this, our great motherland.

There are among us at the present day certain reformers who want to reform our religion or rather turn it topsyturvy with a view to the regeneration of the Hindu nation. There are, no doubt, some thoughtful people among them, but there are also many who follow others blindly and act most foolishly, not knowing what they are about. This class of reformers are very enthusiastic in introducing foreign ideas into our religion. They have taken hold of the word "idolatry", and aver that Hinduism is not true, because it is idolatrous. They never seek to find out what this so-called "idolatry" is, whether it is good or bad; only taking their cue from others, they are bold enough to shout down Hinduism as untrue. There is another class of men among us who are intent upon giving some slippery scientific explanations for any and every Hindu custom, rite, etc., and who are always talking of electricity, magnetism, air vibration, and all that sort of thing. Who knows but they will perhaps some day define God Himself as nothing but a mass of electric vibrations! However, Mother bless them all! She it is who is having Her work done in various ways through multifarious natures and tendencies.

In contradistinction to these, there is that ancient class who say, "I do not know, I do not care to know or understand all these your hair-splitting ratiocinations; I want God, I want the Âtman, I want to go to that Beyond, where there is no universe, where there is no pleasure or pain, where dwells the Bliss Supreme"; who say, "I believe in salvation by bathing in the holy Gangâ with faith"; who say, "whomsoever you may worship with singleness of faith and devotion as the one God of the universe, in whatsoever form as Shiva, Râma, Vishnu, etc., you will get Moksha"; to that sturdy ancient class I am proud to belong.

Then there is a sect who advise us to follow God and the world together. They are not sincere, they do not express what they feel in their hearts. What is the teaching of the Great Ones?—"Where there is Rama, there is no Kâma; where there is Kama, there Rama is not. Night and day can never exist together." The voice of the ancient sages proclaim to us, "If you desire to attain God, you will have to renounce Kâma-Kânchana (lust and possession). The Samsâra is unreal, hollow, void of substance. Unless you give it up, you can never reach God, try however you may. If you cannot do that, own that you are weak, but by no means lower the Ideal. Do not cover the corrupting corpse with leaves of gold!" So according to them, if you want to gain spirituality, to attain God, the first thing that you have to do is to give up this playing "hide-and-seek with your ideas", this dishonesty, this "theft within the chamber of thought".

What have I learnt? What have I learnt from this ancient sect? I have learnt:

दुर्लभं त्रयमेवैतत् देवानुग्रहहेतुकम् ।
मनुष्यत्वं मुमुक्षुत्वं महापुरुषसंश्रयः ॥

—"Verily, these three are rare to obtain and come only through the grace of God—human birth, desire to obtain Moksha, and the company of the great-souled ones." The first thing needed is Manushyatva, human birth, because it only is favourable to the attainment of Mukti. The next is Mumukshutva. Though our means of realisation vary according to the difference in sects and individuals—though different individuals can lay claim to their special rights and means to gain knowledge, which vary according to their different stations in life—yet it can be said in general without fear of contradiction that without this Mumukshutâ, realisation of God is impossible. What is Mumukshutva? It is the strong desire for Moksha—earnest yearning to get out of the sphere of pain

452   SWAMI VIVEKANANDA'S WORKS

and pleasure—utter disgust for the world. When that
intense burning desire to see God comes, then you should
know that you are entitled to the realisation of the
Supreme.

Then another thing is necessary, and that is the coming
in direct contact with the Mahâpurushas, and thus mould-
ing our lives in accordance with those of the great-souled
ones who have reached the Goal. Even disgust for the
world and a burning desire for God are not sufficient.
Initiation by the Guru is necessary. Why? Because it is
the bringing of yourself into connection with that great
source of power which has been handed down through
generations from one Guru to another, in uninterrupted
succession. The devotee must seek and accept the Guru
or spiritual preceptor as his counsellor, philosopher, friend,
and guide. In short, the Guru is the *sine qua non* of
progress in the path of spirituality. Whom then shall I
accept as my Guru? श्रोत्रियोऽवृजिनोऽकामहतो यो ब्रह्मवित्तमः
—"He who is versed in the Vedas, without taint, unhurt by
desire, he who is the best of the knowers of Brahman."
Shrotriya—he who is not only learned in the Shâstras, but
who knows their subtle secrets, who has realised their
true import in his life. "Reading merely the various scriptures, they have become only parrots, and not Pandits.
He indeed has become a Pandit who has gained Prema
(Divine Love) by reading even one word of the Shâstras."
Mere book-learned Pandits are of no avail. Nowadays,
everyone wants to be a Guru; even a poor beggar wants
to make a gift of a lakh of rupees! Then the Guru must
be without a touch of taint, and he must be Akâmahata
—unhurt by any desire—he should have no other motive
except that of purely doing good to others, he should be
an ocean of mercy-without-reason and not impart religious teaching with a view to gaining name or fame, or
anything pertaining to selfish interest. And he must be
the intense knower of Brahman, that is, one who has

realised Brahman even as tangibly as an Âmalaka-fruit in the palm of the hand. Such is the Guru, says the Shruti. When spiritual union is established with such a Guru, then comes realisation of God—then god-vision becomes easy of attainment.

After initiation there should be in the aspirant after Truth, Abhyâsa or earnest and repeated attempt at practical application of the Truth by prescribed means of constant meditation upon the Chosen Ideal. Even if you have a burning thirst for God, or have gained the Guru, unless you have along with it the Abhyasa, unless you practise what you have been taught, you cannot get realisation. When all these are firmly established in you, then you will reach the Goal.

Therefore, I say unto you, as Hindus, as descendants of the glorious Âryans, do not forget the great ideal of our religion, that great ideal of the Hindus, which is, to go beyond this Samsara—not only to renounce the world, but to give up heaven too; ay, not only to give up evil, but to give up good too; and thus to go beyond all, beyond this phenomenal existence, and ultimately realise the Sat-Chit-Ânanda Brahman—the Absolute Existence-Knowledge-Bliss, which is Brahman.

THE RELIGION WE ARE BORN IN

At an open-air meeting convened at Dacca, on the 31st March, 1901, the Swamiji spoke in English for two hours on the above subject before a vast audience. The following is a translation of the lecture from a Bengali report of a disciple:

In the remote past, our country made gigantic advances in spiritual ideas. Let us, today, bring before our mind's eye that ancient history. But the one great danger in meditating over long-past greatness is that we cease to exert ourselves for new things, and content ourselves with vegetating upon that by-gone ancestral glory and priding ourselves upon it. We should guard against that. In ancient times there were, no doubt, many Rishis and Maharshis who came face to face with Truth. But if this recalling of our ancient greatness is to be of real benefit, we too must become Rishis like them. Ay, not only that, but it is my firm conviction that we shall be even greater Rishis than any that our history presents to us. In the past, signal were our attainments—I glory in them, and I feel proud in thinking of them. I am not even in despair at seeing the present degradation, and I am full of hope in picturing to my mind what is to come in the future. Why? Because I know the seed undergoes a complete transformation, ay, the seed as seed is seemingly destroyed before it develops into a tree. In the same way, in the midst of our present degradation lies, only dormant for a time, the potentiality of the future greatness of our religion, ready to spring up again, perhaps more mighty and glorious than ever before.

Now let us consider what are the common grounds of agreement in the religion we are born in. At first sight we undeniably find various differences among our sects. Some

are Advaitists, some are Vishishtâdvaitists, and others are
Dvaitists.   Some believe in Incarnations of God, some in
image-worship, while others are upholders of the doctrine
of the Formless.   Then as to customs also, various differences are known to exist.   The Jâts are not outcasted
even if they marry among the Mohammedans and
Christians.   They can enter into any Hindu temple without hindrance.   In many villages in the Punjab, one who
does not eat swine will hardly be considered a Hindu.   In
Nepal, a Brâhmin can marry in the four Varnas; while in
Bengal, a Brahmin cannot marry even among the subdivisions of his own caste.   So on and so forth.   But in the
midst of all these differences we note one point of unity
among all Hindus, and it is this, that no Hindu eats
beef.   In the same way, there is a great common
ground of unity underlying the various forms and sects
of our religion.

First, in discussing the scriptures, one fact stands out
prominently—that only those religions which had one or
many scriptures of their own as their basis advanced by
leaps and bounds and survive to the present day notwithstanding all the persecution and repression hurled against
them.   The Greek religion, with all its beauty, died out in
the absence of any scripture to support it; but the religion
of the Jews stands undiminished in its power, being based
upon the authority of the Old Testament.   The same is the
case with the Hindu religion, with its scripture, the Vedas,
the oldest in the world.   The Vedas are divided into the
Karma Kânda and the Jnâna Kânda.   Whether for good or
for evil, the Karma Kanda has fallen into disuse in
India, though there are some Brahmins in the Deccan who
still perform Yajnas now and then with the sacrifice of
goats; and also we find here and there, traces of the Vedic
Kriyâ Kânda in the Mantras used in connection with our
marriage and Shrâddha ceremonies etc.   But there is no
chance of its being rehabilitated on its original footing.

III—30

Kumârila Bhatta once tried to do so, but he was not successful in his attempt.

The Jnana Kanda of the Vedas comprises the Upanishads and is known by the name of Vedanta, the pinnacle of the Shrutis, as it is called. Wherever you find the Âchâryas quoting a passage from the Shrutis, it is invariably from the Upanishads. The Vedanta is now the religion of the Hindus. If any sect in India wants to have its ideas established with a firm hold on the people it must base them on the authority of the Vedanta. They all have to do it, whether they are Dvaitists or Advaitists. Even the Vaishnavas have to go to Gopâlatâpini Upanishad to prove the truth of their own theories. If a new sect does not find anything in the Shrutis in confirmation of its ideas, it will go even to the length of manufacturing a new Upanishad, and making it pass current as one of the old original productions. There have been many such in the past.

Now as to the Vedas, the Hindus believe that they are not mere books composed by men in some remote age. They hold them to be an accumulated mass of endless divine wisdom, which is sometimes manifested and at other times remains unmanifested. Commentator Sâyanâchârya says somewhere in his works यो वेदेभ्योऽखिलं जगत् निर्ममे —"Who created the whole universe out of the knowledge of the Vedas". No one has ever seen the composer of the Vedas, and it is impossible to imagine one. The Rishis were only the discoverers of the Mantras or Eternal Laws; they merely came face to face with the Vedas, the infinite mine of knowledge, which has been there from time without beginning.

Who are these Rishis? Vâtsyâyana says, "He who has attained through proper means the direct realisation of Dharma, he alone can be a Rishi even if he is a Mlechchha by birth." Thus it is that in ancient times, Vasishtha, born of an illegitimate union, Vyâsa, the son of a fisherwoman, Nârada, the son of a maidservant with uncertain parentage, and many others of like nature attained to Rishihood. Truly speaking, it comes to this then, that no distinction should be made with one who has realised the Truth. If the persons just named all became Rishis, then, O ye Kulin Brahmins of the present day, how much greater Rishis you can become! Strive after that Rishihood, stop not till you have attained the goal, and the whole world will of itself bow at your feet! Be a Rishi—that is the secret of power.

This Veda is our only authority, and everyone has the right to it.

यथेमां वाचं कल्याणीमावदानि जनेभ्यः ।
ब्रह्मराजन्याभ्यां शूद्राय चार्याय च स्वाय चारणाय ॥

—Thus says the Shukla Yajur Veda (XXVI. 2). Can you show any authority from this Veda of ours that everyone has not the right to it? The Purânas, no doubt, say that a certain caste has the right to such and such a recension of the Vedas, or a certain caste has no right to study them, or that this portion of the Vedas is for the Satya Yuga and that portion is for the Kali Yuga. But, mark you, the Veda does not say so; it is only your Puranas that do so   But can the servant dictate to the master? The Smritis, Puranas, Tantras—all these are acceptable only so far as they agree with the Vedas; and wherever they are contradictory, they are to be rejected as unreliable. But nowadays we have put the Puranas on even a higher pedestal than the Vedas! The study of the Vedas has almost disappeared from Bengal. How I wish that day will soon come when in every home the Veda will be worshipped together with Shâlagrâma, the household Deity, when the young, the old, and the women will inaugurate the worship of the Veda!

I have no faith in the theories advanced by Western savants with regard to the Vedas. They are today fixing the antiquity of the Vedas at a certain period, and again tomorrow upsetting it–and bringing it one thousand years

forward, and so on. However, about the Puranas, I have
told you that they are authoritative only in so far as they
agree with the Vedas, otherwise not. In the Puranas we
find many things which do not agree with the Vedas. As
for instance, it is written in the Puranas that some one
lived ten thousand years, another twenty thousand years,
but in the Vedas we find: शतायुर्वै पुरुषः —"Man lives indeed a hundred years." Which are we to accept in this case?
Certainly the Vedas. Notwithstanding statements like
these, I do not depreciate the Puranas. They contain
many beautiful and illuminating teachings and words of
wisdom on Yoga, Bhakti, Jnâna, and Karma; those, of
course, we should accept. Then there are the Tantras.
The real meaning of the word Tantra is Shâstra, as for
example, Kâpila Tantra. But the word Tantra is generally
used in a limited sense. Under the sway of kings who
took up Buddhism and preached broadcast the doctrine
of Ahimsâ, the performances of the Vedic Yâga-Yajnas became a thing of the past, and no one could kill any animal
in sacrifice for fear of the king. But subsequently
amongst the Buddhists themselves—who were converts
from Hinduism—the best parts of these Yaga-Yajnas were
taken up, and practised in secret. From these sprang up
the Tantras. Barring some of the abominable things in
the Tantras, such as the Vâmâchâra etc., the Tantras are
not so bad as people are inclined to think. There are
many high and sublime Vedantic thoughts in them. In
fact, the Brâhmana portions of the Vedas were modified
a little and incorporated into the body of the Tantras.
All the forms of our worship and the ceremonials of the
present day, comprising the Karma Kanda, are observed
in accordance with the Tantras.

Now let us discuss the principles of our religion a little.
Notwithstanding the differences and controversies existing
among our various sects, there are in them, too, several
grounds of unity. First, almost all of them admit the

existence of three things—three entities—Ishvara, Atman, and the Jagat. Ishvara is He who is eternally creating, preserving and destroying the whole universe. Excepting the Sânkhyas, all the others believe in this. Then the doctrine of the Atman and the reincarnation of the soul; it maintains that innumerable individual souls, having taken body after body again and again, go round and round in the wheel of birth and death according to their respective Karmas; this is Samsâravâda, or as it is commonly called the doctrine of rebirth. Then there is the Jagat or universe without beginning and without end. Though some hold these three as different phases of one only, and some others as three distinctly different entities, and others again in various other ways, yet they are all unanimous in believing in these three.

Here I should ask you to remember that Hindus, from time immemorial, knew the Atman as separate from Manas, mind. But the Occidentals could never soar beyond the mind. The West knows the universe to be full of happiness, and as such, it is to them a place where they can enjoy the most; but the East is born with the conviction that this Samsara, this ever-changing existence, is full of misery, and as such, it is nothing, nothing but unreal, not worth bartering the soul for its ephemeral joys and possessions. For this very reason, the West is ever especially adroit in organised action, and so also the East is ever bold in search of the mysteries of the internal world.

Let us, however, turn now to one or two other aspects of Hinduism. There is the doctrine of the Incarnations of God. In the Vedas we find mention of Matsya Avatâra, the Fish Incarnation only. Whether all believe in this doctrine or not is not the point; the real meaning, however, of this Avatâravâda is the worship of Man—to see God in man is the real God-vision. The Hindu does not go through nature to nature's God—he goes to the God of man through Man.

Then there is image-worship. Except the five Devatâs who are to be worshipped in every auspicious Karma as enjoined in our Shâstras, all the other Devatas are merely the names of certain states held by them. But again, these five Devatas are nothing but the different names of the one God only. This external worship of images has, however, been described in all our Shastras as the lowest of all the low forms of worship. But that does not mean that it is a wrong thing to do. Despite the many iniquities that have found entrance into the practices of image-worship as it is in vogue now, I do not condemn it. Ay, where would I have been if I had not been blessed with the dust of the holy feet of that orthodox, image-worshipping Brahmin!

Those reformers who preach against image-worship, or what they denounce as idolatry—to them I say, "Brothers, if you are fit to worship God-without-form discarding all external help, do so, but why do you condemn others who cannot do the same? A beautiful, large edifice, the glorious relic of a hoary antiquity has, out of neglect or disuse, fallen into a dilapidated condition; accumulations of dirt and dust may be lying everywhere within it, maybe, some portions are tumbling down to the ground. What will you do to it? Will you take in hand the necessary cleansing and repairs and thus restore the old, or will you pull the whole edifice down to the ground and seek to build another in its place, after a sordid modern plan whose permanence has yet to be established? We have to reform it, which truly means to make ready or perfect by necessary cleansing and repairs, not by demolishing the whole thing. There the function of reform ends. When the work of renovating the old is finished, what further necessity does it serve? Do that if you can, if not, hands off!" The band of reformers in our country want, on the contrary, to build up a separate sect of their own. They have, however, done good work; may the blessings of God be showered on their heads! But why should you, Hindus, want to separate yourselves from the great common fold? Why should you feel ashamed to take the name of Hindu, which is your greatest and most glorious possession? This national ship of ours, ye children of the Immortals, my countrymen, has been plying for ages, carrying civilisation and enriching the whole world with its inestimable treasures. For scores of shining centuries this national ship of ours has been ferrying across the ocean of life, and has taken millions of souls to the other shore, beyond all misery. But today it may have sprung a leak and got damaged, through your own fault or whatever cause it matters not. What would you, who have placed yourselves in it, do now? Would you go about cursing it and quarrelling among yourselves! Would you not all unite together and put your best efforts to stop the holes? Let us all gladly give our hearts' blood to do this; and if we fail in the attempt, let us all sink and die together, with blessings and not curses on our lips.

And to the Brahmins I say, "Vain is your pride of birth and ancestry. Shake it off. Brahminhood, according to your Shastras, you have no more now, because you have for so long lived under Mlechchha kings. If you at all believe in the words of your own ancestors, then go this very moment and make expiation by entering into the slow fire kindled by Tusha (husks), like that old Kumarila Bhatta, who with the purpose of ousting the Buddhists first became a disciple of the Buddhists and then defeating them in argument became the cause of death to many, and subsequently entered the Tushânala to expiate his sins. If you are not bold enough to do that, then admit your weakness and stretch forth a helping hand, and open the gates of knowledge to one and all, and give the downtrodden masses once more their just and legitimate rights and privileges."

REPORTS IN AMERICAN NEWSPAPERS

INDIA: HER RELIGION AND CUSTOMS

(*Salem Evening News*, August 29, 1893)

In spite of the warm weather of yesterday afternoon, a goodly number of members of the Thought and Work club, with guests, gathered in Wesley chapel to meet Swami Vive Kanonda,[1] a Hindoo monk, now travelling in this country, and to listen to an informal address from that gentleman, principally upon the religion of the Hindoos as taught by their Vedar[2] or sacred books. He also spoke of caste, as simply a social division and in no way dependent upon their religion.

The poverty of the majority of the masses was strongly dwelt upon. India with an area much smaller than the United States, contains twenty three hundred millions [sic] of people, and of these, three hundred millions [sic] earn wages, averaging less than fifty cents per month. In some instances the people in whole districts of the country subsist for months and even years, wholly upon flowers,[3] produced by a certain tree which when boiled are edible.

In other districts the men eat rice only, the women and children must satisfy their hunger with the water in which the rice is cooked. A failure of the rice crop means famine. Half the people live upon one meal a day, the other half know not whence the next meal will come. According to Swami Vive Kyonda, the need of the people of India is not more religion, or a better one, but as he expresses it, "practicality", and it is with the hope of interesting the American people in this great need of the suffering, starving millions that he has come to this country

---

[1] In those days Swami Vivekananda's name was spelt in various ways by the U.S.A. newspapers, and the reports were inaccurate mostly owing to the novelty of the subjects.

[2] Vedas.   [3] Mohua.

He spoke at some length of the condition of his people and their religion. In course of his speech he was frequently and closely questioned by Dr. F. A. Gardner and Rev. S. F. Nobbs of the Central Baptist Church. He said the missionaries had fine theories there and started in with good ideas, but had done nothing for the industrial condition of the people. He said Americans, instead of sending out missionaries to train them in religion, would better send some one out to give them industrial education.

Asked whether it was not a fact that Christians assisted the people of India in times of distress, and whether they did not assist in a practical way by training schools, the speaker replied that they did it sometimes, but really it was not to their credit for the law did not allow them to attempt to influence people at such times.

He explained the bad condition of woman in India on the ground that Hindoo men had such respect for woman that it was thought best not to allow her out. The Hindoo women were held in such high esteem that they were kept in seclusion. He explained the old custom of women being burned on the death of their husbands, on the ground that they loved them so that they could not live without the husband. They were one in marriage and must be one in death.

He was asked about the worship of idols and the throwing themselves in front of the juggernaut car, and said one must not blame the Hindoo people for the car business, for it was the act of fanatics and mostly of lepers.

The speaker explained his mission in his country to be to organize monks for industrial purposes, that they might give the people the benefit of this industrial education and thus elevate them and improve their condition.

This afternoon Vive Kanonda will speak on the children of India to any children or young people who may be pleased to listen to him at 166 North street, Mrs. Woods kindly offering her garden for that purpose. In person he is a fine looking man, dark but comely, dressed in a long robe of a yellowish red colour confined at the waist with a cord, and wearing on his head a yellow turban. Being a monk he has no caste, and may eat and drink with anyone.

*   *   *

(*Daily Gazette*, August 29, 1893)

Rajah[1] Swami Vivi Rananda of India was the guest of the Thought and Work Club of Salem yesterday afternoon in the Wesley church.

A large number of ladies and gentlemen were present and shook hands, American fashion, with the distinguished monk. He wore an orange colored gown, with red sash, yellow turban, with the end hanging down on one side, which he used for a handkerchief, and congress shoes.

He spoke at some length of the condition of his people and their religion. In course of his speech he was frequently and closely questioned by Dr. F. A. Gardner and Rev. S. F. Nobbs of the Central Baptist church. He said the missionaries had fine theories there and started in with good ideas, but had done nothing for the industrial condition of the people. He said Americans, instead of sending out missionaries to train them in religion, would better send someone out to give them industrial education.

Speaking at some length of the relations of men and women, he said the husbands of India never lied and never persecuted, and named several other sins they never committed.

Asked whether it was not a fact that Christians assisted the people of India in times of distress, and whether they did not assist in a practical way by training

---

[1] American reporters added all sorts of epithets like "Rajah", "Brahmin", "priest", etc., for which they alone were responsible.

schools, the speaker replied that they did it sometimes, but really it was not to their credit, for the law did not allow them to attempt to influence people at such times.

He explained the bad condition of women in India on the ground that Hindoo men had such respect for woman that it was thought best not to allow her out. The Hindoo women were held in such high esteem that they were kept in seclusion. He explained the old custom of women being burned on the death of their husbands, on the ground that they loved them so that they could not live without the husband. They were one in marriage and must be one in death.

He was asked about the worship of idols and the throwing themselves in front of the juggernaut car, and said one must not blame the Hindoo people for the car business, for it was the act of fanatics and mostly of lepers.

As for the worship of idols he said he had asked Christians what they thought of when they prayed, and some said they thought of the church, others of G-O-D. Now his people thought of the images. For the poor people idols were necessary. He said that in ancient times, when their religion first began, women were distinguished for spiritual genius and great strength of mind. In spite of this, as he seemed to acknowledge, the women of the present day had degenerated. They thought of nothing but eating and drinking, gossip and scandal.

The speaker explained his mission in his country to be to organize monks for industrial purposes, that they might give the people the benefit of this industrial education and thus to elevate them and improve their condition.

*   *   *

(*Salem Evening News,* September 1, 1893)

The learned Monk from India who is spending a few days in this city, will speak in the East Church Sunday evening at 7-30. Swami (Rev.) Viva Kananda preached in the Episcopal church at Annisquam last Sunday evening, by invitation of the pastor and Professor Wright of Harvard, who has shown him great kindness.

On Monday night he leaves for Saratoga, where he will address the Social Science association. Later on he will speak before the Congress in Chicago. Like all men who are educated in the higher Universities of India, Viva Kananda speaks English easily and correctly. His simple talk to the children on Tuesday last concerning the games, schools, customs and manners of children in India was valuable and most interesting. His kind heart was touched by the statement of a little miss that her teacher had "licked her so hard that she almost broke her finger". . . . As Viva Kananda, like all monks, must travel over his land preaching the religion of truth, chastity and the brother-hood of man, no great good could pass unnoticed, or terrible wrong escape his eyes. He is extremely generous to all persons of other faiths, and has only kind words for those who differ from him.

*   *   *

(*Daily Gazette*, September 5, 1893)

Rajah Swami Vivi Rananda of India spoke at the East church Sunday evening, on the religion of India and the poor of his native land. A good audience assembled, but it was not so large as the importance of the subject or the interesting speaker deserved. The monk was dressed in his native costume, and spoke about forty minutes. The great need of India today, which is not the India of fifty years ago, is, he said, missionaries to educate the people industrially and socially and not religiously. The Hindoos have all the religion they want, and the Hindoo religion is the most ancient in the world. The monk is a very pleasant speaker and held the close attention of his audience.

* * *

(*Daily Saratogian*, September 6, 1893)

. . . The platform was next occupied by Vive Kananda, a Monk of Madras, Hindoostan, who preached throughout India. He is interested in social science and is an intelligent and interesting speaker. He spoke on Mohammedan rule in India.

The program for today embraces some very interesting topics, especially the paper on "Bimetallism", by Col. Jacob Greene of Hartford. Vive Kananda will again speak, this time on the Use of Silver in India.

HINDUS AT THE FAIR

(*Boston Evening Transcript*, September 30, 1893)

Chicago, Sept. 23:

There is a room at the left of the entrance to the Art Palace marked "No. 1—keep out." To this the speakers at the Congress of Religions all repair sooner or later, either to talk with one another or with President Bonney, whose private office is in one corner of the apartment. The folding doors are jealously guarded from the general public, usually standing far enough apart to allow peeping in. Only delegates are supposed to penetrate the sacred precincts, but it is not impossible to obtain an "open sesame", and thus to enjoy a brief opportunity of closer relations with the distinguished guests than the platform in the Hall of Columbus affords.

The most striking figure one meets in this anteroom
is Swami Vivekananda, the Brahmin monk. He is a large,
well-built man, with the superb carriage of the Hindu-
stanis, his face clean shaven, squarely moulded regular
features, white teeth, and with well-chiselled lips that are
usually parted in a benevolent smile while he is conversing.
His finely poised head is crowned with either a lemon
colored or a red turban, and his cassock (not the technical
name for this garment), belted in at the waist and falling
below the knees, alternates in a bright orange and rich
crimson. He speaks excellent English and replied readily
to any questions asked in sincerity.

Along with his simplicity of manner there is a touch
of personal reserve when speaking to ladies, which sug-
gests his chosen vocation. When questioned about the
laws of his order, he has said, "I can do as I please,
I am independent. Sometimes I live in the Himalaya
Mountains, and sometimes in the streets of cities. I
never know where I will get my next meal, I never keep
money with me. I come here by subscription." Then
looking round at one or two of his fellow-countrymen
who chanced to be standing near he added, "They will
take care of me," giving the inference that his board
bill in Chicago is attended to by others. When asked
if he was wearing his usual monk's costume, he said,
"This is a good dress; when I am home I am in rags,
and I go barefooted. Do I believe in caste? Caste is
a social custom; religion has nothing to do with it; all
castes will associate with me."

It is quite apparent, however, from the deportment,
the general appearance of Mr. Vivekananda that he was
born among high castes—years of voluntary poverty and
homeless wanderings have not robbed him of his birthright of gentleman; even his family name is unknown;
he took that of Vivekananda in embracing a religious
career, and "Swami" is merely the title of reverend

accorded to him. He cannot be far along in the thirties, and looks as if made for this life and its fruition, as well as for meditation on the life beyond. One cannot help wondering what could have been the turning point with him.

"Why should I marry," was his abrupt response to a comment on all he had renounced in becoming a monk, "when I see in every woman only the divine Mother? Why do I make all these sacrifices? To emancipate myself from earthly ties and attachments so that there will be no re-birth for me. When I die I want to become at once absorbed in the divine, one with God. I would be a Buddha."

Vivekananda does not mean by this that he is a Buddhist. No name or sect can lebel him. He is an outcome of the higher Brahminism, a product of the Hindu spirit, which is vast, dreamy, self-extinguishing, a Sanyasi or holy man.

He has some pamphlets that he distributes, relating to his master, Paramhansa Ramakrishna, a Hindu devotee, who so impressed his hearers and pupils that many of them became ascetics after his death. Mozoomdar also looked upon this saint as his master, but Mozoomdar works for holiness in the world, in it but not of it, as Jesus taught.

Vivekananda's address before the parliament was broad as the heavens above us, embracing the best in all religions, as the ultimate universal religion—charity to all mankind, good works for the love of God, not for fear of punishment or hope of reward. He is a great favorite at the parliament, from the grandeur of his sentiments and his appearance as well. If he merely crosses the platform he is applauded, and this marked approval of thousands he accepts in a childlike spirit of gratification, without a trace of conceit. It must be a strange experience too for this humble young Brahmin monk, this sudden transition from poverty and self-effacement to affluence and aggrandizement. When asked if he knew anything of those brothers in the Himalayas so firmly believed in by the Theosophists, he answered with the simple statement, "I have never met one of them," as much as to imply, "There may be such persons, but though I am at home in the Himalayas, I have yet to come across them."

AT THE PARLIAMENT OF RELIGIONS

(The Dubuque, Iowa, *Times,* September 29, 1893)

WORLD'S FAIR, Sept. 28.—(Special.)—The Parliament of religions reached a point where sharp acerbities develop. The thin veil of courtesy was maintained, of course, but behind it was ill feeling. Rev. Joseph Cook criticised the Hindoos sharply and was more sharply criticised in turn. He said that to speak of a universe that was not created is almost unpardonable nonsense, and the Asiatics retorted that a universe which had a beginning is a self-evident absurdity. Bishop J. P. Newman, firing at long range from the banks of the Ohio, declared that the orientals have insulted all the Christians of the United States by their misrepresentations of the missionaries, and the orientals, with their provokingly calm and supercilious smile, replied that this was simply the bishop's ignorance.

BUDDHIST PHILOSOPHY

In response to the question direct, three learned Buddhists gave us in remarkably plain and beautiful language their bed-rock belief about God, man and matter.

[Following this is a summary of Dharmapala's paper on "The World's Debt to Buddha", which he prefaced, as we learn from another source, by singing a Singhalese song of benediction. The article then continues:]

His [Dharmapala's] peroration was as pretty a thing as a Chicago audience ever heard. Demosthenes never exceeded it.

CANTANKEROUS REMARKS

Swami Vivekananda, the Hindoo monk, was not so fortunate. He was out of humor, or soon became so, apparently. He wore an orange robe and a pale yellow turban and dashed at once into a savage attack on Christian nations in these words: "We who have come from the east have sat here day after day and have been told in a patronizing way that we ought to accept Christianity because Christian nations are the most prosperous. We look about us and we see England the most prosperous Christian nation in the world, with her foot on the neck of 250,000,000 Asiatics. We look back into history and see that the prosperity of Christian Europe began with Spain. Spain's prosperity began with the invasion of Mexico. Christianity wins its prosperity by cutting the throats of its fellow men. At such a price the Hindoo will not have prosperity."

And so they went on, each succeeding speaker getting more cantankerous, as it were.

* * *

(*Outlook*, October 7, 1893)

. . . The subject of Christian work in India calls Vivekananda, in his brilliant priestly orange, to his feet. He criticises the work of Christian missions. It is evident that he has not tried to understand Christianity, but neither, as he claims, have its priests made any effort to understand *his* religion, with its ingrained faiths and race-prejudices of thousands of years' standing. They have simply come, in his view, to throw scorn on his most sacred beliefs, and to undermine the morals and spirituality of the people he has been set to teach.

*   *   *

(*Critic*, October 7, 1893)

But the most impressive figures of the Parliament were the Buddhist priest, H. Dharmapala of Ceylon, and the Hindoo monk, Suami Vivekananda. "If theology and dogma stand in your way in search of truth," said the former incisively, "put them aside. Learn to think without prejudice, to love all beings for love's sake, to express your convictions fearlessly, to lead a life of purity, and the sunlight of truth will illuminate you." But eloquent as were many of the brief speeches at this meeting, whose triumphant enthusiasm rightly culminated in the superb rendering by the Apollo Club of the Hallelujah chorus, no one expressed so well the spirit of the Parliament, its limitations and its finest influence, as did the Hindoo monk. I copy his address in full, but I can only suggest its effect upon the audience, for he is an orator by divine right, and his strong intelligent face in its picturesque setting of yellow and orange was hardly less interesting than these earnest words and the rich, rhythmical utterance he gave them. . . . [After quoting the greater part of Swamiji's Final Address, the article continues:]

Perhaps the most tangible result of the congress was the feeling it aroused in regard to foreign missions. The impertinence of sending half-educated theological students to instruct the wise and erudite Orientals was never brought home to an English-speaking audience more forcibly. It is only in the spirit of tolerance and sympathy that we are at liberty to touch their faith, and the exhorters who possess these qualities are rare. It is necessary to realize that we have quite as much to learn from the Buddhists as they from us, and that only through harmony can the highest influence be exerted.

Chicago, 3 Oct., 1893.   LUCY MONROE.

*   *   *

[To a request of the *New York World* of October 1, 1893, for "a sentiment or expression regarding the significance of the great meeting" from each representative, Swamiji replied with a quotation from the Gita and one from Vyâsa:]

"I am He that am in every religion—like the thread that passes through a string of pearls." "Holy, perfect and pure men are seen in all creeds, therefore they all lead to the same truth—for how can nectar be the outcome of poison?"

PERSONAL TRAITS

(*Critic*, October 7, 1893)

. . . It was an outgrowth of the Parliament of Religions, which opened our eyes to the fact that the philosophy of the ancient creeds contains much beauty for the moderns. When we had once clearly perceived this, our interest in their exponents quickened, and with characteristic eagerness we set out in pursuit of knowledge. The most available means of obtaining it, after the close of the Parliament, was through the addresses and lectures of Swami Vivekananda, who is still in this city [Chicago]. His original purpose in coming to this country was to interest Americans in the starting of new industries among the Hindoos, but he has abandoned this for the present, because he finds that, as "the Americans are the most charitable people in the world," every man with a purpose comes here for assistance in carrying it out. When asked about the relative condition of the poor here and in India, he replied that our poor would be princes there, and that he had been taken through the worst quarter of the city only to find it, from the standpoint of his knowledge, comfortable and even pleasant.

A Brahmin of the Brahmins, Vivekananda gave up his rank to join the brotherhood of monks, where all pride of caste is voluntarily relinquished. And yet he bears the mark of race upon his person. His culture, his eloquence, and his fascinating personality have given us a new idea of Hindoo civilization. He is an interesting figure, his fine, intelligent, mobile face in its setting of yellows, and his deep, musical voice prepossessing one at once in his favor. So it is not strange that he has been taken up by the literary clubs, has preached and lectured in churches, until the life of Buddha and the doctrines of his faith have grown familiar to us. He speaks without notes, presenting his facts and his conclusions with the greatest art, the most convincing sincerity; and rising at times to a rich, inspiring eloquence. As learned and cultivated, apparently, as the most accomplished Jesuit, he has also something Jesuitical in the character of his mind; but though the little sarcasms thrown into his discourses are as keen as a rapier, they are so delicate as to be lost on many of his hearers. Nevertheless his courtesy is unfailing, for these thrusts are never pointed so directly at our customs as to be rude. At present he contents himself with enlightening

us in regard to his religion and the words of its philosophers. He looks forward to the time when we shall
pass beyond idolatry—now necessary in his opinion to
the ignorant classes—beyond worship, even, to a knowledge of the presence of God in nature, of the divinity
and responsibility of man. "Work out your own salvation," he says with the dying Buddha; "I cannot help
you. No man can help you. Help yourself."

                                        LUCY MONROE.

REINCARNATION

(*Evanston Index*, October 7, 1893)

At the Congregational Church, during the past week,
there have been given a course of lectures which in nature
much resembled the Religious Parliament which has just
been completed. The lecturers were Dr. Carl von Bergen
of Sweden, and Suami Vivekananda, the Hindu monk. . . .
Suami Vivekananda is a representative from India to the
Parliament of Religions. He has attracted a great deal
of attention on account of his unique attire in Mandarin
colors, by his magnetic presence and by his brilliant
oratory and wonderful exposition of Hindu philosophy.
His stay in Chicago has been a continual ovation. The
course of lectures was arranged to cover three evenings.
[The lectures of Saturday and Tuesday evenings are
listed without comment; then the article continues:]
On Thursday evening Oct. 5, Dr. von Bergen spoke
on "Huldine Beamish, the Founder of the King's
Daughters of Sweden," and "Reincarnation" was the
subject treated by the Hindu monk. The latter was very
interesting; the views being those that are not often

heard in this part of the world. The doctrine of reincarnation of the soul, while comparatively new and little understood in this country, is well-known in the east, being the foundation of nearly all the religions of those people. Those that do not use it as dogma, do not say anything against it. The main point to be decided in regard to the doctrine is, as to whether we have had a past. We know that we have a present and feel sure of a future. Yet how can there be a present without a past? Modern science has proved that matter exists and continues to exist. Creation is merely a change in appearance. We are not sprung out of nothing. Some regard God as the common cause of everything and judge this a sufficient reason for existence. But in everything we must consider the phenomena; whence and from what matter springs. The same arguments that prove there is a future prove that there is a past. It is necessary that there should be causes other than God's will. Heredity is not able to give sufficient cause. Some say that we are not conscious of a former existence. Many cases have been found where there are distinct reminiscences of a past. And here lies the germ of the theory. Because the Hindu is kind to dumb animals many believe that we believe in the reincarnation of souls in lower orders. They are not able to conceive of kindness to dumb animals being other than the result of superstition. An ancient Hindu priest defines religion as anything that lifts one up. Brutality is driven out, humanity gives way to divinity. The theory of incarnation does not confine man to this small earth. His soul can go to other, higher earths where he will be a loftier being, possessing, instead of five senses, eight, and continuing in this way he will at length approach the acme of perfection, divinity, and will be allowed to drink deep of oblivion in the "Islands of the Blest".

HINDU CIVILISATION

[Although the lecture at Streator on October 9 was well attended, the *Streator Daily Free Press* of October 9 ran the following somewhat dreary review:]

The lecture of this celebrated Hindoo at the Opera House, Saturday night, was very interesting. By comparative philology, he sought to establish the long admitted relationship between the Aryan races and their descendants in the new world. He mildly defended the caste system of India which keeps three-fourths of the people in utter and humiliating subjection, and boasted that the India of today was the same India that had watched for centuries the meteoric nations of the world flash across the horizon and sink into oblivion. In common with the people, he loves the past. He lives not for self, but for God. In his country a premium is placed on beggary and tramps, though not so distinguished in his lecture. When the meal is prepared, they wait for some man to come along who is first served, then the animals, the servants, the man of the house and lastly the woman of the household. Boys are taken at 10 years of age and are kept by professors for a period of ten to twenty years, educated and sent forth to resume their former occupations or to engage in a life of endless wandering, preaching, and praying, taking along only that which is given them to eat and wear, but never touching money. Vivekananda is of the latter class. Men approaching old age withdraw from the world, and after a period of study and prayer, when they feel themselves sanctified, they also go forward spreading the gospel. He observed that leisure was necessary for intellectual development and scored Americans for not educating the Indians whom Columbus found in a state of savagery. In this he exhibited a lack of knowledge of conditions.

His talk was lamentably short and much was left unsaid
of seeming greater importance than much that was said.[1]

AN INTERESTING LECTURE

(Wisconsin State Journal, November 21, 1893)

The lecture at the Congregational Church [Madison]
last night by the celebrated Hindoo monk, Vivekananda,
was an extremely interesting one, and contained much of
sound philosophy and good religion. Pagan though he
be, Christianity may well follow many of his teachings.
His creed is as wide as the universe, taking in all religions,
and accepting truth wherever it may be found. Bigotry
and superstition and idle ceremony, he declared, have no
place in "the religions of India".

THE HINDOO RELIGION

(Minneapolis Star, November 25, 1893)

"Brahminism" in all its subtle attraction, because of
its embodiment of ancient and truthful principles, was the
subject which held an audience in closest attention last
evening at the First Unitarian Church [Minneapolis],
while Swami Vive Kananda expounded the Hindoo faith.
It was an audience which included thoughtful women and
men, for the lecturer had been invited by the "Peripatet-
ics," and among the friends who shared the privilege
with them were ministers of varied denominations, as

---

[1] It is clear from the above report that the American Press,
for one reason or another, did not always give Swamiji an enthusiastic reception.

well as students and scholars. Vive Kananda is a Brahmin priest, and he occupied the platform in his native garb, with caftan on head, orange colored coat confined at the waist with a red sash, and red nether garments.

He presented his faith in all sincerity, speaking slowly and clearly, convincing his hearers by quietness of speech rather than by rapid action. His words were carefully weighed, and each carried its meaning direct. He offered the simplest truths of the Hindoo religion, and while he said nothing harsh about Christianity, he touched upon it in such a manner as to place the faith of Brahma before all. The all-pervading thought and leading principle of the Hindoo religion is the inherent divinity of the soul; the soul is perfect, and religion is the manifestation of divinity already existing in man. The present is merely a line of demarkation between the past and future, and of the two tendencies in man, if the good preponderates he will move to a higher sphere, if the evil has power, he degenerates. These two are continually at work within him; what elevates him is virtue, that which degenerates is evil.

Kananda will speak at the First Unitarian Church tomorrow morning.

*   *   *

(*Des Moines News*, November 28, 1893)

Swami Vivekananda, the talented scholar from the far-off India, spoke at the Central church last night [November 27]. He was a representative of his country and creed at the recent parliament of religions assembled in Chicago during the world's fair. Rev. H. O. Breeden introduced the speaker to the audience. He arose and after bowing to his audience, commenced his lecture, the subject of which was "Hindoo Religion". His lecture was not confined to any line of thought but consisted more of some of his own philosophical views relative to his religion and others. He holds that one must embrace all the religions to become the perfect Christian. What is not found in one religion is supplied by another. They are all right and necessary for the true Christian. When you send a missionary to our country he becomes a Hindoo Christian and I a Christian Hindoo. I have often been asked in this country if I am going to try to convert the people here. I take this for an insult. I do not believe in this idea of conversion.[1] To-day we have a sinful man; tomorrow according to your idea he is converted and by and by attains unto holiness. Whence comes this change? How do you explain it? The man has not a new soul for the soul must die. You say he is changed by God. God is perfect, all powerful and is purity itself. Then after this man is converted he is that same God minus the purity he gave that man to become holy. There is in our country two words which have an altogether different meaning than they do in this country. They are "religion" and "sect". We hold that religion embraces all religions. We tolerate everything but intoleration. Then there is that word "sect". Here it embraces those sweet people who wrap themselves up in their mantle of charity and say, "We are right; you are wrong." It reminds me of the story of the two frogs. A frog was born in a well and lived its whole life in that well. One day a frog from the sea fell in that well and they commenced to talk about the sea. The frog whose home was in the well asked the visitor how large the sea was, but was unable to get an intelligent answer. Then the at home frog jumped from one corner of the well to another and asked his visitor if the sea was that large.

---

[1] Although in spots, as will be seen, the reporter woefully failed to follow Swamiji's argument regarding conversion, he captured enough of it to enable the reader who is familiar with Swamiji's thought to comprehend his meaning.

He said yes. The frog jumped again and said, "Is the sea that large?" and receiving an affirmative reply, he said to himself, "This frog must be a liar; I will put him out of my well." That is the way with these sects. They seek to eject and trample those who do not believe as they do.

THE HINDOO MONK

(Appeal-Avalanche, January 16, 1894)

Swami Vive Kananda, the Hindoo monk, who is to lecture at the Auditorium [Memphis] tonight, is one of the most eloquent men who has ever appeared on the religious or lecture platform in this country. His matchless oratory, deep penetration into things occult, his cleverness in debate, and great earnestness captured the closest attention of the world's thinking men at the World's Fair Parliament of Religion, and the admiration of thousands of people who have since heard him during his lecture tour through many of the states of the Union.

In conversation he is a most pleasant gentleman; his choice of words are the gems of the English language, and his general bearing ranks him with the most cultured people of Western etiquette and custom. As a companion he is a most charming man, and as a conversationalist he is, perhaps, not surpassed in the drawing-rooms of any city in the Western World. He speaks English not only distinctly, but fluently, and his ideas, as new as sparkling, drop from his tongue in a perfectly bewildering overflow of ornamental language.

Swami Vive Kananda, by his inherited religion or early teachings, grew up a Brahmin, but becoming converted to the Hindoo religion he sacrificed his rank and became a Hindoo priest, or as known in the country of oriental ideality, a sanyasin. He had always been a close student of the wonderful and mysterious works of nature as drawn from God's high conception, and with years spent as both a student and teacher in the higher colleges of that eastern country, he acquired a knowledge that has given him a worldwide reputation as one of the most thoughtful scholars of the age.

His wonderful first address before the members of the World's Fair Parliament stamped him at once as a leader in that great body of religious thinkers. During the session he was frequently heard in defence of his religion, and some of the most beautiful and philosophical gems that grace the English language rolled from his lips there in picturing the higher duties that man owed to man and to his Creator. He is an artist in thought, an idealist in belief and a dramatist on the platform.

Since his arrival in Memphis he has been guest of Mr. Hu L. Brinkley, where he has received calls day and evening from many in Memphis who desired to pay their respects to him. He is also an informal guest at the Tennessee Club and was a guest at the reception given by Mrs. S. R. Shepherd, Saturday evening. Col. R. B. Snowden gave a dinner at his home at Annesdale in honor of the distinguished visitor on Sunday, where he met Assistant Bishop Thomas F. Gailor, Rev. Dr. George Patterson and a number of other clergymen.

Yesterday afternoon he lectured before a large and fashionable audience composed of the members of the Nineteenth Century Club in the rooms of the club in the Randolph Building. Tonight he will be heard at the Auditorium on "Hindooism".

PLEA FOR TOLERANCE

(*Memphis Commercial*, January 17, 1894)

An audience of fair proportions gathered last night at the Auditorium to greet the celebrated Hindu monk, Swami Vive Kananda, in his lecture on Hinduism.

He was introduced in a brief but informing address by Judge R. J. Morgan, who gave a sketch of the development of the great Aryan race, from which development have come the Europeans and the Hindus alike, so tracing a racial kinship between the people of America and the speaker who was to address them.

The eminent Oriental was received with liberal applause, and heard with attentive interest throughout. He is a man of fine physical presence, with regular bronze features and form of fine proportions. He wore a robe of pink silk, fastened at the waist with a black sash, black trousers and about his head was gracefully draped a turban of yellow India silk. His delivery is very good, his use of English being perfect as regards choice of words and correctness of grammar and construction. The only inaccuracy of pronunciation is in the accenting of words at times upon a wrong syllable. Attentive listeners, however, probably lost few words, and their attention was well rewarded by an address full of original thought, information and broad wisdom. The address might fitly be called a plea for universal tolerance, illustrated by remarks concerning the religion of India. This spirit, he contended, the spirit of tolerance and love, is the central inspiration of all religions which are worthy, and this, he thinks, is the end to be secured by any form of faith.

His talk concerning Hinduism was not strictly circumstantial. His attempt was rather to give an analysis of its spirit than a story of its legends or a picture of its forms. He dwelt upon only a few of the distinctive credal

or ritual features of his faith, but these he explained most
clearly and perspicuously. He gave a vivid account of
the mystical features of Hinduism, out of which the so
often misinterpreted theory of reincarnation has grown.
He explained how his religion ignored the differentiations
of time, how, just as all men believe in the present and
the future of the soul, so the faith of Brahma believes in
its past. He made it clear, too, how his faith does not
believe in "original sin," but bases all effort and aspiration on the belief of the perfectibility of humanity.
Improvement and purification, he contends, must be
based upon hope. The development of man is a return
to an original perfection. This perfection must come
through the practice of holiness and love. Here he
showed how his own people have practiced these qualities, how India has been a land of refuge for the oppressed, citing the instance of the welcome given by the
Hindus to the Jews when Titus sacked Jerusalem and
destroyed the Temple.

In a graphic way he told that the Hindus do not
lay much stress upon forms. Sometimes every member
of the family will differ in their adherence to sects, but
all will worship God by worshipping the spirit of love
which is His central attribute. The Hindus, he says,
hold that there is good in all religions, that all religions
are embodiments of man's inspiration for holiness, and
being such, all should be respected. He illustrated this
by a citation from the Vedas [?], in which varied religions are symbolized as the differently formed vessels
with which different men came to bring water from a
spring. The forms of the vessels are many, but the water
of truth is what all seek to fill their vessels with. God
knows all forms of faith, he thinks, and will recognize his
own name no matter what it is called, or what may be
the fashion of the homage paid him.

The Hindus, he continued, worship the same God

III—32

as the Christians. The Hindu trinity of Brahma, Vishnu, Siva is merely an embodiment of God the creator, the preserver and the destroyer. That the three are considered three instead of one is simply a corruption due to the fact that general humanity must have its ethics made tangible. So likewise the material images of Hindu gods are simply symbols of divine qualities.

He told, in explanation of the Hindu doctrine of incarnation, the story of Krishna, who was born by immaculate conception and the story of whom greatly resembles the story of Jesus. The teaching of Krishna, he claims, is the doctrine of love for its own sake, and he expressed [it] by the words "If the fear of the Lord is the beginning of religion, the love of God is its end."

His entire lecture cannot be sketched here, but it was a masterly appeal for brotherly love, and an eloquent defense of a beautiful faith. The conclusion was especially fine, when he acknowledged his readiness to accept Christ but must also bow to Krishna and to Buddha; and when, with a fine picture of the cruelty of civilization, he refused to hold Christ responsible for the crimes of progress.

MANNERS AND CUSTOMS IN INDIA

(*Appeal-Avalanche*, January 21, 1894)

Swami Vive Kananda, the Hindoo monk, delivered a lecture at La Salette Academy [Memphis] yesterday afternoon. Owing to the pouring rain, a very small audience was present.

The subject discussed was "Manners and Customs in India." Vive Kananda is advancing theories of religious thought which find ready lodgment in the minds of some

of the most advanced thinkers of this as well as other
cities of America.

His theory is fatal to the orthodox belief, as taught
by the Christian teachers. It has been the supreme effort
of Christian America to enlighten the beclouded minds
of heathen India, but it seems that the oriental splendor
of Kananda's religion has eclipsed the beauty of the old-
time Christianity, as taught by our parents, and will find
a rich field in which to thrive in the minds of some of the
better educated of America.

This is a day of "fads," and Kananda seems to be
filling a "long felt want." He is, perhaps, one of the
most learned men of his country, and possesses a wonderful amount of personal magnetism, and his hearers are
charmed by his eloquence. While he is liberal in his
views, he sees very little to admire in the orthodox
Christianity. Kananda has received more marked attention
in Memphis than almost any lecturer or minister that
has ever visited the city.

If a missionary to India was as cordially received as
the Hindoo monk is here the work of spreading the
gospel of Christ in heathen lands would be well advanced.
His lecture yesterday afternoon was an interesting one
from a historic point of view. He is thoroughly familiar
with the history and traditions of his native country, from
very ancient history up to the present, and can describe
the various places and objects of interest there with
grace and ease.

During his lecture he was frequently interrupted by
questions propounded by the ladies in the audience, and
he answered all queries without the least hesitancy, except
when one of the ladies asked a question with the purpose
of drawing him out into a religious discussion. He refused
to be led from the original subject of his discourse and
informed the interrogator that at another time he would
give his views on the "transmigration of the soul," etc.

In the course of his remarks he said that his grand-father was married when he was 3 years old and his father married at 18, but he had never married at all. A monk is not forbidden to marry, but if he takes a wife she becomes a monk with the same powers and privileges and occupies the same social position as her husband.[1]

In answer to a question, he said there were no divorces in India for any cause, but if, after 14 years of married life, there were no children in the family, the husband was allowed to marry another with the wife's consent, but if she objected he could not marry again. His description of the ancient mausoleums and temples were beautiful beyond comparison, and goes to show that the ancients possessed scientific knowledge far superior to the most expert artisans of the present day.

Swami Vivi Kananda will appear at the Y. M. H. A. Hall to-night for the last time in this city. He is under contract with the "Slayton Lyceum Bureau," of Chicago, to fill a three-years' engagement in this country. He will leave tomorrow for Chicago, where he has an engagement for the night of the 25th.

(*Detroit Tribune*, February 15, 1894)

Last evening a good sized audience had the privilege of seeing and listening to the famous Hindu Monk of the Brahmo Samaj, Swami Vive Kananda, as he lectured at the Unitarian Church under the auspices of the Unity Club. He appeared in native costume and made with his handsome face and stalwart figure a distinguished appear-ance. His eloquence held the audience in rapt attention

---

[1] It is quite unlikely that Swamiji made the remark attributed to him regarding the marriage of monks. This must have been an aberration on the part of the reporter, for, as is well known, if a Sannyasin takes a wife he is considered by the Hindu society to be a fallen person and beyond the pale.

and brought out applause at frequent intervals. He spoke
of the "Manners and Customs of India" and presented
the subject in the most perfect English. He said they
did not call their country India nor themselves Hindus.
Hindostan was the name of the country and they were
Brahmans. In ancient times they spoke Sanscrit. In that
language the reason and meaning of a word was explained
and made quite evident but now that is all gone. Jupiter
in Sanscrit meant "Father in Heaven." All the languages
of northern India were now practically the same, but if
he should go into the southern part of that country he
could not converse with the people. In the words father,
mother, sister, brother, etc.; the Sanscrit gave very similar
pronunciations. This and other facts lead him to think
we all come from the common stock, Aryans. Nearly all
branches of this race have lost their identity.

There were four castes, the priests, the landlords and
military people, the trades people and the artisans,
laborers and servants. In the first three castes the boys
as the ages of ten, eleven and thirteen respectively are
placed in the hands of professors of universities and
remain with them until thirty, twenty-five and twenty
years old, respectively. ... In ancient times both boys and
girls were instructed, but now only the boys are favored.
An effort, however, is being made to rectify the long-
existing wrong. A good share of the philosophy and laws
of the land is the work of women during the ancient
times, before barbarians started to rule the land. In the
eyes of the Hindu the woman now has her rights. She
holds her own and has the law on her side.

When the student returns from college he is allowed
to marry and have a household. Husband and wife must
bear the work and both have their rights. In the military
caste the daughters oftentimes can choose their husbands,
but in all other cases all arrangements are made by the
parents. There is a constant effort now being made to

remedy infant marriage. The marriage ceremony is very beautiful, each touches the heart of the other and they swear before God and the assemblage that they will prove faithful to each other. No man can be a priest until he marries. When a man attends public worship he is always attended by his wife. In his worship the Hindu performs five ceremonies, worship of his God, of his forefathers, of the poor, of the dumb animals, and of learning. As long as a Hindu has anything in the house a guest must never want. When he is satisfied then the children, then father and mother partake. They are the poorest nation in the world, yet except in times of famine no one dies of hunger. Civilization is a great work. But in comparison the statement is made that in England one in every 400 is a drunkard, while in India the proportion is one to every million. A description was given of the ceremony of burning the dead. No publicity is made except in the case of some great nobleman. After a fifteen days' fast gifts are given by the relatives in behalf of the forefathers to the poor or for the formation of some institution. On moral matters they stand head and shoulders above all other nations.

HINDOO PHILOSOPHY

(Detroit Free Press, February 16, 1894)

The second lecture of the Hindoo monk, Swami Vive Kananda, was given last evening at the Unitarian church to a large and very appreciative audience. The expectation of the audience that the speaker would enlighten them regarding "Hindoo Philosophy," as the lecture was entitled, was gratified to only a limited extent. Allusions were made to the philosophy of Buddha, and the speaker was applauded when he said that Buddhism was the first missionary religion of the world, and that it had secured the largest number of converts without the shedding of a drop of blood; but he did not tell his audience anything about the religion or philosophy of Buddha. He made a number of cute little jabs at the Christian religion, and alluded to the trouble and misery that had been caused by its introduction into heathen countries, but he skilfully avoided any comparison between the social condition of the people in his own land and that of the people to whom he was speaking. In a general way he said the Hindoo philosophers taught from a lower truth to a higher; whereas, a person accepting a newer Christian doctrine is asked and expected to throw his former belief all away and accept the newer in its entirety. "It is an idle dream when all of us will have the same religious views," said he. "No emotion can be produced except by clashing elements acting upon the mind. It is the revulsion of change, the new light, the presentation of the new to the old, that elicits sensation."

[As the first lecture had antagonised some people, the *Free Press* reporter was very cautious. Fortunately, however, the *Detroit Tribune* consistently upheld Swamiji, and thus in its report of February 16 we get some idea of his lecture on "Hindu Philosophy," although the *Tribune* reporter seems to have taken somewhat sketchy notes:]

(*Detroit Tribune,* February 16, 1894)

The Brahman monk, Swami Vive Kananda, again lectured last evening at the Unitarian church, his topic being "Hindu Philosophy." The speaker dealt for a time with general philosophy and metaphysics, but said that he would devote the lecture to that part pertaining to religion. There is a sect that believes in a soul, but are agnostic in relation to God. Buddahism [sic] was a great moral religion, but they could not live long without believing in a god. Another sect known as the giants [Jains] believe in the soul, but not in the moral government of the country. There were several millions of this sect in India. Their priests and monks tie a handkerchief over their faces believing if their hot breath comes in contact with man or beast death will ensue.

Among the orthodox, all believe in the revelation. Some think every word in the Bible comes directly from God. The stretching of the meaning of a word would perhaps do in most religions, but in that of the Hindus they have the Sanscrit, which always retains the full meaning and reasons of the world.

The distinguished Oriental thought there was a sixth sense far greater than any of the five we know we possess. It was the truth of revelation. A man may read all the books on religion in the world and yet be the greatest blackguard in the country. Revelation means later reports of spiritual discoveries.

The second position some take is a creation without beginning or end. Suppose there was a time when the world did not exist; what was God doing then? To the Hindus the creation was only one of forms. One man is born with a healthy body, is of good family and grows up a godly man. Another is born with a maimed and crooked body and develops into a wicked man and pays the penalty. Why must a just and holy god create one with so many advantages and the other with disadvantages? The person has no choice. The evildoer has a consciousness of his guilt. The difference between virtue and vice was expounded. If God willed all things there would be an end to all science. How far can man go down? Is it possible for man to go back to brute again?

Kananda was glad he was a Hindu. When Jerusalem was destroyed by the Romans several thousand [Jews] settled in India. When the Persians were driven from

their country by the Arabs several thousand found refuge
in the same country and none were molested. The
Hindus believe all religions are true, but theirs antedates
all others. Missionaries are never molested by the Hindus.
The first English missionaries were prevented from landing in that country by English and it was a Hindu that
interceded for them and gave them the first hand. Religion is that which believes in all. Religion was compared
to the blind men and the elephant. Each man felt of a
special part and from it drew his conclusions of what an
elephant was. Each was right in his way and yet all
were needed to form a whole. Hindu philosophers say
"truth to truth, lower truth to higher." It is an idle dream
of those who think that all will at some time think alike,
for that would be the death of religion. Every religion
breaks up into little sects, each claiming to be the true
one and all the others wrong. Persecution is unknown
in Buddahism. They sent out the first missionaries and
are the only ones who can say they have converted
millions without the shedding of a single drop of blood.
Hindus, with all their faults and superstitions, never per-
secute. The speaker wanted to know how it was the
christians allowed such iniquities as are everywhere present in christian countries.

MIRACLES

(Evening News, February 17, 1894)

"I cannot comply with the request of The News to
work a miracle in proof of my religion," said Vive
Kananda to a representative of this paper, after being
shown The News editorial on the subject. "In the first
place, I am no miracle worker, and in the second place
the pure Hindoo religion I profess is not based on mira-

cles. We do not recognize such a thing as miracles. There are wonders wrought beyond our five senses, but they are operated by some law. Our religion has nothing to do with them. Most of the strange things which are done in India and reported in the foreign papers are sleight-of-hand tricks or hypnotic illusions. They are not the performances of the wise men. These do not go about the country performing their wonders in the market places for pay. They can be seen and known only by those who seek to know the truth, and not moved by childish curiosity."

THE DIVINITY OF MAN

(*Detroit Free Press*, February 18, 1894)

Swami Vive Kananda, Hindoo philosopher and priest, concluded his series of lectures, or rather, sermons, at the Unitarian church last night, speaking on "The Divinity of God" [sic].[1] In spite of the bad weather, the church was crowded almost to the doors half an hour before the eastern brother—as he likes to be called—appeared. All professions and business occupations were represented in the attentive audience—lawyers, judges, ministers of the gospel, merchants, rabbi—not to speak of the many ladies who have by their repeated attendance and rapt attention shown a decided inclination to shower adulation upon the dusky visitor whose drawing-room attraction is as great as his ability in the rostrum.

The lecture last night was less descriptive than preceding ones, and for nearly two hours Vive Kananda wove a metaphysical texture on affairs human and divine

[1] Actually the subject was "The Divinity of Man".

so logical that he made science appear like common sense. It was a beautiful logical garment that he wove, replete with as many bright colors and as attractive and pleasing to contemplate as one of the many-hued fabrics made by hand in his native land and scented with the most seductive fragrance of the Orient. This dusky gentleman uses poetical imagery as an artist uses colors, and the hues are laid on just where they belong, the result being somewhat bizarre in effect, and yet having a peculiar fascination. Kaleidoscopic were the swiftly succeeding logical conclusions, and the deft manipulator was rewarded for his efforts from time to time by enthusiastic applause.

The lecture was prefaced with the statement that the speaker had been asked many questions. A number of these he preferred to answer privately, but three he had selected, for reasons which would appear, to answer from the pulpit. They were: [1]

"Do the people of India throw their children into the jaws of the crocodiles?"

"Do they kill themselves beneath the wheels of the juggernaut?"

"Do they burn widows with their husbands?"

The first question the lecturer treated in the vein that an American abroad would answer inquiries about Indians running around in the streets of New York and similar myths which are even to-day entertained by many persons on the continent. The statement was too ludicrous to give a serious response to it. When asked by certain well-meaning but ignorant people why they gave only female children to the crocodiles, he could only ironically reply that probably it was because they were softer and more tender and could be more easily masticated by the inhabitants of the rivers in the benighted country. Regarding

[1]This and the next four paragraphs appear in Vol. IV of the *Complete Works* under the heading, "Is India a Benighted Country?"

the juggernaut legend the lecturer explained the old practice in the sacred city and remarked that possibly a few
in their zeal to grasp the rope and participate in the drawing of the car slipped and fell and were so destroyed.
Some such mishaps had been exaggerated into the distorted version from which the good people of other countries shrank with horror. Vive Kananda denied that the
people burned widows. It was true, however, that widows
had burned themselves. In the few cases where this had
happened, they had been urged not to do so by the priests
and holy men who were always opposed to suicide.
Where the devoted widows insisted, stating that they
desired to accompany their husbands in the transformation that had taken place, they were obliged to submit
to the fiery test. That is, they thrust their hands within
the flames and if they permitted them to be consumed no
further opposition was placed in the way of the fulfilment
of their desires. But India is not the only country where
women who have loved have followed immediately the
loved one through the realms of immortality; suicide in
such cases have occurred in every land. It is an uncommon bit of fanaticism in any country; as unusual in India
as elsewhere. No, the speaker repeated, the people do
not burn women in India; nor have they ever burned
witches.

Proceeding to the lecture proper, Vive Kananda proceeded to analyze the physical, mental and soul attributes of life. The body is but a shell; the mind something that acts but a brief and fantastic part; while the
soul has distinct individuality in itself. To realize the
infinity of self is to attain "freedom" which is the Hindoo
word for "salvation." By a convincing manner of argument the lecturer showed that every soul is something
independent, for if it were dependent, it could not acquire
immortality. He related a story from the old legends of
his country to illustrate the manner in which the realiza-

tion of this may come to the individual. A lioness leap-
ing towards a sheep in the act gave birth to a cub. The
lioness died and the cub was given suck by the sheep
and for many years thought itself a sheep and acted like
one. But one day another lion appeared and led the first
lion to a lake where he looked in and saw his resemblance
to the other lion. At that he roared and realized the full
majesty of self. Many people are like the lion masquerad-
ing as a sheep and get into a corner, call themselves
sinners and demean themselves in every imaginable
fashion, not yet seeing the perfection and divinity which
lies in self. The ego of man and woman is the soul.
If the soul is independent, how then can it be isolated
from the infinite whole? Just as the great sun shines on
a lake and numberless reflections are the result, so the
soul is distinct like each reflection, although the great
source is recognized and appreciated. The soul is sexless. When it has realized the condition of absolute freedom, what could it have to do with sex which is physical?
In this connection the lecturer delved deeply into the
water of Swedenborgian philosophy, or religion, and the
connection between the conviction of the Hindoo and
the spiritual expressions of faith on the part of the more
modern holy man was fully apparent. Swedenborg
seemed like a European successor of an early Hindoo
priest, clothing in modern garb an ancient conviction;
a line of thought that the greatest of French philosophers
and novelists [Balzac?] saw fit to embody in his elevating
tale of the perfect soul. Every individual has in himself
perfection. It lies within the dark recesses of his physical
being. To say that a man has become good because
God gave him a portion of His perfection is to conceive
the Divine Being as God minus just so much perfection
as he has imparted to a person on this earth. The in-
exorable law of science proves that the soul is individual
and must have perfection within itself, the attainment

of which means freedom, not salvation, and the realiza-
tion of individual infinity. Nature! God! Religion! It
is all one.

The religions are all good. A bubble of air in a glass
of water strives to join with the mass of air without; in
oil, vinegar and other materials of differing density its
efforts are less or more retarded according to the liquid.
So the soul struggles through various mediums for the
attainment of its individual infinity. One religion is best
adapted to a certain people because of habits of life,
association, hereditary traits and climatic influences.
Another religion is suited to another people for similar
reasons. All that is, is best seemed to be the substance
of the lecturer's conclusions. To try abruptly to change a
nation's religion would be like a man who sees a river
flowing from the Alps. He criticizes the way it has taken.
Another man views the mighty stream descending from
the Himalayas, a stream that has been running for generations and thousands of years, and says that it has not
taken the shortest and best route. The Christian pictures
God as a personal being seated somewhere above us.
The Christian cannot necessarily be happy in Heaven
unless he can stand on the edge of the golden streets and
from time to time gaze down into the other place and
see the difference. Instead of the golden rule, the
Hindoo believes in the doctrine that all non-self is good
and all self is bad, and through this belief the attainment
of the individual infinity and the freedom of the soul at
the proper time will be fulfilled. How excessively
vulgar, stated Vive Kananda, was the golden rule! Always
self! always self! was the Christian creed. To do unto
others as you would be done by! It was a horrible,
barbarous, savage creed, but he did not desire to decry
the Christian creed, for those who are satisfied with it to
them it is well adapted. Let the great stream flow on,
and he is a fool who would try to change its course,

when nature will work out the solution. Spiritualist (in
the true acceptance of the word) and fatalist, Vive
Kananda emphasized his opinion that all was well and
he had no desire to convert Christians. They were
Christians; it was well. He was a Hindoo; that, also,
was well. In his country different creeds were formulated
for the needs of people of different grades of intelligence,
all this marking the progress of spiritual evolution. The
Hindoo religion was not one of self; ever egotistical in
its aspirations, ever holding up promises of reward or
threats of punishment. It shows to the individual he may
attain infinity by non-self. This system of bribing men
to become Christians, alleged to have come from God,
who manifested Himself to certain men on earth, is atro-
cious. It is horribly demoralizing and the Christian creed,
accepted literally, has a shameful effect upon the moral
natures of the bigots who accept it, retarding the time
when the infinity of self may be attained.

*   *   *

[The *Tribune* reporter, perhaps the same who had
earlier heard "giants" for "Jains," this time heard "bury"
for "burn"; but otherwise, with the exception of
Swamiji's statements regarding the golden rule, he seems
to have reported more or less accurately:]

(*Detroit Tribune*, February 18, 1894)

Swami Vive Kananda at the Unitarian Church last
night declared that widows were never buried [burned]
alive in India through religion or law, but the act in all
cases had been voluntary on the part of the women. The
practice had been forbidden by one emperor, but it had
gradually grown again until a stop was put to it by the
English government. Fanatics existed in all religions, the
Christian as well as the Hindu. Fanatics in India had

been known to hold their hands over their heads in
penance for so long a time that the arm had gradually
grown stiff in that position, and so remained ever after.
So, too, men had made a vow to stand still in one position. These persons would in time lose all control of
the lower limbs and never after be able to walk. All
religions were true, and the people practiced morality,
not because of any divine command, but because of its
own good. Hindus, he said, did not believe in conversion, calling it perversion. Associations, surroundings and
educations were responsible for the great number of religions, and how foolish it was for an exponent of one
religion to declare that another man's belief was wrong.
It was as reasonable as a man from Asia coming to
America and after viewing the course of the Mississippi
to say to it: "You are running entirely wrong. You will
have to go back to the starting place and commence it
all over again." It would be just as foolish for a man
in America to visit the Alps and after following the course
of a river to the German Sea to inform it that its course
was too tortuous and that the only remedy would be to
flow as directed. The golden rule, he declared, was as
old as the earth itself and to it could be traced all rules
of morality [sic]. Man is a bundle of selfishness. He
thought the hell fire theory was all nonsense. There could
not be perfect happiness when it was known that suffering existed. He ridiculed the manner some religious persons have while praying. The Hindu, he said, closed his
eyes and communed with the inner spirit, while some
Christians he had seen had seemed to stare at some point
as if they saw God seated upon his heavenly throne. In
the matter of religion there were two extremes, the bigot
and the atheist. There was some good in the atheist, but
the bigot lived only for his own little self. He thanked
some anonymous person who had sent him a picture of
the heart of Jesus. This he thought a manifestation of

bigotry. Bigots belong to no religion. They are a singular phenomena [sic].

THE LOVE OF GOD[1]

(*Detroit Tribune,* February 21, 1894)

The First Unitarian Church was crowded last night to hear Vive Kananda. The audience was composed of people who came from Jefferson Avenue and the upper part of Woodward Avenue. Most of it was ladies who seemed deeply interested in the address and applauded several remarks of the Brahman with much enthusiasm.

The love that was dwelt upon by the speaker was not the love that goes with passion, but a pure and holy love that one in India feels for his God. As Vive Kananda stated at the commencement of his address the subject was "The Love the Indian Feels for His God." But he did not preach to his text. The major portion of his address was an attack on the Christian religion. The religion of the Indian and the love of his God was the minor portion. The points in his address were illustrated with several applicable anecdotes of famous people in the history. The subjects of the anecdotes were renowned Mogul emperors of his native land and not of the native Hindu kings.

The professors of religion were divided into two classes by the lecturer, the followers of knowledge and the followers of devotion. The end in the life of the followers of knowledge was experience. The end in the life of the devotee was love.

Love, he said, was a sacrifice. It never takes, but it

[1] The *Detroit Free Press* report of this lecture is printed in Vol. VIII of the *Complete Works.*

always gives. The Hindu never asks anything of his God, never prayed for salvation and a happy hereafter, but instead lets his whole soul go out to his God in an entrancing love. That beautiful state of existence could only be gained when a person felt an overwhelming want of God. Then God came in all of His fullness.

There were three different ways of looking at God. One was to look upon Him as a mighty personage and fall down and worship His might. Another was to worship Him as a father. In India the father always punished the children and an element of fear was mixed with the regard and love for a father. Still another way to think of God was as a mother. In India a mother was always truly loved and reverenced. That was the Indian's way of looking at their God.

Kananda said that a true lover of God would be so wrapt up in his love that he would have no time to stop and tell members of another sect that they were following the wrong road to secure the God, and strive to bring him to his way of thinking.

* * *

(Detroit Journal)

If Vive Kananda, the Brahmin monk, who is delivering a lecture course in this city could be induced to remain for a week longer, the largest hall in Detroit would not hold the crowds which would be anxious to hear him. He has become a veritable fad, as last evening every seat in the Unitarian church was occupied, and many were compelled to stand throughout the entire lecture.

The speaker's subject was, "The Love of God". His definition of love was "something absolutely unselfish; that which has no thought beyond the glorification and adoration of the object upon which our affections are bestowed." Love, he said, is a quality which bows down and worships and asks nothing in return. Love of God,

REPORTS IN AMERICAN NEWSPAPERS 505

he thought, was different. God is not accepted, he said, because we really need him, except for selfish purposes. His lecture was replete with story and anecdote, all going to show the selfish motive underlying the motive of love for God. The Songs of Solomon were cited by the lecturer as the most beautiful portion of the Christian Bible and yet he had heard with deep regret that there was a possibility of their being removed. "In fact," he declared, as a sort clinching argument at the close, "the love of God appears to be based upon a theory of 'What can I get out of it?' Christians are so selfish in their love that they are continually asking God to give them something, including all manner of selfish things. Modern religion is, therefore, nothing but a mere hobby and fashion and people flock to church like a lot of sheep."

THE WOMEN OF INDIA

(*Detroit Free Press*, March 25, 1894)

Kananda lectured last night at the Unitarian church on "The Women of India." The speaker reverted to the women of ancient India, showing in what high regard they are held in the holy books, where women were prophetesses. Their spirituality then was admirable. It is unfair to judge women in the east by the western standard. In the west woman is the wife; in the east she is the mother. The Hindoos worship the idea of mother, and even the monks are required to touch the earth with their foreheads before their mothers. Chastity is much esteemed.

The lecture was one of the most interesting Kananda has delivered and he was warmly received.

*   *   *

(*Detroit Evening News*, March 25, 1894)

Swami Vive Kananda lectured at the Unitarian
Church last night on "The Women of India, Past,
Medieval and the Present." He stated that in India the
woman was the visible manifestation of God and that her
whole life was given up to the thought that she was a
mother, and to be a perfect mother she must be chaste.
No mother in India ever abandoned her offspring, he said,
and defied any one to prove the contrary. The girls of
India would die if they, like American girls, were obliged
to expose half their bodies to the vulgar gaze of young
men. He desired that India be judged from the standard
of that country and not from this.

*   *   *

(*Tribune, April* 1, 1894)

While Swami Kananda was in Detroit he had a number of conversations, in which he answered questions
regarding the women of India. It was the information he
thus imparted that suggested a public lecture from him
on this subject. But as he speaks without notes, some
of the points he made in private conversation did not
appear in his public address. Then his friends were in a
measure disappointed. But one of his lady listeners has
put on paper some of the things he told in his afternoon
talks, and it is now for the first time given to the press:

To the great tablelands of the high Himalaya mountains first came the Aryans, and there to this day abides
the pure type of Brahman, a people which we westerners
can but dream of. Pure in thought, deed and action, so
honest that a bag of gold left in a public place would be
found unharmed twenty years after; so beautiful that,
to use Kananda's own phrase, "to see a girl in the fields
is to pause and marvel that God could make anything so
exquisite." Their features are regular, their eyes and hair

dark, and their skin the color which would be produced by the drops which fell from a pricked finger into a glass of milk. These are the Hindus in their pure type, untainted and untrammeled.

As to their property laws, the wife's dowry belongs to her exclusively, never becoming the property of the husband. She can sell or give away without his consent. The gifts from any one to herself, including those of the husband, are hers alone, to do with as she pleases.

Woman walks abroad without fear; she is as free as perfect trust in those about her can render her. There is no zenana in the Himalayas, and there is a part of India which the missionaries never reach. These villages are most difficult of access. These people, untouched by Mahometan influence, can but be reached by wearisome and toilsome climbing, and are unknown to Mahometan and Christian alike.

India's First Inhabitants

In the forest of India are found races of wild people—very wild, even to cannibalism. These are the original Indians and never were Aryan or Hindu.

As the Hindus settled in the country proper and spread over its vast area, corruptions of many kinds found home among them. The sun was scorching and the men exposed to it were dark in color.

Five generations are but needed to change the transparent glow of the white complexion of the dwellers of the Himalaya Mountains to the bronzed hue of the Hindu of India.

Kananda has one brother very fair and one darker than himself. His father and mother are fair. The women are apt to be, the cruel etiquette of the Zenana established for protection from the Mohammedans keeping them within doors, fairer. Kananda is thirty-one years old.

A CLIP AT AMERICAN MEN

Kananda asserts with an amused twinkle in his eye that American men amuse him. They profess to worship woman, but in his opinion they simply worship youth and beauty. They never fall in love with wrinkles and gray hair. In fact he is under a strong impression that American men once had a trick—inherited, to be sure—of burning up their old women. Modern history calls this the burning of witches. It was men who accused and condemned witches, and it was usually the old age of the victim that led her to the stake. So it is seen that burning women alive is not exclusively a Hindu custom. He thought that if it were remembered that the Christian church burned old women at the stake, there would be less horror expressed regarding the burning of Hindu widows.

BURNINGS COMPARED

The Hindu widow went to her death agony amid feasting and song, arrayed in her costliest garments and believing for the most part that such an act meant the glories of Paradise for herself and family. She was worshipped as a martyr and her name was enshrined among the family records.

However horrible the rite appears to us, it is a bright picture compared to the burning of the Christian witch who, considered a guilty thing from the first, was thrown in a stifling dungeon, tortured cruelly to extort confession, subjected to an infamous trial, dragged amid jeering to the stake and consoled amid her sufferings by the bystander's comfort that the burning of her body was but the symbol for hell's everlasting fires, in which her soul would suffer even greater torment.

MOTHERS ARE SACRED

Kananda says the Hindu is taught to worship the principle of motherhood. The mother outranks the wife. The mother is holy. The motherhood of God is more in his mind than the fatherhood.

All women, whatever the caste, are exempt from corporal punishment. Should a woman murder, her head is spared. She may be placed astride a donkey facing his tail. Thus riding through the streets a drummer shouts her crime, after which she is free, her humiliation being deemed sufficient punishment to serve as a preventive for further crime.

Should she care to repent, there are religious houses open to her, where she can become purified or she can at her own option at once enter the class of monks and so become a holy woman.

The question was put to Mr. Kananda whether the freedom thus allowed in the joining the monks without a superior over them did not tend to hypocrisy among the order, as he claims, of the purest of Hindu philosophers. Kananda assented, but explained that there is no one between the people and the monk. The monk has broken down all caste. A Brahmin will not touch the low-caste Hindu but let him or her become a monk and the mightiest will prostrate himself before the low-caste monk.

The people are obliged to take care of the monk, but only as long as they believe in his sincerity. Once condemned for hypocrisy he is called a liar and falls to the depths of mendicancy—a mere wandering beggar—inspiring no respect.

OTHER THOUGHTS

A woman has the right of way with even a prince. When the studious Greeks visited Hindustan to learn of the Hindu, all doors were open to them, but when the

Mohammedan with his sword and the Englishman with his bullets came their doors were closed. Such guests were not welcomed. As Kananda deliciously words it: "When the tiger comes we close our doors until he has passed by."

The United States, says Kananda, has inspired him with hopes for great possibilities in the future, but our destiny, as that of the world, rests not in the lawmakers of today, but in the women. Mr. Kananda's words: "The salvation of your country depends upon its women."

BUDDHISTIC INDIA[1]

(Delivered at the Shakespeare Club, Pasadena, California, on February 2, 1900)

Buddhistic India is our subject tonight. Almost all of you, perhaps, have read Edwin Arnold's poem on the life of Buddha, and some of you, perhaps, have gone into the subject with more scholarly interest, as in English, French and German, there is quite a lot of Buddhistic literature. Buddhism itself is the most interesting of subjects, for it is the first historical outburst of a world religion. There have been great religions before Buddhism arose, in India and elsewhere, but, more or less, they are confined within their own races. The ancient Hindus or ancient Jews or ancient Persians, every one of them had a great religion, but these religions were more or less racial. With Buddhism first begins that peculiar phenomenon of religion boldly starting out to conquer the world. Apart from its doctrines and the truths it taught and the message it had to give, we stand face to face with one of the tremendous cataclysms of the world. Within a few centuries of its birth, the barefooted, shaven-headed missionaries of Buddha had spread over all the then known civilised world, and they penetrated even further—from Lapland on the one side to the Philippine Islands on the other. They had spread widely within a few centuries of Buddha's birth; and in India itself, the religion of Buddha had at one time nearly swallowed up two-thirds of the population.

The whole of India was never Buddhistic. It stood outside. Buddhism had the same fate as Christianity had with the Jews; the majority of the Jews stood aloof. So the old Indian religion lived on. But the comparison stops here. Christianity, though it could not get within its fold

[1] Reproduced from the *Swami Vivekananda Centenary Memorial Volume*, published by the Swami Vivekananda Centenary, Calcutta, in 1963. The additions in square brackets have been made for purposes of clarification. Periods indicate probable omissions.—*Publisher*.

all the Jewish race, itself took the country. Where the old religion existed—the religion of the Jews—that was conquered by Christianity in a very short time and the old religion was dispersed, and so the religion of the Jews lives a sporadic life in different parts of the world. But in India this gigantic child was absorbed, in the long run, by the mother that gave it birth, and today the very name of Buddha is almost unknown all over India. *You* know more about Buddhism than ninety-nine per cent of the Indians. At best, they of India only know the name—"Oh, he was a great prophet, a great Incarnation of God"—and there it ends. The island of Ceylon remains to Buddha, and in some parts of the Himalayan country, there are some Buddhists yet. Beyond that there are none. But [Buddhism] has spread over all the rest of Asia.

Still, it has the largest number of followers of any religion, and it has indirectly modified the teachings of all the other religions. A good deal of Buddhism entered into Asia Minor. It was a constant fight at one time whether the Buddhists would prevail or the later sects of Christians. The [Gnostics] and the other sects of early Christians were more or less Buddhistic in their tendencies, and all these got fused up in that wonderful city of Alexandria, and out of the fusion under Roman law came Christianity. Buddhism in its political and social aspect is even more interesting than its [doctrines] and dogmas; and as the first outburst of the tremendous world-conquering power of religion, it is very interesting also.

I am mostly interested in this lecture in India as it has been affected by Buddhism; and to understand Buddhism and its rise a bit, we have to get a few ideas about India as it existed when this great prophet was born.

There was already in India a vast religion with an organised scripture—the Vedas; and these Vedas existed as a mass of literature and not a book—just as you find the Old Testament, the Bible. Now, the Bible is a mass of literature of different ages; different persons are the writers, and so on. It is a collection. Now, the Vedas are a vast collection. I do not know whether, if the texts were all found—nobody has found all the texts, nobody even in India has seen all the books—if all the books were known, this room would contain them. It is a huge mass of literature, carried down from generation to generation from God, who gave the scriptures. And the idea about the scriptures in India became tremendously orthodox. You complain of your orthodoxies in book-worship. If you get the Hindus' idea, where will you be? The Hindus think the Vedas are the direct knowledge of God, that God has created the whole universe in and through the Vedas, and that the whole universe exists because it is in the Vedas. The cow exists outside because the word "cow" is in the Vedas; man exists outside because of the word in the Vedas. Here you see the beginning of that theory which later on Christians developed and expressed in the text: "In the beginning was the Word and the Word was with God." It is the old, ancient theory of India. Upon that is based the whole idea of the scriptures. And mind, every word is the power of God. The word is only the external manifestation on the material plane. So, all this manifestation is just the manifestation on the material plane; and the Word is the Vedas, and Sanskrit is the language of God. God spoke once. He spoke in Sanskrit, and that is the divine language. Every other language, they consider, is no more than the braying of animals; and to denote that they call every other nation that does not speak Sanskrit [Mlechchhas], the same word as the barbarians of the Greeks. They are braying, not talking, and Sanskrit is the divine language.

Now, the Vedas were not written by anybody; they were eternally coexistent with God. God is infinite. So is knowledge, and through this knowledge is created the world. Their idea of ethics is [that a thing is good] because the law says so. Everything is bounded by that book

—nothing [can go] beyond that, because the knowledge of God—you cannot get beyond that. That is Indian orthodoxy.

In the latter part of the Vedas, you see the highest, the spiritual. In the early portions, there is the crude part. You quote a passage from the Vedas—"That is not good", you say. "Why?" "There is a positive evil injunction"—the same as you see in the Old Testament. There are numbers of things in all old books, curious ideas, which we would not like in our present day. You say: "This doctrine is not at all good; why, it shocks my ethics!" How did you get your idea? [Merely] by your own thought? Get out! If it is ordained by God, what right have you to question? When the Vedas say, "Do not do this; this is immoral", and so on, no more have you the right to question at all. And that is the difficulty. If you tell a Hindu, "But our Bible does not say so", [he will reply] "Oh, your Bible! it is a babe of history. What other Bible could there be except the Vedas? What other book could there be? All knowledge is in God. Do you mean to say that He teaches by two or more Bibles? His knowledge came out in the Vedas. Do you mean to say that He committed a mistake, then? Afterwards, He wanted to do something better and taught another Bible to another nation? You cannot bring another book that is as old as Vedas. Everything else—it was all copied after that." They would not listen to you. And the Christian brings the Bible. They say: "That is fraud. God only speaks once, because He never makes mistakes."

Now, just think of that. That orthodoxy is terrible. And if you ask a Hindu that he is to reform his society and do this and that, he says: "Is it in the books? If it is not, I do not care to change. You wait. In five [hundred] years more you will find this is good." If you say to him, "This social institution that you have is not right", he says, "How do you know that?" Then he says: "Our social institutions in this matter are the better. Wait five [hundred] years and

your institutions will die. The test is the survival of the
fittest. You live, but there is not one community in the
world which lives five hundred years together. Look here!
We have been standing all the time." That is what they
would say. Terrible orthodoxy! And thank God I have
crossed that ocean.

This was the orthodoxy of India. What else was there?
Everything was divided, the whole society, as it is today,
though in a much more rigorous form then—divided into
castes. There is another thing to learn. There is a tendency
to make castes just [now] going on here in the West. And
I myself—I am a renegade. I have broken everything. I do
not believe in caste, individually. It has very good things
in it. For myself, Lord help me! I would not have any
caste, if He helps me. You understand what I mean by
caste, and you are all trying to make it very fast. It is a
hereditary trade [for] the Hindu. The Hindu said in olden
times that life must be made easier and smoother. And what
makes everything alive? Competition. Hereditary trade
kills. You are a carpenter? Very good, your son can be only
a carpenter. What are you? A blacksmith? Blacksmithing
becomes a caste; your children will become blacksmiths. We
do not allow anybody else to come into that trade, so you
will be quiet and remain there. You are a military man, a
fighter? Make a caste. You are a priest? Make a caste. The
priesthood is hereditary. And so on. Rigid, high power!
That has a great side, and that side is [that] it really rejects
competition. It is that which has made the nation live
while other nations have died—that caste. But there is a
great evil: it checks individuality. I will have to be a carpenter because I am born a carpenter; but I do not like it.
That is in the books, and that was before Buddha was born.
I am talking to you of India as it was before Buddha. And
you are trying today what you call socialism! Good things
will come; but in the long run you will be a [blight] upon
the race. Freedom is the watchword. Be free! A free body,

a free mind, and a free soul! That is what I have felt all my life; I would rather be doing evil freely than be doing good under bondage.

Well, these things that they are crying for now in the West, they have done ages before there. Land has been nationalised . . . by thousands all these things. There is blame upon this hide-bound caste. The Indian people are intensely socialistic. But, beyond that, there is a wealth of individualism. They are as tremendously individualistic— that is to say, after laying down all these minute regulations. They have regulated how you should eat, drink, sleep, die! Everything is regulated there; from early morning to when you go to bed and sleep, you are following regulations and law. Law, law. Do you wonder that a nation should [live] under that? Law is death. The more of the law in a country, the worse for the country. [But to be an individual] we go to the mountains, where there is no law, no government. The more of law you make, the more of police and socialism, the more of blackguards there are. Now this tremendous regulation of law [is] there. As soon as a child is born, he knows that he is born a slave: slave to his caste, first; slave to his nation, next. Slave, slave, slave. Every action—his drinking and his eating. He must eat under a regular method ; this prayer with the first morsel, this prayer with the second, that prayer with the third, and that prayer when he drinks water. Just think of that! Thus, from day to day, it goes on and on.

But they were thinkers. They knew that this would not lead to real greatness. So they left a way out for them all. After all, they found out that all these regulations are only for the world and the life of the world. As soon as you do not want money [and] you do not want children—no business for this world—you can go out entirely free. Those that go out thus were called Sannyasins—people who have given up. They never organised themselves, nor do they now; they are a free order of men and women who refuse to marry, who refuse to possess property, and they have no law—not even the Vedas bind them. They stand on [the] top of the Vedas. They are [at] the other pole [from] our social institutions. They are beyond caste. They have grown beyond. They are too big to be bound by these little regulations and things. Only two things [are] necessary for them: they must not possess property and must not marry. If you marry, settle down, or possess property, immediately the regulations will be upon you; but if you do not do either of these two, you are free. They were the living gods of the race, and ninety-nine per cent of our great men and women were to be found among them.

In every country, real greatness of the soul means extraordinary individuality, and that individuality you cannot get in society. It frets and fumes and wants to burst society. If society wants to keep it down, that soul wants to burst society into pieces. And they made an easy channel. They say: "Well, once you get out of society, then you may preach and teach everything that you like. We only worship you from a distance. So there were the tremendous, individualistic men and women, and they are the highest persons in all society. If one of those yellow-clad shaven-heads comes, the prince even dare not remain seated in his presence; he must stand. The next half hour, one of these Sannyasins might be at the door of one of the cottages of the poorest subjects, glad to get only a piece of bread. And he has to mix with all grades; now he sleeps with a poor man in his cottage; tomorrow [he] sleeps on the beautiful bed of a king. One day he dines on gold plates in kings' palaces; the next day, he has not any food and sleeps under a tree. Society looks upon these men with great respect; and some of them, just to show their individuality, will try to shock the public ideas. But the people are never shocked so long as they keep to these principles: perfect purity and no property.

These men, being very individualistic, they are always

trying new theories and plans—visiting in every country. They must think something new; they cannot run in the old groove. Others are all trying to make us run in the old groove, forcing us all to think alike. But human nature is greater than any human foolishness. Our greatness is greater than our weakness; the good things are stronger than the evil things. Supposing they succeeded in making us all think in the same groove, there we would be—no more thought to think; we would die.

Here was a society which had almost no vitality, its members pressed down by iron chains of law. They were forced to help each other. There, one was under regulations [that were] tremendous: regulations even how to breathe: how to wash face and hands; how to bathe; how to brush the teeth; and so on, to the moment of death. And beyond these regulations was the wonderful individualism of the Sannyasin. There he was. And every day a new sect was rising amongst these strong, individualistic men and women. The ancient Sanskrit books tell about their standing out—of one woman who was very quaint, queer old woman of the ancient times; she always had some new thing; sometimes [she was] criticised, but always people were afraid of her, obeying her quietly. So, there were those great men and women of olden times.

And within this society, so oppressed by regulations, the power was in the hands of the priests. In the social scale, the highest caste is [that of] the priest, and that being a business—I do not know any other word, that is why I use the word "priest". It is not in the same sense as in this country, because our priest is not a man that teaches religion or philosophy. The business of a priest is to perform all these minute details of regulations which have been laid down. The priest is the man who helps in these regulations. He marries you; to your funeral he comes to pray. So at all the ceremonies performed upon a man or a woman, the priest must be there. In society the ideal is marriage.

[Everyone] must marry. It is the rule. Without marriage, man is not able to perform any religious ceremony; he is only half a man; [he] is not competent to officiate—even the priest himself cannot officiate as a priest, except he marries. Half a man is unfit within society.

Now, the power of the priests increased tremendously. . . . The general policy of our national law-givers was to give the priests this honour. They also had the same social-istic plan [you are] just ready to [try] that checked them from getting money. What [was] the motive? Social honour. Mind you, the priest in all countries is the highest in the social scale, so much so in India that the poorest Brâhmin is greater than the greatest king in the country, by birth. He is the nobleman in India. But the law does not allow him ever to become rich. The law grinds him down to poverty— only, it gives him this honour. He cannot do a thousand things; and the higher is the caste in the social scale, the more restricted are its enjoyments. The higher the caste, the less the number of kinds of food that man can eat, the less the amount of food that man may eat, the less the number of occupations [he may] engage in. To you, his life would be only a perpetual train of hardships—nothing more than that. It is a perpetual discipline in eating, drinking, and everything; and all [penalties] which are required from the lower caste are required from the higher ten times more. The lowest man tells a lie; his fine is one dollar. A Brah-min, he must pay, say, a hundred dollars—[for] he knows better.

But this was a grand organisation to start with. Later on, the time came when they, these priests, began to get all the power in their hands; and at last they forgot the secret of their power: poverty. They were men whom society fed and clad so that they might simply learn and teach and think. Instead of that, they began to spread out their hands to clutch at the riches of society. They became "money-grabbers"—to use your word—and forgot all these things.

Then there was the second caste, the kingly caste, the military. Actual power was in their hands. Not only so— they have produced all of our great thinkers, and not the Brahmins. It is curious. All our great prophets, almost without one exception, belong to the kingly caste. The great man Krishna was also of that caste; Rama, he also, and all our great philosophers, almost all [sat] on the throne; thence came all the great philosophers of renunciation. From the throne came the voice that always cried, "Renounce". These military people were their kings; and they [also] were the philosophers; they were the speakers in the Upanishads. In their brains and their thought, they were greater than the priests they were more powerful, they were the kings—and yet the priests got all the power and tried to tyrannise over them. And so that was going on: political competition between the two castes, the priests and the kings.

Another phenomenon is there. Those of you that have been to hear the first lecture already know that in India there are two great races: one is called the Aryan; the other, the non-Aryan. It is the Aryan race that has the three castes; but the whole of the rest are dubbed with one name, Shudras—no caste. They are not Aryans at all. (Many people came from outside of India, and they found the Shudras [there], the aborigines of the country). However it may be, these vast masses of non-Aryan people and the mixed people among them, they gradually became civilised and they began to scheme for the same rights as the Aryans. They wanted to enter their schools and their colleges; they wanted to take the sacred thread of the Aryans; they wanted to perform the same ceremonies as the Aryans, and wanted to have equal rights in religion and politics like the Aryans. And the Brahmin priest, he was the great antagonist of such claims. You see, it is the nature of priests in every country—they are the most conservative people, naturally. So long as it is a trade, it must be; it is to their interest to be conservative. So this tide of murmur outside the Aryan pale, the priests were trying to check with all their might. Within the Aryan pale, there was also a tremendous religious ferment, and [it was] mostly led by this military caste.

There was already the sect of Jains [who are a] conservative [force] in India [even] today. It is a very ancient sect. They declared against the validity of the scriptures of the Hindus, the Vedas. They wrote some books themselves, and they said: "Our books are the only original books, the only original Vedas, and the Vedas that now are going on under that name have been written by the Brahmins to dupe the people." And they also laid the same plan. You see, it is difficult for you to meet the arguments of the Hindus about the scriptures. They also claimed [that] the world has been created through those books. And they were written in the popular language. The Sanskrit, even then, had ceased to be a spoken language—[it had] just the same relation [to the spoken language] as Latin has to modern Italian. Now, they wrote all their books in Pali; and when a Brahmin said, "Why, your books are in Pali!", they said, "Sanskrit is a language of the dead."

In their methods and manners they were different. For, you see, these Hindu scriptures, the Vedas, are a vast mass of accumulation—some of them crude—until you come to where religion is taught, only the spiritual. Now, that was the portion of the Vedas which these sects all claimed to preach. Then, there are three steps in the ancient Vedas: first, work; second, worship; third, knowledge. When a man purifies himself by work and worship, then God is within that man. He has realised He is already there. He only can have seen Him because the mind has become pure. Now, the mind can become purified by work and worship. That is all. Salvation is already there. We don't know it. Therefore, work, worship, and knowledge are the three steps. By work, they mean doing good to others. That has, of course, something in it, but mostly, as to the Brahmins, work means to perform these elaborate ceremonials: killing of cows and killing of bulls, killing of goats and all sorts of animals, that are taken fresh and thrown into the fire, and so on. "Now" declared the Jains, "that is no work at all, because injuring others can never be any good work"; and they said; "This is the proof that your Vedas are false Vedas, manufactured by the priests, because you do not mean to say that any good book will order us [to be] killing animals and doing these things. You do not believe it. So all this killing of animals and other things that you see in the Vedas, they have been written by the Brahmins, because they alone are benefited. It is the priest only [who] pockets the money and goes home. So, therefore, it is all priest-craft."

It was one of their doctrines that there cannot be any God: "The priests have invented God, that the people may believe in God and pay them money. All nonsense! there is no God. There is nature and there are souls, and that is all. Souls have got entangled into this life and got round them the clothing of man you call a body. Now, do good work." But from that naturally came the doctrine that everything that is matter is vile. They are the first teachers of asceticism. If the body is the result of impurity, why, therefore the body is vile. If a man stands on one leg for some time—"All right, it is a punishment". If the head comes up bump against a wall—"Rejoice, it is a very good punishment". Some of the great founders of the [Franciscan Order]—one of them St. Francis—were going to a certain place to meet somebody; and St. Francis had one of his companions with him, and he began to talk as to whether [the person] would receive them or not, and this man suggested that possibly he would reject them. Said St. Francis: "That is not enough, brother, but if, when we go and knock at the door, the man comes and drives us away, that is not enough. But if he orders us to be bound and gives us a thorough whipping, even that is not enough. And then, if he binds us hand and foot and whips us until we bleed at every pore and throws us outside in the snow, that would be enough."

These [same] ascetic ideas prevailed at that time. These Jains were the first great ascetics; but they did some great work. "Don't injure any and do good to all that you can, and that is all the morality and ethics, and that is all the work there is, and the rest is all nonsense—the Brahmins created that. Throw it all away." And then they went to work and elaborated this one principle all through, and it is a most wonderful ideal: how all that we call ethics they simply bring out from that one great principle of non-injury and doing good.

This sect was at least five hundred years before Buddha, and he was five hundred and fifty years before Christ.[1] Now the whole of the animal creation they divide into five sections: the lowest have only one organ, that of touch; the next one, touch and taste; the next, touch, taste, and hearing; the next, touch, taste, hearing, and sight. And the next, the five organs. The first two, the one-organ and the two-organ, are invisible to the naked eye, and they are everywhere in water. A terrible thing, killing these [low forms of life]. This bacteriology has come into existence in the modern world only in the last twenty years and theretofore nobody knew anything about it. They said, the lowest animals are only one-organ, touch; nothing else. The next greater [were] also invisible. And they all knew that if you boiled water these animals were all killed. So these monks, if they died of thirst, they would never kill these animals by drinking water. But if [a monk] stands at your door and you give him a little boiled water, the sin is on you of killing the animals—and he will get the benefit. They carry these ideas to ludicrous extremes. For in-

[1] The dates of the Jaina and Buddha were not known accurately in those days.

stance, in rubbing the body—if he bathes—he will have to kill numbers of animalcules; so he never bathes. He gets killed himself; he says that is all right. Life has no care for him; he will get killed and save life.

These Jains were there. There were various other sects of ascetics; and while this was going on, on the one hand, there was the political jealousy between the priests and the kings. And then these different dissatisfied sects [were] springing up everywhere. And there was the greater problem: the vast multitudes of people wanting the same rights as the Aryans, dying of thirst while the perennial stream of nature went flowing by them, and no right to drink a drop of water.

And that man was born—the great man Buddha. Most of you know about him, his life. And in spite of all the miracles and stories that generally get fastened upon any great man, in the first place, he is one of the most historical prophets of the world. Two are very historical: one, the most ancient, Buddha, and the other, Mohammed, because both friends and foes are agreed about them. So we are perfectly sure that there were such persons. As for the other persons, we have only to take for granted what the disciples say—nothing more. Our Krishna—you know, the Hindu prophet—he is very mythological. A good deal of his life, and everything about him, is written only by his disciples; and then there seem to be, sometimes, three or four men, who all loom into one. We do not know so clearly about many of the prophets; but as to this man, because both friends and foes write of him, we are sure that there was such a historical personage. And if we analyse through all the fables and reports of miracles and stories that generally are heaped upon a great man in this world, we will find an inside core; and all through the account of that man, he never did a thing for himself—never! How do you know that? Because, you see, when fables are fastened upon a man, the fables must be tinged with that man's general

character. Not one fable tried to impute any vice or any
immorality to the man. Even his enemies have favourable
accounts.

When Buddha was born, he was so pure that whosoever looked at his face from a distance immediately gave
up the ceremonial religion and became a monk and became saved. So the gods held a meeting. They said, "We
are undone". Because most of the gods live upon the ceremonials. These sacrifices go to the gods and these sacrifices
were all gone. The gods were dying of hunger and [the
reason for] it was that their power was gone. So the gods
said: "We must, anyhow, put this man down. He is too
pure for our life." And then the gods came and said: "Sir,
we come to ask you something. We want to make a great
sacrifice and we mean to make a huge fire, and we have
been seeking all over the world for a pure spot to light the
fire on and could not find it, and now we have found it.
If you will lie down, on your breast we will make the huge
fire." "Granted," he says, "go on." And the gods built the
fire high upon the breast of Buddha, and they thought he
was dead, and he was not. And then they went about and
said, "We are undone." And all the gods began to strike
him. No good. They could not kill him. From underneath,
the voice comes: "Why [are you] making all these vain
attempts?" "Whoever looks upon you becomes purified and
is saved, and nobody is going to worship us." "Then, your
attempt is vain, because purity can never be killed." This
fable was written by his enemies, and yet throughout the
fable the only blame that attaches to Buddha is that he was
so great a teacher of purity.

About his doctrines, some of you know a little. It is his
doctrines that appeal to many modern thinkers whom you
call agnostics. He was a great preacher of the brotherhood
of mankind: "Aryan or non-Aryan, caste or no caste, and
sects or no sects, every one has the same right to God and
to religion and to freedom. Come in all of you." But as to

other things, he was very agnostic. "Be practical." There came to him one day five young men, Brahmin born, quarrelling upon a question. They came to him to ask him the way to truth. And one said: "My people teach this, and this is the way to truth." The other said: "I have been taught this, and this is the only way to truth." "Which is the right way, sir?" "Well, you say your people taught this is truth and is the way to God?" "Yes." "But did you see God?" "No, sir." "Your father?" "No, sir." "Your grandfather?" "No, sir." "None of them saw God?" "No." "Well, and your teachers—neither [any] of them saw God?" "No." And he asked the same to the others. They all declared that none had seen God. "Well," said Buddha, "in a certain village came a young man weeping and howling and crying: 'Oh, I love her so! oh my, I love her so!' And then the villagers came; and the only thing he said was he loved her so. 'Who is she that you love?' 'I do not know.' 'Where does she live?' 'I do not know'—but he loved her so. 'How does she look?' 'That I do not know; but oh, I love her so.'" Then asked Buddha: "Young man, what would you call this young man?" "Why, sir, he was a fool!" And they all declared: "Why, sir, that young man was certainly a fool, to be crying and all that about a woman, to say he loved her so much and he never saw her or knew that she existed or anything?" "Are you not the same? You say that this God your father or your grandfather never saw, and now you are quarrelling upon a thing which neither you nor your ancestors ever knew, and you are trying to cut each other's throats about it." Then the young men asked: "What are we to do?" "Now, tell me: did your father ever teach that God is ever angry?" "No, sir." "Did your father ever teach that God is evil?" "No, sir; He is always pure." "Well, now, if you are pure and good and all that, do you not think that you will have more chance to come near to that God than by discussing all this and trying to cut each other's throats? Therefore,

say I: be pure and be good; be pure and love everyone."
And that was [all].

You see that non-killing of animals and charity towards
animals was an already existing doctrine when he was born;
but it was new with him—the breaking down of caste, that
tremendous movement. And the other thing that was new:
he took forty of his disciples and sent them all over the
world, saying, "Go ye; mix with all races and nations and
preach the excellent gospel for the good of all, for the benefit of all." And, of course, he was not molested by the
Hindus. He died at a ripe old age. All his life he was a
most stern man: he never yielded to weakness. I do not
believe many of his doctrines; of course, I do not. I believe
that the Vedantism of the old Hindus is much more
thoughtful, is a grander philosophy of life. I like his
method of work, but what I like [most] in that man is that,
among all the prophets of mankind, here was a man who
never had any cobwebs in his brain, and [who was] sane
and strong. When kingdoms were at his feet, he was still
the same man, maintaining "I am a man amongst men."

Why, the Hindus, they are dying to worship somebody.
You will find, if you live long enough, I will be worshipped
by our people. If you go there to teach them something,
before you die you will be worshipped. Always trying to
worship somebody. And living in that race, the world-
honoured Buddha, he died always declaring that he was
but man. None of his adulators could draw from him one
remark that he was anything different from any other man.

Those last dying words of his always thrilled through
my heart. He was old, he was suffering, he was near his
death, and then came the despised outcaste—he lives on
carrion, dead animals; the Hindus would not allow them
to come into cities—one of these invited him to a dinner
and he came with his disciples, and the poor Chanda, he
wanted to treat this great teacher according to what he
thought would be best; so he had a lot of pig's flesh and a

lot of rice for him, and Buddha looked at that. The disciples were all [hesitating], and the Master said: "Well, do not eat, you will be hurt." But he quietly sat down and ate. The teacher of equality must eat the [outcaste] Chanda's dinner, even the pig's flesh. He sat down and ate it.

He was already dying. He found death coming on, and he asked, "Spread for me something under this tree, for I think the end is near." And he was there under the tree, and he laid himself down; he could not sit up any more. And the first thing he did, he said: "Go to that Chanda and tell him that he has been one of my greatest benefactors; for his meal, I am going to Nirvâna." And then several men came to be instructed, and a disciple said, "Do not go near now, the Master is passing away". And as soon as he heard it, the Lord said, "Let them come in". And somebody else came and the disciples would not [let them enter]. Again they came, and then the dying Lord said: "And O, thou Ânanda, I am passing away. Weep not for me. Think not for me. I am gone. Work out diligently your own salvation. Each one of you is just what I am. I am nothing but one of you. What I am today is what I made myself. Do you struggle and make yourselves what I am. . . ."

These are the memorable words of Buddha: "Believe not because an old book is produced as an authority. Believe not because your father said [you should] believe the same. Believe not because other people like you believe it. Test everything, try everything, and then believe it, and if you find it for the good of many, give it to all." And with these words, the Master passed away.

See the sanity of the man. No gods, no angels, no demons—nobody. Nothing of the kind. Stern, sane, every brain-cell perfect and complete, even at the moment of death. No delusion. I do not agree with many of his doctrines. You may not. But in my opinion—oh, if I had only one drop of that strength! The sanest philosopher the world ever saw. Its best and its sanest teacher. And never that man bent before even the power of the tyrannical Brahmins. Never that man bent. Direct and everywhere the same: weeping with the miserable, helping the miserable, singing with the singing, strong with the strong, and everywhere the same sane and able man.

And, of course, with all this I can [not] understand his doctrine. You know he denied that there was any soul in man—that is, in the Hindu sense of the word. Now, we Hindus all believe that there is something permanent in man, which is unchangeable and which is living through all eternity. And that in man we call Âtman, which is without beginning and without end. And [we believe] that there is something permanent in nature [and that we call Brahman, which is also without beginning and without end]. He denied both of these. He said there is no proof of anything permanent. It is all a mere mass of change; a mass of thought in a continuous change is what you call a mind. . . . The torch is leading the procession. The circle is a delusion. [Or take the example of a river.] It is a continuous river passing on; every moment a fresh mass of water passing on. So is this life; so is all body, so is all mind.

Well, I do not understand his doctrine—we Hindus never understood it. But I can understand the motive behind that. Oh, the gigantic motive! The Master says that selfishness is the great curse of the world; that we are selfish and that therein is the curse. There should be no motive for selfishness. You are [like a river] passing [on]—a continuous phenomenon. Have no God; have no soul; stand on your feet and do good for good's sake—neither for fear of punishment nor for [the sake of] going anywhere. Stand sane and motiveless. The motive is: I want to do good, it is good to do good. Tremendous! Tremendous! I do not sympathise with his metaphysics at all; but my mind is jealous when I think of the moral force. Just ask your minds which one of you can stand for one hour, able and

daring like that man. I cannot for five minutes. I would
become a coward and want a support. I am weak—a
coward. And I warm to think of this tremendous giant.
We cannot approach that strength. The world never saw
[anything] compared to that strength. And I have not yet
seen any other strength like that. We are all born cowards.
If we can save ourselves [we care about nothing else]. Inside
is the tremendous fear, the tremendous motive, all the
time. Our own selfishness makes us the most arrant
cowards; our own selfishness is the great cause of fear and
cowardice. And there he stood: "Do good because it is
good; ask no more questions; that is enough. A man made
to do good by a fable, a story, a superstition—he will be
doing evil as soon as the opportunity comes. That man
alone is good who does good for good's sake, and that is
the character of the man."

"And what remains of man?" was asked of the Master.
"Everything—everything. But what is in the man? Not the
body not the soul, but character. And that is left for all
ages. All that have passed and died, they have left for us
their characters, eternal possessions for the rest of humanity;
and these characters are working—working all through."
What of Buddha? What of Jesus of Nazareth? The world
is full of their characters. Tremendous doctrine!

Let us come down a little—we have not come to the
subject at all. (*Laughter.*) I must add not a few words
more this evening. . . .

And then, what he did. His method of work: organisation. The idea that you have today of church is his character. He left the church. He organised these monks and made
them into a body. Even the voting by ballot is there five
hundred and sixty years before Christ. Minute organisation.
The church was left and became a tremendous power, and
did great missionary work in India and outside India. Then
came, three hundred years after, two hundred years before
Christ, the great emperor Asoka, as he has been called by

your Western historians, the divinest of monarchs, and that man became entirely converted to the ideas of Buddha, and he was the greatest emperor of the world at that time. His grandfather was a contemporary of Alexander, and since Alexander's time, India had become more intimately connected with Greece. . . . Every day in Central Asia some inscription or other is being found. India had forgotten all about Buddha and Asoka and everyone. But there were pillars, obelisks, columns, with ancient letters which nobody could read. Some of the old Mogul emperors declared they would give millions for anybody to read those; but nobody could. Within the last thirty years·those have been read; they are all written in Pali.

The first inscription is: ". . ."

And then he writes this inscription, describing the terror and the misery of war; and then he became converted to religion. Then said he: "Henceforth let none of my descendants think of acquiring glory by conquering other races. If they want glory, let them help other races; let them send teachers of sciences and teachers of religion. A glory won by the sword is no glory at all." And next you find how he is sending missionaries even to Alexandria. . . . You wonder that you find all over that part of the country sects rising immediately, called Theraputae, Essenes, and all those—extreme vegetarians, and so on. Now this great Emperor Asoka built hospitals for men and for animals. The inscriptions show they are ordering hospitals, building hospitals for men and for animals. That is to say, when an animal gets old, if I am poor and cannot keep it any longer, I do not shoot it down for mercy. These hospitals are maintained by public charity. The coasting traders pay so much upon every hundredweight they sell, and all that goes to the hospital; so nobody is touched. If you have a cow that is old—anything—and do not want to keep it, send it to the hospital; they keep it, even down to rats and mice and anything you send. Only, our ladies try to kill these animals sometimes, you know. They go in large numbers to see them and they bring all sorts of cakes; the animals are killed many times by this food. He claimed that the animals should be as much under the protection of the government as man. Why should animals be allowed to be killed? [There] is no reason. But he says, before prohibiting the killing of animals for food even, [people] must be provided with all sorts of vegetables. So he sent and collected all kinds of vegetables and planted them in India; and then, as soon as these were introduced, the order was: henceforth, whosoever kills an animal will be punished. A government is to be a government; the animals must be protected also. What business has a man to kill a cow, a goat, or any other animal for food?

Thus Buddhism was and did become a great political power in India. Gradually it also fell to pieces—after all, this tremendous missionary enterprise. But to their credit it must be said, they never took up the sword to preach religion. Excepting the Buddhistic religion, there is not one religion in the world which could make one step without bloodshed—not one which could get a hundred thousand converts just by brain power alone. No, no. All through. And this is just what you are going to do in the Philippines. That is your method. Make them religious by the sword. That is what your priests are preaching. Conquer and kill them that they may get religion. A wonderful way of preaching religion!

You know how this great emperor Asoka was converted. This great emperor in his youth was not so good. [He had a brother.] And the two brothers quarrelled and the other brother defeated this one, and the emperor in vengeance wanted to kill him. The emperor got the news that he had taken shelter with a Buddhistic monk. Now, I have told you how our monks are very holy; no one would come near them. The emperor himself came. He said, "Deliver the man to me" Then the monk preached to him: "Vengeance

is bad. Disarm anger with love. Anger is not cured by
anger, nor hatred by hatred. Dissolve anger by love. Cure
hatred by love. Friend, if for one evil thou returnest
another, thou curest not the first evil, but only add one
evil more to the world." The emperor said: "That is all
right, fool that you are. Are you ready to give your life—to
give your life for that man?" "Ready, sir." And he came
out. And the emperor drew his sword, and he said: "Get
ready." And just [as he] was going to strike, he looked at
the face of the man. There was not a wink in those eyes.
The emperor stopped, and he said: "Tell me, monk, where
did you learn this strength, poor beggar, not to wink?"
And then he preached again. "Go on, monk", he said,
"That is nice", he said. Accordingly, he [fell under] the
charm of the Master—Buddha's charm.

There have been three things in Buddhism: the
Buddha himself, his law, his church. At first it was so
simple. When the Master died, before his death, they said:
"What shall we do with you?" "Nothing." "What monu-
ments shall we make over you?" He said: "Just make a
little heap if you want, or just do not do anything." By
and by, there arose huge temples and all the paraphernalia.
The use of images was unknown before then. I say they
were the first to use images. There are images of Buddha
and all the saints, sitting about and praying. All this paraphernalia went on multiplying with this organisation.
Then these monasteries became rich. The real cause of the
downfall is here. Monasticism is all very good for a few; but
when you preach it in such a fashion that every man or
woman who has a mind immediately gives up social life,
when you find over the whole of India monasteries, some
containing a hundred thousand monks, sometimes twenty
thousand monks in one building—huge, gigantic buildings,
these monasteries, scattered all over India and, of course,
centres of learning, and all that—who were left to procreate
progeny, to continue the race? Only the weaklings. All the

strong and vigorous minds went out. And then came national decay by the sheer loss of vigour.

I will tell you of this marvellous brotherhood. It is great. But theory and idea is one thing and actual working is another thing. The idea is very great: practising non-resistance and all that, but if all of us go out in the street and practise non-resistance, there would be very little left in this city. That is to say, the idea is all right, but nobody has yet found a practical solution [as to] how to attain it.

There is something in caste, so far as it means blood; such a thing as heredity there is, certainly. Now try to [understand]—why do you not mix your blood with the Negroes, the American Indians? Nature will not allow you. Nature does not allow you to mix your blood with them. There is the unconscious working that saves the race. That was the Aryan's caste. Mind you, I do not say that they are not equal to us. They must have the same privileges and advantages, and everything; but we know that if certain races mix up, they become degraded. With all the strict caste of the Aryan and non-Aryan, that wall was thrown down to a certain extent, and hordes of these outlandish races came in with all their queer superstitions and manners and customs. Think of this: not decency enough to wear clothes, eating carrion, etc. But behind him came his fetish, his human sacrifice, his superstition, his diabolism. He kept it behind, [he remained] decent for a few years. After that he brought all [these] things out in front. And that was degrading to the whole race. And then the blood mixed; [intermarriages] took place with all sorts of unmixable races. The race fell down. But, in the long run, it proved good. If you mix up with Negroes and American Indians, surely this civilisation will fall down. But hundreds and hundreds years after, out of this mixture will come a gigantic race once more, stronger than ever; but, for the time being, you have to suffer. The Hindus believe—that is a peculiar belief, I think; and I do not know, I have nothing to say to the contrary, I have not found anything to the contrary—they believe there was only one civilised race: the Aryan. Until he gives his blood, no other race can be civilised. No teaching will do. The Aryan gives his blood to a race, and then it becomes civilised. Teaching alone will not do. He would be an example in your country: would you give your blood to the Negro race? Then he would get higher culture.

The Hindu loves caste. I may have little taint of that superstition—I do not know. I love the Master's ideal. Great! But, for me, I do not think that the working was very practical; and that was one of the great causes that led to the downfall of the Indian nation, in the long run. But then it brought about this tremendous fusion. Where so many different races are all fusing, mingling—one man white like you, or yellow, while another man as black as I am, and all grades between these two extremes, and each race keeping their customs, manners, and everything—in the long run a fusion is taking place, and out of this fusion surely will come a tremendous upheaval; but, for the time being, the giant must sleep. That is the effect of all such fusion.

When Buddhism went down that way, there came the inevitable reaction. There is but one entity in the whole world. It is a unit world. The diversity is only eye-service. It is all one. The idea of unity and what we call monism—without duality—is the idea in India. This doctrine has been always in India; [it was] brought forward whenever materialism and scepticism broke down everything. When Buddhism broke down everything by introducing all sorts of foreign barbarians into India—their manners and customs and things—there was a reaction, and that reaction was led by a young monk [Shankarâchârya]. And [instead] of preaching new doctrines and always thinking new thoughts and making sects, he brought back the Vedas

III—35

to life: and modern Hinduism has thus an admixture of ancient Hinduism, over which the Vedantists predominate. But, you see, what once dies never comes back to life, and those ceremonials of [Hinduism] never came back to life. You will be astonished if I tell you that, according to the old ceremonials, he is not a good Hindu who does not eat beef. On certain occasions he must sacrifice a bull and eat it. That is disgusting now. However they may differ from each other in India, in that they are all one—they never eat beef. The ancient sacrifices and the ancient gods, they are all gone; modern India belongs to the spiritual part of the Vedas.

Buddhism was the first sect in India. They were the first to say: "Ours is the only path. Until you join our church, you cannot be saved." That was what they said: "It is the correct path." But, being of Hindu blood, they could not be such stony-hearted sectarians as in other countries. There will be salvation for you: nobody will go wrong for ever. No, no. [There was] too much of Hindu blood in them for that. The heart was not so stony as that. But you have to join them.

But the Hindu idea, you know, is not to join anybody. Wherever you are, that is a point from which you can start to the centre. All right. It—Hinduism—has this advantage: its secret is that doctrines and dogmas do not mean anything; what you are is what matters. If you talk all the best philosophies the world ever produced, [but] if you are a fool in your behaviour, they do not count; and if in your behaviour you are good, you have more chances. This being so, the Vedantist can wait for everybody. Vedantism teaches that there is but one existence and one thing real, and that is God. It is beyond all time and space and causation and everything. We can never define Him. We can never say what He is except [that] He is Absolute Existence, Absolute Knowledge, Absolute Blissfulness. He is the only reality. Of everything He is the reality; of you and me, of

the wall and of [everything] everywhere. It is His knowledge upon which all our knowledge depends: it is His
blissfulness upon which depends our pleasure; and He is
the only reality. And when man realises this, he knows that
"I am the only reality, because I am He—what is real in
me is He also". So that when a man is perfectly pure and
good and beyond all grossness, he finds, as Jesus found:
"I and my Father are one." The Vedantist has patience to
wait for everybody. Wherever you are, this is the highest:
"I and my Father are one." Realise it. If an image helps,
images are welcome. If worshipping a great man helps you,
worship him. If worshipping Mohammed helps you, go on.
Only be sincere; and if you are sincere, says Vedantism, you
are sure to be brought to the goal. None will be left. Your
heart, which contains all truth, will unfold itself chapter
after chapter, till you know the last truth, that "I and my
Father are one". And what is salvation? To live with God.
Where? Anywhere. Here this moment. One moment in
infinite time is quite as good as any other moment. This
is the old doctrine of the Vedas, you see. This was revived.
Buddhism died out of India. It left its mark on their
charity, its animals, etc. in India; and Vedantism is recon-
quering India from one end to the other.

INDEX

Abhih (seè fearlessness), 237, 318, 386
Aborigines, 292-93, 520
Absolute (s), 2, 7, 11, 37, 42, 93, 261, 335, 453; Existence-Knowledge-Bliss, 12, 18; two 7; worship of, 77
Âchârya, 36
Address of Welcome, at Almora, 350; at Calcutta, 305; at Colombo, 103-04; at Jaffna, 116-17; at Kumbakonam, 176; at Madras, 200; at Madura, 169; at Pamban, 135-36; at Paramakudi, 155; at Ramnad, 144-45

Adhikârabheda, 397
Âditya, 61
Advaita, 129, 161-62, 190-91, 229, 236, 342, 395-97, 403, 413, 430-33; explains morality, 425; and hopes of dualists, 40; ideal of, 190; its practicality, 425-28; to rouse up hearts of men, 191; three systems merge in, 397; way of reconciliation, 191
Advaitin, 60, 442
Advaitism (see non-dualism), 242, 375, 415; and Buddhist Kshanika Vijnâna Vâda, 404-05, 410-16; and final evolution, 439; moral aspect of, 419-26; scientific region, 423-24
Advaitist (see non-dualist), 9, 14, 20, 22, 230, 233-34, 239, 299, 323-25, 335, 337, 341, 347-48, 424, 455-56
Afghanistan, 293
Africa(n), 192, 243, 292
Agnostic(s), 61, 422, 525
Ahamkâra, 402, 412
Âhâra (see food)
Ahimsâ, 67-68, 458
Akâsha, 400
Akbar, 328
Alexander,. 237, 340, 530
Alexandria, 322, 512, 531
Alice in Wonderland, 23

Allah, 154, 369
Allopanishad, 328
Almora, 350, 355
Alps, 52
America, 103, 107-08, 116, 144-45, 169, 176-78, 189, 191-92, 207-09, 214, 220, 223, 226, 272, 276, 290, 292, 351, 433, 442, 444
American(s), 307, 310, 314, 318; practical Vedantists, 428
Anabhidhyâ, 67
Ânanda, 528
Anarchism, 204
Angels, 23, 119, 528
Anger, to be conquered by love, 532
Anglo-Saxon, 441-42
Animâ, 41, 334
Animal(s), charity towards, 526; creation, five sections of, 523; hospitals for, 531; non-killing of, 526, 530
Annisquam, 469
Antahkarana (see mind, organ), 399, 401-03
Antioch, 322
Anurakti, 36
Appeal-Avalanche, 48¾
Arab(s), 109, 154
Âranyaka, 394
Aristocracy, 297
Ârjava, 67
Arjuna (see Kunti, son of), 77, 445
Arnold, Edwin, 511
Ârya(s), 114, 368, 426, 453; Samâj, 366
Aryan(s), 168, 186, 263, 286, 307, 317, 340, 351, 409, 418, 434, 437, 480, 486, 506-07, 520-21, 524-25, 534; analytical by nature, 434; and Dravidians, 292-93, 299; Indo-269, 350; and non-Aryans, 198, 253, 520, 525, 534
Âryâvarta, 136, 202, 255, 366
Asceticism, 344, 522
Asia, 287, 440; Central, 293, 512
Asia Minor, 512

540   SWAMI VIVEKANANDA'S WORKS

Asoka, 276, 530-31 ; his conversion, story of, 532-33 ; greatest emperor of the world, 530 ;'s reign, 530-32
Aspirant, 46 ; qualifications of, 47-53
Astronomy, 2, 85, 255, 349
Atavism, 239
Atheist, 15, 44, 265, 278-79, 304, 411, 502
Athens, 2, 322
Atlantic, 310
Ātman (see Self, soul), 11, 19-20, 22, 25-26, 31, 35, 39, 60, 68-69, 74, 126, 159, 224, 236, 241-42, 254, 283, 320, 331, 345, 364, 374, 401-05, 409-10, 418, 450, 458-59, 529 ; Jiv-, Param-, 416
Auguste Comte, 61
Austria, 430
Avatâra (see Incarnation), 53, 184, 249, 459, worship of, 54, 332
Avidyâ (see ignorance)

Baal, 112, 186 ; -Merodach, 112, 186
Babylon, 185
Babylonian(s) gods, 112, 186 ; souls with, 436
Baluchis, 265, 296
Barrows, Dr., 182, 217
Beef, eating of, 173-74, 535
Bengal, 211, 266, 306, 325-27, 333, 336, 340, 345, 457 ; Eastern, 448 ; reformers, 212 ; youth of, 320, 445
Bengali(s), 312, 339-40, 440, 442, 449, 454 ; credited with imagination, 318
Bergen, Dr. Carl von, 478
Besant, Mrs., 208, 442
Beyond (see Brahman, God), 1-3, 126, 128, 236, 253, 450
Bhâgavata (Purâna), 40-41, 53, 183, 255-56, 363-64
Bhakta (devotee), 19, 27-28, 37, 42-43, 50, 65, 68-69, 71, 79-88, 233, 350, 365, 391
Bhakti (see love), 36, 42, 60-61, 66, 115, 128, 266, 357-65, 385-92, 458 ; advantage and disadvantage of, 32 ; begins with and ends in, 36 ; definition of, 31-36 ; forms of, 86 ; greater than Karma, Yoga, 31 ;

Bhakti—Contd.
ideal of 385-86 ; instrument of liberation, 34 ; material helps in, 388 ; its own fruition, 32 ; potency of, 130 ; and Pranidhâna, 35-36 ; preparatory (Gauni), 33, 43 ; Supreme (Parâ-), 33, 43, 70-100, 365 ; triangle of, 391-92 ; in Upanishads, 230-31
Bhakti-aphorisms, 31
Bhakti-yoga, 63, 68, 74-76 ; aim of, 42-44 ; definition of, 31 ; its method and means, 63-69 ; its naturalness and central secret, 77-79 ; as science of higher love, 73
Bhârata, 313, 350
Bhartrihari, 226
Bhoja, 36
Bible, 48, 332-33, 394, 438, 494, 505, 513-14
Bigotry, 202
Biology, 2
Birth and Death, 36, 126-27, 130, 422
Bliss, 4, 348, 450 ; eternal, 128, 427 ; -fulness, 536
Bodhâyana, 326-27
Body, 77, 83, 127, 158, 281, 309, 334, 349, 515, 522, 529-30 ; finer and grosser, 66 ; soul and mind (see soul), 401, 416, 421, 436 ; as temple of God, 388
Bombay, 344
Bondage, 9-10, 15, 17, 28, 72, 78, 85, 128, 139, 516
Bonney, President, 470
Book(s) (see scriptures), 52, 72, 92, 114-15, 150, 240, 271, 289-90, 319, 343, 346, 377, 416, 435, 521 ; as breath of God, 375 ; inadequacy of, 45 ; old, 111 ; and religions, 118, 253 ; worship, 513-14
Boston Evening Transcript, 470
Brahmâ, 36, 39, 57, 363, 400 ; -varta, 366
Brahmacharya, 134
Brahmaloka, 66, 417
Brahman, 11, 16, 37-38, 51, 59-60, 80, 85, 123, 154, 282, 327, 342, 347-48, 362, 417-18, 424, 426, 429, 452-53, 529 ; anthropomorphic idea of, 42 ; each soul is, 7 ; one Infinite Whole, 432 ; perception of,

Philosophy—*Contd.*
171, 189, 201, 214, 225, 234-
35, 254, 273, 285, 310, 327-28,
341-43, 395-96, 435, 445, 518,
527, 536
Physics, 2
Pilgrimage (see holy place),
141, 143
Pitri, worship of, 161
Plato, 434
Pleasure, 157, 348, 536 ; intellectual, 71-72 ; and pain, 18,
25, 78, 83, 451-52 ; of senses,
71-72
Pole, North, 293
Politics, 107-08, 137, 146, 149,
177, 179, 204, 220-21, 241,
314, 520
Pontifex Maximus, 217
Poor, the, of Bengal, 445 ; lift
up, 192 ; in India and
America, 477 ; as Nârâyana,
391 ; see Shiva in, 141 ; ty-
ranny over, 211 ; worship
God in, 246
Portuguese, 116, 290
Power, 80, 284, 298, 317, 319,
358 ; Âtman has all, 409-10 ;
and God, 95, 320, 373 ; of
liberated souls, 37-39, 41 ;
military, 108, 137 ; and
people, 320 ; in souls, 126,
334-35, 443 ; of thought, 227
Prahlâda, 36, 40, 358, 371, 386
Pralaya, 123, 407, 437
Prâna (s), 399
Pranidhâna, 36
Prasthânas, 395-96
Pratika (s), 59-61, 65, 122
Pratimâ (s), 59
Pravritti, 150
Prayer, 141
Priest (s), 158, 243, 262, 264,
281, 283, 492, 515, 518-20,
522, 524, 532 ; craft, 68, 414,
522 ; -hood, 513 ; and kings,
524
Privilege (s), 245-46, 294, 297,
443, 461
Progress, 5, 172, 174, 198, 222,
276, 367, 381, 393, 440-41 ;
crimes of, 488 ; Hindu's
quota to, 109 ; infinite, 4 ;
practical realisation of, 196 ;
and spiritual thought, 3
Prophet (s), 131, 183-84, 249,
266, 313, 362, 519-20, 524,
527

III—36

Protestantism, 217 ; idolatry
and images in, 61, 362
Psychology (see Kapila), 81,
188, 299, 327, 391, 395, 398 ;
Indian and Western, 334-35
Public opinion, 215, 219
Punjab, 326, 357, 455
Purâna (s), 60, 111, 121, 173,
221, 229, 231-32, 238, 243,
248, 275, 278, 332, 385-89 ;
and Vedas, 457-58
Purity, 64, 67, 360-61, 517 ;
can never be killed, 525
Pythagoras, 434

Qualified, monism (see Vishishtâdvaita), 230 ; monist, 7,
119, 191, 229, 287, 320, 323,
438, 442 ; non-dualist (see
Vishishtâdvaita), 397

Race ((s), 105, 111, 142, 220,
286, 531, 534 ; each has a
mission, 108 ; fusion of, 535 ;
Hindu, 195 ; mission of our,
369 ; our, 228 ; religions in
different, 112
Râdhâ, 364
Radicals, 108
Raja of Ramnad (see Ramnad),
put the idea of going to
Chicago in my brain, 139,
146-47, 170
Rajas, 65, 256, 337-38, 408
Râja-Yoga, and Bhakti, 32
Râja-Yogi, his renunciation, 70-
71
Râma (Chandra), 64, 144, 213,
255, 263, 358, 450-51, 520
Ramakrishna (Bhagavân, Paramahamsa) (see Master, my),
49, 56, 63, 103, 144, 218, 268,
308, 312-16, 344, 348, 472
Râmânuja (Bhagavân), 35, 38,
59, 281, 325-27, 329, 336, 344,
348-49, 394, 396, 439 ; his
attempt to raise the lower
classes, 290 ; on contraction
and expansion of soul, 239,
284, 337 ; on food, 64-65,
337-39 ; his heart, 265-66 ;
his *Shri Bhâshya*, 36, 326 ;
his system, 39
Râmâyana, 64, 217, 219
Rameswaram, 141
Ramnad, 144-46 ; Raja of (see
Raja), 136-37, 139, 146, 151

Rawalpindi, 357

Realisation, 38, 44, 69, 91, 345, 377-79, 451-53, 456 ; divine, 66 ; religious, 76, 283 ; spiritual, 42-44

Realism, 156

Reality, 15, 24

Reason, 1, 5, 17, 225, 253, 347, 424 ; and realisation, 42-43, 378

Reform, reformer, 44, 146, 151, 172, 194-96, 208, 210-16, 218-21, 225, 244, 265, 314, 383-84, 450, 460 ; Buddhistic and Jain, 447 ; fanatical, 214 ; and growth, 213 ; radical, 216 ; root-and-branch, 213 ; secret of, 383-84 ; spiritual, 384

Reincarnation (s), 43, 334, 459, 478-79, 487

Religion (s), 1-5, 22, 43, 49, 51-52, 111, 113, 134, 137-38, 144-48, 158-59, 161, 169, 175, 177, 200-07, 217-18, 220, 224, 228, 233, 243, 245, 249-52, 262, 265, 273-76, 279-80, 283-90, 306-09, 317, 351-54, 357-60, 364, 367, 511-12, 518, 520-21, 524-25, 531-32 ; all all are good, true, 495, 500, 502 ; arguments against Indian, 179 ; based on principles, not persons, 249-51 ; is being and becoming, 253 ; books as basis of, 118-19 ; and bread, 3, 433 ; Buddhistic, converted without bloodshed, 532 ; and caste, 465 ; changing a nation's, 500 ; common grounds of, 454 ; comparative, 185, 307 ; development of, 112 ; in England, 221 ; essentials of, 68 ; is evolution, 218 ; exists in love, and not ceremony, 141 ; fanatical forms of, 44 ; forms of, 1, 92 ; founders of, 105, 182-83, 280 ; not frothy words, 18, grounds of, unity of, 458-59 ; highest aim of man, 50 ; Hindus and (see Hindus) ; ideals of, 252, 254, 261, 453 ; and India (see India) ; in India and other countries, nations, 107, 179, 203-04, 467, 469 ; is keynote of Indian life, 287 ; and kit-

Religion—*Contd.*

chen, 66, 167, 271, 339 ; of love, 91, 93 ; make it dynamic in India, 383 ; manifestations of same Lord, 62 ; and morality, 360 ; mythological and symbological parts of, 43 ; national, 443, 449 ; and national life (see national life) ; one cannot suit all, 358-59 ; as opium-eating, 63 ; our, 132-33 ; as politico-social club life, 62 ; principles of, 121, 279-80, 287, 306, 371, 458 ; proof of, 252 ; no quarrel with, 131-32 ; and realisation, 54, 345, 377-79 ; and renunciation (see renunciation), 148 ; revival of, 117, 172 ; science and, 433 ; search for, of, 81,111 ; and sect, 483, 495 ; Semitic, 436-37 ; teacher of, 46 ; thirst after, 47 ; toleration in, 114 ; unifying power of, 286-90 ; unity, the goal of, 1-5 ; universal (see universal) ; universality of, 185 ; we are born in, 454-61 ; in the West, 110 ; world's great, 27

Religious, conceptions, 307 ; culture, 66 ; liberalism, 63 ; persecution, 114 ; practices change, 121 ; realisation, 283 ; sects, 67 ; work, 177 ; world, 155

Renaissance, 109

Renunciation (see Vairâgya), 17, 137, 148, 150, 156, 197, 256, 353-54, 418, 431, 446, 453, 520 ; Bhakta's, 73-76 ; and enjoyment, 206 ; and India, 148, 343 ; preparatory, 70-73 ; and religion, 148, 205, 343 ; and spirituality, our ideal, 152

Repression or suppression, 73

Republican, 108

Resignation (see self-surrender) 83-85

Revelation, 494

Reverence, 79, 95

Rishi (s), 112, 119, 139, 155, 175, 197-98, 252-55, 282-84, 296, 301-02, 353, 381, 410, 436-37, 447, 454, 456-57

Ritual (s), 70, 72, 169 ; -ism, 44 ; -istic, 60-61